Flash MX Upgrade Essentials

Sham Bhangal

friendsof

DESIGNER TO DESIGNER™

Flash MX Upgrade Essentials

© 2002 friends of ED

First published March 2002
Latest reprint May 2002

Trademark Acknowledgments

friends of ED has endeavored to provide trademark information about all the companies and products mentioned in this book by the appropriate use of capitals. However, friends of ED cannot guarantee the accuracy of this information.

Published by friends of ED
30-32 Lincoln Road, Olton, Birmingham, B27 6PA, UK.

Printed in USA
ISBN: 1-903450-76-4

Flash MX Upgrade Essentials

Credits

Author
Sham Bhangal

Commissioning Editor
Andy Corsham

Additional Material
aYo Binitie
Hoss Gifford

Technical Editors
Dan Britton
Steve Rycroft

Technical Reviewers
Chris Andrade
Michael Bedar
Sally Cruikshank
Leon Cych
John Davey
Hoss Gifford
Steve McCormick
Jake Smith
Pete Walker

Author Agent
Gaynor Riopedre

Project Manager
Vicky Idiens

Graphic Editors
Chantal Hepworth
Matt Clark
Deb Murray

Proof Readers
Jason Cuthbert
Vicky Idiens
Matthew Knight
Melanie Orgee

Cover and Design
Deb Murray

Managing Editor
Melanie Orgee

Indexer
Fiona Murray

About the Author

Sham Bhangal
Sham Bhangal originally started his career as an engineer specializing in industrial computer-based display and control systems. In his spare time he took up freelance web design, a hobby that grew slowly until it became his main career. He now writes extensively for friends of ED and is engaged in all aspects of web design. Sham now lives in rural Somerset with his partner Karen.

Acknowledgements
This book is dedicated to those people who contributed to my understanding of the new version of Flash during early testing. They are, in no particular order: Andreas Heim, Robert Penner, Philip Kerman, Guy Watson, Hoss Gifford, aYo Binite, Colin Moock, Sam Wan, Jon Kaye, Branden Hall, Sascha Wolter, Josh Ulm, Dave Yang, Dorian Nisinson, Bertrand Saint-Guillain, Waldo Smeets.

It's no coincidence that many of these names have also helped make the Flash community in general the vibrant and creative group it has quickly become. Thank you.

Thanks also to the Macromedia team. The following people, in particular, took time out from their busy schedules to answer my questions, no matter how stupid those questions might seem with hindsight. (Again in no particular order) – Nigel 'Dark lord' Pegg, Peter Santangeli, Mike Williams, Mike Chambers, Troy 'Major Player' Evans, Matt Wobensmith, Jeremy Clark, Gary Grossman, Scot Drier, Erica 'Quality' Norton, Sharon 'Fact of Life' Sheldon, Lily Khong, Chris 'Software Guy' Thilgen, Tinic Uro, Rebecca Sun.

Table of Contents

Table of Contents

01   Macromedia Flash MX Overview   1

Macromedia Flash MX in context 1
A tour of Macromedia Flash MX..2
   The Flash player...2
   Workflow and user interface 3
      Panels...4
      The Property inspector..7
      The timeline and library..8
      User interface extensibility 9
   Browser control and accessibility...9
   Content creation...10
      Distort and envelope modifiers...11
      Fonts and text..12
      Components 14
      Video 15
      Templates 15
   Scripting...17
      Many multimedia and graphic elements are now objects 18
      The drawing API...18
      Advanced ActionScripting 20
  Summary 20
  How to use this book...21
   Layout conventions 21
   Support 22

02   The User Interface   25

Overview of the Flash MX user interface..25
   What's disappeared? 27
   Panels 28
      Docking areas 28
   New panel functionality 32
      The Actions panel 32
      The Components and Component Parameters panels.....................35
      The Color Mixer panel...36
      The Accessibility panel..36
   The Property inspector 37
      Shape, Group, and Tool properties 38
      Document properties 40
      Media properties 41
      Symbol properties 42
      Text properties 43
      Component properties..45
      Frame properties 45
  Summary 45

03   The Timeline and the Library   47

The timeline 47
   The timeline panel 48
   Layer folders...48
   Distribute to layers..51
The library 54
   The library panel...55
   Creating symbols...55
   Sharing library assets 57
      Sharing during authoring..58
      Runtime sharing 63
Summary 66

04   Tools   69

The toolbox..69
   Free transform tool 69
   Distort modifier 72
      Creating faux 3D graphics...73
      Isometric 3D graphics...76
   The envelope modifier..77
      Creating morphing animations 80
      Conforming text to a path 84
   Fill transform tool..88
   Linear fill...88
   Radial fill...90
      Producing realistic light source highlights 92
Summary 93

05   The Scripting Environment   95

The Actions panel 96
   Line numbering...99
   Pinning the actions editor 99
   Preferences..100
      Basic appearance 101
      Code formatting 102
   Help features 103
      Check syntax 103
      Auto format 104
      Auto complete 104
      Code hinting 105
   Default naming conventions 106
   The Reference panel 107
Advanced configuration of the scripting environment 108
Summary 110

06   Building Blocks   **113**

Text enhancements 113
　Font mapping 113
　Font formatting..115
　　Kerning..115
　　Tracking 116
　　Text type..116
　　More text format options 117
　Text objects 118
Movie clip masks..121
　Dynamic masking..123
Button movie clips 126
　Advantages of the button movie clip..131
　　Animated buttons 131
　　Animated hit areas 131
　　A real timeline 132
The switch action 136
　Using switch with motion graphics 138
Summary 139

07   Introducing Flash Objects: Buttons and Text   **141**

What's the big deal with objects? 141
The button object 142
　Setting up a Flash MX button 142
　New button-related techniques 144
　　Enabling and disabling a button 144
　　Button over cursor 146
　　Button visibility..147
　ActionScript-based button animations..148
The text object..151
　The text field object 151
　　Password style..153
　　Background color 153
　　Text events..153
　The text format object 164
Summary 171

08   MX Objects: Movie Clips and Sketches   **173**

Introducing the Flash MX movie clip 173
The global level 174
　When to use globals 176
　Global functions 176
　Global depth 177
　　What global is, and what it isn't! 178
The movie clip object 179
　Creating new movie clips..180

Flash MX Upgrade Essentials

Using new movie clip events and properties..181
The drawing API..189
Turtle graphics...189
Lines...191
Curves...194
A simple tool for drawing lines and curves..196
Fills...201
Summary...204

09   Introducing Components   207

New component functionality...208
The component environment 209
Using components 209
Using the default components..212
'Drag and drop' components 213
Components that associate via linkage...216
The scroll pane 216
Components that require event handlers 219
The checkbox 220
Using change handlers..221
The push button..224
The radio button 226
The list box...230
The combo box..234
Creating custom Flash MX components for Flash 5 users 236
Creating the Flash 5 file 236
Installing the components 237
Summary 239

10   Browser Control: Flash and the User   243

You and your user..243
The Flash stage and browser window 245
Dynamically resizing the stage..248
The back button and bookmarks 249
Direct loading of images and sounds...251
Streaming sound 252
Accessibility..253
Local shared objects...257
Summary 263

11   Debugging   267

Existing debug options outside the debugger 267
The debugging environment 268
The SWD file 269
The debugger window 269
Using the debugger 271
Summary 285

12   Video   287

The Video object 287
    Sorenson Spark and Sorenson Squeeze...287
    The Flash player and video 288
Video Workflow 289
    Importing video 289
    Adding video to Flash timelines..295
        Streaming video 295
        Preloading video 298
Summary 302

13   Events   305

Event scripting techniques 305
Events as methods in Flash..306
The Macromedia Flash MX event model 311
    Listeners 311
    Timer events 318
    The sound completion event 323
        How to use onSoundComplete 324
Summary 329

14   Advanced Components   331

Customizing the default components 331
    Using the FstyleFormat object 332
        Changing the global style 332
        Creating and defining a custom style 333
Skinning components..335
    Customizing skins 344
Setting up advanced components 349
    Stage 1: Drag and drop 349
    Stage 2: Adding the script 353
    Stage 3: Adding a live preview 355
Summary 360

15   Advanced Objects   365

Flash and object-oriented design 365
Extending classes 367
    Prototypes...367
    Inheritance 367
    Using prototypes to create custom classes 369
Using functions without OOP 372
    OOP and components..374
    Modifying the default object prototypes 381

Watchers 386
Summary 393

16   Departure Lounge   395

The Oracle, by aYo Binitie..395
    Creation...396
        Ray of energy 397
        Bugs..397
        Flies 399
        The Oracle's 'being' 400
        Lines of Force 402
        Sound 402
        Covering boards...403
    Completion...404
Spank, the Monkey, by Hoss Gifford 408
    Who needs Generator?...409
    Spank the Monkey MX 409
        The set up 410
        Acquiring a new image 410
        Drawing an outline for the mask 412
        Creating the mask 412
        Ready to start spanking 414
    Reflections 415

Appendix: Common Errors   417

Errors caused by scope 417
    The global level...417
    Callback events 418
    Scope of #initclip 419
Errors caused by enhancements to events 419
    Callbacks 419
    Object.watch 420
        sound.OnSoundComplete 420
    Depth and the drawing API..421
    Components and text fields 421
Summary 421

Index   423

Table of Contents

Chapter 1

Macromedia Flash MX: Overview

This book assumes throughout that you've previously been using Macromedia Flash 5, and that you want to learn about all the new Macromedia Flash MX stuff without having to wade through information you already know.

In preparation for writing this book, we've been working with Macromedia Flash MX since its early stages of development, becoming familiar with all the enhancements, and gaining practical insights on how to use it efficiently. Now we want to pass all this information on to you in the form you need it most – quickly and concisely, with emphasis on the real-world use of new features.

Accordingly, we'll be looking at Macromedia Flash MX from two angles, tackling the two distinct areas of Flash – the *designer's environment* and the *scripting environment*.

> The code-junkies amongst us may feel inclined to jump straight to the scripting content, but we advise you to first have a look at Chapters 2 and 3. The Macromedia Flash MX user interface is significantly different from previous versions and we don't want to lose anyone along the way!

Macromedia Flash MX in context

Flash started out as the simple timeline-based web graphics application *FutureSplash*. Since then, its compact plug-in and compressed vector-based format has made it the number one rich media delivery system for the web.

On the face of it, Macromedia Flash MX may look like a vibrant new interface and not much else. In fact, there's a heck of a lot to be found beneath the surface! As you dig down into the details, a very different picture soon emerges. Although Flash 5 was a big step forward from Flash 4, its workflow wasn't so hot. Now, with an optimized workflow and numerous new features hiding behind the interface, Macromedia Flash MX is easily the most different revision of Flash so far; so different in fact that we'll spend this entire first chapter previewing the main enhancements – you should regard this chapter as a sample of what's to come in this book.

As well as the useful additions of a new **Property inspector** based user interface, there are an amazing number of major refinements in *all* areas of the Flash environment, important examples of which include **components** (MX's major enhancement of smart clips), and support for video importing. Flash 5 concentrated on the scripting side of design and development, and indeed Macromedia Flash MX refines scripting even further to make it significantly more powerful. Unlike

Flash 5, however, this latest software revision also applies the same level of fine-tuning to the standard animation and drawing tools, so non-programmers are also invited to party with this release!

Flash MX is not just different – it is *fundamentally different* from previous revisions. Macromedia have taken a long hard look at the way Flash 5 was used, and have completely redefined the workflow to make utilizing it simpler and more direct, irrespective of whether you are an animator-designer or serious scripter.

Backwards compatibility is a big concern, and it's worth noting that a surprisingly large number of the new additions will work on legacy Flash players as well.

A tour of Macromedia Flash MX

In this introductory chapter we'll take a quick tour of the additional features that you can expect to meet in later chapters of this book. Hold on tight – it's a long and action-packed ride!

The Flash player

The Flash plug-in has undergone some pretty big changes itself, and the new version is significantly bigger (although the zipped download file is still less than 400kb). In parallel, the *performance* of the Flash player has increased dramatically. Macromedia have re-written much of the Flash 5 plug-in such that much of it is now *totally* different to the lower level stuff, and this major re-engineering has led to a highly *robust* product.

As you may or may not be aware, all Flash actions are eventually converted to a form called `ASNative` which, in turn, calls low-level native commands. In Flash 5, there were no ASNative commands to handle *array*, *string*, and *XML* objects (in fact, some of the beta-code for this functionality did find its way into Flash 5 as an 'undocumented feature', for those devious enough to find it!). These objects were handled via a long and inefficient route in the past; they're now hard coded in to the Flash player plug-in, making them blindingly fast in comparison to the previous edition of Flash.

Furthermore, the Flash player plug-in now includes an embedded video codec (more on this later) as well as something so subtle that you might at first miss it – **SWF compression**. A Flash MX SWF is compressed during publishing and then decompressed at run-time by the player. This makes existing Flash 5 FLAs that are republished in Flash MX *significantly* smaller. Compression works particularly well with ActionScript; a compressed ActionScript-heavy site can be as little as 25% the size of its Flash 5 version. So, practically speaking, the user has to wait a quarter of the time for download! Alternatively, you can get 400% more stuff in for the equivalent download size!

> *The compression used by MX (ZLib) is great for uncompressed content (such as scripts), but may not be effective in certain FLAs where you are streaming in content that is already heavily compressed (MP3, Sorenson video, and so on). In these cases, the file size reduction (of the SWF) should be compared against the slight loss in performance caused by the decompression, and a decision on whether to compress should be taken on a per-FLA basis.*

Best of all, adding compression simply requires checking Compress Movie in File>Publish Settings>Flash. You need to make no changes to the content.

As we hinted earlier, backward compatibility with Flash 5 and even earlier versions is fully supported as far as practicable, and is actually almost *total*.

A particular difference between Macromedia Flash and Macromedia Director is the fact that deprecated commands continue to be supported in Flash. In Director, deprecated translates as *'stop using this command because we may not support it in the future'*. In Flash, deprecated essentially means *'avoid using this command because there is a better way of doing it, but your old FLAs that do use it will always continue to work'*. Backward compatibility is rated highly by Macromedia, so unlike many other applications, there are expected to be very few *previously supported* actions or methods dropped with each software upgrade, even if they are no longer commonly used by the design community.

There are however a very small number of *unsupported* actions that will no longer work in Flash MX, but these are generally undocumented features that the hackers (and the 'curious' developers!) got to know about in Flash 5, including some direct calls to ASNative and some undocumented FsCommand actions. If you don't know what we're alluding to, you don't need to worry; all your Flash 5 content should still work!

> *Use of* FsCommand *to save data to a hard drive has also been removed. It was trial beta code that has been omitted because of potential security violations - the user had no way of stopping access. However, the new shared objects of Flash MX allow writing to a user's drive in a controlled manner, as we'll see later in the book.*

Let's now dive right in to Flash MX, starting with an examination of the new UI.

Workflow and user interface

One thing to notice when you first open Flash MX is that the Quick Launch bar is no more. Although you may find this to be a major step backwards to start with, you will soon realize you no longer need it!

The screenshot below shows the user interface (UI) display that you'll see when you first start Flash MX:

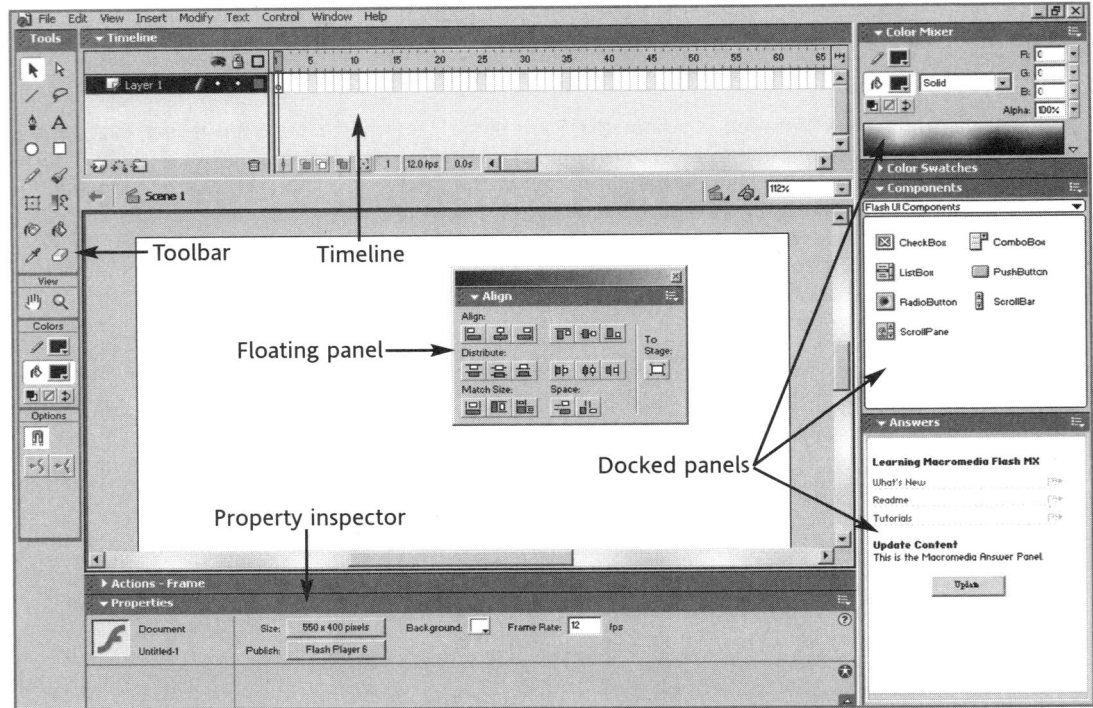

Panels

The Flash 5 floating panels tended to create clutter, with panels all over the stage area. To combat this, Flash MX now allows panels to dock with the new interface. The timeline and toolbar also inherit some of this new panel functionality.

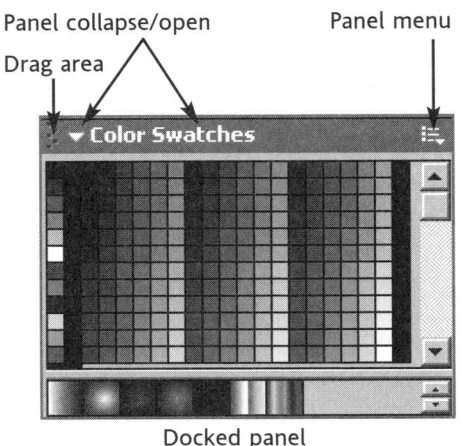

Docked panel

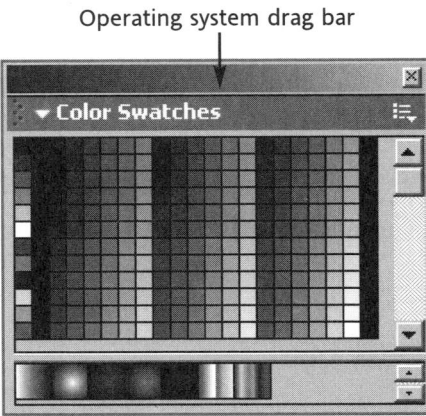

Floating panel

The default layout (select Window>Panel Sets>Default Layout) will result in a number of docked panels appearing at the far right margin of the screen. To undock a panel, drag it away from the docked area via the knurled drag area. To re-dock a panel, drag it back via the same drag area. Dragging a panel with the operating system drag bar (which differs in appearance slightly depending on which operating system you are using - see Chapter 2) will *not* cause the panel to re-dock.

You can also dock/undock the timeline and Property inspector to/from their default positions in this fashion. Practice with the docking feature and see if you can do the following:

- Find all the areas that panels will dock to
- Find out how to dock floating panels to each other thus creating floating docking stacks

You can open/collapse a panel via the little down-arrow or the title area next to it. This will also work for the timeline and Property inspector:

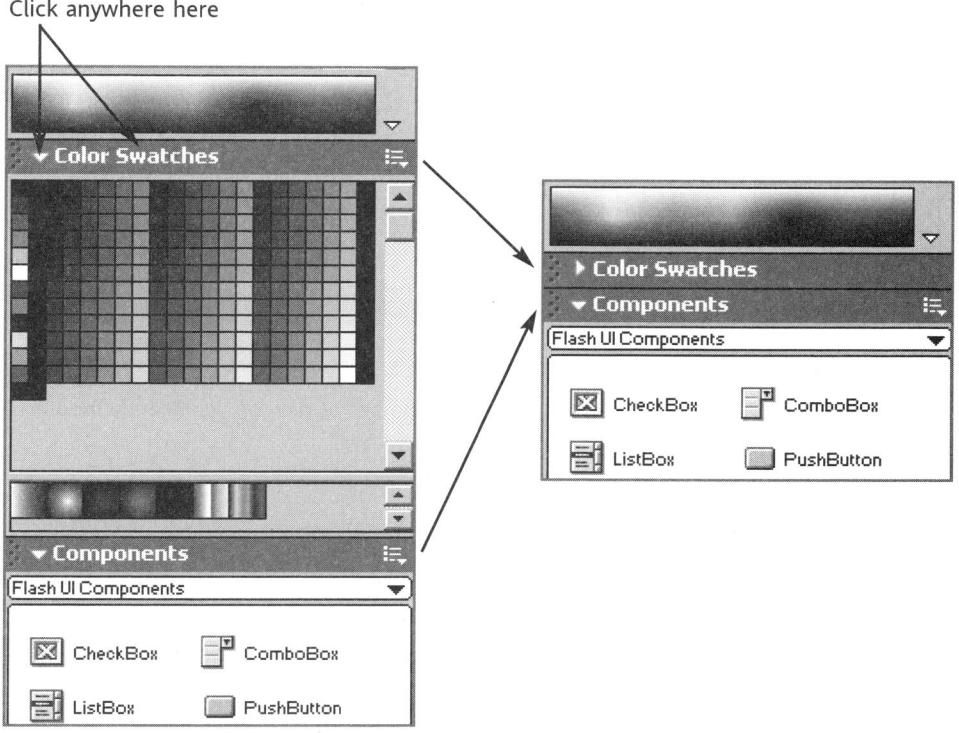

Open Color Swatches panel   Collapsed Color Swatches panel

By collapsing both the Property inspector and timeline unless needed, you gain the *maximum* available screen 'real estate' for the stage, thus allowing room to build up those intricate hand-drawn animation keyframes. As we shall soon see, the Property inspector actually replaces many of the common content creation panels, so most of the time artists only need to access the timeline,

Property inspector and toolbar, plus a few specialized panels, which can be tucked away in a corner as collapsed floaters that are only a single click away:

As well as the new panel interface, there are also a number of new or significantly modified panels, which include:

- The Color Mixer panel (modified)

- The Components panel (new) – components replace Flash smart clips, and are discussed at length later in this book

- The Accessibility panel (new) – allows you to add accessibility features to meet current and potentially important future changes to the specifications of the *Americans with Disabilities Act* (ADA)

- The Answers Panel (new) – replaces the old Flash 5 *Macromedia Dashboard*

- The Reference panel (new) – used in association with the Actions panel

The Property inspector

Anyone who has used Dreamweaver or Director will know what a Property inspector is (it's sometimes referred to as a 'PI'). It is a small panel that displays the properties of the object currently selected, as well as a context sensitive help icon and the Actions panel quick-launch icon that was previously part of the taskbar in Flash 5:

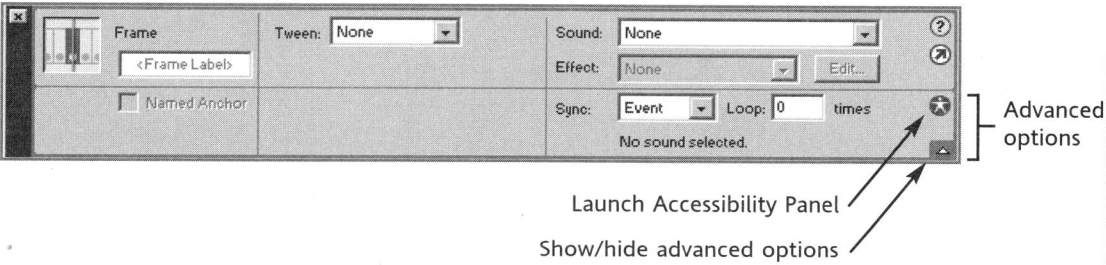

Launch Accessibility Panel

Show/hide advanced options

Rather than having to open several different panels in readiness to work with a stage or timeline element, the PI changes to reflect the item that you have currently selected, so it is always displaying the information you need when you want it! This *context sensitive* information directly relating to whatever you are engaged in improves the workflow radically.

Sometimes, however, too much information is a curse, so Macromedia have added a little **show/hide** arrow at the bottom right for those of us who want to choose whether we want to know the full story or not. Expanding the PI with this arrow reveals some extra details, including an icon to bring up the new accessibility panel:

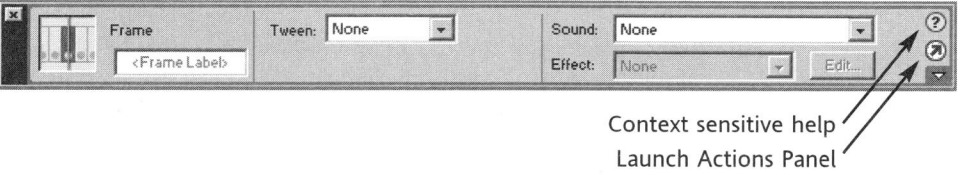

Context sensitive help

Launch Actions Panel

> Note that you can use CTRL+F3 to toggle the visibility of the Property inspector.

Using the PI reduces the number of panels you need to have open, and you will soon find that many of the old Flash 5 panels are no longer needed at all once you embrace the Flash MX PI.

The timeline and library

Although the new version of Flash no longer allows you to go back to the full Flash 4 style timeline (as did Flash 5), it does have some new features that more than make up for it. Let's take a quick look at the timeline of a typical Flash MX FLA:

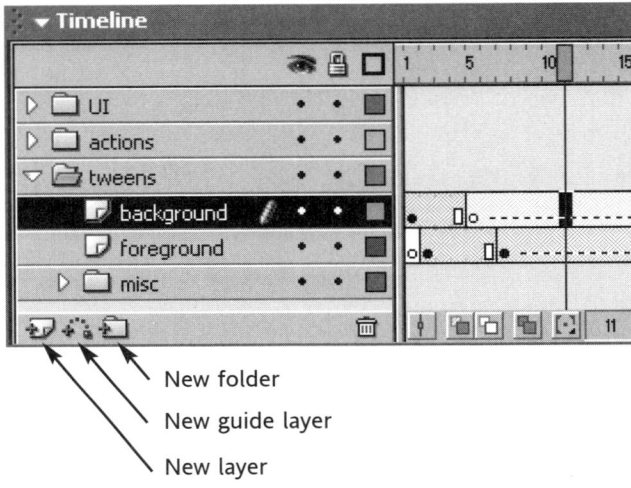

New folder

New guide layer

New layer

Anyone who has tried to create complex Flash content will know how quickly an FLA can end up with a large numbers of layers. Well, now you can arrange the layers into **folders**. Not only does this produce a more structured timeline, but it comes at no cost to the final SWF size, so feel free to go mad with folders!

In fact, Macromedia are effectively encouraging the use of more layers now that they can be organized more efficiently. For example, the **break apart** functionality now allows you to distribute the split elements into new layers, which, as any animator knows, puts them just how you want them (with one symbol per layer) to create tweens.

We should emphasize that Break Apart and Distribute to Layers are actually distinct commands. You would select a symbol or group to break apart, and then after breaking it apart you can distribute its constituent parts to layers. Note also that distributing to layers can give two of the newly created layers the same name, so you might sometimes have to edit the names. If you break apart and distribute the word Macromedia, for example, you will end up with two layers called a – so get in quick and alter some layer names before you forget!

Try it yourself; create a static text box and enter 'Flash' (or whatever) in it. Highlight your text, and break it apart with Modify>Break Apart, or CTRL+B. Notice that the break has separated the letters out rather than converting to fills and lines (if you actually want separated fills and lines, simply hit CTRL+B again). Now select Modify>Distribute to Layers, or CTRL+SHIFT+D, to do the distribution. You'll see 'F' in layer F, 'l' in layer l, and so on.

The **library** window has also gone through some subtle changes that enhance its usability. Folder structure is now maintained if you copy library contents between different FLA files, and there are some enhancements to shared libraries. More specifically:

- Because folder structures are maintained between libraries, you can simply drag and drop stuff during authoring. Flash will tell you if you are about to overwrite a file of the same name via drag and drop.

- Enhanced compilation-time use of shared libraries allows you to use a library from another SWF during the creation process. This is ideal because if you need to change a symbol in many SWFs within a site, all you have to do is change the library SWF and recompile them all. This function works across a network, which is really good for multi-team projects!

We'll look at these enhancements in detail in Chapter 3.

User interface extensibility

Finally, not only has Macromedia tweaked the interface, but they have also opened it up so that you can customize both the *position* of panels and the actual *contents* of certain windows. The Actions panel, for instance, can be customized via a set of XML documents that you are free to edit. For example, you can delete all deprecated actions so that you are never tempted to use them. We'll learn about how flexible the Flash MX UI is in Chapter 5.

Browser control and accessibility

In previous editions of Flash, one of the biggest irritations was the lack of support for the browser Back button. Furthermore, there was no support for bookmarking specific places within the SWF in the same way you can with HTML. As we all know, Flash produces motion graphics, so surely you can't bookmark within an animation? Well, you can now! As we'll see in Chapter 10, all that it requires is giving a keyframe a name (thus making it a label), and then clicking the Named Anchor checkbox on the frame Property inspector, and you're away!

The scaling and position of the Flash movie can now be altered or read directly via ActionScript. You can also tell when the browser has just been resized, allowing dynamic control of the appearance of your site.

Just as HTML separates formatting (the HTML document) from images (the JPG, GIF, and PNG files), in Flash MX you can now do the same with images and sound. Flash MX allows direct import of a number of media types *during run-time,* allowing you the same level of flexibility as HTML documents. You just write the SWF framework and let the *client* update the associated images and sound themselves, whenever they wish. We'll see specific examples of this in Chapters 10 and 16, after which it'll become clear that it also gives more options for conditional or structured loading of Flash content into the browser.

Accessibility can be added to a Flash site via the Accessibility panel:

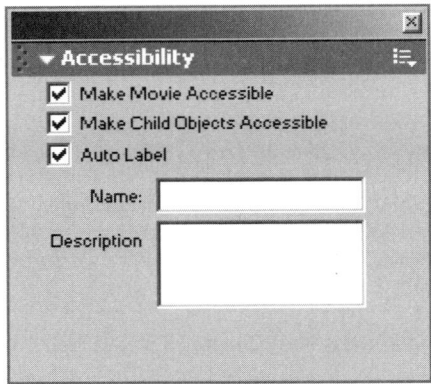

This allows auto-readers used by the vision-impaired to decode your site via the appropriate software. Such accessibility is a feature that may soon become a legal requirement in the USA, so it's something to start doing if you aren't already – clients are sure to start adding it to their site design requirements.

Content creation

Now let's delve into the real 'hands-on' tools to gain some concrete insights into the new design functionality that Flash MX offers. There are all sorts of little tweaks to the standard tools and workflow, such as the Break Apart function that we mentioned earlier, which breaks text into individual letters the first time you apply it, and to individual shapes if you do it again.

Irate users of Flash 4 who realized that Flash 5 overwrote files so that previous versions could no longer access them need not worry. Flash MX actually warns you about such matters, so you can use Flash MX with confidence. It's this sort of thoughtful refinement that has gone on behind the scenes that confirms that Macromedia have actually listened long and hard to folks who sent stuff to the wish-flash@macromedia mailing list, and we'll be describing all such changes throughout this book, whether they're the totally obvious new features, or the more subtle modifications.

As a teaser of what's to come, we'll take a brief look at enhancements under the following headlines in the next few sections:

- Distort and envelope modifiers

- Fonts and text

- Components

- Video

- Templates

Distort and envelope modifiers

The **Transform** tool now has some neat new and advanced modifiers hidden in the Options area of the toolbar. Blink and you'll miss them, which is a shame because they are really power tools for animation:

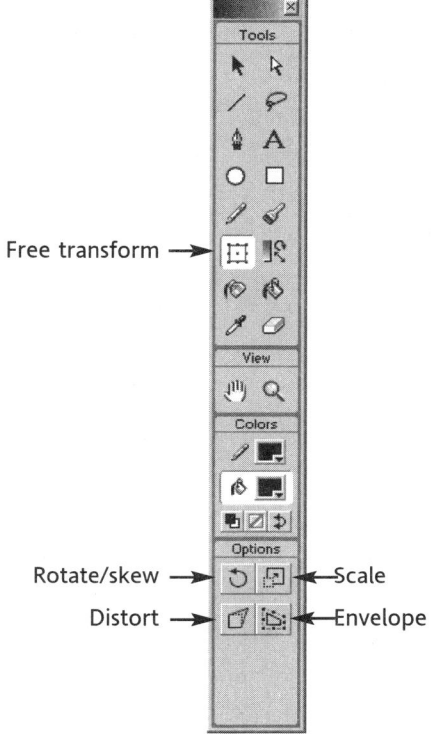

Free transform

Rotate/skew — Scale

Distort — Envelope

In Chapter 4 we'll be learning how to use the **distort** modifier to alter text however we see fit, as shown below:

As you can probably already guess, this is an invaluable tool for creating 3D animations for the keyframe animator who doesn't want to have to jump through Swift3D, 3DMax, or math-ActionScript hoops!

Envelope is cooler still; instead of distorting via a rectangle we can use **curves** to modify our selections to create whatever customized shapes we want:

The envelope modifier is a very useful tool that can clearly be used to create lifelike shape tweens:

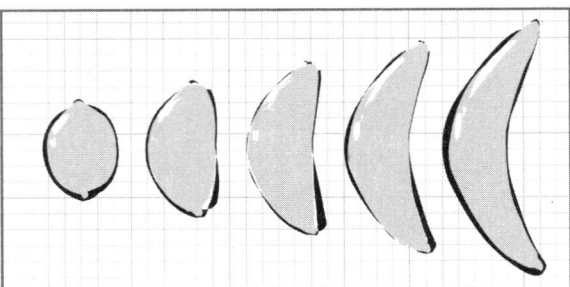

From swaying trees to flexing muscles and mouth movements during speech, the envelope modifier will be a real bonus for the skilled traditional animator. Who says ActionScript junkies get all the good stuff?

Fonts and text

We'll examine text enhancements at length in Chapter 6. Flash now supports Unicode UTF8 and vertical text (useful for non-western text).

You can also have scrolling text areas for input fields, plus some advanced text-formatting options, as shown below:

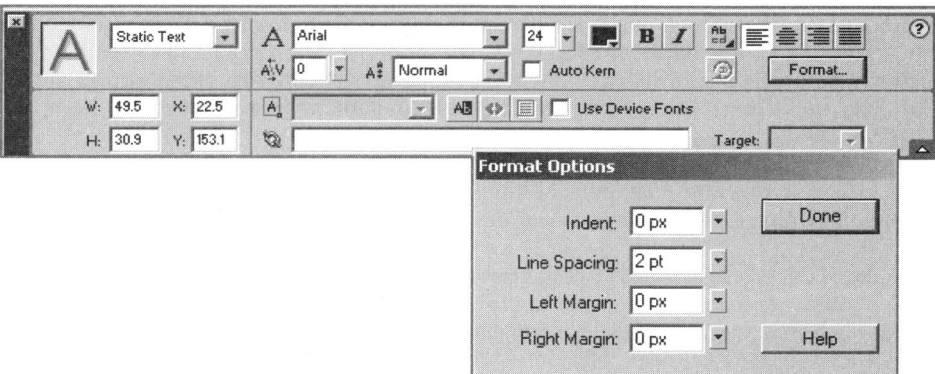

We don't have advanced text transform effects like *conform to path*, but you can easily do such text effects (which would normally require an import from a package like Illustrator or Freehand) with the envelope modifier. With this new version of Flash, Macromedia have given us a rather advanced set of *general editing tools:*

Another small but relevant new feature relates to *pixel-snapping*. Although anti-aliasing is cool for getting rid of 'jaggies', it can blur certain designs, particularly those that use the small text fonts that have been very popular lately. A good workaround in Flash 5 was to place text on an exact pixel boundary. This could be difficult to do because it was not always obvious whether a graphic element was actually on a pixel boundary. In Macromedia Flash MX, not only can you snap to pixels as you create content (View>Snap to Pixels) but, if you zoom in far enough, you can actually see the pixel grid appear. The images below show a pixel-snapped text area (top), and a non-snapped instance (bottom):

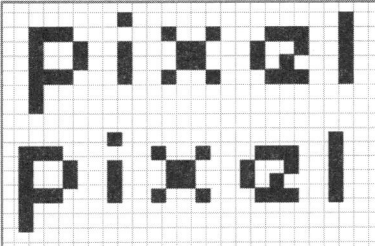
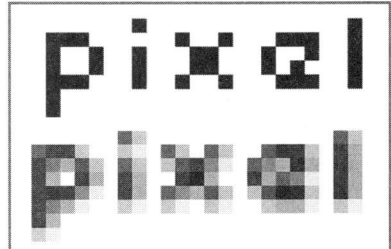

The difference in the real-time rendering of the two text areas shows quite a change in crispness and legibility.

Components

Flash 5 introduced a new kind of movie clip – the smart clip, with which a scripter could create clips that were configurable. A designer could take the ready-built smart clip and, by setting a few parameters, configure it to their particular application without having to know about what was actually inside the clip in terms of code. With **components**, Macromedia have followed this idea through in a natural evolution. A component is a 'super smart clip' that allows you to do the same kind of thing, but is much better integrated to the Flash authoring environment.

As we'll see in Chapter 9, using the standard components that ship with Flash couldn't be easier. For example, by simply click-dragging the ScrollBar icon from the Components panel onto a textbox we can include fully functional scrollbars in our designs.

The benefits of this are clear – by the simple act of dragging and dropping it, the scrollbar effectively *knows* that you want to scroll the text you dropped it on, and in that specific area. Once you have done those two things, the scrollbar is intelligent enough to look after itself!

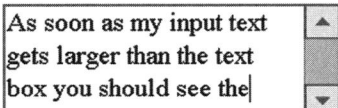 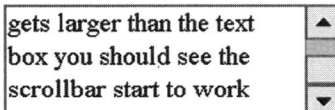

Looking at the other standard UI components, you will see that you have all the building blocks there for a fairly complex site. All you have to do is place them on the stage, perhaps add a small bit of scripting (nothing too taxing), and you're away!

> *Components are indeed a pretty cool improvement to the Flash workflow, and the default UI ones are actually just the tip of the iceberg! The true beauty of components is that one designer can create them, and then everyone can use them!*

The more discerning of you might be thinking 'OK, but I don't like the look of the standard components... I want them to be styled in a blue chrome effect so I can use them in my personal designs!' In fact, those nice folks at Macromedia have already considered this – via a process called **skinning**, you can change the look of components without affecting the way they work by creating your own graphics (called a *skin*). We'll learn how to skin our components in Chapter 14.

Even better, you can add further components built by Macromedia (or by anyone else who might have written some). You never have to know how they work – just how to use them, which means that you don't even have to get into the detailed scripting. This is the non-programming designer's heaven! We can expect more components to appear on the Web soon, including pre-loaders and text effect engines.

Video

Enhanced video import functionality is a great new feature, which we'll study in Chapter 12; its importance will no doubt become obvious simply by looking at some of your favorite sites on the Web in the coming months. This is *not* a simple 'import loads of frames as separate images' deal, but a true embedded video codec that resides within the Flash player, so there's no need for any other plug-in as was the case with Flash 5 and Quicktime. Not only does Flash MX support video pictures, there's the option of synchronized audio as well, if the original video source included it.

Macromedia Flash MX video import acts just like standard bitmap or sound import in Flash 5. Simply select File>Import and make All Video Formats the file-type filter. Once you have chosen and imported your video, it will appear as a symbol in your library; imagine the artistic possibilities of overlaying vector graphic animations onto video as it plays, or dragging multiple instances of the same video clip onto the stage to create video walls:

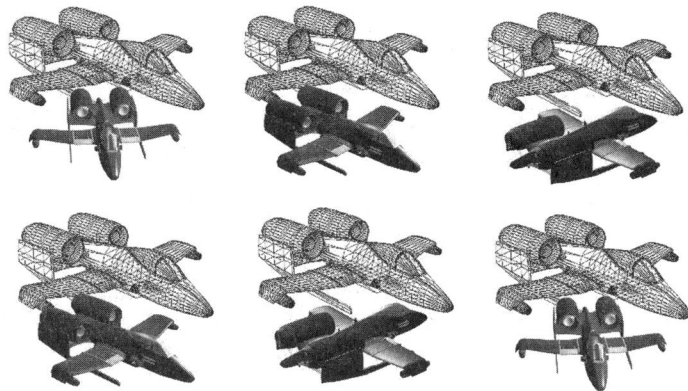

Imported video clips in Flash can also use most (but not quite all) of the effects that you can apply to a normal movie clip. However, you cannot just apply ActionScript in the same way as you can with movie clips, and the dynamic manipulation of an imported movie is restricted to the basics like sizing, scaling, skewing, and so on. It's also worth mentioning that real-time decompression of the video is rather intensive on the player.

Flash also has some new sound options. Although using most of these features involves ActionScript (discussed later in the book), you do gain a new sound compression type for speech - the Nellymoser speech codec (curious readers can find out more about it at www.nellymoser.com). This codec works well with speech at very low bit-rates, allowing you to compress sound files that only contain speech to smaller sizes than other sound compression types allow.

Templates

The inclusion of standard templates in Macromedia Flash MX enables quick and easy content creation. For standard sites and corporate presentations that you have to do in a hurry, there are default templates installed ready for you to load up and use.

Just select File>New From Template... and add your own content to your chosen template:

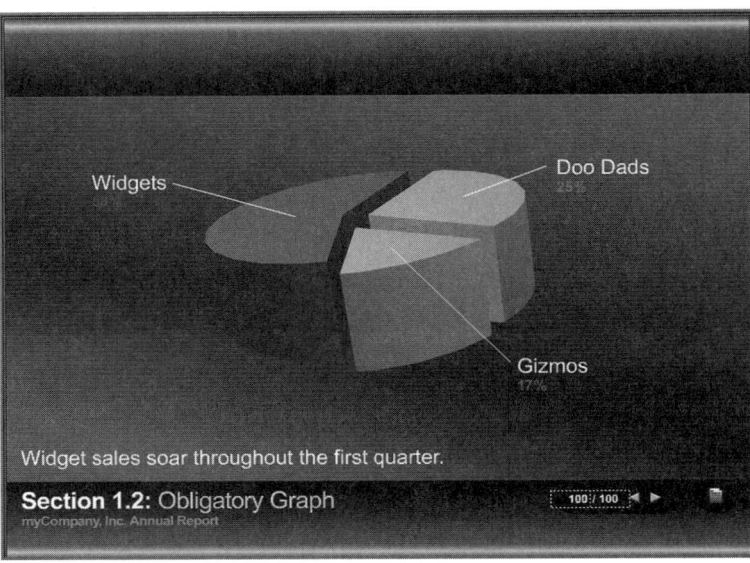

Of course, this is not just a workflow tool for the designer. Most Flash applications and sites that I construct tend to have a first layer that contains labels and comments, then one that contains scripts, and so on. Wouldn't it be nice if these were included at the start of every new FLA as a template? Well, now you can even create such a standard 'programmer's timeline' (complete with a tidy folder structure) just by using File>Save as template... once you have created your default FLA configuration:

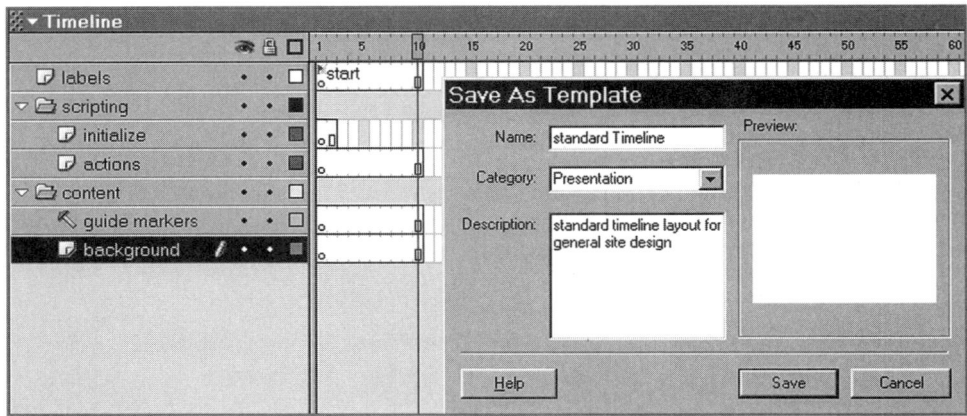

Scripting

Now it's time to take a glance at the more technical advancements made by Macromedia Flash MX and see what's new on the *scripting* side of Flash. The first thing you may notice is that the Actions panel looks remarkably similar to the Flash 5 version, but don't be fooled – there are indeed a number of new features that Macromedia have added. Although this panel can be docked, it is usually too small to be useful, so after hitting F2 to bring it up, undock and enlarge it. The Actions panel has been seriously reworked, but hides its new powers well. We won't give it all away just yet because there's a lot to show you, but rest assured, there are some really striking features added behind the seemingly dull façade – we'll cover these enhancements when we come to look specifically at the scripting environment, in Chapter 5.

There is also a reworked debugger in Flash MX that allows us to use **breakpoints**. A problem with the old Flash 5 debugger was that although it showed us everything that was going on, we could never pause or stop it in mid-execution. Sometimes the particular condition we want to debug only lasts for a single frame, or even worse, for the duration of a loop, or within a fleeting function. Breakpoints can force the SWF to pause, which allows us to look at the wealth of information offered by the debugger at our leisure before un-pausing and moving on. We'll familiarize ourselves with the Macromedia Flash MX debugging functionality in Chapter 11.

In terms of scripting actions, the easiest way to get some indication of the number of new Flash MX actions is as follows. In File>Publish Settings>Flash select Flash Player 5 as the version. Almost all Flash MX-only actions will now be highlighted in yellow in the Actions panel (signifying that Flash 5 can't use them). Bring up the Actions panel, and click on Index in the left pane (which lists all actions alphabetically). Scrolling down this list will give you an indication of all the new actions and, as you will soon see, there is a sea of yellow on your screen meaning that we have lots of new ones to play with:

- attributes (XML)
- autoSize (TextField)
- background (FStyleFormat)
- background (TextField)
- backgroundColor (TextField)
- backgroundDisabled (FStyleF...
- BACKSPACE (Key)
- beginFill (MovieClip)
- beginGradientFill (MovieClip)
- blockIndent (TextFormat)
- bold (TextFormat)
- Boolean
- border (TextField)
- borderColor (TextField)
- bottomScroll (TextField)
- break
- bullet (TextFormat)
- call
- call (Function)
- callee (arguments)
- caller (arguments)
- capabilities (System)
- CAPSLOCK (Key)

Let's take a moment to have a look at the nature of some of these new actions and modified objects.

Many multimedia and graphic elements are now objects

You may have noticed by now that the Property inspector allows you to add instance names for text fields. It will actually allow you to do this for a number of other elements. In fact, everything that can be placed on stage (except a static graphic symbol) is now an object, and has properties similar to those of the `movie clip`. This means that, just as you can with a `movie clip`, you can animate or control these new objects via their properties. More importantly, each of the new objects has an associated set of *methods*, which allow to interact with them and get them to *do things* – there's much more on this throughout the rest of the book. Ultimately, the link between the graphic environment and ActionScript is much stronger because the level of control through scripting has greatly improved.

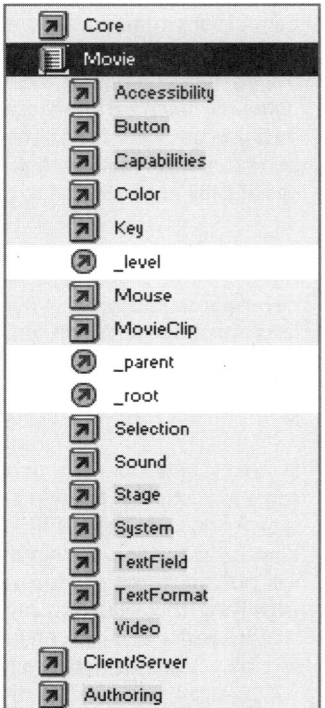

You can see the full list of objects from within the Actions panel by looking in Objects>Movie set of actions:

As well as the ubiquitous `MovieClip`, you now have some other neat multimedia objects. Notice that the `Button` is now also an object, as is the `Stage`. There is even a `Capabilities` object whose methods will tell you about the capabilities of the computer your SWF is running on, thus allowing you to tailor the Flash site to the user display and system resources. `Video` is another important object; it lets you control video playback interactively via scripting.

We've come a long way from the humble movie clip; Chapters 7 and 8 of this book are devoted to an overview of the new Flash MX objects, and Chapter 15 describes some advanced scripting techniques associated with objects. In fact, as we'll see in the next section, we can now even get Flash to draw the graphic content within these empty clips as well.

The drawing API

In the past, one of the problems with Flash was that although you could alter the visual properties a `movie clip` (such as its alpha, position, dimensions, and so on), you could not change its actual content. For example, you could not make a movie clip that contained a blue circle change into one that looked like a red triangle – some features, such as number of lines, fill colors, and so on, were fixed.

Well, that's all changed! You can create empty movie clips and get ActionScript to add the lines and fills to create totally new content inside each clip *dynamically*. The commands to do this are reminiscent of turtle graphics (remember your school days?), where you can draw lines and filled areas with a 'virtual pen'. So now ActionScript doesn't even need you to have defined the graphic symbols – it can draw them on the fly! Furthermore, because SWF compression will seriously compress any actions you use to draw such graphics, the final SWF may turn out to be tiny.

The drawing API is a subset of the `MovieClip` object methods and, as shown below, not only can you draw lines and fills, but you can also set gradients and draw curves. Take a look in the Objects>Movie>MovieClip>Drawing Methods folder of the Actions panel:

The ability to create a movie clip on the fly, build graphics inside it, and then add text and sound completely opens up the effects that can be created with ActionScript. Accordingly, we'll demonstrate the power of the drawing API in Chapter 8:

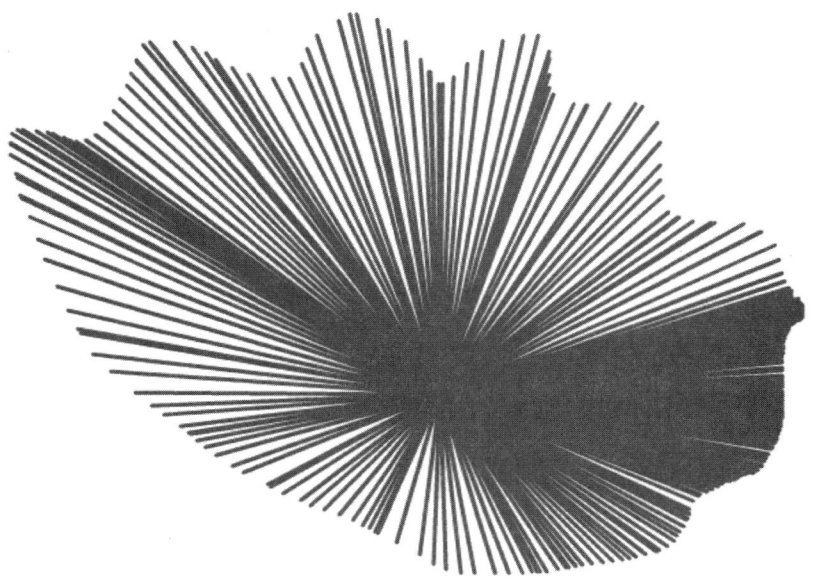

There are even more surprises for the major ActionScript users out there – new scripting features include the following:

- Closer compliance with JavaScript

- A true **global** level, which has implications to the scope of your variables and functions

- The ability to modify all objects (including the default ones such as the movie clip) to create your own object classes or custom methods (you could actually do this in Macromedia Flash 5, but it's better documented now)

- A new event model called **listeners**

- New Flash 'super-cookies' called **shared objects**

- Closer support for browser control without having to use JavaScript

And that's not even all of them!

Advanced ActionScripting

The final set of enhancements constitutes dynamite for the intermediate or advanced scripter. We will reserve the detailed discussion for later chapters, especially Chapter 15; for the moment it's sufficient to say that these changes include a totally reworked **event model** and major additions to the object model so that you can, for example, do the following:

- Modify existing default objects (like the movie clip and video, for instance) to add *custom methods*.

- Create new objects and methods that appear in the Actions panel and appear to be part of the ActionScript language via components. You could, for example, create an ActionScript 3D object that uses the drawing API to represent a vector 3D world.

- Create a hierarchy of handlers that respond to a particular event via the new *listener* actions. This would, for example, allow a number of movie clips to respond to events that occur to a third movie clip. This is *extremely* useful for advanced interactive control.

Finally, Macromedia Flash MX ActionScript now has a true global level, making it much more like other languages. In fact, some of the missing commands and features that JavaScript includes, functionality that didn't make it into Flash 5, are now included with Flash MX.

Summary

As you can see, there are a lot of new features in Macromedia Flash MX. Learning how to utilize this varied and feature-rich bag of tricks will take time because the possibilities are endless. Rather than give us specific built-in additions, Macromedia seem to have taken the approach of giving us a few definitive additions (such as video and the drawing API), and lots of useful general tools. In fact, enhancements to the general workflow and customizability of Flash give us the capacity to create anything else we might want *for ourselves!*

The developers at Macromedia have thoroughly listened to user requests for Flash 5 and made numerous changes to the workflow and user interface to get us where we want to be in the most efficient way possible. The new ways may seem a little odd at first, but trust us – we have persevered with it and the view from the top of the mountain is breathtaking!

How to use this book

As we emphasized at the start of this chapter, this book is aimed at designers with a solid background in Flash 5 who want to upgrade to Flash MX as quickly and painlessly as possible. Accordingly, we'll be covering each new topic at a fairly swift pace – so, to get the most out of this book, it's worth spending a moment familiarizing yourself with some of the standard styles and layout that we will use.

Layout conventions

We've tried to keep this book as clear and easy to follow as possible, so we've only used a few layout styles to avoid confusion. Let's take a quick look at them:

- If I introduce a new **important term** it will be in bold.

- I'll use different styles to emphasize things that appear on the screen, `pieces of code`, **`changes to pieces of code`**, as well as hyperlinks and `file names`.

> *If there's something you shouldn't miss, I'll highlight it like this - so when you see the bubble, pay attention!*

Practical exercises will appear with this heading style:

Example heading

And the exercises themselves will be broken down into logical steps, like this:

1. If you see the exercise numbers get ready for some real Flash action

2. Follow the steps through and check the screenshots and diagrams for more hints

3. When you get to the end, test it out to make sure it works!

- When we're showing ActionScript code blocks that should be referred to in the source code files, I'll use this style:

```
for (i=0; i<10; i++) {
  _root.attachMovie("monkey", "monkey"+i, 1000+i);
```

continues overleaf

```
        jump.apply(_root["monkey"+i]);
    }
```

- Where ActionScript is too wide to fit on the page, I'll indicate that it runs over two lines by using an arrow-like 'continuation' symbol:

```
    // Enable all buttons
    button01.enabled = button02.enabled = button03.enabled =
    ➥button04.enabled = true;
```

- Finally, when I add new code to, or change code in an existing block, it'll be highlighted like this:

```
    red = 0xFF0000;
    green = 0x00FF00;
    popupText = new TextFormat();
    popupText.color = green;
    popupText.align = "center";
```

Support

This friends of ED book is fully supported at www.friendsofed.com – source code files for the book can be downloaded from here, and you can also visit our support forums for help, inspiration, or just to chat.

There are dedicated pages for this book on the site, and the author will be visiting the forums regularly to hold mini 'surgeries'. You'll be able to continue developing and sharing your newfound Flash MX knowledge with like-minded individuals who are as keen to explore MX as you are.

The friends of ED site also has interviews with top designers, information and sample chapters for other books, and much more. The book is just the first part of the experience!

If you run into trouble - perhaps you have a problem with a certain file or tutorial, or you've just got plain muddled, we're right here for you! Leave a message on the forum, use the online feedback form, or drop a mail to support@friendsofed.com – we'll get you back on track in no time.

And even if you don't have problems, let us know what you think. Mail feedback@friendsofed.com or fill out the cute little reply card at the back of the book – that's what it's there for, and we'd love to hear from you!

Now that you're primed and ready to go, you're probably really eager to get your hands dirty and start playing with all the new and enhanced features of Flash MX. We'll get the ball rolling in the next chapter by taking an in-depth look at the new Macromedia Flash MX user interface.

Chapter 2

The User Interface

The user interface of Macromedia Flash MX not only looks different from the previous version, but it also works rather differently. All of the changes have been designed to create a more *streamlined* workflow. In simple terms, this means that the new interface quickly presents the information you need, when you need it.

The user interface (UI) is highly *customizable*, allowing you to configure it to the way you work, rather than the way Macromedia think you *should* be using it.

One particular frustration with the old Macromedia Flash 5 interface was that you often needed to have more than one panel open to achieve what you wanted. Like many other Macromedia products (such as Dreamweaver and Director), the Flash MX interface is now based around the concept of a Property inspector, which is context sensitive and alters its display to give you all the information you need in one place (rather than you having to move between panels of fixed information). This now takes over many functions that were previously in the panels. Don't worry though, many of the panels are still there, but you will quickly realize that you don't *need* some of the older ones that are still hanging on in Flash MX.

It's obvious that too many panels tend to clutter up the work area. To combat this, Macromedia Flash MX has **docking** panels that are designed to stick to the sides of the interface and keep your central stage area uncluttered and maximized.

We'll begin this chapter by examining the general Flash MX UI layout. Before looking at the new panels and the Property inspector, we'll briefly highlight which aspects of Flash 5 have been chopped out of this new interface (so you don't waste time looking for them!).

Overview of the Macromedia Flash MX user interface

In the previous chapter we saw a screenshot (from a Windows system) of the Flash MX UI. If you have tinkered with your copy of Flash MX since then, you can get back to this default state via Window>Panel Sets and then selecting the Default layout. It's also worth noting that there are a number of other designer UI configurations available to choose from here. For the moment, let's stick with the default layout.

Initially, there are a few things to notice. Perhaps most obviously, panels can now be *docked* or *undocked*. You can see the default docked panels on the right-hand side. If you now try to open more panels, such as the Align panel for instance (Window>Align or Ctrl+K), they will open as floating panels over the stage area by default, after which you can position your panels wherever you feel works best - preferably leaving your stage work area uncluttered.

If you were to open *all* the available panels as docked panels you can probably appreciate how docking leads to an uncluttered stage (overleaf):

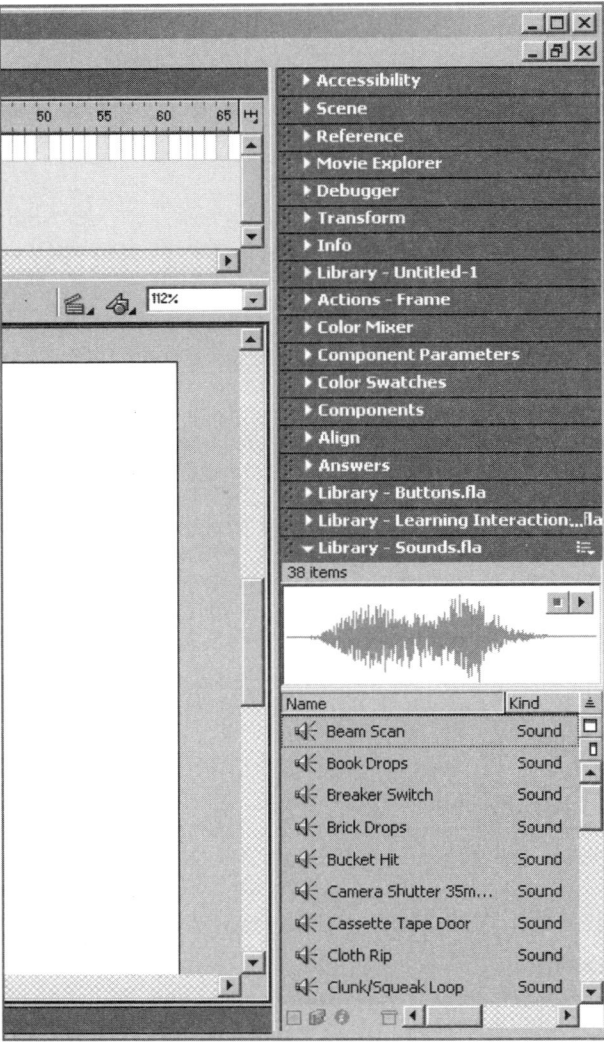

We'll learn more about how to use these new improved panels shortly.

At this point it's worth noting that the features of panels described in this section are specific to the application environment and operating system being used. For instance, although all of the design functionality is fundamentally the same, Mac users working with Flash MX may notice that their panels work somewhat differently from those of a PC user - on the Mac all panels are free-floating, although they can dock to other panels. The following screenshot shows how the Flash MX UI looks on a Mac:

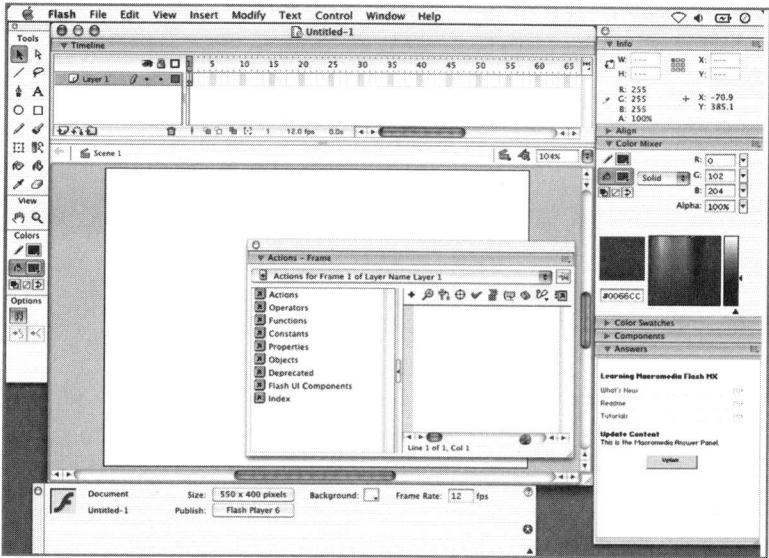

Another important addition to notice is the Property inspector, which indicates the properties of the item that is currently selected (for example, the main document in the screenshot above). You'll find the Property inspector just below the stage in the default layout, and we'll discuss it at length in the latter half of this chapter. From here you can set items such as the publish properties, stage size, and background color. Since these are among the first things you usually want to do when you open a new movie, the Property inspector will usually be your first port of call.

The best way to find out exactly what the Property inspector can do is, like most things, to play around a little. For example, select a tool on the toolbar, and the Property inspector will list all the things you can change before and during the use of that tool. Moreover, go ahead and use the tool you have picked, and then select whatever you have just drawn on the stage. The Property inspector will now show you all the properties of that item you can change - all from one window!

> The key point to remember is that the Property inspector is **context sensitive** - it effectively knows what you are trying to do and always provides the information you need at the time you need it. We'll look at this useful new friend in detail later in this chapter.

What's disappeared?

Perhaps the biggest shock with this release of Flash is that the quick launch icons that were found in the bottom right-hand corner of Flash 5 are no more. Almost every Flash 5 user I have talked to was mourning their loss at first, but then realized within a few days that these icons are just not needed any more.

Another more important feature that's vanished is the Generator icon that allowed you to insert Generator environment variables into Flash 5; Macromedia Generator is *not supported at all* in Flash MX. Although this is indeed a sad loss to many of us, don't worry! We can expect Macromedia to come up with a suitable replacement product soon enough - it's worth keeping an eye on www.friendsofed.com for future developments.

The option to use the *Flash 4 selection style or Flash 4 frame drawing* in the timeline has also disappeared from the preference options in Flash MX (Edit>Preferences...>General). Again, you'll soon find that these are no longer needed.

Now that we have the bad news out of the way let's have a look at the new interface in detail, starting with an outline of the new panel features.

Panels

The new panel functionality allows you to customize how your work area looks in far more useful ways than the old Flash 5 tabbed panels ever did. Not only does Macromedia Flash MX allow a high amount of customization, it also *remembers* what you have done between sessions - for instance, what your layout was like, what mode you were in, and so on. So, unlike an obsessive roommate, Flash won't complain about the way you like your living space organized, and will leave it just the way you want it.

Remember, to return to the default panel layout, simply select Window>Panel sets>Default layout. In this section we'll take a closer look at how to use panels most efficiently.

Docking areas

The typical docked panel title bar looks like this:

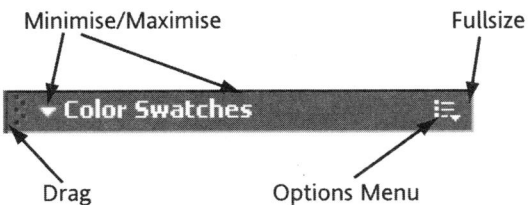

The knurled drag area on the left-hand side of the title bar allows you to drag a panel out of its docking area. For example, use it to drag the Color Mixer panel out of the default docking area on the right and place it on the stage. This panel is now undocked, or floating.

To re-dock the panel, simply drag it again with the same knurled drag area. You will see an outline of the dragged panel follow the cursor, and the various dockable areas will also be highlighted, as shown on the next page for the left-hand margin:

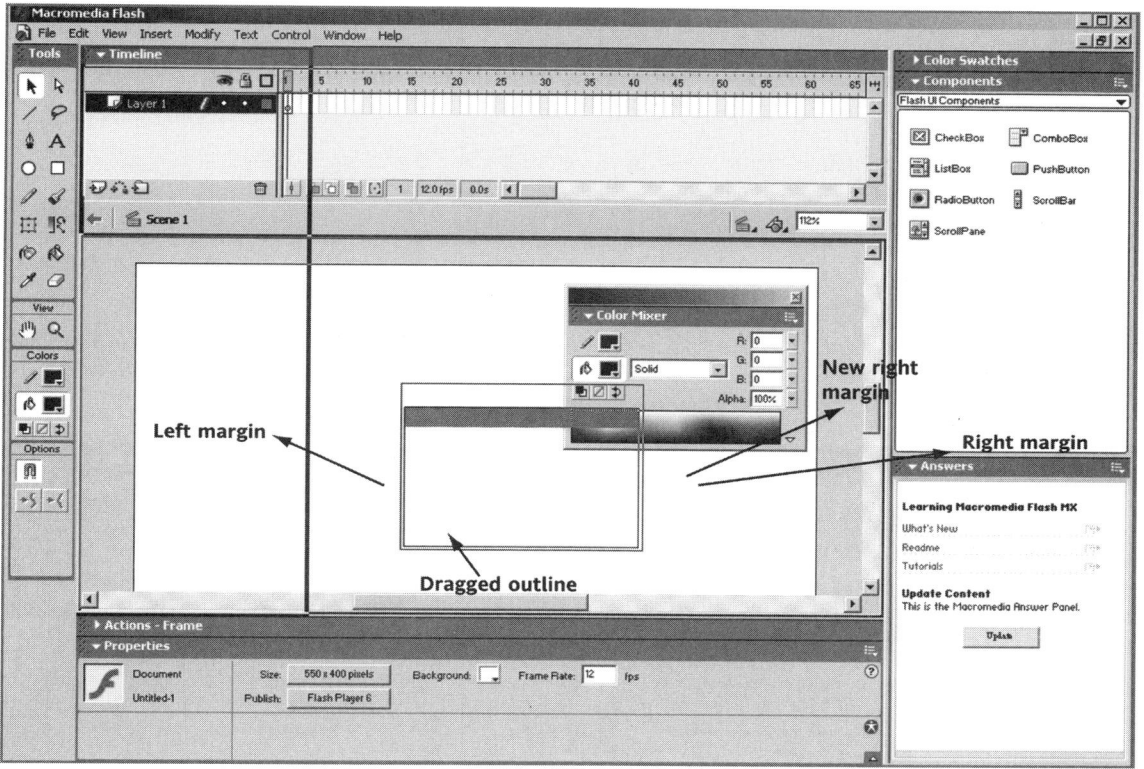

You will soon see that there are four areas that you can now dock a panel to:

- **The left margin** - drag the panel towards the left side of the stage and an outline of the new docking area that will be created will appear. Drop the panel to create this new docking area.
- **The right margin** - drag the panel back to the original docking area. Dropping the panel here will place the panel in the default docking area.
- **The new right margin** - an additional right margin will be created if you drop the panel between the stage and the existing docking area to the right. This will create two docking columns next to each other. Although this is not normally desirable (it reduces the available area for the stage), designers with very large screens may appreciate it.
- **Lower margin** - you can also dock to the lower margin where the Property inspector and Actions panels are found. This margin is more useful for larger panel.

> *Although the Actions and Library panels are called 'windows' in some documentation, they actually act as panels. In this book, we will refer to all items that can be docked in the margins as panels.*

While either docked or floating, you can hit the maximize/minimize switch on any panel to toggle between the maximized and minimized states for that panel. PC users can also alter the width of a docking area by dragging the edge of the docking column. This is particularly useful when you are using large panels like Actions and Color Swatches in the vertical margins.

For instance, with the default panel layout open you might find the Color Swatches panel a little too small to use effectively. You can change this by simply dragging the inner edge of the docking area as shown below:

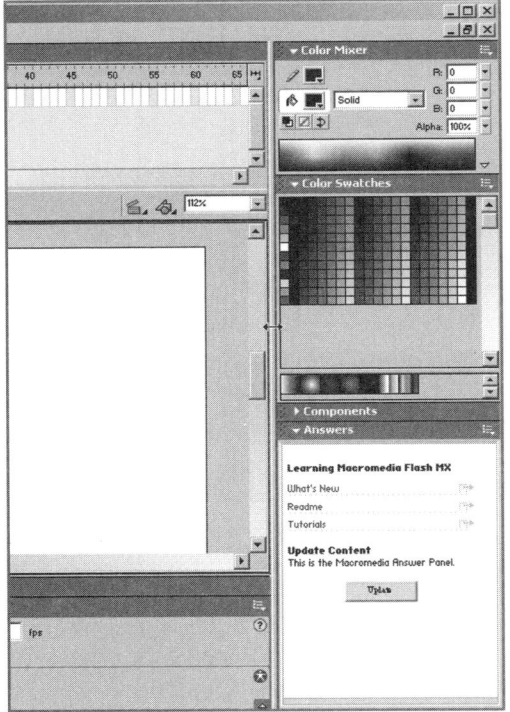 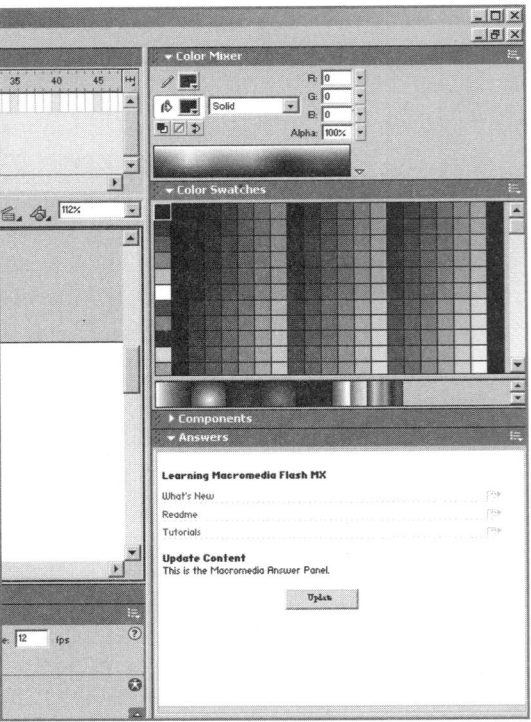

This gives us plenty of room to make use of the Color Swatches panel; notice that it has scaled itself to fit. Once you have used the panel, you can simply reduce the docking area size back to its initial width and continue working on the stage.

> *Note that there is no icon to close a docked panel. To do this you have to select the options menu on the panel (or just right click on it) and choose Close Panel. Alternatively, the same shortcut key that you can use to open a panel will also close it - for example, if you opened the Library panel using Ctrl+L, this shortcut will close it.*

There is one final bit of magic that docked panels allow - you can dock panels together to make a *floating stack*. You might do this, for instance, to group related panels.

Two panels that are made for each other are the Actions panel and Reference panel. You can dock these together as follows: drag the Actions panel from the lower margin onto the stage to make it a floating panel and resize it to whatever dimensions you'd prefer. Next, open the Reference panel (Window>Reference or Shift+F1) and drag it with the knurl bar over the Actions panel (which will become highlighted with a black border), then release it. The Reference panel will dock itself to the bottom of the Actions panel. Finally, the standard OS drag-bar at the top of the stack will allow you to drag both panels as a single unit and position them wherever you want:

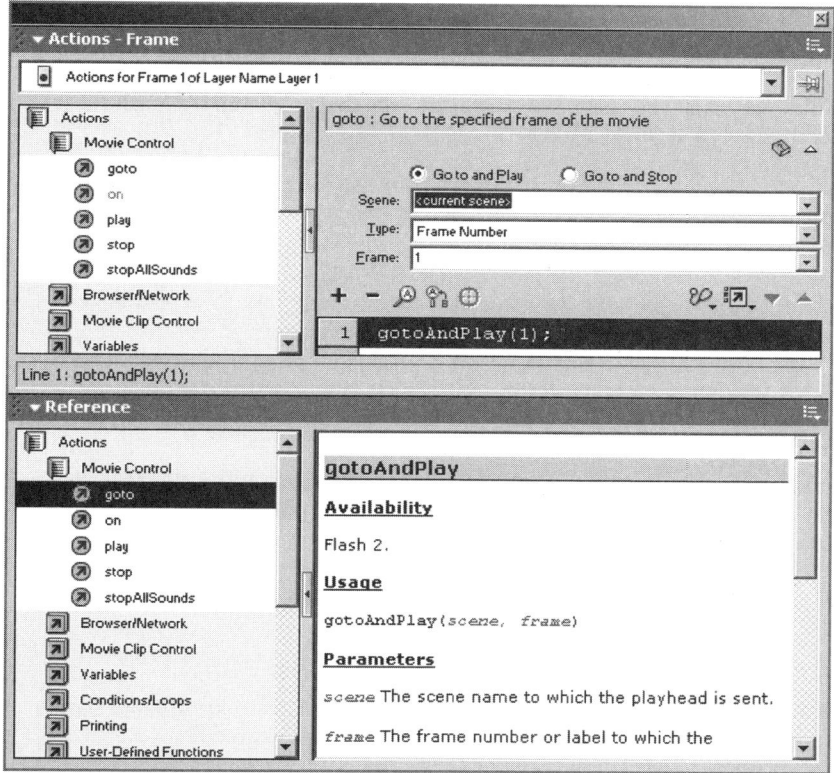

The beauty of this combination is that if you are writing a script and need to know more about a particular action, simply press the little blue reference book icon at the top right of the Actions panel. A full definition of the line you have currently selected (or the action the cursor is on if you are in Expert mode - more on this later) will appear in the Reference panel.

Once you are finished with your scripting, simply minimize both windows by clicking on the title bar of each panel in the floating stack in turn, and tuck it away in a corner of the screen (overleaf):

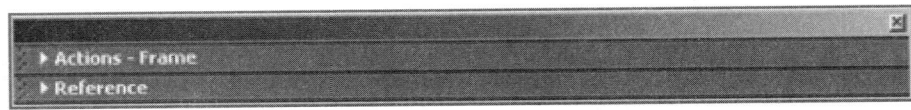

Remember, when moving such stacks, the bar you drag it with will have an effect on what happens:

- Dragging by the top Operating System bar will cause the whole stack to move to the point you drop

- Dragging by the knurled bar of any of the panels will cause that panel to disconnect from the stack

Floating stacks of docked panels are particularly useful if you are using a two-screen setup. In this case, you would set up all your panels in the second window as related stacks and these stacks would be maintained between sessions.

> *The Actions panel in Macromedia Flash MX has had numerous other refinements; we'll soon highlight the major additions in this chapter, and we'll look at them in greater detail when we come to investigate enhancements to the scripting environment, in Chapter 5.*

New panel functionality

There are a few new or significantly modified panels in Flash MX; in the following sections we'll highlight the major new functionality in several of the Flash panels:

- Actions
- Components and Component Parameters
- Color Mixer
- Accessibility

It's also worth noting that we have the Answers panel, which is really just the old Flash 5 *Macromedia Dashboard*, and the debugger, which we'll study at length in Chapter 11.

The Actions panel

The Actions panel has been substantially modified with this release. Most of these modifications are concerned with the following workflow enhancements:

- Increasing the usefulness of the Actions panel during normal workflow
- Allowing user customization
- Making Expert mode more accessible

For the moment we will introduce the new functionality of this panel in Normal mode. Later in this book, in particular in Chapter 5, we'll look at the benefits of using Flash MX in Expert mode.

Select Edit>Preferences...>ActionScript Editor. This gives you a first look at the new ActionScript panel's preferences. In fact, you can make more detailed changes to the Actions panel by playing with some XML files found within your Flash MX installation directories - we'll look at this in Chapter 5. For now, check that your preferences are set up as shown below:

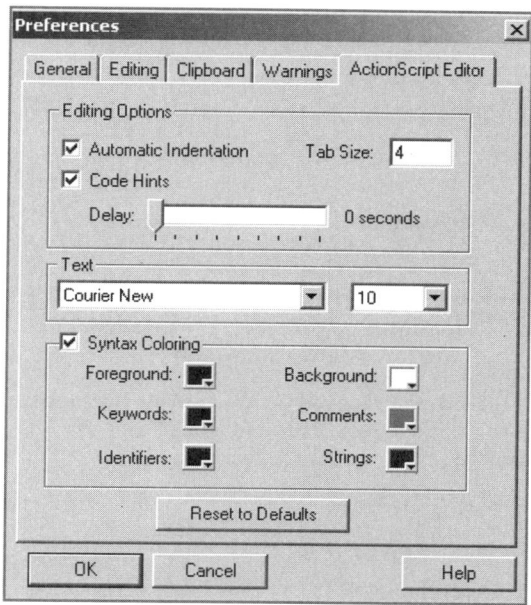

Hitting the Reset to Defaults button will set everything to match the settings shown in the screenshot. Notice that with this window you can change the syntax coloring, font type, and size in the new Actions panel.

Bring up the Actions panel (select Window>Actions or hit F2) if it isn't onscreen already; undock and resize it so that it is comfortable to work with - something like the screenshot below:

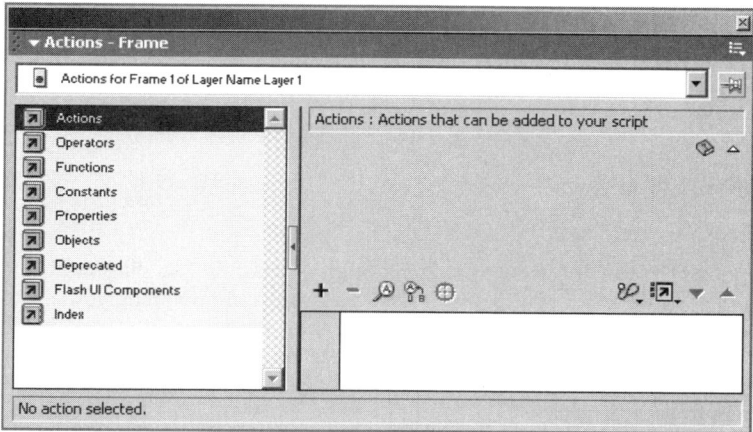

> *Note that here we are assuming that you are in Normal mode - if you are unsure, hit the 'view options' button (see below) and change as appropriate.*

A closer look at the Actions panel toolbar reveals a number of icons:

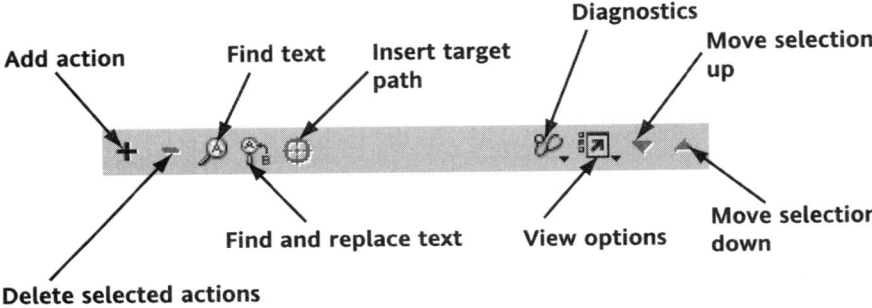

The **add action** and **delete selected actions** buttons work just like the + and − icons in Flash 5. The **find text** and **find and replace text** icons allow you to find/replace text in the current script, as you would expect. Unfortunately, however, there is no global search/replace that lets you change *all* scripts in the FLA.

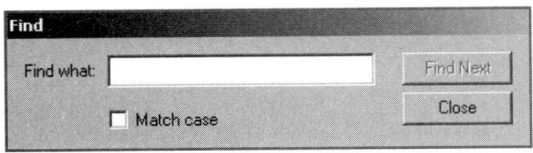

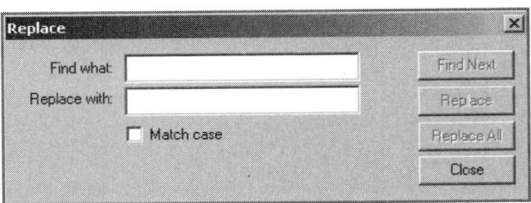

The **insert target path** icon also works much like it did in Flash 5. The **diagnostics** icon allows you to add *breakpoints*. These allow you to stop a SWF part way and (assuming you are testing the SWF via Control>Debug movie) enable you to temporarily stop execution at crucial points in the script and fault find via the debugger. We'll take a more detailed look at the new debugging features in Chapter 11. The **view options** switch allows you to toggle between Normal and Expert mode, and add line numbers to your script.

Turning our attention to the top right-hand corner of the Actions panel we see a little book icon - this allows you to display detailed information about an action in the Reference panel. To the right of this you'll find a little arrow that allows you to toggle a help window giving you one line of help text per action, if required.

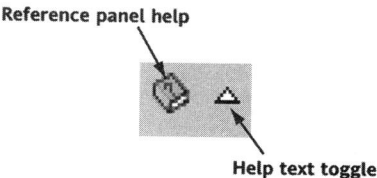

Reference panel help

Help text toggle

The **pin** icon above these two icons is a very cool new feature that allows you to pin the panel. It works as follows - assume that you are editing a script that is attached to a particular keyframe. In Flash 5, you had to keep the keyframe highlighted all the time. Using the pin icon in Flash MX allows you to keep the focus of the actions panel on the keyframe even if you select something else or close and re-open the panel later.

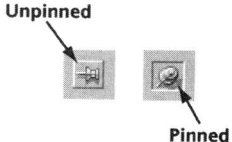

Unpinned

Pinned

The really cool stuff doesn't appear until you go into Expert mode. We will look at this in detail in Chapter 5, but if you are into scripting in a big way and can't wait, you might want to skip over to there to get the lowdown now. Later in this book you'll probably realize that this new stuff actually makes the Expert mode much less daunting to those of us from a non-programming background.

The Components and Component Parameters panels

Components are like super smart clips - ready-made bits of functionality that you can drop into your movies and customize as required. Unlike the smart clips that we became familiar with in Flash 5, components are much more closely linked to both the Flash interface (so that components appear as if they are part of the application itself, rather like plug-ins in browsers), and to ActionScript (new and component-specific actions may appear in the Actions panel).

From the Components panel we can simply drag and drop components onto the stage, and add associated parameters through the Component Parameters panel:

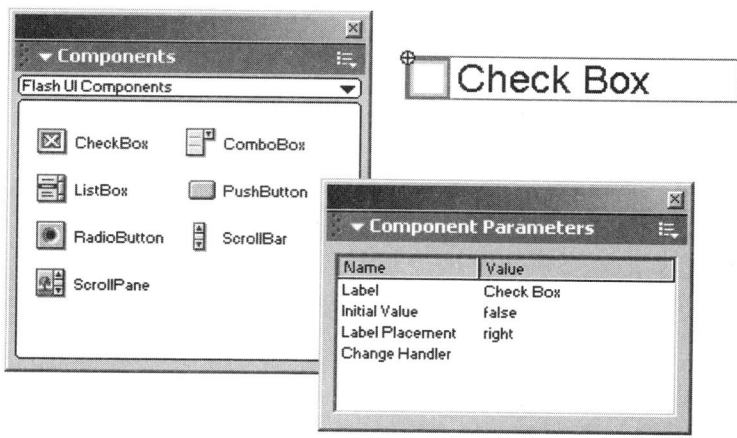

We'll look at using components in Chapter 9, and creating your own components in Chapter 14.

The Color Mixer panel

The Color Mixer panel has been enhanced to include a better color selection method than the one found in Macromedia Flash 5. The color selector is set to the old Flash 5 version by default, but pressing the little down-arrow at the bottom right of the panel changes to the new enhanced version:

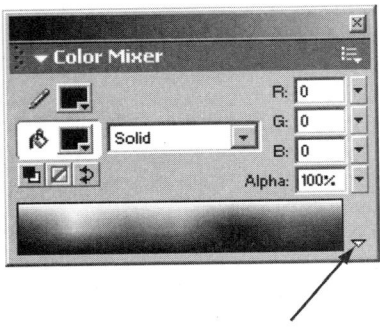 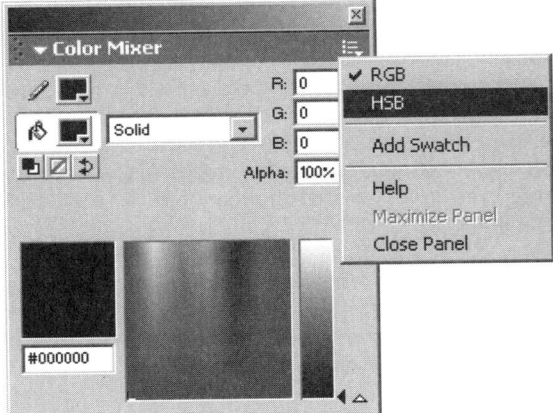

This new color mixer has the following features:

- A large swatch showing the selected color
- Hex values of the chosen color
- A brightness control – moving the caret up/down brightens/darkens the current color being mixed
- The ability to switch between the RGB (red-green-blue) and HSB (hue-saturation-brightness) color models via the panel options menu, as shown above

Once you have mixed your chosen color, you can add it to the Color Swatches panel by selecting Add Swatch on the panel's options menu. The new color mixer also inherits the fill type dropdown menu (the one that currently says Solid on the pictures above), thus integrating all the common color creation features into a single panel.

The Accessibility panel

This panel allows you to associate text with each separate graphic instance on the stage. The text can be accessed by software utilized by sight-impaired users. We'll cover this in more detail in Chapter 10.

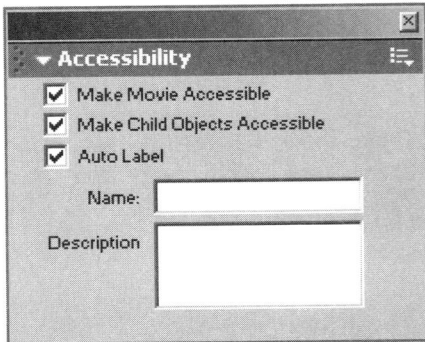

After our overview of all the new panel functionality, here's the punch line – you won't actually need to use them as much as you used to. A lot of their functionality is now embedded in the Property inspector; accordingly, we'll familiarize ourselves with this useful panel in the next section.

The Property inspector

The Property inspector replaces many of the panels you used in Macromedia Flash 5, including:

- The Info panel
- The Transform panel
- The Stroke panel
- All the Text panels (Character, Paragraph, and Text options)
- The Instance panel
- The Effects panel
- The Frame panel
- The Sound panel

The problem with Flash 5 panels was that they arranged information by *subject areas*. This meant that the information relating to a single graphic or movie component might well have been spread around two or more panels. With the Property inspector, this no longer happens because information is presented to you based on *workflow;* it provides the information you need to fulfill the task you are currently working on. This makes life easier for a number of reasons:

- The Property inspector is *context sensitive* and will change its appearance according to the user's active selection
- All information is presented in one place
- Multiple panels are required much less, which clears up much of the clutter that used to build up in Flash 5
- Many tasks can be completed solely with the Property inspector, thus reducing the number of panels you need open

> *Because the Property inspector is such a radical change, it takes some getting used to and you may find yourself returning to using the panels. During the testing stages of Macromedia Flash MX, some of the well-known old hands of Flash were not too fond of the new Property inspector at first, but after a few weeks, everyone found they loved it, so give it a chance!*

The Property inspector itself has a subset of the standard panel functionality and, accordingly, can be minimized/maximized:

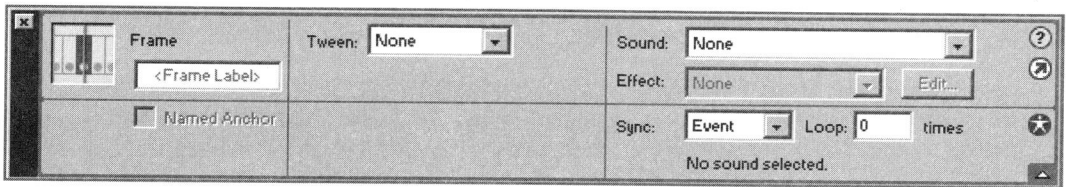

The docked version has a knurled drag area allowing it to be undocked. Unlike panels, however, it loses its title bar once undocked and, because it maintains its width when docked, it is only really very practical in its default docking position at the bottom of the stage area:

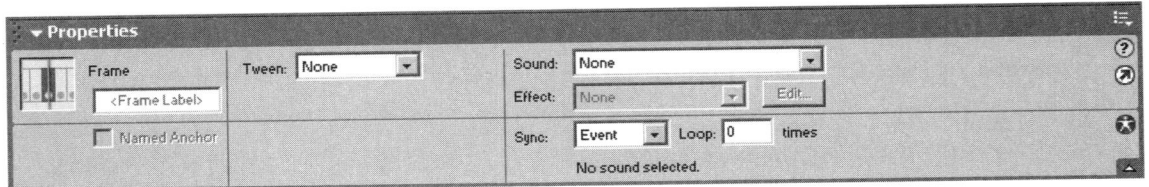

Both variants of the panel have a number of icons on the far right:

- A help button.
- A quick-launch button for the Actions panel (but note that this will only appear if the item you have currently selected can have actions attached to it – a frame or instance, for example).
- A quick-launch button for the Accessibility panel (this will only appear if the item you have currently selected can have accessibility text associated with it – a button or movie clip, for example).
- A show/hide toggle arrow to reveal more detailed options. The Property inspector is split in two by a line running along its length. Items above the line are those that are important to all users because they *must* be defined (or at least left at the default value by choice). Items below the line include detailed or specialized optional items that you may not have to consider at all. You can toggle detailed options via the little up/down arrow toggle at the bottom right corner of the Property inspector to hide/show optional fields.

OK, let's see how the Property inspector works in practice. For completeness, we'll use it with detailed options shown throughout. Although there are several Property inspectors that are invoked depending on what you have just selected (frame, movie clip, tool, etc.), it actually feels like there is one inspector that is intelligently changing to reflect what you are currently doing.

> *Rather than remember the Property inspector for each function, it is better to read through the following sections whilst using the inspector and gain familiarity, taking note of information that is not on the inspector, and where to find it. Generally, the inspector is very intuitive, and you will most likely understand the general way it works very quickly.*

Shape, Group, and Tool properties

If you select a shape or set of shapes on the stage, you will see the shape Property inspector. This inspector has the following features:

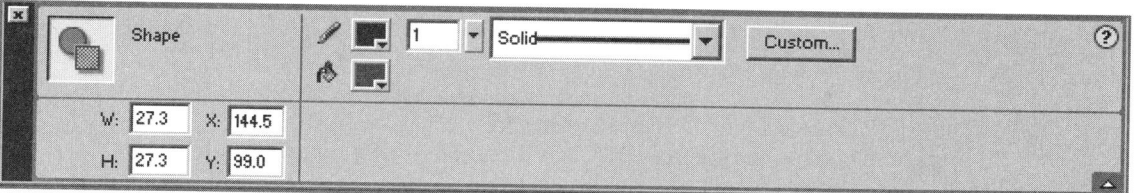

The top half of this inspector contains the stroke and fill colors, plus the stroke thickness and style. Pressing the Custom... button will bring up the Stroke Style window. This gives access to detailed parameters that set the stroke style:

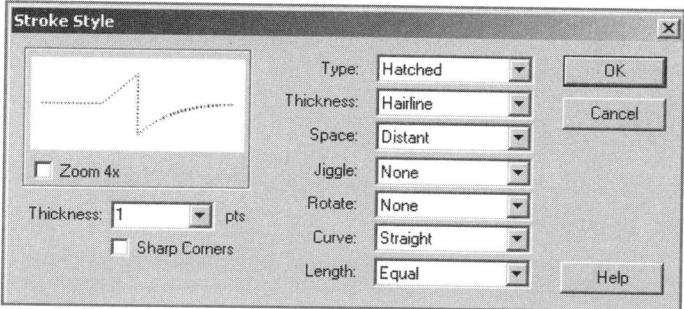

As you can see, there can be a lot of parameters for some styles, but bear in mind that complex line styles can add massively to download time if used excessively.

The bottom half of the inspector contains the width (W), height (H), and horizontal (X) and vertical (Y) positions of the selected graphic. If more than one graphic is selected, then the width/height and center position of the imaginary bounding box that contains all the selection is instead specified.

> These position fields are read/write – as well as reading the values you can scale or move the selection by changing the displayed values.

If you select multiple graphics and group them via Modify>Group or Ctrl+G (or select an existing group), you will see the group Property inspector (which is essentially a cut-down version of the shape Property inspector shown above):

> *An important point to notice about the shape and group Property inspectors is that neither of them allows accessibility text to be added (that is, no accessibility icon appears on them). If you want to create graphics that can have accessibility text attached, each graphic must first be converted to a symbol.*

If you select a tool capable of drawing a graphic on the screen (line, pen, oval, rectangle, pencil, or brush) but have nothing selected on the stage, you will see a *tool-specific* Property inspector, an example of which is shown below:

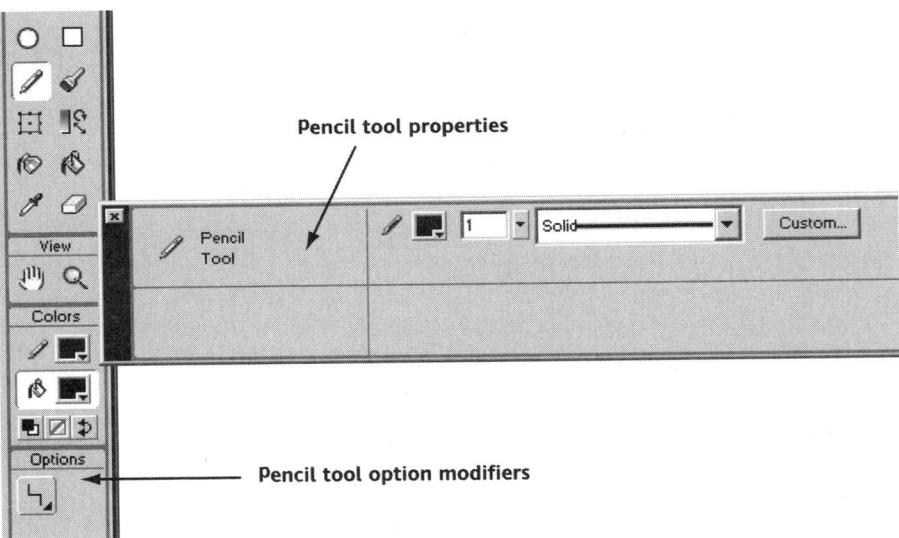

Pencil tool properties

Pencil tool option modifiers

Notice that the tool modifier options still appear in the toolbox (as they did in Flash 5), rather than in the Property inspector.

Document properties

When starting a new document or movie, or at any time you have nothing selected within a movie, the Property inspector shows the properties for the document itself.

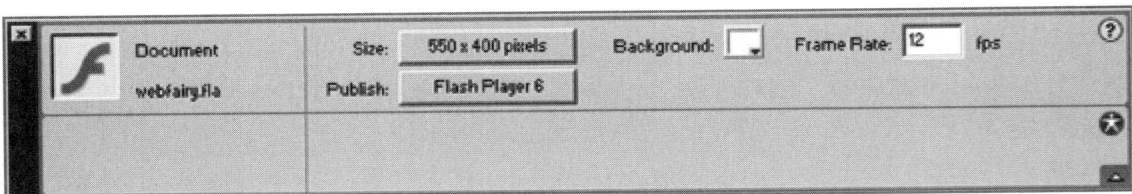

Although the available options are self-explanatory, there are a couple of points worth noting:

- You can add accessibility text for the entire document.
- These options are just a small subset of the total movie options. More detailed options are available in the Publish Settings window (go to File>Publish Settings..., or hit CTRL+SHIFT+F12, then select the HTML or Flash tabs).

Media properties

There are two very similar media inspectors for video and bitmaps. These allow you to change the dimensions and position of the element on the stage via the W, H, X, and Y values.

Options to set the compression rate of video and bitmaps will appear when you first import them via File>Import. You can modify these options by selecting the properties of the element in the library panel, in the same way that you did in Macromedia Flash 5.

You can also swap the current instance for another symbol of the same type via the Swap button, or edit a bitmap via the Edit... button. The Edit button will open the bitmap in your default program associated with that file type (typically, it will open Fireworks, ImageReady, or Photoshop files).

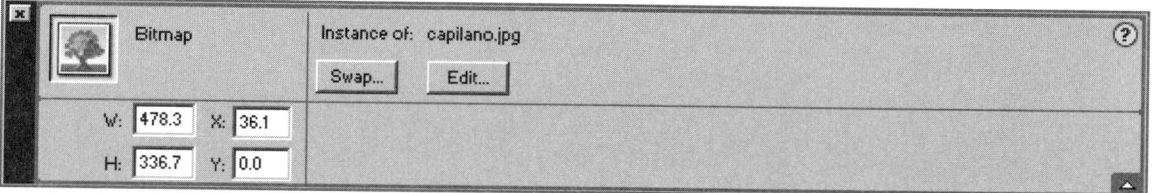

The video symbol can also have an instance name assigned if you intend to control it directly via ActionScript. To do the same thing with a bitmap, you must convert the bitmap to a movie clip first. With the bitmap selected go to Insert>Convert to Symbol..., or hit F8, and change its behavior to a movie clip in the Convert to Symbol dialog that will appear.

> The Convert to Symbol window is shown here in its minimized form. We will look at the advanced options that appear if you maximize it in the next chapter.

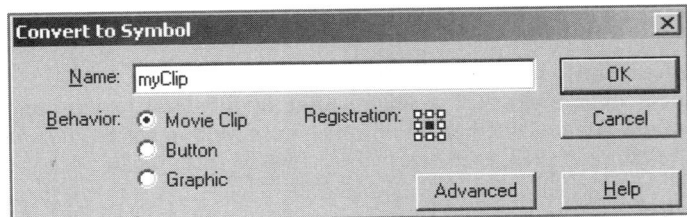

Symbol properties

The symbol inspectors will appear if you select a symbol on the stage. Symbols now include buttons, graphics, and movie clips, as well as text (discussed in the next section).

The graphic, movie clip, and button symbol Property inspectors contain the width, height, and X, Y information plus a Swap button that allows you to exchange the current symbol with any other in the library. The Color dropdown is the old instance effects, allowing you to add tweenable *brightness*, *tint*, *alpha*, or *advanced* effects.

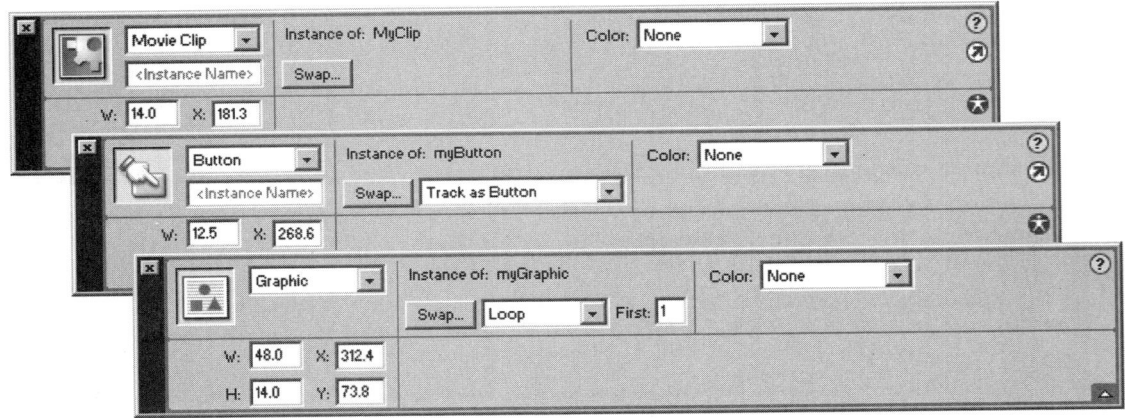

> *Notice that as well as movie clips, buttons and graphics also have instance names. This means that not only does the button now behave a lot like a movie clip, but more subtly (and indeed more powerfully) you can also make a movie clip behave like a button. We'll be returning to this topic later in the book.*

You can also change the behavior of a symbol between graphic, movie clip, and button simply by changing the top left dropdown menu.

Text properties

Dynamic and input text options in Macromedia Flash MX are now made up of fully-fledged symbols rather than graphics, and the **text** Property inspector reflects this by allowing you to add an instance name or instance effects.

The text Property inspector is rather busy, and a considerable amount of all that functionality is new, so we will look at it in detail here. The screenshot below shows the Property inspector for input text:

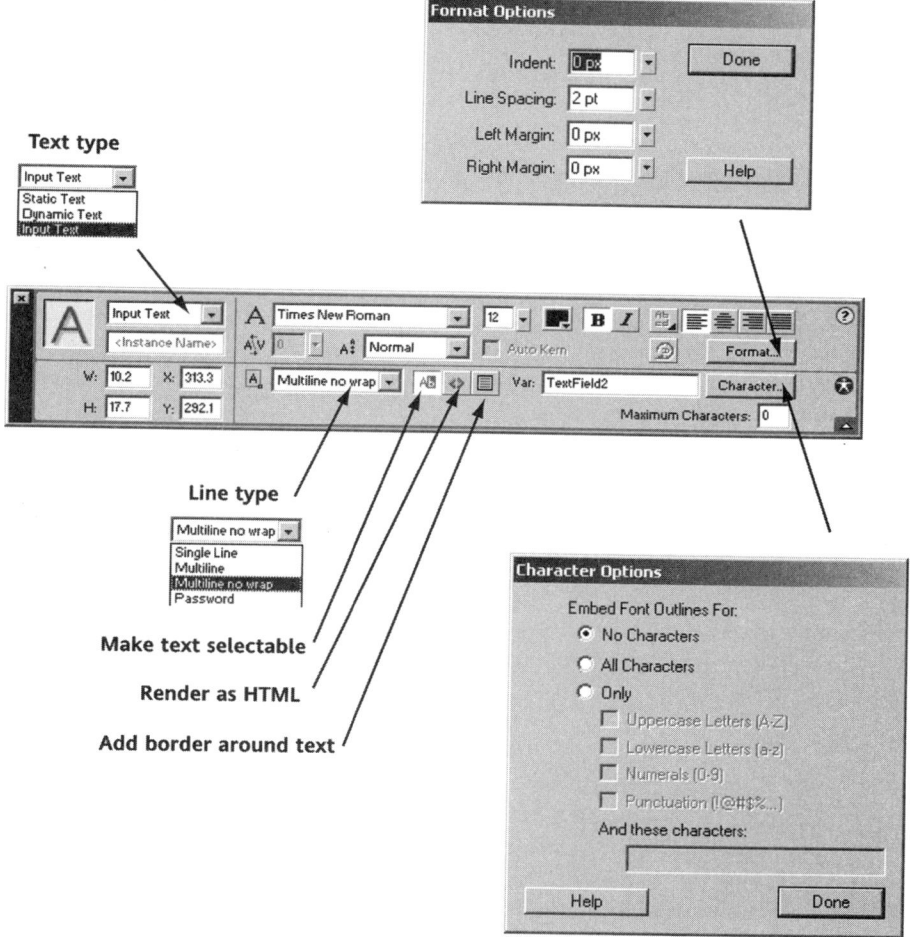

Starting from the top left, the **text type** dropdown menu allows you to select between the three types of text field. The **line type** allows you to specify between **single line** entry, **multi-line** (text will run over to the next line and scroll down if more text is added than the text box can display), or **multi-line no wrap** (text will scroll right using the first line of the text box only).

The **make text selectable**, **render as HTML**, and **add border around text** functions are still there, except that they are now icons rather than the checkboxes of Flash 5.

Hitting the Format... or Character... buttons will open the Format Options window (which allows variation of the text box's default indent, line spacing, and margins) and the Character Options window (allows you to define which parts of the font should be embedded for input or dynamic text).

Let's now look at the Property inspector for static text:

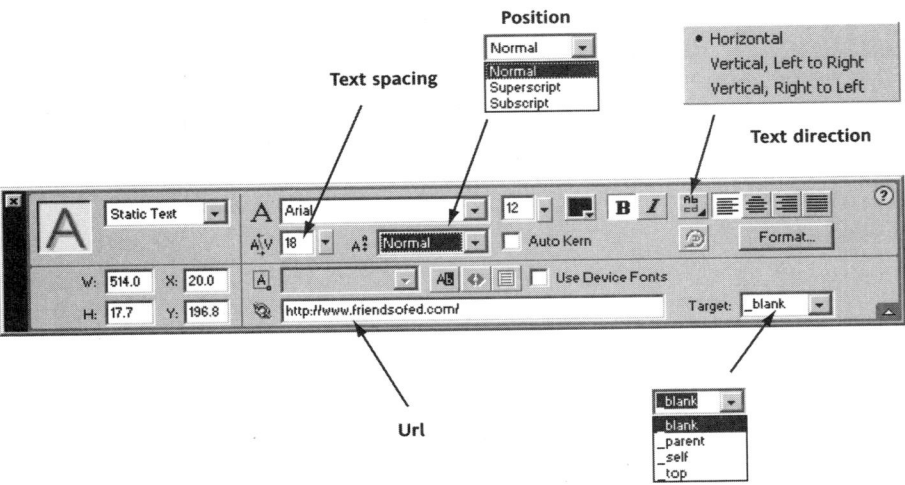

The **position** dropdown menu allows you to define the character position of your text. You can decide between normal, superscript or subscript. Note that while static text will allow you to select any of these three positions, input or dynamic text only allow the normal style.

The **text spacing** value can only be altered for static text. It will change the distance between each character in the font to create, for example, that well spaced out text we all know and love:

r e a l l y   f a s h i o n a b l e

Here we also see the new **text direction** icon, which allows us to change the direction that text runs – useful for certain languages that don't follow the western 'horizontal, left to right' reading pattern. Unfortunately, although you can now create static text in Chinese, you still can't do it with input or dynamic text, so the user will still have to use a western language at some point if you envision a site with dynamic content or input fields.

Finally, the **URL** and **target** fields allow you to make your text a link. Flash renders URL-link text with a dotted underline (but note that this does not translate to the published movie). It will *not* change the color to the standard URL link color, so you need to do that yourself.

Another way to achieve the same result is to use the **render as HTML** icon, and add the URL that way. This second way may appeal to some because it allows you to change the color of text dynamically in a standard way (that is, using HTML tags).

As you can see, not only have all the text formatting/display options migrated to the Property inspector, there are also lots more of them.

Component properties

Components represent a valuable new addition deserving a few chapters all to themselves. Accordingly, we will cover the component Property inspector when we come to look at using components in Chapter 9.

Frame properties

This is the final type of inspector that we'll examine; the frame inspector best demonstrates the advantages of the inspector-based approach over the old Flash 5 panels. Although there's very little that is new here, the Property inspector includes sound, tween, and label fields all together. Everything that you can do to a keyframe is here in one easy to access panel rather than being spread all over the interface:

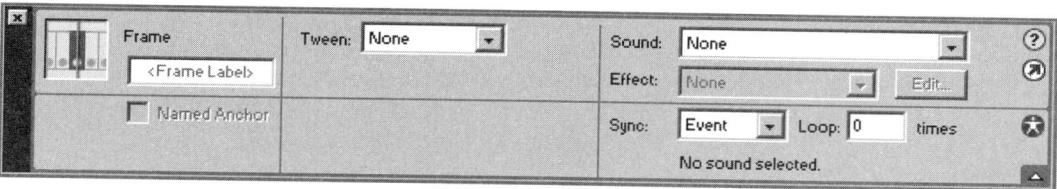

The only new feature is the Named Anchor checkbox. This will create an anchor at the keyframe, which is exactly like an HTML web page as far as the browser is concerned – the back and forward buttons on the browser will jump between anchor keyframes, and the browser will also allow the user to bookmark them. The only thing to remember when using anchors is that you must select the correct HTML template (Flash w/Named Anchors), via File>Publish Settings>HTML, otherwise they will not work.

Summary

Well, that's the basic interface defined. In this chapter we've provided an overview to the major improvements that come with the new user interface of Macromedia Flash MX. More specifically, we've looked at the new docking and undocking procedures of the panels, and the fresh functionality that they offer. We also took a detailed look at the various types of Property inspectors.

You should now be quite familiar with some of the basic new features of the Flash MX user interface. We'll continue our tour of this environment in the next chapter by looking at the timeline and the library.

Chapter 3

The Timeline
and the Library

In this chapter we will examine the remaining fundamental elements that complete our study of the Macromedia Flash MX user interface – the **timeline** and **library** windows. The timeline is the key to enabling cool animations to be produced with Flash, and the library is vital for all aspects of your designs. Although neither of them *looks* much different from their Flash 5 incarnations, there are plenty of changes below the surface. Let's start with the new timeline.

The timeline

The default position for the timeline in Macromedia Flash MX is docked to the top of the stage:

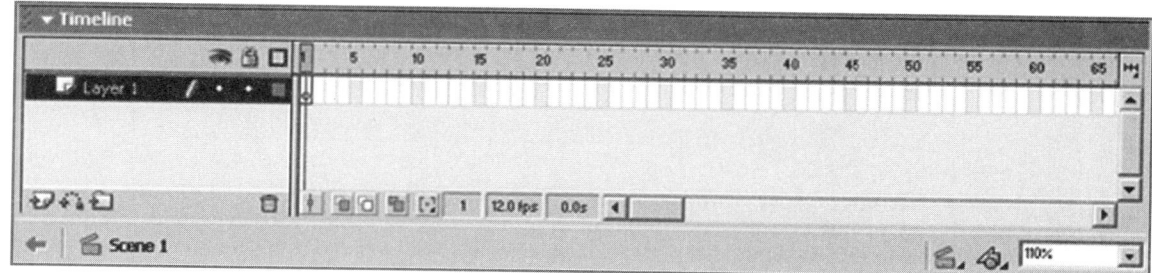

Initially, you'll probably only notice a few minor visual changes to the icons and menus. For instance, the **edit scene** and **edit symbol** icons have moved to the bottom right corner of the timeline, along with the stage-scale dropdown menu.

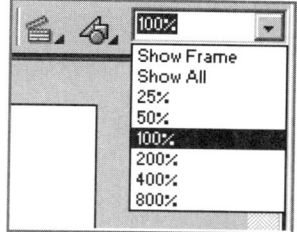

The **insert layer** and **add guide layer** are in the same place as before (bottom left), but now look different, as shown below. There is also a new icon: **insert layer folder**; we'll have a closer look at layer folders shortly:

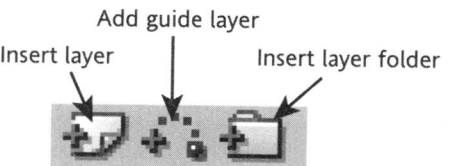

The timeline panel

The docked timeline now has a knurled bar meaning that you can dock and undock it just like the Property inspector (discussed in the previous chapter). The floating timeline looks like this:

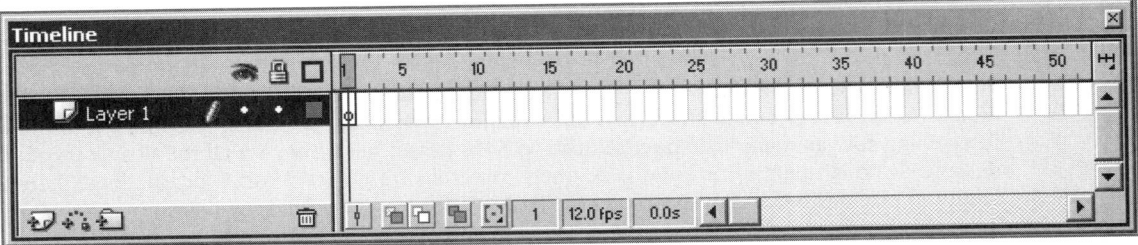

A subtle yet useful feature is that if you undock the timeline and leave it floating, it will toggle on/off with the panels when you hit the Tab key, allowing you to quickly switch to a screen with only the toolbar and stage visible.

Another difference is that, as well as docking back to its default position at the top of the stage, the timeline can also be docked along the bottom of the stage with the Property inspector, or as a new column to the left or right of the stage. If you do this, you can have the timeline tucked into the side, and slide it in or out as it is needed.

Layer folders

It's amazing how quickly a timeline can fill up with layers, especially if you have a lot of tween-based animation going on. In Macromedia Flash 5, the only real way to organize related layers together was to put them into movie clips. Unfortunately, this also changed the way that your site streamed in.

The main timeline will stream in one frame at a time – that is, the next frame will appear as soon as it is loaded into the browser. The first frame of a timeline in a movie clip will only appear when all the frames in the movie clip have been loaded in. Thus, there may be a much longer pause before a timeline in a movie clip will start playing under streaming conditions. Additionally, a frame on the timeline with a movie clip on it will not appear until all the frames in that movie clip have loaded in - this may delay your main timeline considerably.

Many designers aren't aware of these issues and end up relying on a pre-loader. You don't need to do this if your site is carefully designed so that it (or at least the main part of it) can load up a frame at a time. Organizing via layer folders rather than movie clips is the way to go if you want your tween-based animations to stream effectively.

In Flash MX layer folders present an ideal way to organize your timeline. To create a folder, simply click the **insert new layer folder** icon. This will create a layer folder as shown:

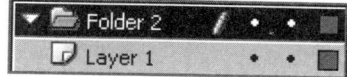

The folder acts just like a folder on your hard drive, and they're just as useful for ordering your content. Create a few more layers – at the moment I have four layers, with an empty and open folder, Folder 2:

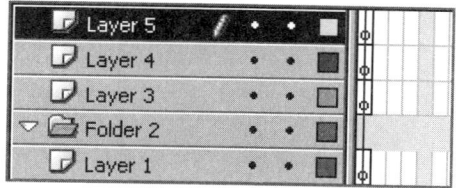

To place a layer in a folder, simply drag it into the folder. Here, I have dragged Layer 4 and Layer 5 into my folder:

Note that by clicking on the little down-arrow next to the folder icon, you can toggle the folder open or closed.

You can also nest folders. Open Folder 2 and highlight one of the layers within it. Click the **insert new layer folder** icon to create a new folder, Folder 6, within Folder 2 (if you wanted to create a folder outside Folder 2, you would have selected any layer that was also outside the folder before creating Folder 6):

Create some new layers and drag them into Folder 6. As you can see, we already have quite a busy set of layers (overleaf):

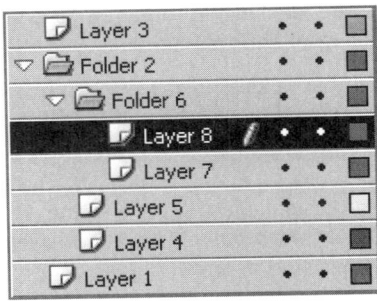

Simply closing all layers gives us a much less cluttered timeline:

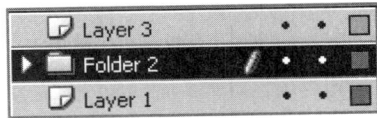

> Note that the final exported SWF is a hugely stripped down version of the FLA, and doesn't contain either folders or folder names (it doesn't, for that matter, contain any layers either), so there's nothing stopping you using as many layers and folders as you want.

Folders have other advantages as well as ordering the timeline layers. If you lock or hide a folder, all the contents of the folder (including the contents of nested folders) also inherit the same settings. Following on from our previous example, locking Folder 2 would also lock layers 4, 5, 7, and 8. Similarly, *hiding* Folder 6 would hide layers 7 and 8:

The stacking order of layers when using folders is the same as the order they appear if you open all the folders. In other words, if you open all the folders and ignore the folder structure, this is the order that your layers appear in.

This becomes more obvious if we present it graphically – the Flash MX timeline below left is equivalent to the Flash 5 timeline to the right, and both will behave exactly the same way in terms of stacking (items in Layer 3 are at the front, Layer 1 is the furthest back).

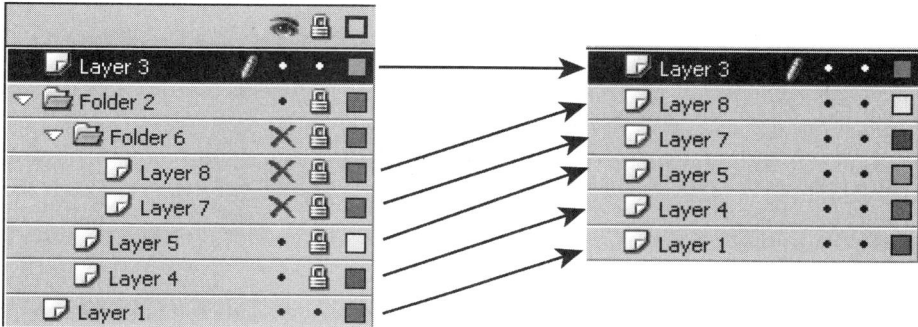

The order of execution of scripts if placed in these layers would also flow from top to bottom:

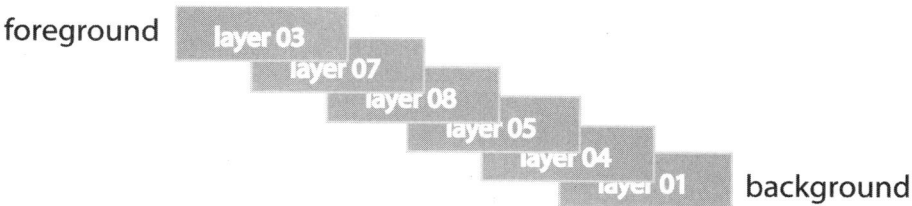

Layer folders can be really useful in keeping the timelines of all your projects neat and tidy, not to mention well structured.

Distribute to layers

There is another extremely useful feature associated with layers and layer folders: **distribute to layers**. After creating a graphic or breaking apart a group or movie clip, you can spread the separate elements across layers. Doing this means that you can then animate the separate layers with ease because tweens only work well if there is one symbol or graphic per layer. This *sounds* a lot more complicated than it actually is, so let's look at an example.

Here's a graphic I created a while back for a site – a record player:

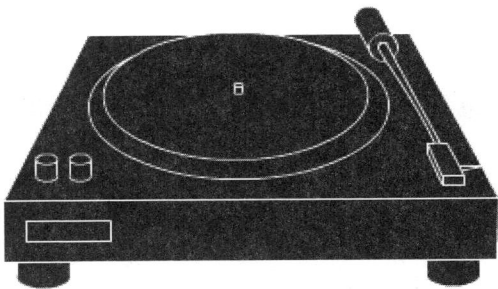

For this simple movie, the record player itself is made up of two separate symbols: the turntable, and the record arm:

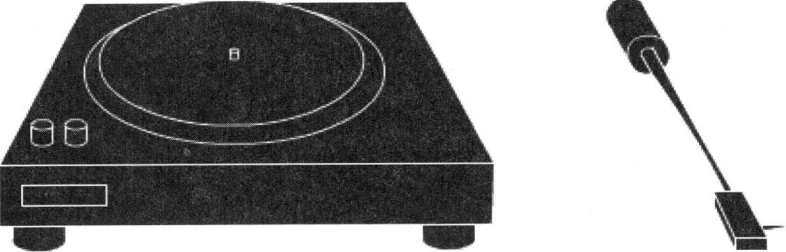

If I want to animate the symbols, the first thing to do is place the whole record player onto the stage. Assuming we're creating a new movie clip with a new timeline, the record player will be placed in Layer 1:

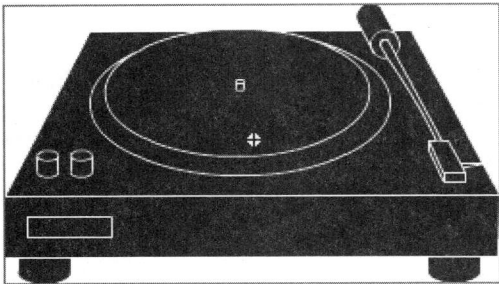

Then, with the record player symbol selected, I break the symbol apart with Modify>Break Apart, or CTRL+B. This will separate the record player out into its two component parts (you should see that both discrete items now have their own bounding box).

Now comes the magic part – with both parts still selected, select Modify>Distribute to Layers, or just CTRL+SHIFT+D:

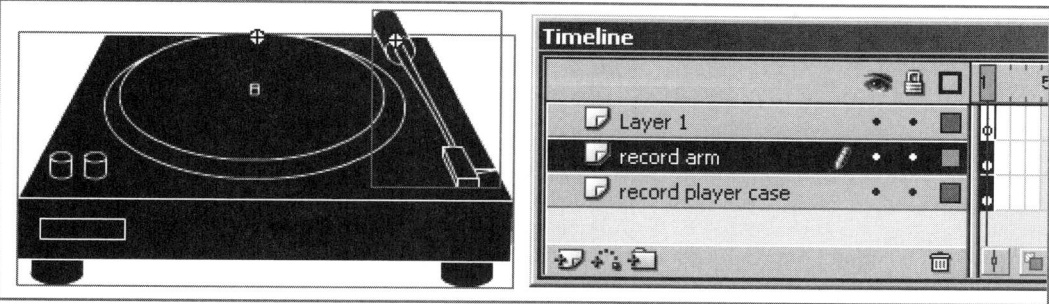

> Note that the Distribute to Layers *function requires that you have selected a group (of symbols or grouped graphics) before you use it, because you cannot distribute a selection consisting of one thing very far! In this case we have created our group by first breaking apart the record player graphic.*

Notice that Flash has created a new layer for each separate item in the player and has also given these layers the name of the symbol it contains. Furthermore, the original layer (Layer 1) is now empty.

I can now put all these layers in their own folder and, for example, swap the record arm for a tween that shows the record arm move onto the record:

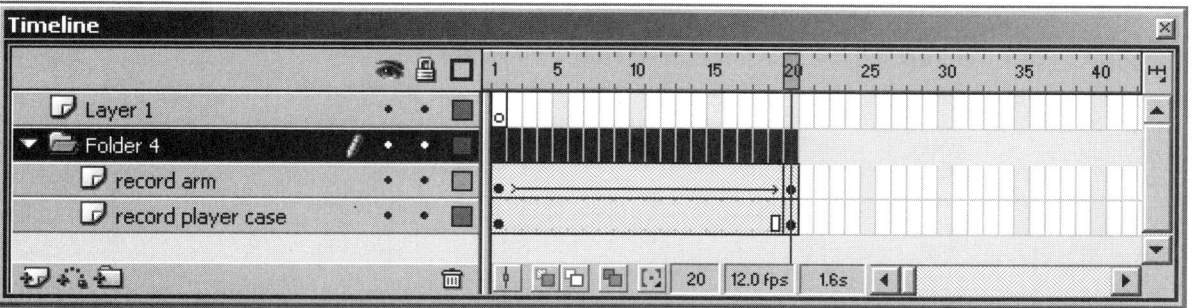

> *Notice that the number of frames that are selected when you click on a folder is equal to the longest layer of frames inside it. This is an easy way of telling how long the layers are inside a closed folder without having to open it.*

Another cool use of the Distribute to Layers feature is when you want to create some text effects through tweening. In Flash 5, this could turn into a long and fiddly job! Take a look at the chapter by the**void** in the first *New Masters of Flash* book to get a feel for the number of timelines that can be involved in creating complex tween-based text effects.

The following example will show how easy it is to tween text in Macromedia Flash MX. Create your text as a single static text field, as shown below:

 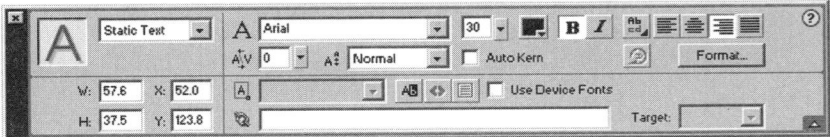

Break apart the text using CTRL+B – this will split the text into individual letters:

Now perform the Distribute to Layers function (remember, CTRL+SHIFT+D). You will see that the letters now arrange themselves onto one unique layer per letter, each appropriately named for the letter it contains:

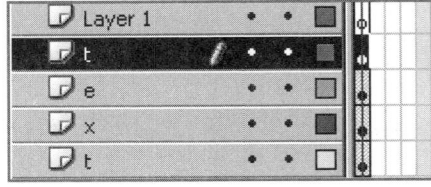

You can now add tweens for each letter to create whatever cool text transition effects you want. Simple!

The library

We'll now turn our attention to the new features of the Flash MX library, which has perhaps the subtlest enhancements of all. On the face of it, nothing much has changed, but as you will soon see, many of the common operations you perform with it have now become faster and more efficient. Unlike the timeline enhancements, where there are new icons that just scream 'I am something cool and new, click me to see what happens!', the library enhancements take a bit more digging around before you even know they are there. Let's start digging!

We'll start with the basics and then move on to some great new functionality associated with library management and sharing.

The library panel

The library panel itself is more or less unchanged – visually, at least. Of course, it's now a dockable panel, which means that it can be docked just like any other standard Flash MX panel. When you first invoke the library (Window>Library or CTRL+L), it will appear as a floating panel, although you can, of course, change this – by docking it to the right docking column, for instance.

The symbol icons are unchanged except for the old smart clip, which now appears as the component 'building block' icon. Here's an example of what the library of a simple movie might look like:

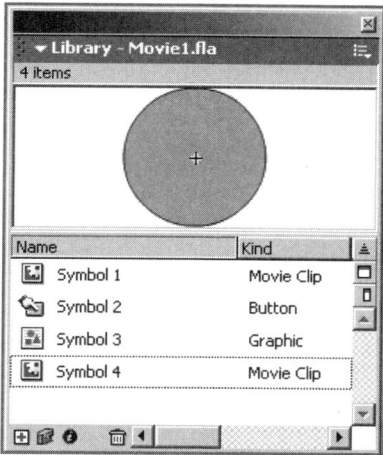

Creating symbols

The symbol creation process has now been refined. The best way to illustrate is by example – create a shape (a square or circle is easiest). Select it and use Insert>Convert to Symbol..., or hit F8. You will see the following rather familiar Convert to Symbol window appear:

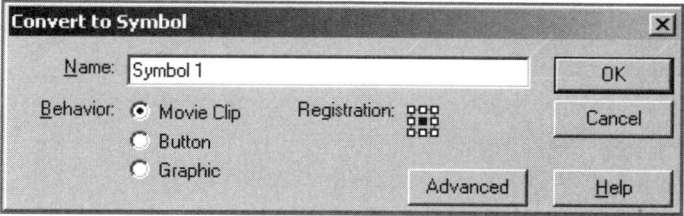

Two things have changed: one is rather obvious, the other is not, so stay sharp! The obvious difference is that you can now move the registration point of the symbol to any of the nine positions denoted by the registration grid. The most common registration points are center (the default) or one of the corner positions (usually top left).

The more subtle change is that in Flash 5, the behavior always appeared as Movie Clip by default. In Macromedia Flash MX, however, the behavior defaults to whatever you chose the *last* time you used the window.

> *Creating symbols via the 'Hit F8, enter the name, hit return, and assume it is a movie clip because that's the default in Flash 5' sequence is an ingrained set of steps that many long-time designers will do in their sleep. Because Flash MX has no default as such, you need to turn off your 'autopilot' when you do this from now on!*

As well as selecting Insert>Convert to symbol or hitting F8, there is a third quick way to create a symbol – simply drag it into the library window. OK, some of you will be saying 'Surely that's a non-feature – hitting F8 is much faster!' True, but the drag and drop method is sensitive to *where* you drag the clip. If you drop it over a particular folder in the library, the new symbol is created in that folder, making it a lot faster when you are using a folder structure (that is, most of the time).

Although Macromedia Flash 5 allowed you to drag symbols between libraries, Flash MX now lets you drag entire folders as well. Although a seemingly small point, this makes the process a whole lot easier. Most libraries have some sort of folder structure so that if, for example, you have all the buttons in a folder called (unsurprisingly) buttons and you wanted to copy the button set you used in one site to another, you'd simply drag the buttons folder over between the library windows of the two movies, and you are done. Not only would the buttons folder and its contents be copied, so would any subfolders:

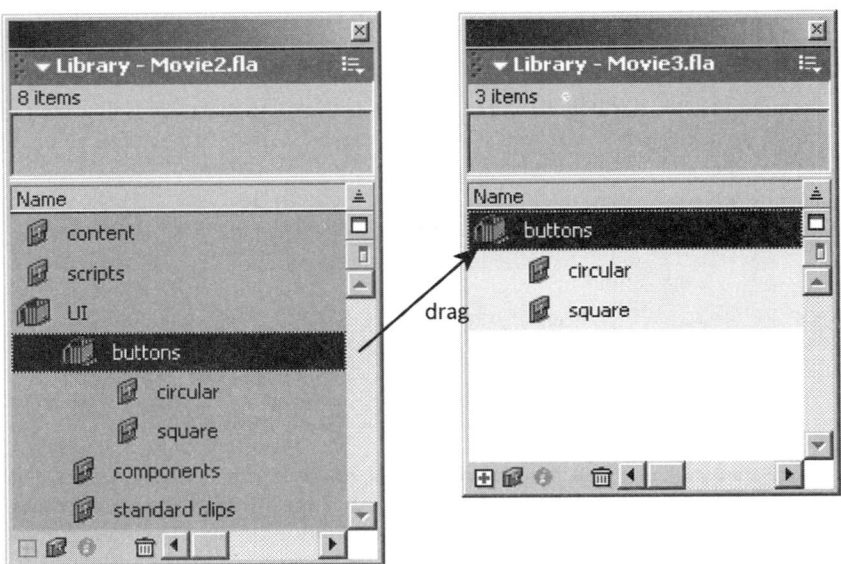

> *Remember in Chapter 1 when we demonstrated how to create a template containing standard timeline folders? Well, you can also add default library folders within the same template (using File>Save as Template...), so that you always start with the same default library folder structure. That way, all your Flash MX sites will have the same set of folders in the library, and you'll be familiar with the structure of each site.*

Coupled with the new drag and drop library enhancements, these features allow you to quickly copy content across from old sites and put it in a standard place in the new library.

Sharing library assets

So, with Macromedia Flash MX you've now got a nice set of features to use if you want to base one site on another, assuming you are the sole designer involved with both sites. This is all well and good, but it's not so relevant to the real world of web design where there are usually *several* designers working on the same site.

> *Let's consider a typical situation in which one designer, let's call him Joe, does the graphics, and another designer, say Jean, works on the ActionScripting to tie it all together. They both work on different machines connected to the design studio network.*

In this scenario, the process described earlier wouldn't work because there's no continuous updating of files. Assuming Joe creates all the buttons and saves them as `library.fla`, Jean can then just open up `library.fla` and drag the buttons folder across. End of story, right? Well, not quite...

If the buttons subsequently change slightly, which is quite common in the real world, the network would only 'see' the old version. For instance, perhaps the artistic director took the button designs to the client who then said that they wanted the button colors to reflect their corporate colors, and not the web-safe ones that Joe chose. So, Joe updates them, but Jean has no way of telling they have been updated unless Joe tells her. A system that requires folks to remember to 'tell people stuff' is always doomed to failure, especially when those people are busy web designers who have people 'telling them stuff' all day long!

Don't worry though, Macromedia have thought this one out – you can share stuff across files automatically *without* having to have both files open. In the next couple of sections we'll take a look at how to share libraries.

Sharing during authoring

Let's work this through with a simple example. First of all, Joe might create his button to look like this:

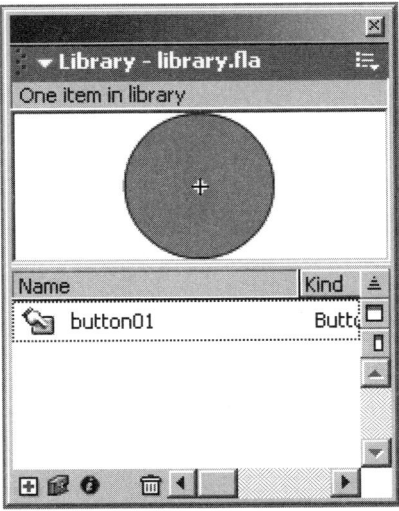

You can see why the company took him on – an artistic diva specializing in understated minimalism. It's a gray circle. Create your own and turn it into a button symbol. Then, as Joe would do, save the whole thing as `library.fla`. Close Joe's FLA and open a new one.

Next, Jean comes along and opens `library.fla` as a library (File>Open as Library... or CTRL+SHIFT+O). You'll now have two library windows: one for `library.fla` and one for the current movie (Movie4 in our case).

For Jean to use `button01` in her FLA, she simply drags it across into her own library, as shown below (or alternatively, she could also drag it onto the stage):

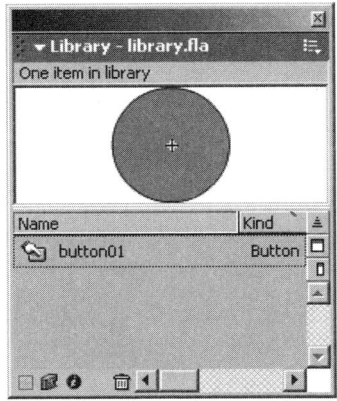

So now that Jean has a copy of Joe's button in her FLA, you can close the library of `library.fla`:

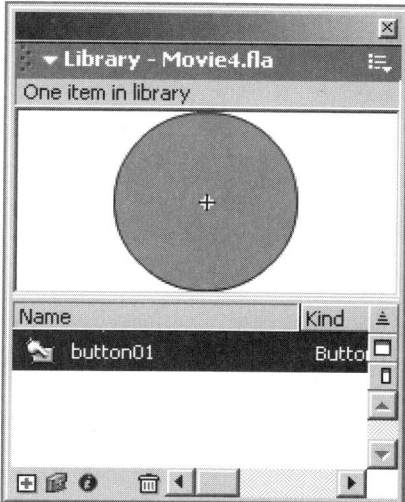

Notice that the active library (that is, the one associated with the currently open FLA) has a white background. Any other library window is gray.

Now comes the cool part – either right-click on `button01` in the library window and select Properties..., or open the windows menu from the top right of the library panel and select Properties.... You will see the familiar Symbol Properties window. To see the best new features of the library you'll have to click the Advanced button.

At this point you should have a maximized Flash MX Symbol Properties window (as seen over the page), containing information that also appeared in the Flash 5 Symbol Linkage Properties and Symbol Properties windows.

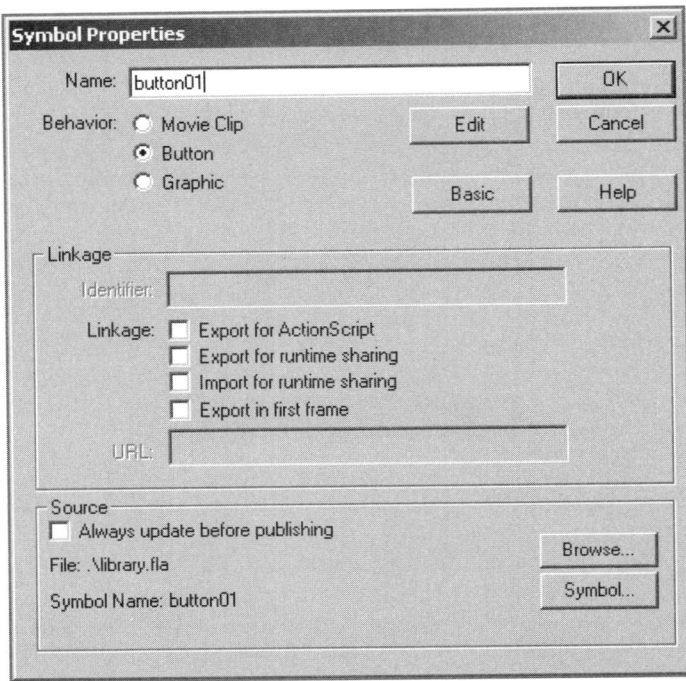

Look at the lower portion – the bit titled Source – of the now expanded Symbol Properties window. The File part will have a pathname to the FLA that you dragged (button01.fla), and if Flash knows where the original button01 comes from, it can *automatically update it*. To do this, check the Always update before publishing checkbox, as indicated above.

OK, to prove that it works, save this FLA as final.fla and, pretending that you are now Joe again, open up library.fla. The art director tells Joe that the button now needs to be black – edit the symbol, resave the FLA, and close library.fla. Finally, as Jean again, test or publish *your* movie and, *voila*, the button is black, reflecting all the changes Joe has made to the library version.

You might agree that this is not a very obvious feature, but it is certainly one that every web designer who works in a team will appreciate. You can now achieve any of the following:

- **A centralized library file:**
  For a set of designers building or maintaining one large corporate site, it's worth creating a centralized FLA file, library.fla, which contains all the standard buttons, icons, and other library stuff. All other FLA files should then have assets linked to library.fla. To change the look and feel of the site, you'd simply update library.fla. After that, any other SWFs published from any of the other FLAs will reflect these changes when they are next published.

- **Easy access to the library**
  You don't need to open `library.fla` if you know its location. Simply click the Browse button in the Symbol Properties dialog to form the linkage between source and destination library directly. If your web design house has a standard directory structure per project, such as `<ReferenceCode>\assets\library.fla`, and you are working on a project with reference code FoED001, you will immediately know that the assets are stored in `FoED001\assets\library.fla`.

- **Multiple libraries**
  Why stop at `library.fla`? – you can also create `content.fla`, `sounds.fla`, `userInterface.fla`, `bitmaps.fla`, and so on.

- **Automatic updating**
  If, for instance, Joe were to check the Export for run-time sharing checkbox (under Linkage in the Symbol Properties window shown above), then the Always update before publishing checkbox will be set in Jean's FLA automatically. Where you are creating FLA files that are shared libraries, checking this linkage option for everything in the library will make the sharing process work without Jean having to do anything other than copy stuff over from the shared library. How's that for workflow?

This new sharing feature means that everything can be maintained in its place and updated automatically – a project manager's Utopia!

> *One point to watch out for is that update only occurs when Joe saves his changes and Jean creates a SWF (via Publish or Test Movie). If Joe is still making the changes when Jean runs the SWF, the changes will not get picked up. It is therefore important for the project manager to make sure that Joe has made all the changes necessary before Jean makes the final customer SWFs.*

A final bit of additional functionality exists that, on the face of it, doesn't seem so useful until you see its real application. Instead of *automatic* update, you can specify which items to update *manually*.

To do this, you would copy your shared assets across in the normal way, but *not check* the Always update when publishing checkbox. You can now choose when you want to update by selecting Update… via the library right-click menu or the library window's main menu. This will bring up the window you see on the next page.

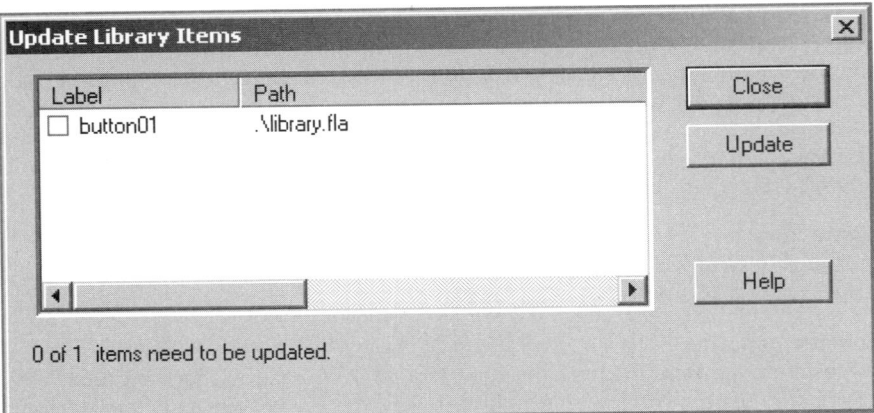

This dialog allows you to selectively update each imported symbol. For the single designer working alone it allows you to selectively *revert* between FLA revisions.

The following sequence illustrates the benefits of the manual update technique:

1. version01.fla is your original.

2. You then create version02.fla, which has all assets linked back to the version01.fla.

3. You alter the library symbols in version02.fla. Hopefully, most of these changes may be beneficial to the design, but some may also be things that are worse than the original (for example, some symbols may have been reworked such that they are now too great a download strain).

4. Using the Update Library Items options, you can revert back to the version01 symbols that didn't work by checking them for update, and retain the ones that worked by un-checking them. Once you are happy with version02.fla, make it version03.fla and start the process again.

Manual update can also be used to *formalize* the update process that Joe and Jean have to go through. The problem with doing it all automatically is that as soon as an automatic update is made on Jean's FLAs, *she may lose the last versions she was working on.*

This means that there is no *version control*. Indeed, Jean will find it difficult to go back to old versions if an automatic update results in the FLAs no longer working. She has no idea what Joe has done and, more crucially, she can't get back to a version that worked! To do that, not only would Jean have to have saved all her old versions, but also all of Joe's. Since Joe is simply making updates and saving, he will not have a clue as to which was the last working version!

This kind of scenario would not become a problem with small teams, or sites that are not so code-rich, but constant and automatic update is the bane of larger projects. In these cases, a *controlled manual update scheme* may be more appropriate because it lets you go back (to fix mistakes) as well as forward.

The workflows seen in this section refer to sharing at authoring time. You can also share files at runtime, that is, when running SWFs, and we'll look at this in the next section. Non-ActionScript designers may not be interested in the next section because it assumes a certain level of scripting knowledge.

Run-time sharing

The library has added a number of *run-time* import/export options since Flash 5, seen in the advanced Symbol Properties window that we came across in the previous section. These are pretty much identical to those seen via Symbol Linkage Properties in Macromedia Flash 5. The only major addition is the Export in first frame checkbox, which we'll describe in this section.

Sometimes, you may want to use ActionScript to dynamically place symbols on stage using attachMovie. In fact, this action caused a lot of confusion in Flash 5, and many people couldn't get it to work. By default, during compilation of a FLA into a SWF *any symbol that does not appear on the stage at compilation time is not included in the SWF* on the assumption that it will not be needed.

However, ActionScript can *dynamically* add symbols to the stage via the attachMovie command. This means that although the symbol may not have been on the stage at compilation time, it *can* be controlled by Actionscript during run-time. Your ActionScript will place the clip onto stage during 'SWF time', rather than explicitly placing it on stage by adding it to a keyframe at authoring time. Obviously, Flash doesn't know if this is what you want to do unless you specifically tell it before compilation, where you must somehow specify that you want to 'export symbols for ActionScript to place on stage later'.

This is when the advanced options in the Symbol Properties window become relevant, and indeed rather useful for run-time sharing – so let's take a moment to emphasize their meanings:

- **Export for ActionScript**
  Usually, Flash doesn't export any symbol in the library that isn't in a keyframe. What Flash doesn't know is whether or not the scripting will place it on stage via the attachMovie method. So, by using Export for ActionScript you are essentially telling Flash 'although it never appears on the stage, I will actually be placing it on stage dynamically, under the control of a script that uses attachMovie'.

- **Export for run-time sharing**
  In simple terms, this means 'put this symbol in the library because other SWFs will pull it from this SWF at run-time'. In effect, the SWF is simply a library of symbols that other SWFs will use (or rather, other FLAs will attach to during compilation).

- **Export in first frame**
  If you place a movie clip onto a keyframe at author time, Flash knows when it is needed, and puts it in the SWF so that it is loaded by the time it first appears on stage. If you attachMovie it onto the stage instead, Flash has no way of knowing when it will appear on stage (and neither will the designer because we usually make it appear in response to the user inputs). In this case Flash can only assume it might be required from frame 1 onwards, and will load it as if it is required at frame 1. With this option, it effectively doesn't matter which frame the script uses it with because it is available for attaching from the start.

Of course, the best way to demonstrate these points is with an example – create a simple movie clip as shown below, consisting of a simple circle that has been made into a movie clip by dragging it into the library and naming it `circle`. Next, delete any instance of `circle` from the stage and then test the movie. Unsurprisingly, you will see that you end up with a movie with nothing in it! There is nothing on the stage because we have added nothing to it. More importantly, there are no symbols exported into the SWF.

You can see an indication of this by looking at the bandwidth profiler (View>Bandwidth Profiler or CTRL+B while testing the movie). Note that the SWF file size is near zero (30 bytes, which is the normal size for an empty SWF file):

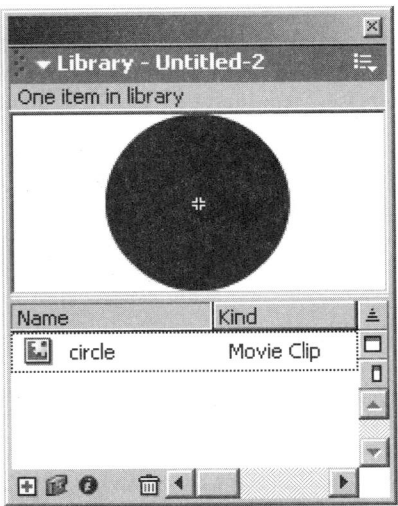
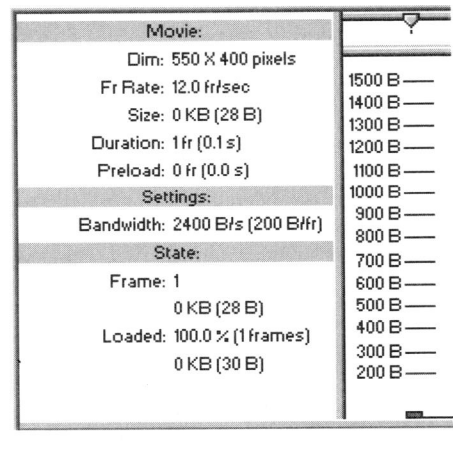

OK, so what if we *want* `circle` to be exported even though it doesn't appear on a timeline, perhaps because we want to put it onto the stage during run-time via scripting? The first step in doing this is to force Flash to export our symbol for ActionScript. Using the library right-click or library window dropdown menu, select Properties..., and then pick the Advanced options. Check the Export for ActionScript checkbox from the Linkage options.

As we highlighted earlier, Flash normally loads every symbol on the frame in which it first appears. For dynamic ActionScript control, if you don't know the first frame that your script will try to attach to a library symbol, the Export in first frame option will force Flash to load the symbol in at frame 1, making sure that it is available for scripting, and overriding Flash's decision to not include it.

It may be that you know when your script will start to attach to the symbol. In that case, you can simply place an instance of the symbol on stage (you can put it off stage or with a `visible` property of `false` if you don't want it to be seen) for at least one frame before you start using `attachMovie`, and you can then get away with not checking Export in first frame.

For our example, however, leave the Linkage options as per the screenshot below:

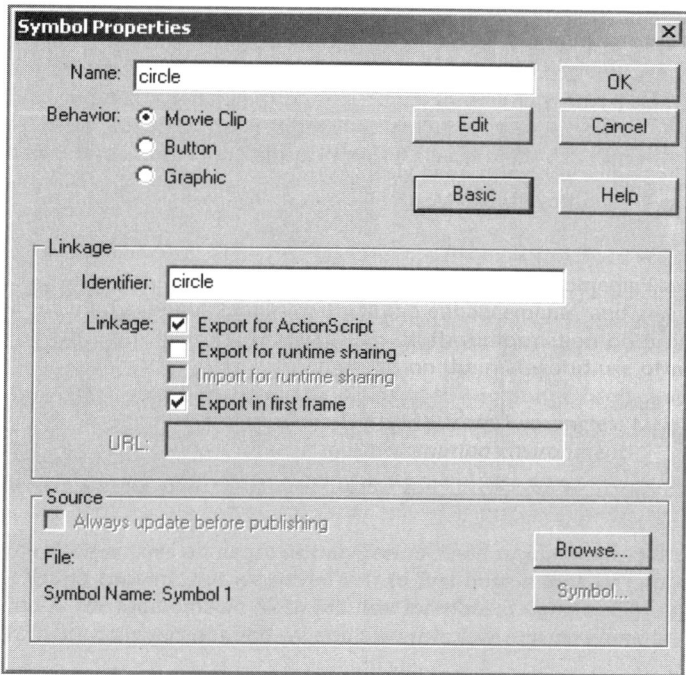

> *Remember, the second option may be preferred if you are attaching many different symbols via attachMovie. If you load them all up on frame 1 your movie will pause for a long time at frame 1 (resulting in a blank browser) while the streaming catches up. It's better to load your symbols in gradually over a number of frames and phase the download over time.*

If you test the FLA now, you will see that the SWF size has gone up on the bandwidth profiler (I get around 150 bytes), signifying that the symbol is now being loaded.

We have now successfully preloaded our symbol for ActionScript. All we have to do now is create some instances on stage via attachMovie.

On frame 1 of your timeline, add this script:

```
attachMovie("circle", "myClip", 10);
myClip._x = 200;
MyClip._y = 200;
```

The first line creates an instance of our `circle` symbol called `myClip` and gives it a depth of 10. The following two lines move `myClip` to an X, Y position of `200, 200`. If you test this movie, you will finally see our circle appear!

You may be thinking, 'Well, that's totally under-whelming... I could have done that in a tenth of the time using a keyframe'. True, but with ActionScript and the dynamic creation of clips, we can utilize some of the really powerful features of Macromedia Flash MX. You need to be familiar with `attachMovie` to use many of them, so we'll return to this topic in Chapter 8 when we start to look at the new Drawing API.

Summary

So what have we really gained with these changes to the UI that Flash MX introduces? Well, for a start we now have an ideally well-structured timeline because of the timeline folders. We've also gained a more intuitive drag and drop functionality in the library that allows us to quickly move symbols around. We've also gained some useful asset sharing features during authoring, plus one or two tweaks to run-time sharing. Last but not least, both the timeline and library follow the standard dockable panel system.

Now that we've finished our tour of the interface, it's time to start getting serious! We'll be looking closer at actual content creation, starting with a look at the new design tools included with Flash MX.

Chapter 4

Tools

Macromedia Flash MX packs in a number of new or enhanced content creation tools. In this chapter we will look specifically at these new features, with practical and inspirational demonstrations of their use throughout.

The toolbox

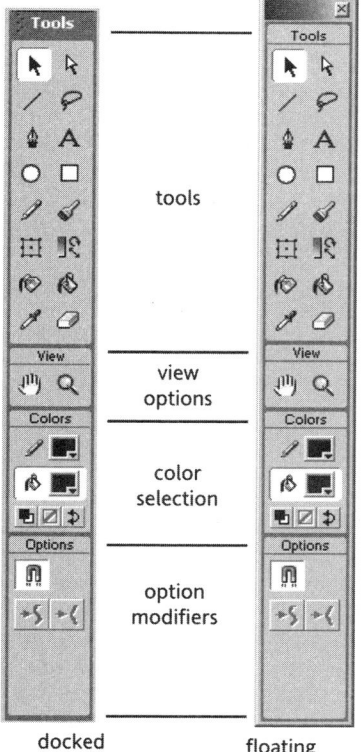

docked   floating

The toolbox is largely unchanged since Flash 5. It has gained the docked panels makeover, and you can now either dock it in its default location (far left of the screen) or move it into any floating panel position. When you click on a tool – assuming that there is nothing selected on the stage – the Property inspector will display all options available for the current tool (remember, the Tool inspector was discussed in Chapter 2).

The major additions to the toolbox of Flash MX are the **free transform** tool and **fill transform** tool. Accordingly, we'll spend the bulk of this chapter demonstrating how powerful they can be when used with their associated modifiers:

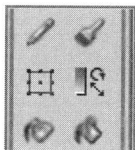

In addition, there are enhancements to functions related to the tools, such as **break apart**, so along the way we'll also learn how they are utilized. Let's dive right in and experiment with the **free transform** tool.

Free transform tool

As well as inheriting the **rotate** and **skew** and **scale functions** (which were previously just options for the arrow selection tool), the free transform tool has two additional modifiers: **distort** and **envelope**. To see how both work, we will first use a graphic that will help us to visualize the effects of both new modifiers – a simple grid.

Make sure that you can see the grid (View>Grid>Show Grid or CTRL+#) and that 'snap to grid' is selected (View>Grid>Snap to Grid or CTRL+SHIFT+#), and draw out a simple 5x5 grid as shown below (or simply use the file `grid.fla` from this book's source code):

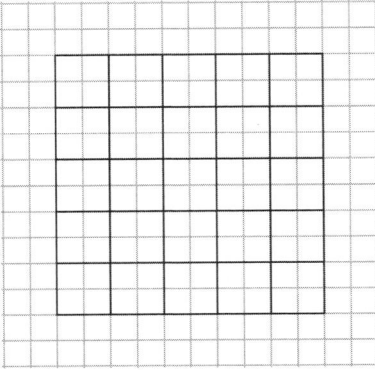

Using the arrow selection tool, select the entire grid (or just click on the current layer in the timeline) and then click on free transform from the toolbox:

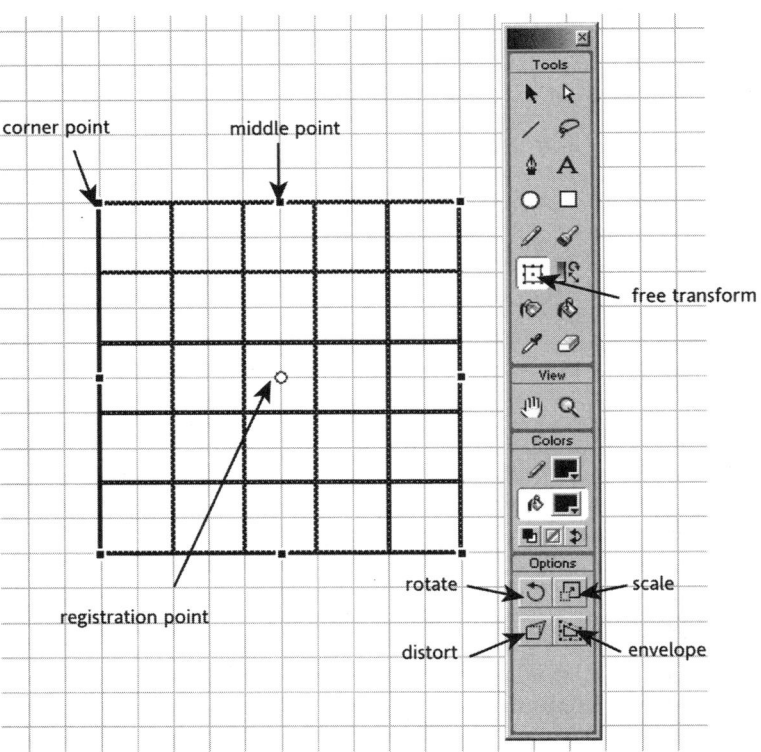

As we've mentioned, the **rotate** and **scale** modifiers are the same as those in Flash 5, except that they are now free transform option modifiers. You don't really even have to select them, because the cursor is context sensitive – more specifically, you can automatically perform the following operations on your selection:

■   **Scale** - if you hover over a corner or middle point, click-drag to scale or SHIFT-click-drag to scale while maintaining proportions:

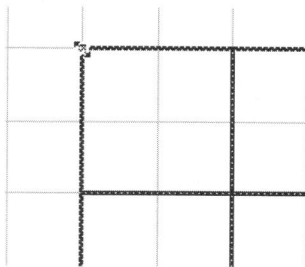

■   **Skew** - if you hover over an outer edge, click-drag to skew:

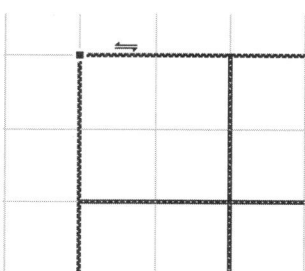

■   **Rotate** - if you hover near a corner point, click-drag to rotate. As always, you can also click-drag the registration point to alter the center of rotation. Note also that holding down SHIFT snaps the rotation to 45-degree increments:

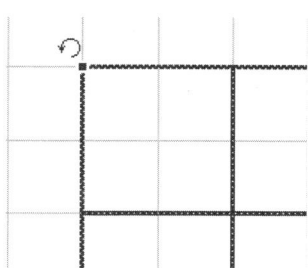

- **Move** - if you hover over any other area containing pixels, click-drag to move:

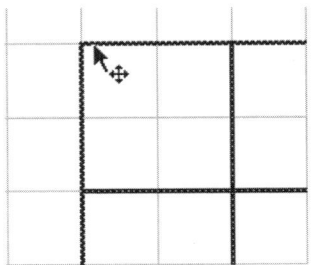

All that functionality was actually available in one form or another in Flash 5. However, the next two modifiers that we'll look at – **distort** and **envelope** – are totally new.

Distort modifier

With your grid selected, click the distort icon. You can now drag corner points individually to distort the bounding box. The grid will distort to fit in the new bounding box:

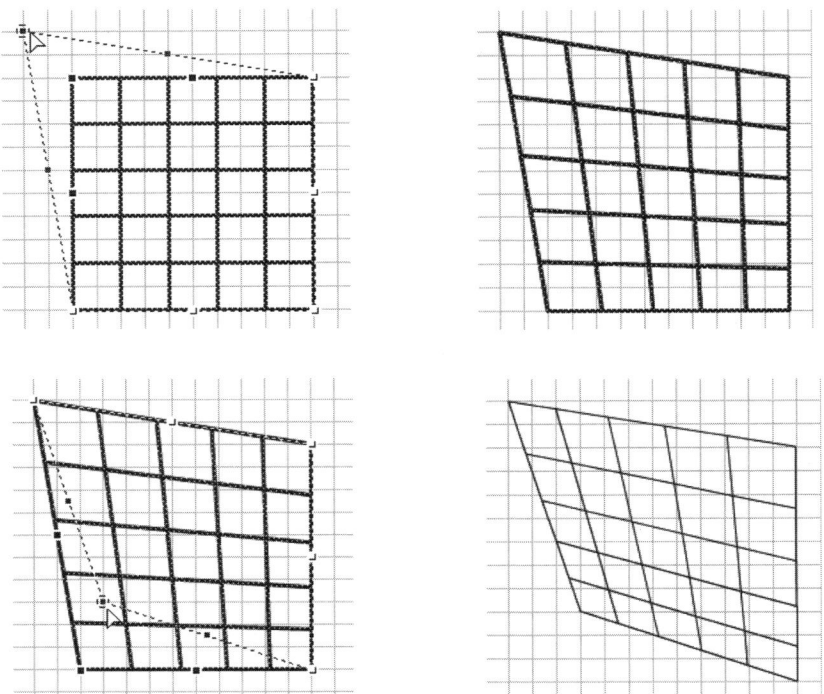

Note that when using the distort tool, you can still scale and skew by click-dragging while over a mid-point or outer edge on the bounding box. Also, SHIFT-dragging a corner will result in the opposite corner also moving to create a taper as shown opposite:

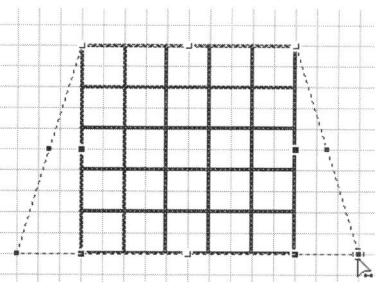 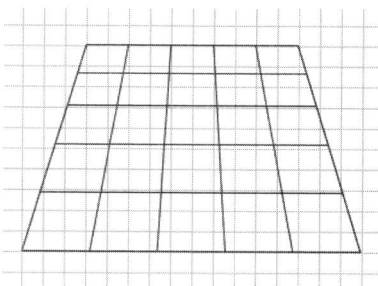

Now let's look at some of the more high-end design possibilities that this tool gives us.

Creating faux 3D graphics

One cool use of the distort modifier is for the creation of simple faux 3D. As you have probably noticed, one of the effects of moving any two corner points of the distort modifier is that it transforms our flat 2D grid such that it looks like it is floating in 3D space.

> *The distort tool has a subtle feature that makes it particularly useful for creating faux 3D perspectives. If you look at the pictures below (where we have moved the bottom right corner point to the left), you can see that the lines of the grid become closer together as you get to the shorter side in the distorted shape. In true 3D, the shortest edge is that which is the furthest away. We can use this effect to our benefit to create realistic pseudo-3D designs.*

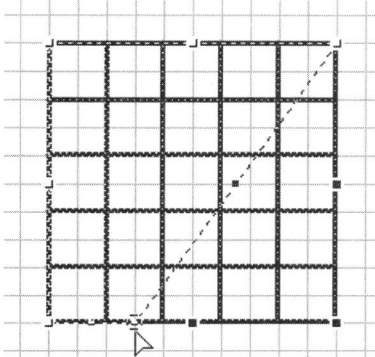 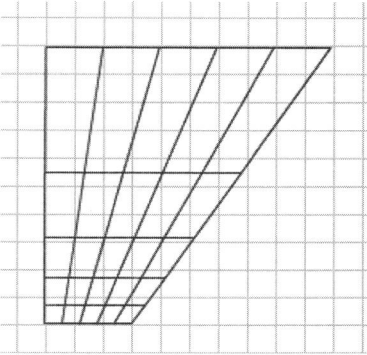

In the following exercise, we will use the distort modifier to create a simple faux 3D cube.

Create two new layers: call the top one lines and the bottom one 3D object. Make the top layer a guide (the easiest way to do this is to right-click on the layer title and select Guide from the pop-up menu that appears):

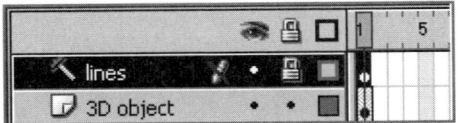

Select Show grid and Snap to grid (remember, CTRL+# and CTRL+SHIFT+#), if they are not already checked. Next go for View>Guides>Show guides (CTRL+;) and View>Guides>Snap to Guides (CTRL+SHIFT+;). Finally, select View>Rulers (CTRL+ALT+SHIFT+R).

By click-dragging on the horizontal and vertical rulers, create a '#' pattern of guides as shown:

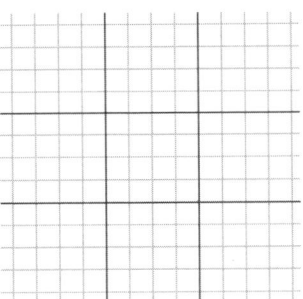

On the lines layer, add lines that go from a point in the top right corner to each of the three nearest corners of the square created by the four guides (as shown in the figure below left). Once you have done this, turn off the grid and grid snap to reveal an image like that shown below right:

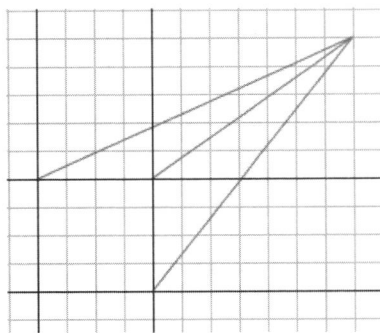 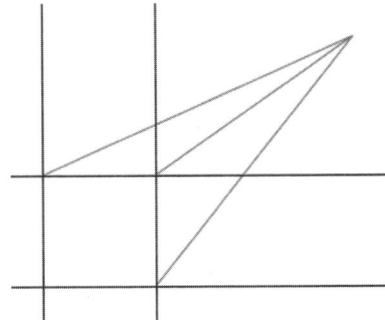

This set of lines represents a good starting point whenever you are creating faux 3D. The three lines we have just added are our perspective lines, and they meet at the vanishing point of our perspective view.

Before you continue, lock the lines layer. Now, using the guides as a reference, add a square in your 3D object layer, as shown below:

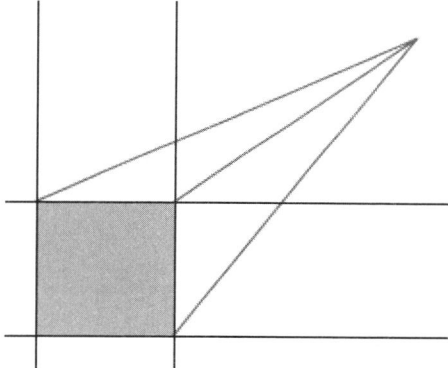

Copy this square, and then paste it back into the 3D object layer above the initial square (as shown below). With the new square still selected, use the distort modifier to move and distort the square so that it follows our perspective lines, as shown in this sequence:

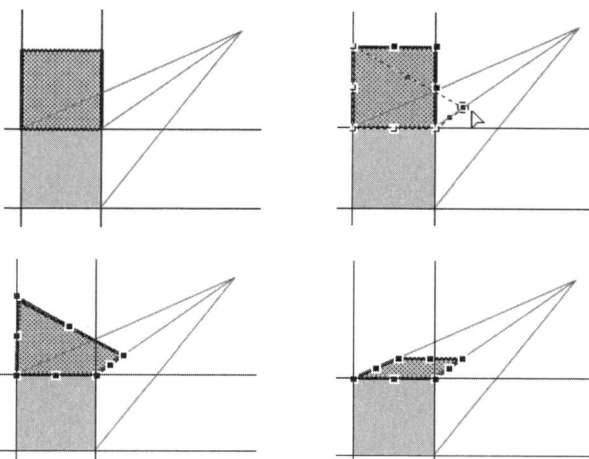

Do the same thing to add the third side of our cube to create the finished object (as shown overleaf).

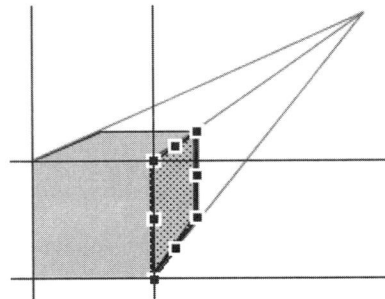

OK, so you could do the same thing with something like Swift3D, so what's the big deal? Well for one thing, although we used a simple gray square as our face, there is nothing stopping us from using a more complex picture or texture instead (but remember that if you want to use a bitmap, you need to convert it to a vector using Modify>Trace Bitmap..., after importing it):

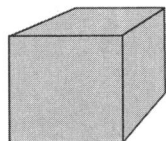 

The distort tool is also useful for building up **isometric** 3D graphics.

Isometric 3D graphics

An isometric view is one where there is no vanishing point, and all perspective lines are at 45 degrees. You can create isometric shapes in exactly the same way as we described in the previous section, but using the distort tool and a guide layer with an isometric view (sometimes also called *pixel 3D*):

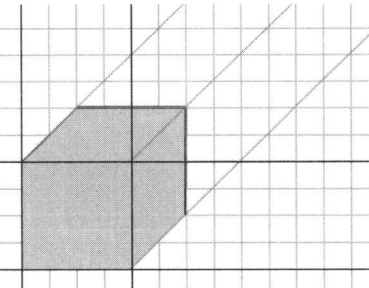

A useful tip for creating isometric graphics it to use the Shift+drag feature when drawing the construction lines, and they will automatically snap to 45 degrees. You can also create views that have 30 or 60 degree construction lines, and the effect will still work.

The beauty of isometric views is that the size of the shapes does not diminish with distance, and 'distant' objects are still clearly represented. Here's an example:

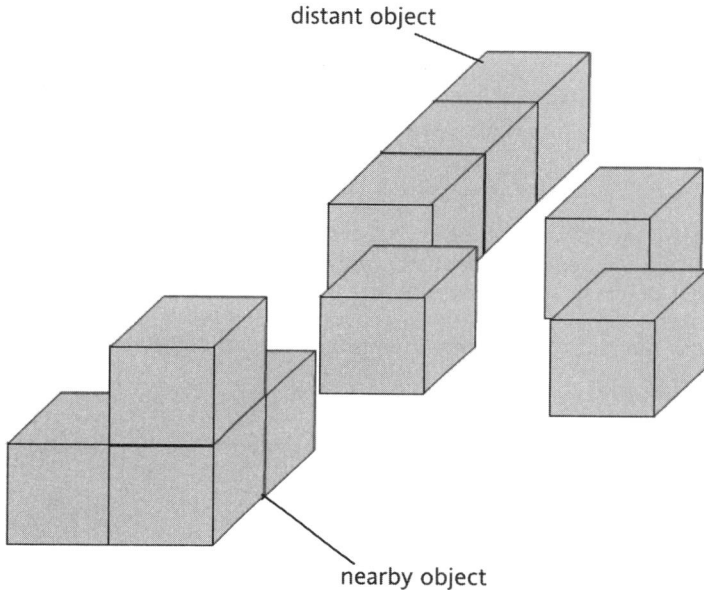

distant object

nearby object

Note that all the squares in the isometric view above are the same symbol, which makes the creation of the scene much easier than if you drew a similar scene using true perspective (where each square would look slightly different, meaning that each one would have to be drawn separately).

> *Using layers in isometric views will allow for automatic removal of hidden lines. Alternatively, you can place the most 'distant' symbols on the stage first, and symbols added later will automatically appear 'in front'.*

Take a look at Andries Odendaal's web site www.wireframe.co.za to see some nice isometric views in action.

The envelope modifier

To see what we can do with the envelope modifier we'll use our grid method again. You can just use the same 5x5 grid that we used with the distort tool earlier. The envelope modifier is an altogether different creature to its distort compatriot; it allows you to reshape things using *curves*, and it uses **bowties** to define curved edges.

> *As a side note, it's worth taking a moment to discuss the terminology we are using here. Bowties present an ideal way in which to manipulate the envelope modifier. The center point of the bowtie is called an **anchor point** (represented by a square), the lines connecting the 'bows' are called **tangent lines**, and the two endpoints of the bowtie are called the **tangent handles** (the circles). A possible source of confusion that is worth noting is that Adobe refers to tangent lines as 'direction lines'.*

A potential problem with the use of this modifier is that when you select it, depending on the scale you've got set, all you will see is a large number of similar looking points. There are actually the same number of anchor points as the distort tool, but each anchor point also has two tangent lines and handles (which forms the 'bowtie' discussed above). Looking at the following screenshot it is rather difficult to make out that the anchor points are actually squares, and the tangent handles are circles:

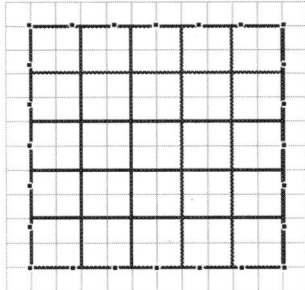

This problem is easily resolved – just change the movie background to a mid-gray to improve the contrast of the points:

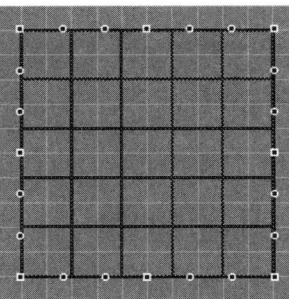

Moving the anchor points (click-drag any square point) causes the edges of your selection to curve such that they pass through each connecting anchor point (a behavior that you might recognize as a Bezier curve). Moving multiple anchor points results in a smoothly deformed graphic:

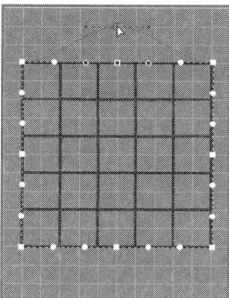 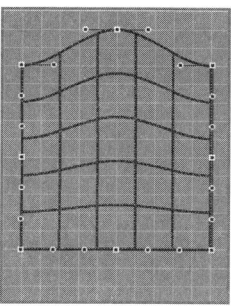 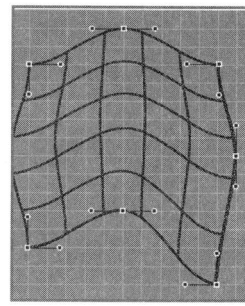

But what happens when we move the tangent handles from their current positions relative to the anchor points? Well, this alters the *direction* of the curve, as you can see below where we drag and drop a tangent handle on the bottom left corner of the envelope:

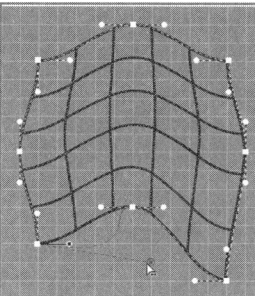 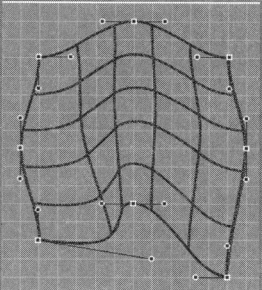

> *The direction of the handle and its associated tangent line defines the direction that the curve will be in as it passes through the anchor point, and the length defines the strength of the curve in that direction. Using the envelope modifier is one of those things that becomes very intuitive once you have tried it yourself a few times.*

It's important to remember that the envelope modifier only works on vector graphic elements (it will not work on symbols or groups, and will not deform a bitmap), but is very versatile when creating either complex shape tweens or transforming text. It is particularly useful for:

- Creating bends in limbs or other objects
- Simulating flexing of organic shapes
- Creating mouth movements in faces
- Conforming one shape to another

We'll look at implementing some of these ideas in the next couple of sections.

Creating morphing animations

The envelope modifier is great for creating organic shape tweens, such as bending or flexing. In this simple example, we will perform a little bit of magic and turn a lemon into a banana using the envelope modifier. You can use any image to follow this example – it's the general techniques that we're interested in learning, rather than some kind of fruit-alchemy! But, if you're interested, you'll find a copy of the lemon image, `lemon.fla`, in this chapter's code folder.

To start with, we want to make our lemon taller. Drag the top and bottom anchor points so that you end up with the stretched shape shown below. As you drag and release each point, you should see the lemon begin to contort to the shape defined by the envelope:

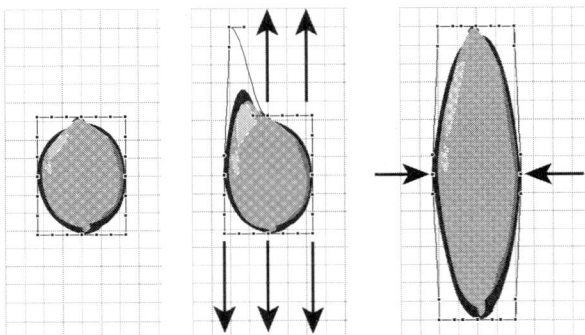

You could actually have stretched the lemon via the normal free transform, but the next step can only be done with the envelope modifier; we now want to bend the shape so that it becomes curved.

> *Be very careful when you're selecting bowties - make sure that you never deselect the envelope (by selecting the stage instead, for example) until you have finished the deformation. Once you've done this you can never bring the current envelope back, and you'll have to start again with a square envelope! Even if you hit undo (CTRL+Z) the envelope will reset itself to a bounding box, which can become highly annoying.*
>
> *You can, however, use undo while the envelope is still selected to move anchor points/tangent handles to their previous positions. Do this if you find you have dragged a handle instead of an anchor, for example.*

We need to change our rectangular envelope into a curve. We will do this in two steps:

    1.   Create a bent '<' shape
    2.   Curve the '<' into a 'c' shape to form our final shape

To form the '<' shape, move the top and bottom anchor points to the left to form the 'bend' (see the screenshot below). The problem here is that the tangent lines are still horizontal and vertical, so you will also have to move them so that you form roughly straight edges for the top and bottom of your envelope:

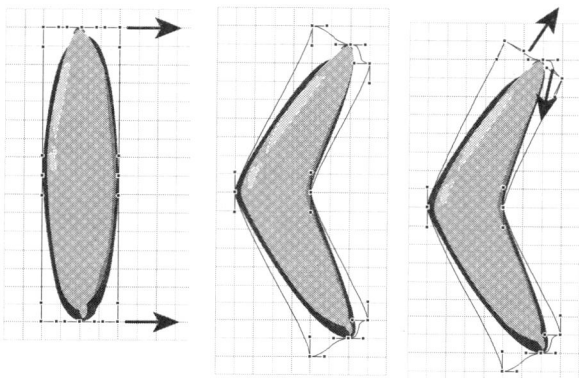

Okay, now we have moved our bowties so that the top and bottom edges of the envelope are straighter (you don't have to be too precise with this), but our banana doesn't exactly curve yet. To fix this, we need to move the handles of the middle anchor points so that the extended tangent lines give us more of a curved effect, as shown below. The final shape is not only bent, but the bend is also nicely curved:

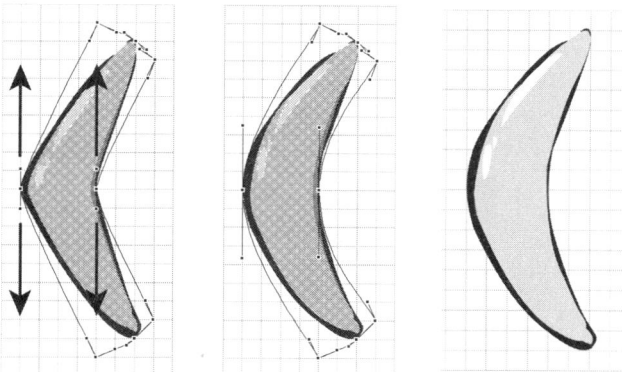

The before and after shapes can be used in a tween animation as shown on the next page, although you will need to do some tweaking of the start and end keyframe to get it to tween successfully without using shape hints.

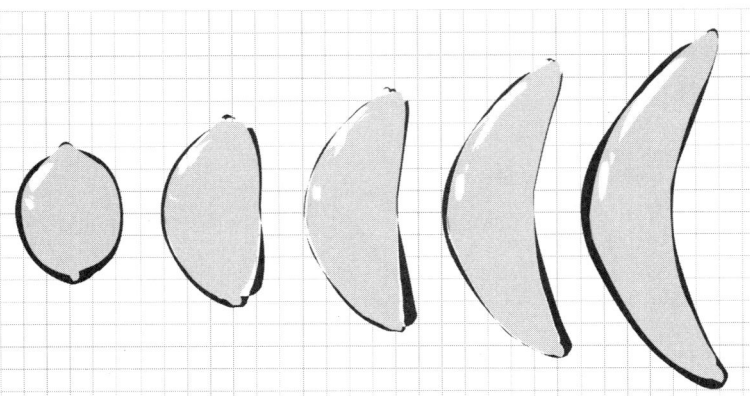

So by now you may be saying, "Well, very nice, but I don't really need to turn lemons into bananas, and I'm pretty sure that it will never appear in a client spec for an animation". While this may well be true, the general principles that we have learned are can be applied to almost anything.

For instance, here I have a running figure, crossing the finishing line, which I'd like to animate:

To bend the front leg as it runs (or any other body part), you can use the envelope modifier in very much the same way as we used it to deform and morph fruit.

Notice how in this case the envelope has the effect of accounting for the muscle compression of the underside of the thigh as the leg bends upwards:

 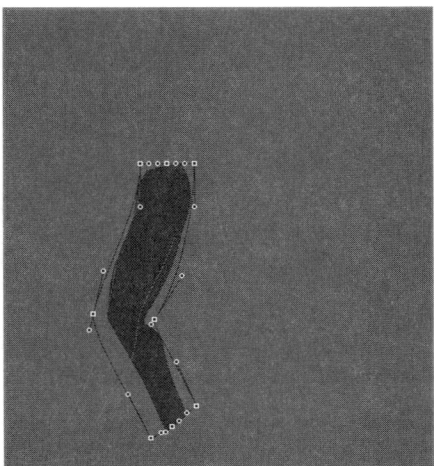

Note that I have taken my own advice here, and temporarily changed the colors of the stage (and figure) such that the envelope modifier is easily visible, and I can tell the difference between an anchor point and its bow tie handles.

Setting this sort of thing up does take a lot of practice and involves splitting the figure into many separate parts – you obviously can't do it by simply applying an envelope modifier to the whole figure. But once you crack it, it's extremely useful for creating lifelike low bandwidth character animation.

Here are a few more tips on using the envelope for this kind of animation:

- Notice that the tangent lines are very short at the lower side of the knee. This is the way to tell the envelope that this point is a corner. You need to make the inside corner sharper than the outer one.
- Be sure to turn grid snap off when using the envelope modifier. As the effect is so sensitive to the positions of tangent handles, you really need a free unsnapped movement (and a steady hand!).
- When starting a limb shape tween using an envelope modifier, make sure that the limb is either horizontal or vertical. Any angle in between, and your envelope will form itself around the bounding box that includes the limb diagonal, as shown overleaf for the figure's left arm – this is less than ideal for animation. In such a scenario you wouldn't know which anchor point you had to move for a given arm position because they are so far away from the arm itself.

- To make sure that you 'steer' your shape tweens properly, you will need to add frequent key frames. Around one every 5-10 frames seems to do the trick.

OK, now some of you are thinking "Hmm... looks cool, but I'm not all that interested in animating running figures either". Well, that's fair enough! The important thing to note here is that we've achieved these nice effects using the transform tool. Although it's not specifically meant to do this, an artist can re-purpose it however they wish. More generally speaking, the examples we've talked about have shown us how to tell the difference between a corner point and an inside curve, something that is not actually very intuitive.

There are two more important uses of the envelope modifier – **distorting text**, which is pretty much self-explanatory as seen below, and **conforming text to a defined path**, which we'll look at in detail in the next section.

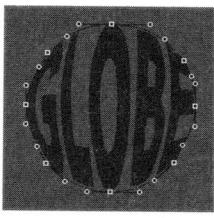 

Conforming text to a path

As well as shaping text as shown above, you can also use the envelope modifier to simulate text that is conformed to a path. First we need to create a guide layer with our path design, and then a static text symbol.

To create a path draw a straight line between the two end points of the desired path using the **line** tool:

With the **arrow** tool, create the basic curve you want for your path by click-dragging any point on the line in between the end points:

Finally, click on the line with the **sub-selection** tool (the white-headed arrow). Your line will now have at least two anchor points, and selecting either one allows you to access that point's tangent line to 'fine-tune' the curve shape:

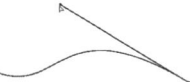

> *Because the envelope lines and tangent handles will be black, it's a good idea to make your path line a distinct color (such as green, or any color that will stand out well against black and your chosen background color).*

Lock the guide layer when you're happy with the path you've created. Next, place the text so that its first letter sits at the start of the path (you may have to zoom in to do this):

> *It's worth keeping in mind a little undocumented feature of Flash 5 that is still with us – holding down CTRL+SPACE and clicking on any area of the stage allows us to zoom in without unselecting the current tool. Then we can use CTRL+SHIFT+SPACE and click to zoom out again (PhotoShop has an analogous feature: CTRL+SPACE to zoom in and ALT+SPACE to zoom out).*

Zoom back out so that you can see both the complete text and the path. It is a good idea to make your background color non-white again at this point so that you will be able to see the points and tangent handles of the envelope modifier when we come to use them.

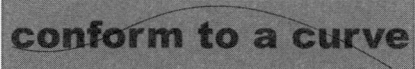

As we've seen in previous examples, we need to make our text a vector graphic using the Break Apart function (CTRL+B) before the envelope modifier will work with it. It's worth noting that this feature now works slightly differently from its Flash 5 equivalent, which would have changed all of the text into shape vectors. Flash MX now breaks the text into individual characters by creating one static text field per character. This is a useful feature for some purposes (such as creating animated text effects using tweening), but not what we want for the current example:

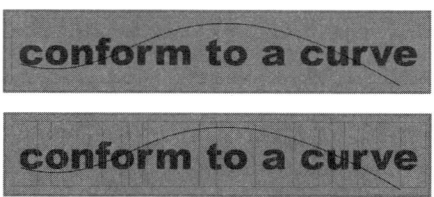

To get to the vector graphics we want, simply hit CTRL+B a second time:

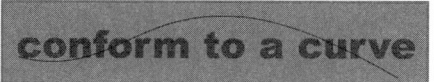

With the text selected, use the free transform tool with the envelope modifier and move the middle anchor points so that they line up with the path, as shown below:

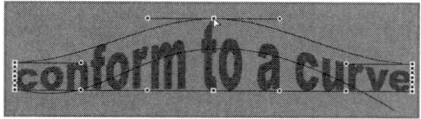

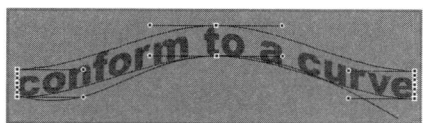

We now need to edit the envelope at the beginning and end of the text. Notice that the text is much shorter than it is wide, therefore the points and tangent handles are all squashed together – there appears to be very little space there to do anything, even if we could reliably select a point!

Remember, earlier we established that we shouldn't unselect our envelope, (to select the zoom tool for instance) because we would lose it for good. The answer is to simply press CTRL+SPACE and click to zoom in again. So go on and zoom in enough to see what you are doing.

You need to make the bottom envelope line up with the path, and make the top and bottom edges of the envelope curve along parallel paths. The left edge of the envelope should be at right angles to the initial path:

Do the same with the right edge of the text:

 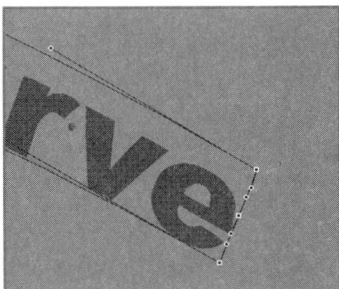

Finished! After zooming back out (CTRL+SHIFT+SPACE+CLICK), here's my final text, plus the path I was trying to conform the text to. Pretty close!

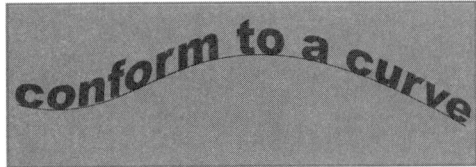

Finally, get rid off the guide, and return the background to its original white.

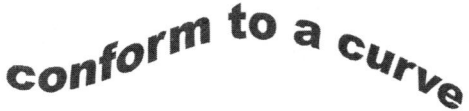

After this whirlwind tour of the free transform tool, and the design possibilities that its associated modifiers give us, let's turn our attention to the other new addition to the Flash toolbox – the **fill transform** tool.

Fill transform tool

The **fill transform** tool allows you to change a fill after you have placed it on the stage. As you'll see, it is useful for fine editing of fills, and is context sensitive based on the fill attributes, which is a very valuable extra. You really need to try it out on every fill type otherwise you will miss some of the neat features it offers!

Select a gray fill color and a black outline stroke, then use the draw oval tool, to create a large circle on the stage (a handy tip here is that holding down the Shift key while dragging ensures that you draw a circle, rather than an oval):

If you now select the fill transform tool (as shown above) and click inside the gray fill, nothing will happen. Don't worry; it isn't broken! You've not yet selected a fill with any modifiable attributes so, obviously, nothing happens. What we need to do is select a **linear** or **radial** fill for the tool to work – we'll study both of these types in the next two subsections.

Linear fill

With the **arrow** tool selected, click on the circle's fill. This highlights the fill, allowing us to edit it. Insert a **linear** fill by clicking on the fill color in the toolbox (or indeed the Property inspector) and selecting the default gradient fill. This will change the fill to linear as shown over the page:

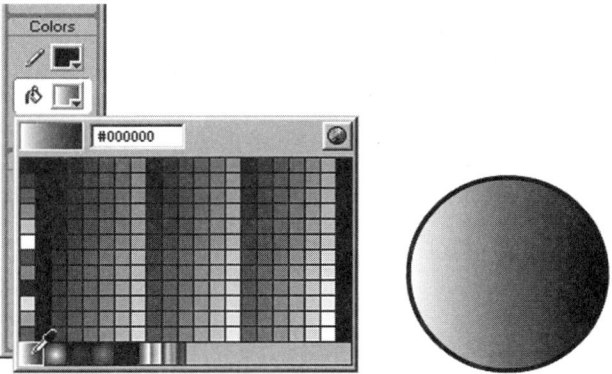

Now select the fill transform tool again, and click on the fill – here we have an altogether different story. There are three points that you can click-drag and visually edit to alter the fill:

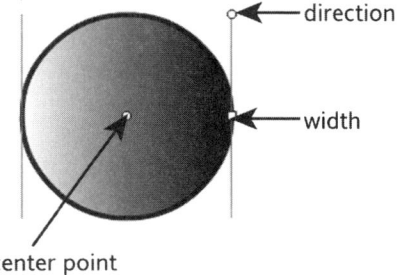

direction

width

center point

> It's worth making that sure snap to grid (CTRL+SHIFT+#) is not checked, to allow for pixel perfect fine-tuning of the fill.

Moving the **center point** alters the position of the fill (top left of next page). Moving the **direction** of the fill rotates the fill around the center point; for example, in the middle picture on the next page, we have rotated the fill of our default circle by a quarter turn. Finally, the **width** allows you to vary the linear spacing of the fill – the picture top right overleaf shows our default circle with the fill width compressed by moving the width point towards the center (overleaf):

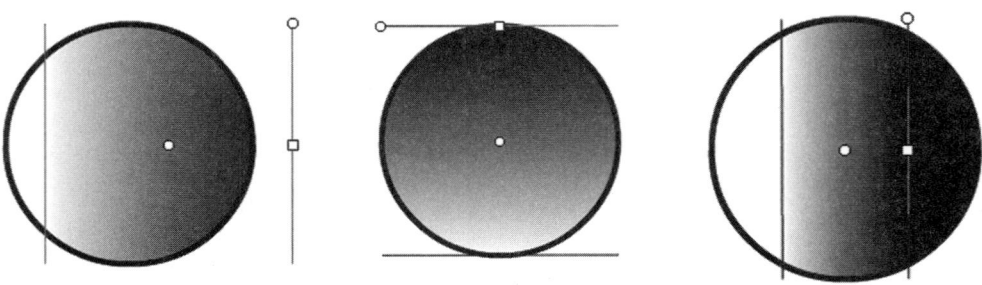

Radial fill

The **radial** fill gives us even more possibilities for creating cool shading in graphics. To apply a radial fill to our circle select the fill with the arrow tool and then choose the fill color and a radial fill. Your circle will now have a radial fill pattern as shown below:

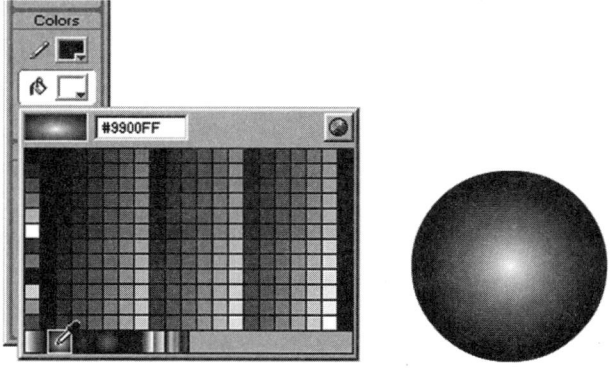

Ignore the #9900FF value we have in our picture; this is the color of the pixel under the cursor at the point you select the fill. For patterned fills, this value is not really significant, and will change depending on the exact pixel under your mouse pointer.

If you select the fill transform tool again, you'll see that the modifiable attributes are now different – with the radial fill there are four click-draggable points:

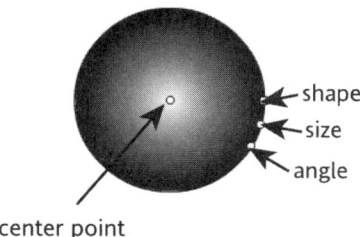

center point

Moving the **center point** does the same thing as last time – it moves the fill:

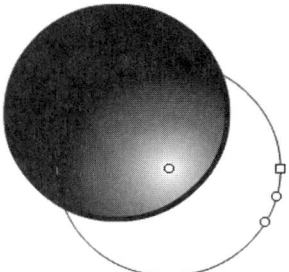

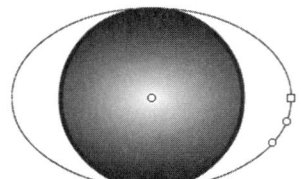

Starting with the default circle again, dragging the **shape** point changes the shape of the *radial* that the fill is based around.

With the radial kept as the oval, drag the **size** point – this changes the size of the radial:

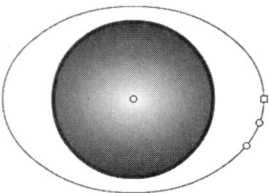

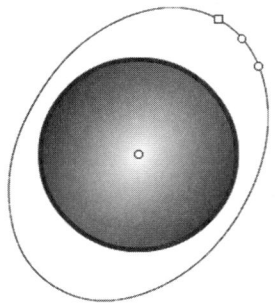

Finally, and unsurprisingly, the **angle** point changes its angle.

Producing realistic light source highlights

You have probably realized by now that if the radial gradient colors are chosen wisely (a radial gradient that gets brighter as you move towards its center, for instance), the gradient actually acts like the highlight from a light source, and associated shadows. The radial envelope is a representation of the spotlight beam that creates the highlight; it is effectively a perfect circle that is seen as an oval due to the viewer's position in 3D space:

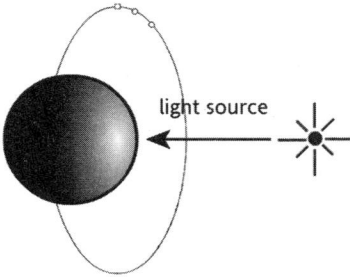

If you are using this effect to mimic a light source, consider using a radial fill which is white (zero alpha) at the edge, and white (100% alpha) at the center, and add it over some of the 3D shapes you have created with the distort tool (which we looked at earlier in this chapter in relation to those faux 3D scenes).

Tomasz Jankowski used radial fills as lighting highlights in his early *Blue Mondo* site versions (see friends of ED's *New Masters Of Flash* book), but the process is now much easier with the ability to fine edit the fill with the fill transform tool so that all your light source highlights appear to come from the same point.

Summary

On the face of it, Macromedia Flash MX has only a couple of completely new graphic creation tools, and they are both really only modifiers to an existing tool. They are, however, very well chosen enhancements that will undoubtedly prove themselves to be powerful additions to your toolbox once you get to grips with what they can actually do.

In this chapter we've looked at the improvements to the standard graphics toolbox that comes with Flash MX, concentrating on utilizing the free transform tool, with its associated distort and envelope modifiers, and the fill transform tool, with both linear and radial fills. From a 3D perspective, through advanced character animation and text effects, to cool new highlighting techniques, these new tools give us a lot of new functionality for tween-based animation or static graphic creation. Get out there and use them!

In the next chapter we're going to get to grips with the use of the Actions panel and the associated features of the enhanced scripting environment that Flash MX gives us.

Chapter 5

The Scripting Environment

The Actions panel changed considerably between versions 4 and 5 of Flash to allow direct typing of scripts, superceding the cumbersome mode of script creation in Flash 4 (or, in fact, in the **Normal** mode of Flash 5). Experience in the field with Flash 5 showed Macromedia that most people were still using Normal mode because of its debug, auto-format, and help facilities. In Normal mode:

- Errors were highlighted in red, and it was not possible to add incorrect actions.
- ActionScript was correctly indented, and semi-colons were automatically added to the end of each line.
- It was obvious which arguments had to be used for an action. For instance, actions like `for...` or `duplicateMovieClip` take a number of arguments, and can be difficult to remember these without Normal mode there to help you with the ones you don't use often.

Because of these issues, even competent Flash users who were using **Expert** mode were occasionally dipping into Normal mode, if only to ensure that their script was free of errors, correctly formatted, and to help them enter actions that required lots of difficult-to-remember arguments.

After validating their code in Normal mode, such users were going back into Expert mode to do some more text entry, and then dropping back into Normal mode every few lines. This is clearly not a very user-friendly experience. Macromedia Flash MX makes this sort of thing a relic of the past by offering an Expert mode with all the advantages of the old Flash 5 Normal *and* Expert modes, but with none of their disadvantages.

Accordingly, we strongly recommend that users with any previous experience of Flash should *forget about Normal mode completely*. As this book is designed for previous Flash 5 users who don't need a foundation book this time round, this more than likely includes you.

In fact, most of the new functionality of Macromedia Flash MX can only be accessed in Expert mode. Although Normal mode tries to compete, we really think it is the beginner's learning mode for Flash MX, and you will be frustrated by its slowness when you come to use the new scripting features of Flash MX.

OK, enough trying to sell Expert mode to you – let's dive right in to our study of the scripting environment by taking a look at the new Actions panel.

The Actions panel

Be sure to select Expert Mode *from the Actions panel menu. Unless otherwise stated, the rest of the book will assume you are in this mode.*

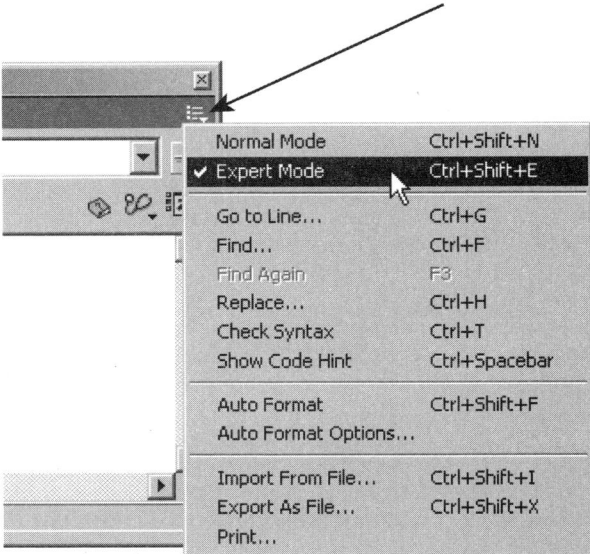

The first thing that has obviously changed is that the Actions panel is dockable, like all the other panels. The default panel set-up (Window>Panel Sets>Default Layout) places the Actions panel in the central docking area below the stage, and it's probably the best place to leave it there to ensure an efficient workflow. Leaving it floating makes for clutter, and leaving it in a side docking area makes it far too cramped.

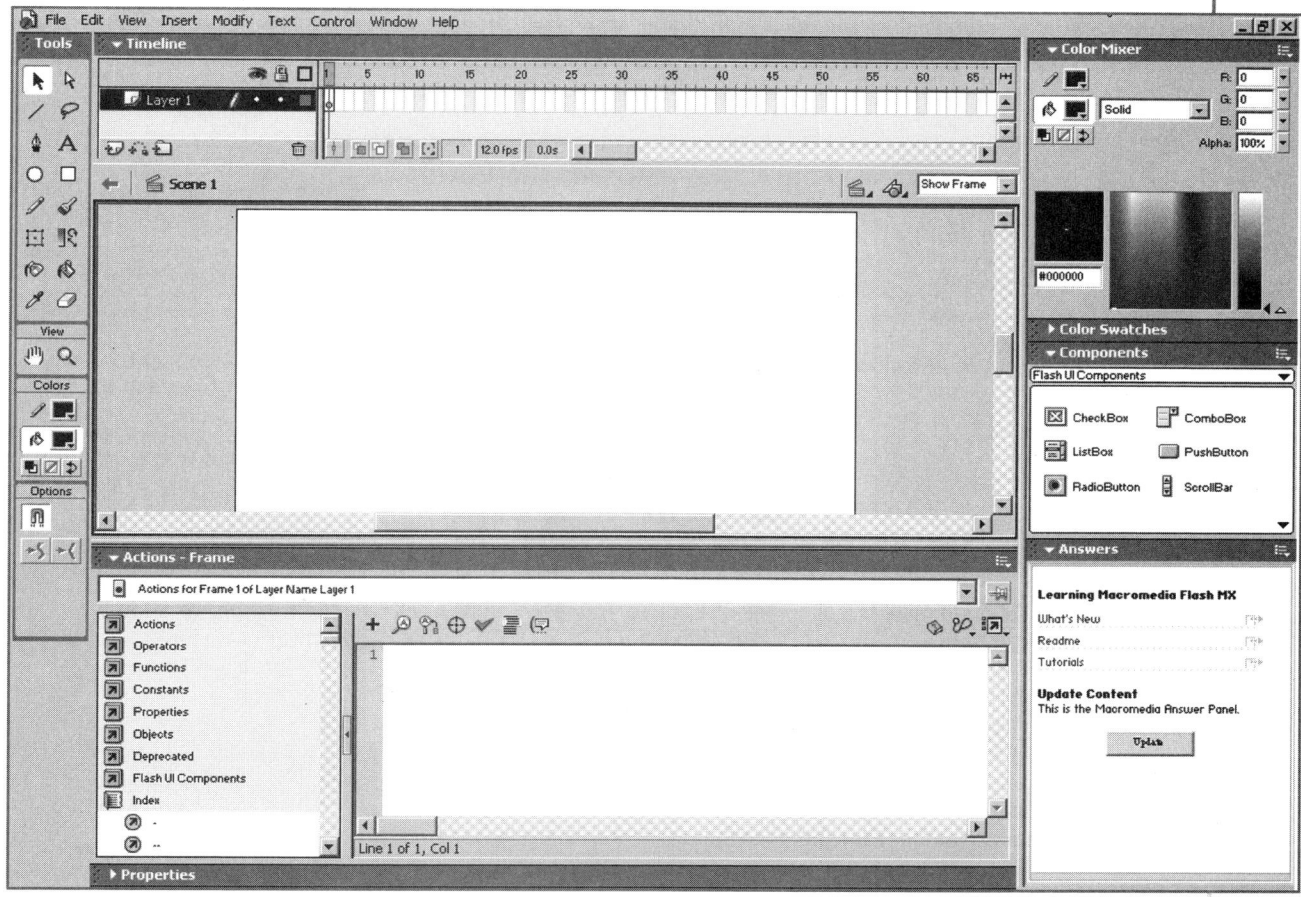

Maximizing the Actions panel makes it grow to fill the lower half of the environment, as shown above, and you can simply minimize it again to tuck it back away when it's not needed. As an aside, we found that leaving the Property inspector floating was the best option, since it is in use at all times. As you familiarize yourself with all the new functionality of Macromedia Flash MX you will, no doubt, develop your own personal preferences for your UI layout.

The standard way of using the Actions panel in the Flash 5 workflow was as a floating panel. You would bring it up from either the quick launch menu or by double-clicking a keyframe in the timeline. If you've already been playing around with Flash MX you might have already noticed that neither of these options will work now – the quick launch icon is no longer where it was, and you cannot double-click a keyframe to bring up the Actions panel.

If, however, you are keen to carry on using the Flash 5 way of doing things, here's how (overleaf).

■ You can use the quick launch icon in the far right edge of the Property inspector. This icon will only appear if the item you have selected can have a script attached to it (such as a frame or movie clip):

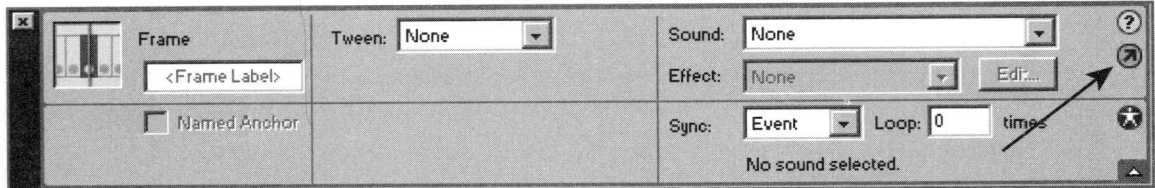

■ Double-clicking on a keyframe now selects the frame span instead of bringing up the Actions panel. For example, if you had your Flash 5 hat on and wanted to attach a script to the keyframe at frame 18...

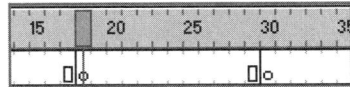

...double-clicking on the required frame will make MX select the *span*, as shown below:

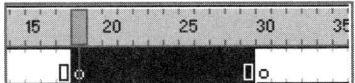

Unlike in Flash 5, you cannot change this selection functionality. A useful alternative way of bringing up the Actions panel in Flash MX is to simply hit F2.

These are just small-fry inconveniences to the new Flash MX Actions editor. They pale into insignificance against the enhancements, most of which are major, but some of which are so subtle you might not even notice them. For example, Flash 5 always opened the **Actions** window to a *default* state as specified in your preferences. MX has a much better brain, and knows better than to mess with your workflow in this way. It opens the Actions window looking the same way it did the last time you used it, whenever that was. How thoughtful!

In the following sections we'll examine the following fundamental features of the new, improved, intelligence-boosted MX Actions panel:

■ Line numbering
■ Pinning the actions editor
■ Preferences
■ Help features
■ The Reference panel

Line numbering

Macromedia Flash MX can now show line numbering. You can turn this feature on and off via the View Options icon, as shown below:

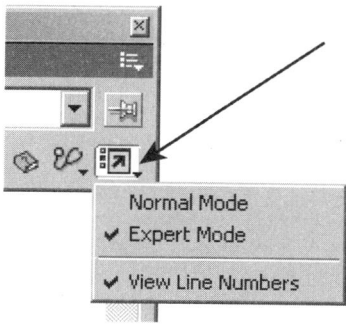

It's a pretty cool feature to leave on, because it allows you to:

- Move through long scripts easily without losing your place.
- Relate errors in the Output window with line numbers in the script (remember, Flash 5 listed errors in terms of the line and frame they appeared in, but only displayed the line number that your cursor was on!).
- Document your code better by referring to line numbers.

Pinning the actions editor

One of the Flash 5 gripes was that you had to have a frame or object selected before you could enter a script. We've probably all tried to enter something into the actions editor when the dreaded Current selection cannot have actions applied to it message appears – clearly, we haven't actually selected anything that we can attach a script to! This is reasonable, but not so obvious when you are working from home at two o'clock in the morning, a few hours before your client progress meeting deadline at dawn...

Even when you already know what the problem is, it's a little annoying having to re-select a keyframe every time you want to change a script. Even though we're used to doing it in Flash 5, you might still be thinking, 'I keep having to go back to that keyframe to change a bit of the script attached to it... why can't the Actions window realize this and just keep it selected?' Well now you can do it the easy way. You can **pin** the Actions panel to a keyframe or object. The best way to demonstrate how to do this is with an example.

How to pin the current script

1. Open a new FLA and create two layers, actions and graphics:

2.   With the Actions panel open, select frame 1 of layer actions and add the following script:

```
// My script
```

OK, this isn't really a script, just a simple comment, but you'll see the point in a moment. While we're here, notice that comments are now colored gray – this is a neat new feature, and we'll show you how to customize the color in the next section.

3.   To pin the window, click on the icon that looks like a notice board pin in the top right of the panel (see below). It will change to indicate that it has pinned down the panel:

4.   Now let's assume you need to tweak some graphics. Select the graphics layer and add some circles, lines, or whatever. Notice that the script does not disappear from the Actions panel. Now go back in the Actions panel with layer graphics still selected, and add the following line:

```
// Some more script
```

So, you can focus the Actions window on the thing you are attaching your scripts to, go away and do some other stuff with the graphics, keeping the scripts still visible, and drop back to the scripting where you left off, whenever you want.

For long-suffering Flash 5 users, this is such a nice new feature it makes you wonder why we put up with the old way for so long!

Preferences

Rather like the T-shirts that are sold as a 'one size fits all' garment that really means 'one size fits everyone equally badly', the Actions window in Flash 5 had three font sizes: small (impossible to read!), medium, and large (perhaps only useful for those with very large monitors, or for people who stand well back).

It also had preset colors that you could not change, which made matters worse. Although any ASP and C++ programmers that I know do in fact use small text sizes, they set their editors to display white text on a black background, allowing the text to remain small but legible because of the high contrast. A few of them actually use green text on a black background (perhaps under the impression that they are actually characters in *The Matrix*!).

Additionally, the previous releases of Flash didn't let you vary the default tabs and other settings for the 'auto format' features, and you were largely stuck with them.

The lack of preference settings in Flash 5 made for a very inflexible editing environment. Many scripters instead used a text editor of their own choice (either a basic ASCII editor, or one that recognized JavaScript syntax and formatting), and one or two particularly disgruntled souls actually built their own external ActionScript editors. Well, with Flash MX you now can script within the luxury of your own integral, customized scripting environment – let's take a look at this environment, and at how we can customize it to suit our personal needs.

Basic appearance

You can change the basic appearance of the Actions window editor, allowing you to alter it from the sublime...

...to the somewhat ridiculous:

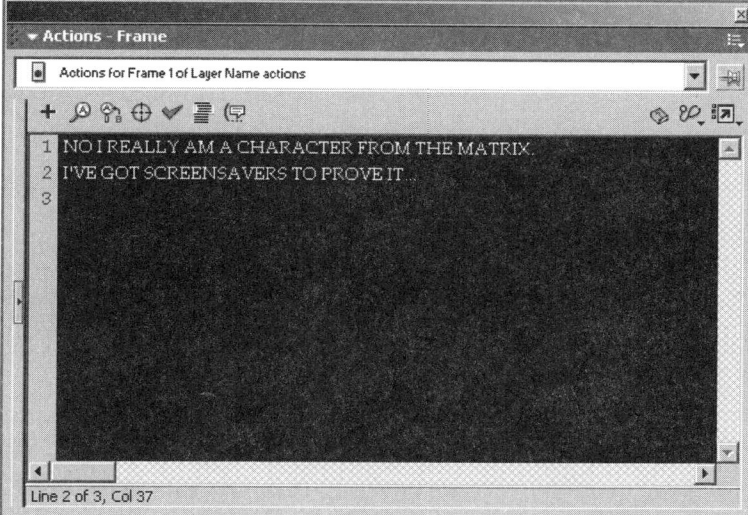

To modify the appearance, select Preferences... from the panel's drop-down (you can also use Edit>Preferences...>ActionScript Editor):

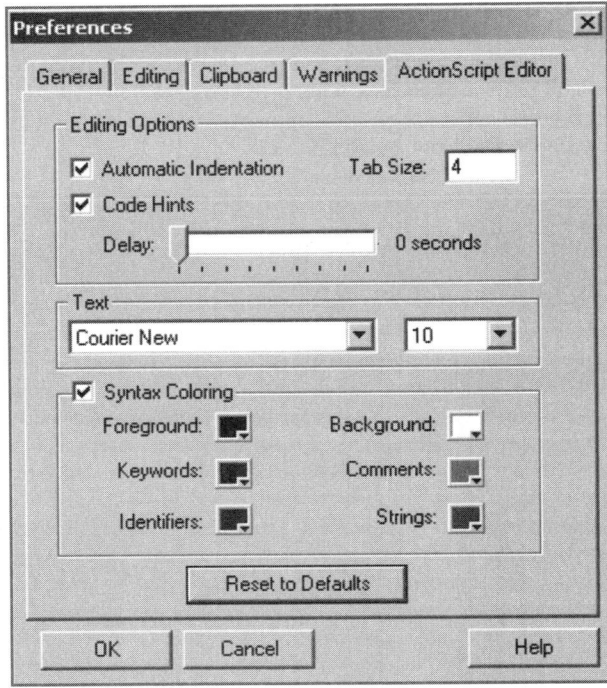

You can change the syntax coloring (or disable it completely by un-checking this function), as well as the font and font size.

> *If you want to go back to the font used in Flash 5, select Lucida Console as your text font.*

The other settings are fairly self-explanatory – you can set the tab size and whether Flash will indent your scripts, which is useful if you want to limit the width of your scripts in the window. We will look at code hinting shortly when we come to look at the help features built into Macromedia Flash MX.

Code formatting

You can alter the automatic code formatting that Flash applies to ActionScript through the Auto Format Options window (you'll find this option in the drop-down menu of the Actions panel).

Again, this window is pretty self-explanatory. Simply check each option, and if you like what it does, keep it. The scripts are presented in this book using the default code formatting though, so return your formatting to the default preferences once you have slated your curiosity on what *cuddling* a brace ('}') actually means!

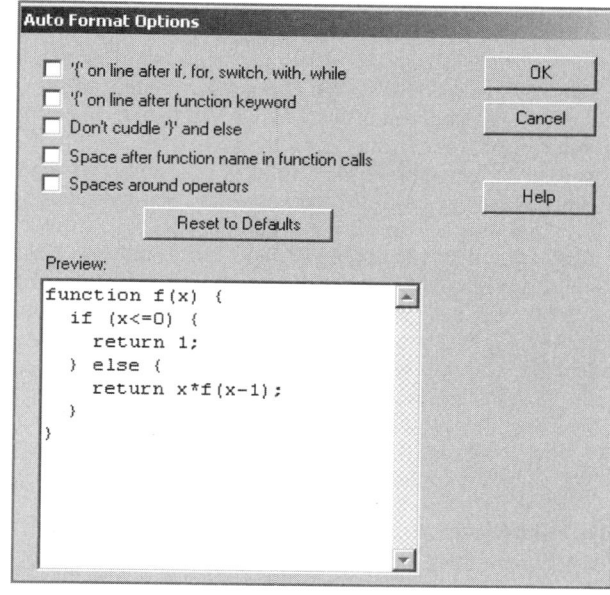

```
function f(x) {
  if (x<=0) {
    return 1;
  } else {
    return x*f(x-1);
  }
}
```

Help features

The toolbar of the Actions panel looks like this:

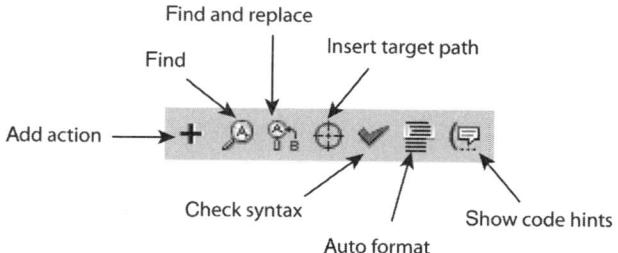

From the left, the first four icons are simply repositioned versions of Flash 5 functionality. The real magic is in the last three icons. As we mentioned earlier, the reason many people could not break the umbilical from the Normal mode was the benefit of syntax checking, auto formatting, and the ability to see which arguments were needed. These features are all brought over into the Expert environment via the last three icons, so don't touch that Normal mode! Additionally, there's another help feature without an icon, **auto complete**, so we will have a look at this as well.

Check syntax

The check syntax function will perform a check of the script currently shown in the Actions window. Because it is simply a click away, I have already got used to hitting it every three or four lines of code. When an error is detected, the errors and relevant line numbers will be listed in the Output window.

Auto format

Every structured language I've ever been involved with from PASCAL upwards has certain formatting standards to aid readability. This is a good idea, and it works well, but it's a real pain having to do it manually as you code; this was a good reason for people – even scripting superheroes – to sneak into Normal mode to let it do the formatting, and then just as quickly sneak back into Expert mode. You no longer have to do this, and can keep your ego intact; simply click the AUTO FORMAT button every time the script is starting to look like it needs a spring clean.

Auto format has another excellent (but subtle) use: when you hit ENTER after the end of a line of code, and the auto formatting gets it wrong by going to the wrong tab space, you know it's because the line you just typed has an error in it. There will usually be a missed bracket or something small, something that you would otherwise have missed. Like most one-finger-typing programmers, I tend to enter code at breakneck speed, not looking up at the screen until three lines later. When I do look up, the first thing I ask myself in Flash MX is 'Has the auto formatting accepted it?' If so, then I'm more confident that I haven't missed a pesky bracket or something. I know, I know, I shouldn't propagate my own bad habits, but I'm a realist – that's the way a lot of us work after six weeks with any scripting application!

Auto complete

Now, what's the name of the method that allows you to duplicate movie clips? Well, I'll tell you that it's `duplicateMovieClip`. If I *didn't* know this, with Flash MX I'd no longer have to reach for the ActionScript dictionary – thanks to the auto complete feature: auto complete checks to see what you are writing, and as soon as it thinks it knows what you are trying to enter it will list all the permissible options for what to type next. For example, if you enter `_root.`, the next thing you will enter must be a movie clip method.

Try it now – we want to enter `_root.duplicateMovieClip`. The text will be black until Flash recognizes that we have entered a keyword `_root`, at which point (assuming you have kept the default syntax colors), it will turn blue. Now comes the really cool bit. Add the period '.':

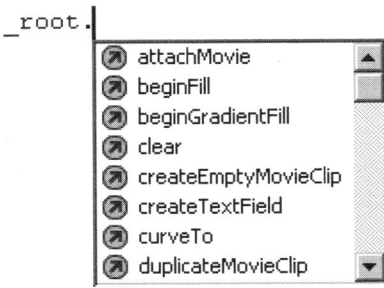

Flash then lists all the methods that we could possibly want to add next. The method we want doesn't appear in the visible part of the list box yet, so let's give Flash another clue. Add the 'd':

```
_root.d
```

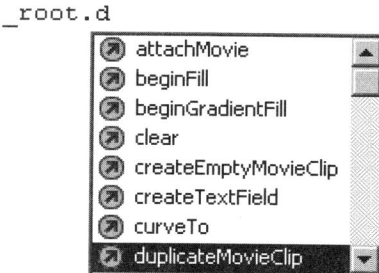

There it is! Hit ENTER to add the full `duplicateMovieClip` method syntax to the end of `_root`. The fun hasn't ended yet though, because Flash MX knows that I am a lost cause when it come to ActionScript, and there's yet more help on its way…

Code hinting

OK, so I've cheated my way this far. Even though I might not have know how to spell `duplicateMovieClip`, the auto complete function has helped me to find my required method. The next problem is even bigger – although I have a vague idea of how to use this method, I can't remember the exact order or number of arguments.

This is where code hinting comes in:

```
_root.duplicateMovieClip(
```

```
MovieClip.duplicateMovieClip( newName, depth [, initObject] )
```

> *Where the lists of methods and parameters are particularly large, or there are different groups of them, you may want to navigate through your methods and parameters. Hitting* CONTROL+LEFTARROW / CONTROL+RIGHTARROW *allows you to do this. This is an undocumented feature introduced by Macromedia, and well worth knowing.*

The help text that pops up as soon as the `duplicateMovieClip` has appeared gives you a hint as to how to complete the line. Note that if you've changed your window/application you can get the help text line back again by hitting the *show code hint* icon.

As you enter each argument, the hint text moves on to the next argument by showing it in bold. The final argument is in square brackets signifying that it is optional (in this case, it's actually a new feature added to this method in Flash MX), so we won't put it in for now (overleaf):

```
_root.duplicateMovieClip("myClip",
```

> MovieClip.duplicateMovieClip(newName, **depth** [, initObject])

```
_root.duplicateMovieClip("myClip", 10);
```

The help features are not infallible though, and this example is actually designed to show this. The resulting line is *syntactically* correct, but it doesn't necessarily follow that it will *work*. We have told Flash to duplicate _root, which is a nonsense instruction.

We should actually specify a movie clip, rather than the main timeline, as the thing to duplicate. We need to enter something like this:

```
_root.myOtherClip.duplicateMovieClip("myClip", 10);
```

So should we have used Normal mode instead? Well, no. Neither modes will trap errors like this, but as long as you know what the *logic* and *intent* of a method or action is, they will help enormously.

Don't worry though, because there is one final bit of help that will actually tell us this – the Reference panel, which we'll see in a moment.

Default naming conventions

As a quick aside let's look at naming conventions briefly. Macromedia have designed a default naming convention for use within ActionScript, and if you stick to it, auto complete will make life *much* easier for you.

The conventions are as follows:

Object	Naming convention
Movie clips and/or timelines	_mc, _level, _parent or _root
Array	_array
String	_str
Button	_btn
Text field	_txt
Text format	_fmt
Date	_date
Sound	_sound
XML	_xml
XML sockets	_xmlsocket
Color	_color
Video	_video

So how does this work? Well, suppose you were using a sound object: you could call it anything you liked, but if you use _sound at the end of the name, the Actions panel will automatically deduce that the object is a sound object, and will filter its help accordingly.

For example, in the Actions panel, enter this:

```
tune_sound
```

Now add the '.':

```
tune_sound.
```

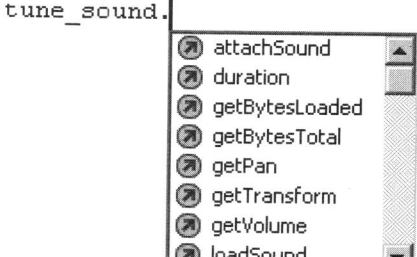

Flash MX now only lists those specific methods that relate to the sound object. That's what I call *intelligent* help.

If you feel you need an extra level of help via this sort of filtering, make sure that you use the naming conventions.

But what if, like me, you are a bit of a maverick and want to use your own conventions? Well, Flash MX is actually extremely *configurable*, and you can alter a lot of its functionality using a set of built-in files – we'll have a look at these towards the end of this chapter. These files can change the way Flash works at a very detailed level, and you can alter the way all parts of the Flash UI look, work, and feel.

The Reference panel

The *reference* icon is on the right of the Actions window:

If you leave your text cursor somewhere within the `duplicateMovieClip` action we looked at a few moments ago, and then hit the reference icon, you will see the full entry of the method appear in the Reference panel:

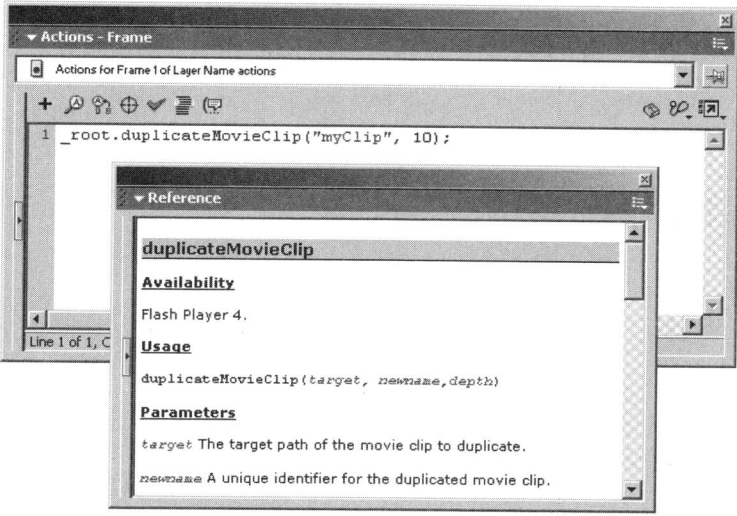

The Reference panel includes all the entries in the Macromedia ActionScript dictionary. With this reference guide at hand you are far less likely to try to duplicate _root now... as if you ever would do that in the first place!

Advanced configuration of the scripting environment

The actions editor's functionality is based on a number of default naming conventions, and on assumptions about coding style. Macromedia have assumed that we are all typical users, and given us a typical environment. We are only typical users when we are learning, though - after that it's all down to what we want to do, and the way we tend to use the Actions panel. Macromedia have given us a path to alter the interface to suit our own needs.

> *Although you can do little harm to the configuration of Flash, the documents that we are about to look at are in a location that also houses other files that define how the configurable portions of the whole Flash UI operate (and not just the Actions panel). Be careful not to alter anything else without knowing what the implications are!*

Have a look inside the \Configuration folder of your Flash installation. You should see a file called Configuration_ReadMe.htm. Open it up – this will tell you the location of the configuration files. For example, on my current machine (Windows 2000) the location is:

C:\Documents and Settings\<user name>\Application Data\Macromedia\Flash MX

Navigate to this folder and to the \Configuration\ActionsPanel directory within it. You should see the following three files: ActionsPanel.xml, AsCodeHints.xml and AsColorSyntax.xml. These files are XML documents that define the detailed way in which the Actions panel works:

You can edit these documents to change the way that the actions panel works. For example, have a look at `AsCodeHints.xml`:

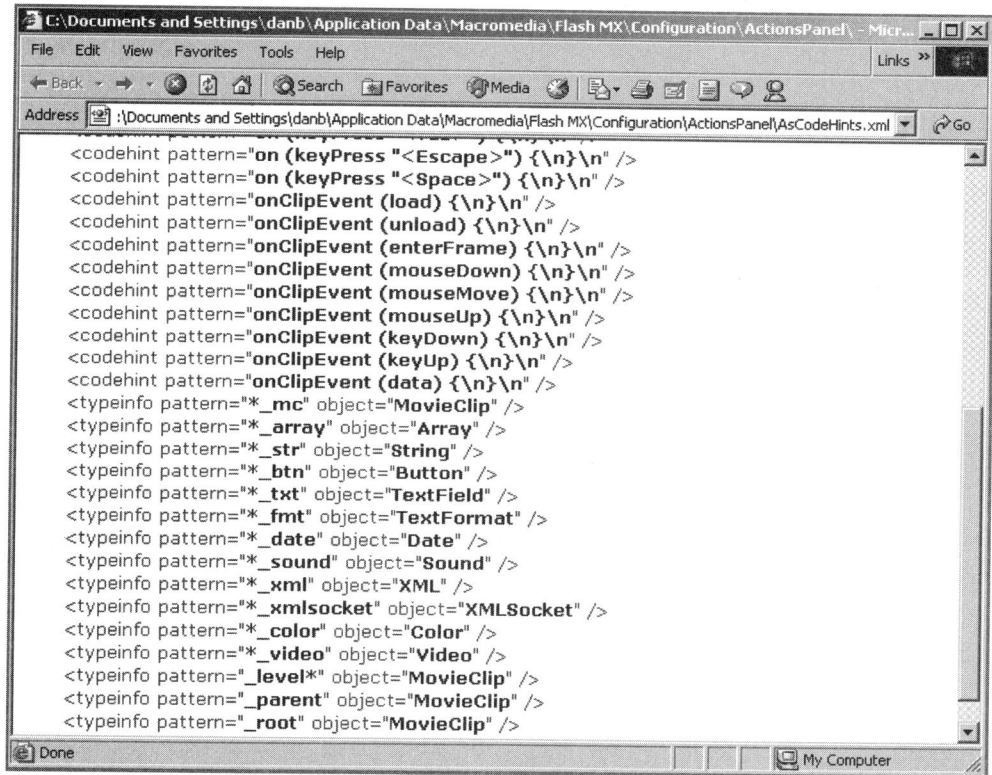

You can clearly see the lines that define the default naming conventions. If you wanted to change the convention for the movie clip name from `something_mc` to `mcSomething`, for example, you can do so by opening the file up in the text editor of your choice (Notepad, for example) and change the pattern `*_mc` to `mc*`.

What if you get it all wrong or corrupt the XML file? Easy, just delete the file. Flash MX searches for these files on start up, and if it doesn't find them, it will recreate the default files.

> *Note that we've ignored the* `ActionScriptErrors.xml` *file. In the Macromedia ActionScript reference there is an appendix that tabulates each brief error message and gives a fuller description. Replacing the original error messages means we lose this useful cross-reference.*

Summary

In this chapter we've highlighted the major enhancements that have been made to the scripting environment, focusing on the differences between the Normal and Expert scripting modes in Macromedia Flash MX compared to the previous version.

It seems that the folks at Macromedia have really listened to users' experiences, and drawn on this feedback to fix all the glaring UI issues. They have taken care of the common little niggles that break the workflow, made Expert mode much more approachable for mere mortals, and allowed a high level of control of the way we want the software to handle our scripting experience. With these enrichments, Flash MX gives us everything we need for a highly personalized, efficient and helpful scripting environment.

In the next chapter we'll take a look at the upgrades to some of the basic design building blocks for our content: **text enhancements**, **dynamic masking**, **movie clips**, and **buttons**.

Chapter 6

Building Blocks

Although the new user interface is the most noticeable change in Macromedia Flash MX, the really fundamental changes have occurred behind the scenes. One change is that links between advanced scripting and symbols have become a lot tighter: this is something we will look at closely in the coming chapters. Before we get ahead of ourselves though, we will concentrate here on the new features of Macromedia Flash MX that can be used to aid design in a tween-based site, or one using minimal scripting.

One of the major new areas of enhancement is **text**, and we will look at this in detail. **Masking** has also been updated, a feature which, although under-utilized, can actually create some stunning effects.

In Flash 5, the movie clip became the most important symbol because it was just so *versatile*. There were, however, a few things it couldn't do, and one of them was 'act like a button'. In Flash MX, the boundaries between the movie clip and button have been blurred – they are both now **objects**, which is something that we will look at in more depth in the next two chapters. As an early example of this strange new behavior, later in this chapter we'll make some cool new building blocks – weird new Flash MX entities that are neither movie clips nor buttons, but something in between. Spooky!

Text enhancements

Macromedia Flash MX now supports a number of enhancements to text. Although static text is essentially the same, dynamic and input text elements are now objects in the same way movie clips were in Flash 5. There are new actions that can be applied to text (or for the scripters out there, the **text object** has a full set of new methods to go with it). First though, we will start off at the easy end with new additions to text formatting and font substitution.

Font mapping

We've probably all had this same problem with fonts: you take some work-in-progress home to work on over the weekend. You open the FLA on your home machine, and the text that was supposed to look like this (if we ignore for the moment my total dislike of the overused Pipe character – '|')...

home | products | about | contact

...now looks like this instead:

This anomaly is due to your office machine having the *Humanist* font installed, and your home machine having a different set of fonts installed – a set that doesn't include Humanist. Flash will pick the next best match, and assumes that your operating system has fonts installed that know which font family they are in. Unfortunately, not all computers have their fonts correctly configured. It can go drastically wrong, and you end up with Humanist replaced with a specialized or decorative font, as shown above.

One way out of this mess is replacing all the Humanist text with Arial to tide you over, wasting a lot of time, and then when you get back to the office you will have to spend more time changing them all back to Humanist – this is far from ideal!

Macromedia have realized that FLAs should be more portable between machines. It now warns of impending font substitution, and allows you to have a say in it. As soon as you load an FLA with references to fonts that your machine doesn't have installed, you will see the following warning appear:

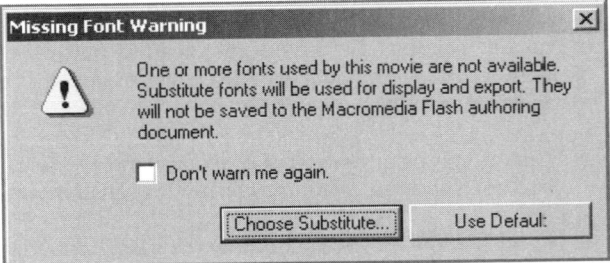

If you choose Use Default Flash will try to choose the best match as it did in previous versions of the software. If you know that Flash has a habit of getting it wrong on your machine because of the weird and wonderful fonts you have installed, you can now choose the substitute yourself with the rather appropriately titled Choose Substitute....

Note that if you have previously checked the Don't warn me again checkbox and want to get the option back, you can do so via Edit>Preferences... by selecting the Warnings tab and making sure Warn on missing fonts is checked.

If you hit Choose Substitute..., you will see the Font Mapping window below. In the example shown, Flash is telling me that the FLA is expecting *Helvetica* but it is not on my current machine. Initially, the System Default Font is the suggested replacement, which is Flash's best guess, but you can override this by selecting another font via the Substitute Font drop-down menu:

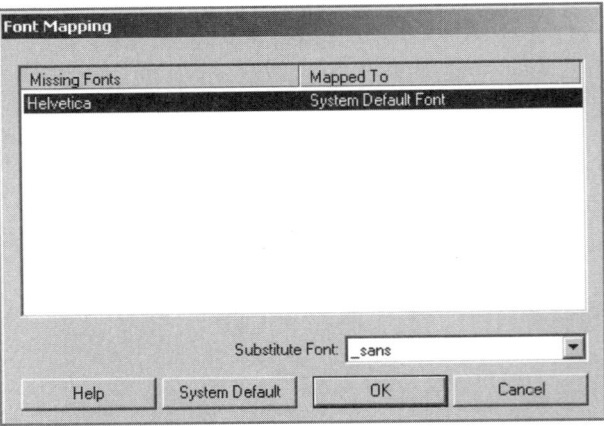

This gains me one big advantage – if I now run the FLA on the office machine on Monday morning, the correct fonts will be available, and *Flash will switch back to the originals automatically*. Specifying a substitution does not cause a permanent substitution in the actual FLA; as soon as Flash sees the fonts are now available, it will switch back to the originals.

Font formatting

There are also new text formatting options available. Using font formatting may be a little new to some Flash designers who have never got into print design, so we will look at the uses as well as the function of some of the more esoteric options. Here are some of the features of the format options window:

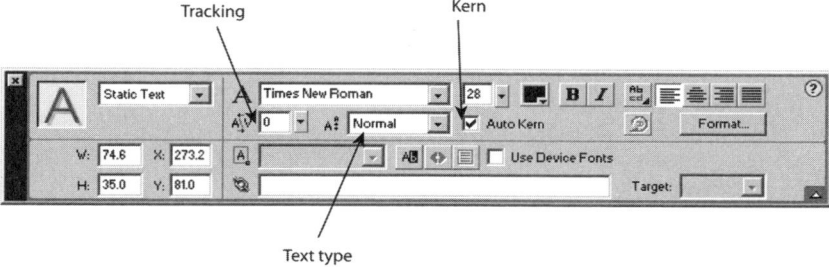

Kerning

Kerning refers to the amount of space between two letters. Although most letter pairs have very similar spacing, for a font to look right, certain letter pairs have a *custom* spacing. Particular letter pairs that need special attention include AW and AV. The kerning information is actually included as part of the font you are using, but if you do not want to use kerning, un-check the Auto Kern checkbox. Reasons for not wanting auto-kerning might include:

- You have increased the **tracking** (see next section) such that kerning is no longer an issue.

- You are using a decorative font (such as Dingbats) mixed with a text font.

- You are using a public domain font with poor kerning.

> *Bad kerning is actually a common fault with some public domain fonts. If you have this problem, you can either load up the font in Macromedia Fontographer and fix it yourself (not as difficult an option as you might think), or use tracking on individual letters (see below) to fix the problem.*

Assuming you're using a non-decorative font that will be read (rather than just looked at), you would normally have auto-kerning enabled. Without it, your text may appear too spaced out between certain letter pairs (such as certain combinations of L, A, V and W):

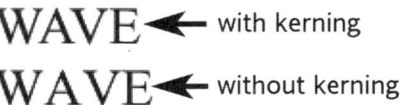

Some fonts have no kerning information (they are mono-spaced fonts, which means that each letter takes up the same space, and kerning is not needed for correct display of the font). In this case, Flash will gray out the auto-kern checkbox.

Tracking

Tracking is the amount of space between characters, and you can vary it by altering the AV slider. A value of zero maintains the default font value, *positive* values add space between characters, and *negative* values reduce it. By highlighting an individual letter, you can vary the tracking distance between it and the next character. This allows you to add manual kerning if you are not happy with the default kerning of your font. (Note that kerning relates to the distance between *two* characters, whereas tracking relates to the distance between *all* selected characters.)

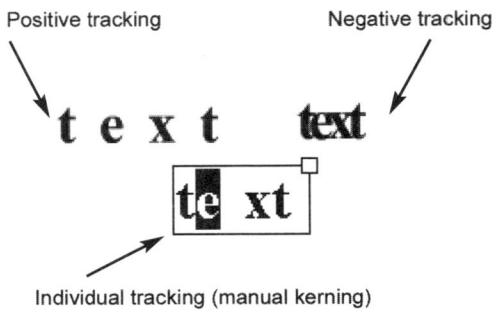

Positive tracking   Negative tracking

Individual tracking (manual kerning)

Setting a non-default tracking value is useful when you're creating logos (these rarely have standard tracking – this is to make them stand out from normal text). Good examples of positive tracking are found in fashion magazines (for instance, all perfume and designer labels seem to like large positive tracking values in logos). Beware of using large tracking values in large text sections that are intended for reading – large spacing can make text difficult to read. As the horizontal distance between letters increases, it reduces the readability because the vertical distance between lines (the **line spacing**, which we will look at in a moment) becomes less prominent, particularly for small fonts (where the line spacing may be smaller to start off with).

A good Flash-centric use of tracking is differentiating between the Up and Over states of a textual button. This certainly makes a refreshing change from boring bold!

about ⟵————— Default tracking (button up state)

a b o u t ⟵——— Positive tracking (button over and down state)

Text type

This is a fairly self-explanatory format option in which the text type can be normal, superscript or subscript.

More text format options

Hit the Format... button (it's among the font formatting options) and bring up the final set of new text formatting features via the Format Options window. These options are most useful where you have a block of text.

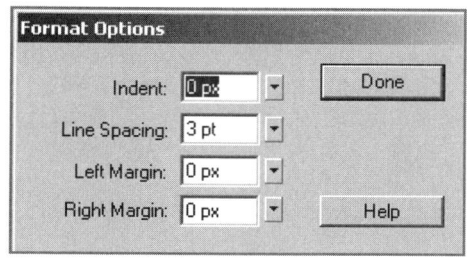

Indent controls the distance of the text from the first margin. If you want to apply this to one line only, highlight that line before setting the indent value. If you do not select a line first, the indent will be applied to all lines in the text field. Although this is fine, you would be better off setting the left margin to achieve an indent on *all* text in a field.

The **line spacing** is the distance between each line of text. The font freaks amongst us will usually refer to **leading**, which is *not* the same thing. For the record, leading refers to the font height *plus* the line spacing, as shown below:

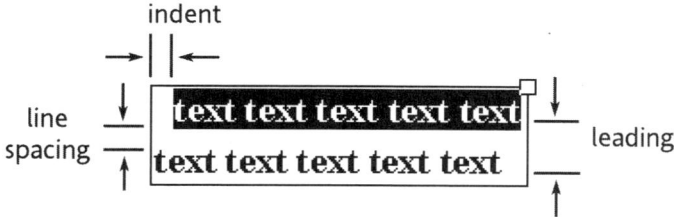

> *You may be confused by a line spacing of zero, which you may expect to cause lines of text to start touching because there is 'zero space' between them. In fact, a line spacing of zero does not mean 'zero space between lines' – it means that Flash is using the default spacing specified by the font. Hence, the real line spacing is (strictly speaking) the default line spacing plus the value shown in the* Format Options *window.*

There's another point worth noting here – using a line spacing of zero means you are using the line spacing recommended by the font creator and, because most fonts are actually designed for print, reading from a screen can be a little harder. So, don't be afraid to increase the line spacing slightly if the readability isn't what you might consider perfect.

Increasing the line spacing can make large blocks of text more readable by adding more white space and making each individual line stand out from each other, particularly if you are using small font sizes. Decreasing the line spacing may allow more text to be shown in a given area, but be careful that you don't also decrease readability – web audiences are very fickle and won't plough through such text for long!

Another tip is to increase the line spacing between the first and second line of a text section if the first line is a title. This is something that would have required two separate text fields to achieve in Flash 5.

Finally, the left and right margins, as you might expect, allow you to set margins to the left and right of the text area:

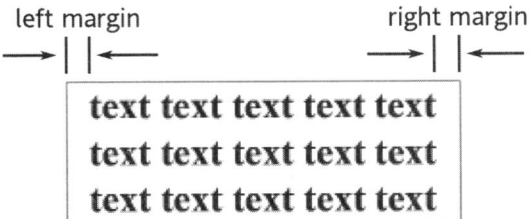

The addition of total control of the spacing of text within Flash will please many people, particularly web designers with a graphic design background. For those of you who doubt the value of careful use of type format in design, look no further than the Flash 5 carton graphics. They were designed by one *Neville Brody* (www.researchstudios.com, www.myfonts.com), a graphic designer who made his name by his smart use of fonts and layout in magazine design (such as *The Face,* a British music magazine, and the precursor of many ideas still in use in print today).

> *Remember that you can also emulate text that conforms to a path via the envelope modifier, so there are plenty of font-related design building blocks available in the new release!*

Text objects

There are changes in the way dynamic and input text elements work. They are now actually **objects** (we'll be looking at objects more closely in Chapter 7). For now, we will look at one simple consequence of this 'objectification of text' – the ability to reference dynamic or input text directly as if it were a movie clip. First we need to create a suitable text field to play with.

Accessing text dynamically

1.   Create two layers called actions and text:

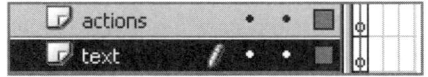

2. In the text layer, create a dynamic text field as shown below, entering the text 'spin me around' (or whatever you want) inside it. Set the field initially filled with <Instance Name> to myText, and change the Var field to text01:

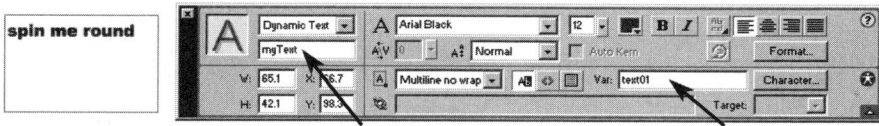

3. With frame 1 of layer actions selected (make sure you are in Expert mode), hit the 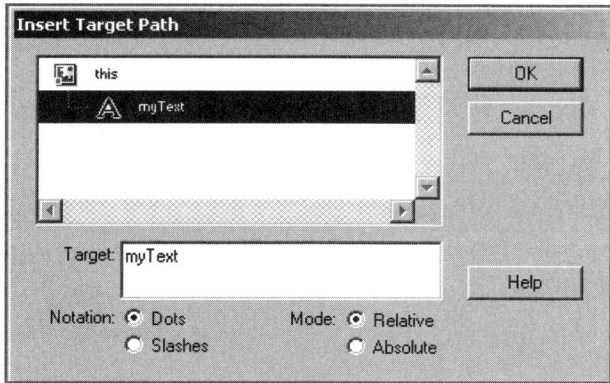 icon in the Actions panel to bring up the Insert Target Path window. Notice that this instance has a new icon against it: a letter 'A' symbol to show it is a **text instance**. Select instance myText and hit OK.

So far, you should have the following script in the Actions window:

myText

4. Add the following to complete the line:

myText._rotation += 45;

This will rotate the text by 45 degrees.

5. To enable Flash to perform this transformation, we need to not only give the font information, but also allow Flash to store the vector outlines of the text in the exported SWF. To do this, hit the Character... button in the Property inspector (after ensuring that the text field is still selected), and then select All Characters in the Character Options window:

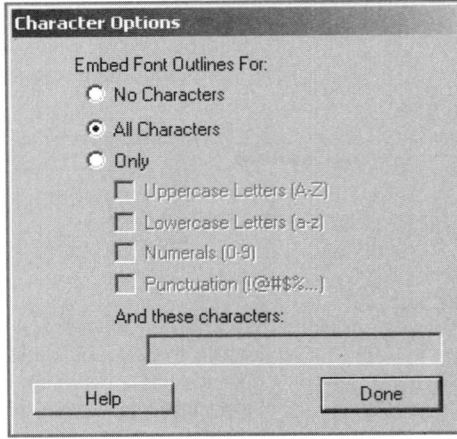

You can now test the FLA.

6. We can also change the text by accessing the variable text01. Add the following action to change the text:

```
text01 = "hello world";
```

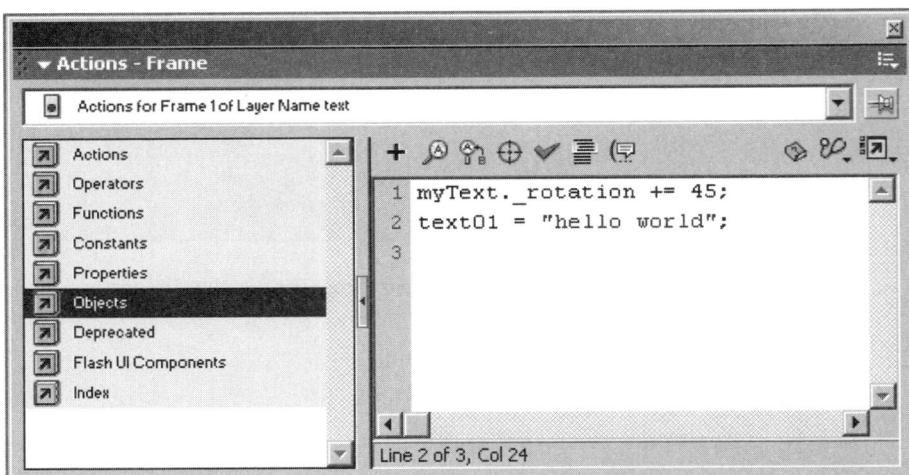

If you test the FLA now, the text will have changed to the new message.

You may have expected the text field variable to also act like a movie clip symbol, where you would have to write:

```
myText.text01 = "hello world!";
```

Where myText is the instance name and text01 is a variable that exists within myText. Obviously, this is not what we have done – we have simply referenced myText directly. The reason for this is simple – *a text field has no timeline*. The variable `text01` exists on the timeline you put the text on (in this case `_root`).

This may seem like a simple rule (it is actually how dynamic text worked in Flash 5, so is nothing new), but it does throw up another problem. If you place a text field in a button, not only does the text field not have a timeline, but neither does the button! This means that you will not be able to reference the text field instance at all (although you can reference its variable, which will be on the same timeline as the button), so as a rule, *always place a dynamic or input text field on `_root` or a movie clip timeline.*

Movie clip masks

Masking in Flash 5 only really worked if the mask was a static symbol. If you tried to use a movie clip as a mask, two things would happen:

1. Only frame 1 of the movie clip would be used as a mask, thus preventing the creation of animated masks.

2. If any actions were attached to the movie clip, they would be ignored and not executed. This made it difficult to create ActionScript controlled dynamic masks. There were several workarounds to the problem, but they tended to be rather obscure to say the least.

Flash MX loses these two constraints, and we'll present an example of each here.

Animated masking

1. Create a new movie clip and call it `mc.aniMask`. We'll create a simple shape tween within this movie clip. Within `mc.aniMask`, make frame 20 a keyframe, so that you now have keyframes at frames 1 and 20. In frame 1, draw a circle:

2. In frame 20, draw a square of similar size:

3. Add a shape tween between frames 1 and 20 to give you a simple 'circle becomes square' shape tween. We do this by selecting frame 1 and changing Tween to Shape in the Property inspector:

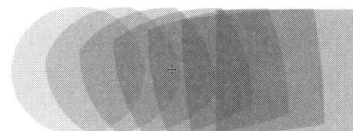

The tween will work best if you don't use strokes around the shapes.

4. Go back to the main timeline. Rename Layer 1 to masked, and add a new layer called mask:

5. In layer masked, add the graphic to be masked. I have added a simple rectangle with a gradient fill, but if you want to add a bitmap or something more esoteric or funky, we'll leave it to you. Just make sure that it contains no large areas of background color (white), otherwise the mask animation may not be as clear as it could be:

6. In layer mask, place an instance of mc.aniMask so that it overlaps the gradient (without going outside it):

7. Finally, turn layer mask into a mask layer by right-clicking on it and selecting Mask:

8. Now run the movie. You should see the 'circle to square' animation play at the same time as acting as a mask for the background graphic.

Note that you can see the change between Flash 5 and Flash MX by selecting File>Publish Settings>Flash and setting the Player Version dropdown menu to Flash 5. Notice that if you now test the movie, only the first frame of mc.aniMask plays.

> *Don't forget to change the publishing settings back to Flash MX before continuing, otherwise the next effect won't work!*

Dynamic masking

In this example, we'll create an effect called *moiré*. It can be created by superimposing two identical patterns that are shifted slightly from each other.

One of the simplest graphic patterns that will cause *moiré* is that of concentric circles, so this is what we'll create. If you find – like me – that these kind of circles make your eyes feel strange, you'll probably find it easier to download the finished file, moireFinal.fla, from this book's source code, available from http://www.friendsofed.com/code.html.

Otherwise, the following tips should help you to make a nice concentric pattern.

1. Select View>Grid>Edit Grid... and set the horizontal and vertical grid spacings to 10 pixels. With Snap to Grid and Show Grid set, draw an unfilled circle in the center of the stage.

2. You now need to draw a new circle concentric with the one you just drew. Imagine a 45 degree diagonal line going up from the center of the original circle. The point where it crosses the top left corner of the first free grid square that is not touching the circle is where you need to start dragging as you create the next circle. This is more clearly described visually:

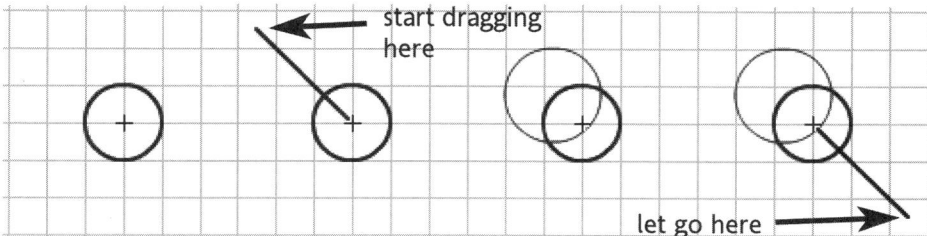

3. Next, drag the mouse so that it is the same distance away from the circle on the other side of the diagonal line, and release. Keep doing this, and you should build up a set of concentric circles:

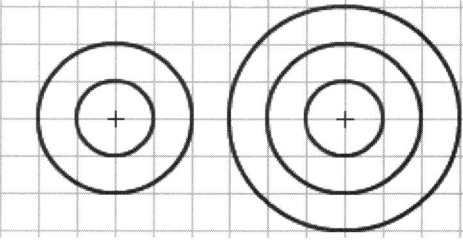

4. Eventually you should have more or less covered the stage with circles, as shown below:

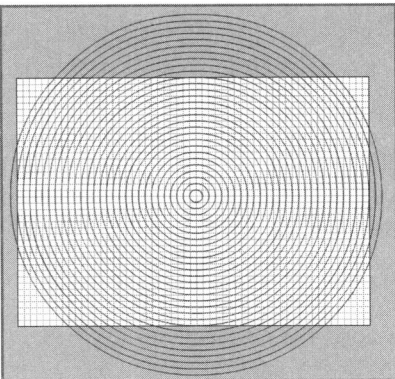

5. Using the fill tool, fill every alternate ring formed by the concentric circles:

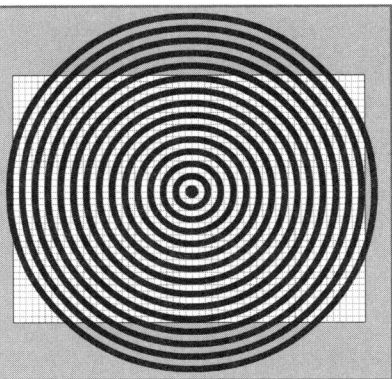

6. The circle strokes are now no longer needed (and will slow down the effect if you leave them in), so carefully delete them while retaining the filled areas.

> *Unfortunately, masking doesn't allow you to create masks with holes in them. This would be a real problem, if it wasn't for the next devious step...*

7. With the arrow tool, select a thin strip passing through the center of the ring mask. Delete it by hitting the delete key on your keyboard.

8. Now, hit CONTROL+A to select all the circles. Hit F8 to make the circles a single symbol, and make it a movie clip called mc.moire. Rename the layer that mc.moire is on to masked, and with mc.moire still selected, hit CONTROL+C to copy it.

9. Create a new layer called mask, and paste in place a copy of mc.moire. As before, make mask a mask layer.

10. Lock layer masked and unlock mask. Select the instance of mc.moire on this layer and, using the Actions Panel (again, in Expert mode), attach the following script to it:

```
onClipEvent (load) {
  startDrag(this, true);
}
```

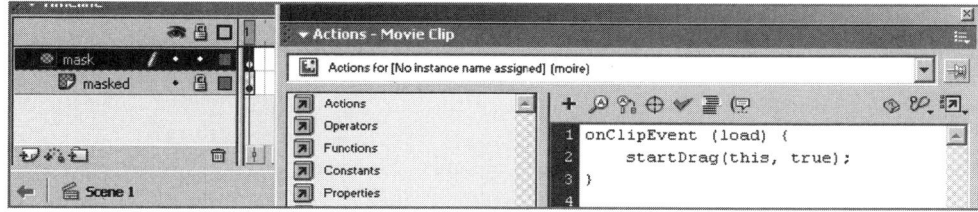

This script will cause the mask to become draggable, with the mouse at its center point. Test the movie to see the resulting patterns as you move the mouse:

Groovy!

> *Because masking is processor intensive, consider making the movie small or the aliasing quality low.*

You can also create similar patterns by masking straight lines with a slightly rotated version of themselves, plus all sorts of other combinations. You can also make both the mask and masked clips follow the mouse with different inertia constants (such that one is slower than the other) to make a strange animated mouse pointer. As with most masking effects, the more you think about masking, the more possibilities appear!

Button movie clips

Although there is only one explicit new symbol type – the *component* type, which replaces the smart clip – there are a number of new and useful variations that affect the movie clips you can build. Some of these are wildly different from anything that Flash 5 could do, and will most likely find wide use in Flash MX content. To save you time in working it out, here's the first one – a button movie clip.

The first question of course has to be 'But there's already a button symbol! Why make a movie clip into a button?' Making a button movie clip has a major advantage over the standard button symbol – *it has a timeline*. There are also several additional features that make it a 'super-button', which we'll see as we progress through this section.

Building a button movie clip

1. Start a new movie (File>New). Create a new symbol in the library and define the symbol behavior as a movie clip; call it `mc.button` (CONTROL+L to bring up the library panel if you haven't already got it visible). This will be our button movie clip.

2. Double-click on `mc.button` in the library to edit it. Rename Layer 1 to states, and add keyframes at frames 2 and 3.

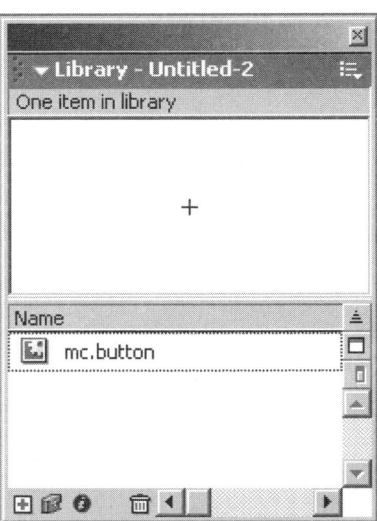

3. Create new layers called hit and actions. Your timeline at this point should look like this:

4. Select frame 1 of states. Using the Property inspector, give the frame a label name of _up, and press ENTER:

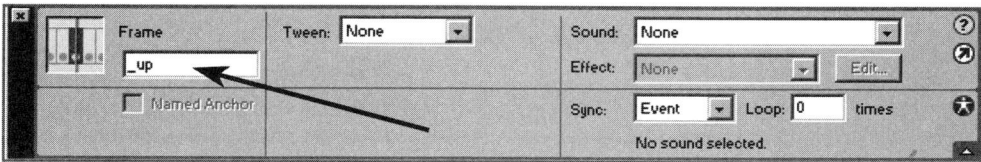

5. In the same way, select frames 2 and 3 and give them label names of _over and _down, respectively. These three keyframes are exactly the same as our standard button Up, Over, and Down states. The final state, Hit, defines the button hit area. We won't define this with a _hit keyframe: instead, we can use a much more flexible approach in which we can either:

   ■ *Not define the hit state at all*. In this case, the hit area will be assumed to be all non-zero pixels currently displayed by the movie clip. That's OK if your button is a solid shape (such as the circle below), but causes problems if your button is text or another shape with gaps. Although the same problem occurs with standard buttons, it's worth keeping in mind as you grapple with this new hybrid symbol type for the first time:

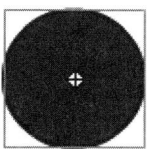
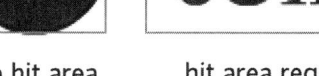

no hit area
needed

hit area required
because of the gaps
in the text

   ■ *Define a second movie clip as our hit area*. This is great because we can *change* the hit area by animating the second movie clip. This feature allows us to do all sorts of things that are just not possible with the standard button.

We'll create a button that consists of text, because it will allow us to show off one really cool feature of buttons that have a timeline.

6. In the _up keyframe, add a static text field with some text in it. Do the same in the _down and _over states, but make the text bold (remember, the easiest way to do this is probably to copy and Paste in Place, using CONTROL+SHIFT+V):

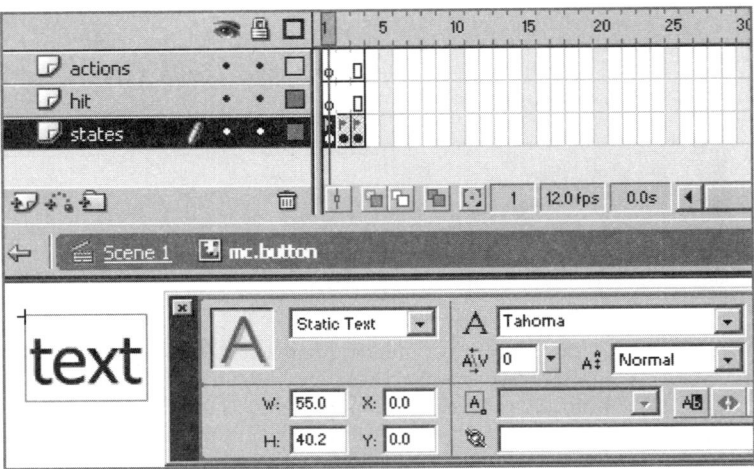

7. Now we need a hit state. In layer hit, add a filled rectangle that covers the text. This will form our button hit area:

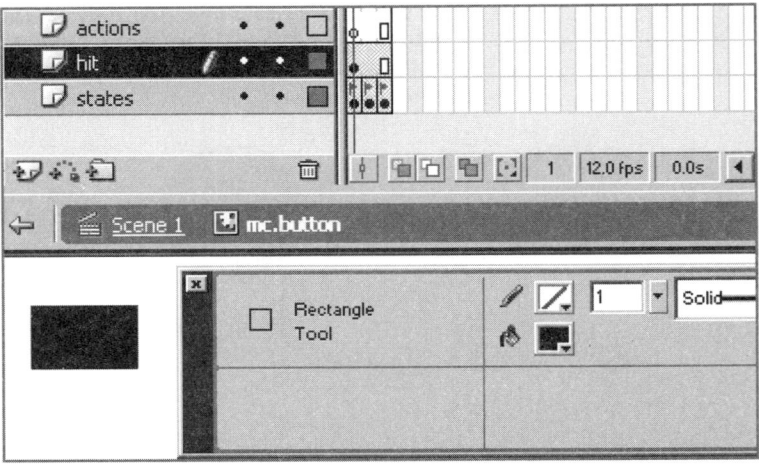

Notice that I haven't given my rectangle an outline. Although it doesn't matter if you add one, your hit area simply has to be an area of pixels, so using a fill only is sufficient.

8. Convert your rectangle into a movie clip by hitting F8. Call it `mc.hitRectangle`, and then double-click on it to edit in place. Rename the existing Layer 1 to hitArea, and add a new layer called actions:

> *Notice that the edit in place feature now has a* Back *button (it's the little blue arrow at the bottom left hand corner of the picture above). This allows you to go back a level in the timeline hierarchy. You can, of course, also click on* Scene 1, `mc.button` *or* `mc.hitRectangle` *to get you where you want to go directly. Although it may seem a small feature, the complexity of some Flash sites, with embedded clips being three or four deep, was crying out for this!*

9. With frame 1 of the actions layer selected, bring up the Actions panel (F2) in Expert mode and add the following line:

```
_parent.hitArea = this;
```

As soon as you enter `_parent.` you will see this menu appear:

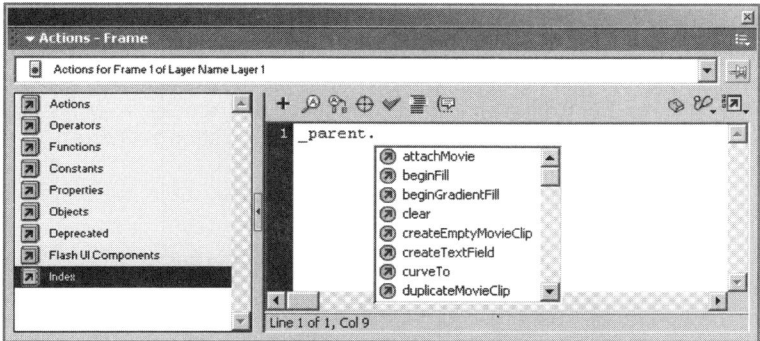

This is actually a useful new feature called **code hints**; Flash will list all the actions that you might want to add after `_parent.` In this case, since you know what you want to add, you can ignore it as you type.

10. Next, enter the second line as follows:

```
this._visible = false;
```

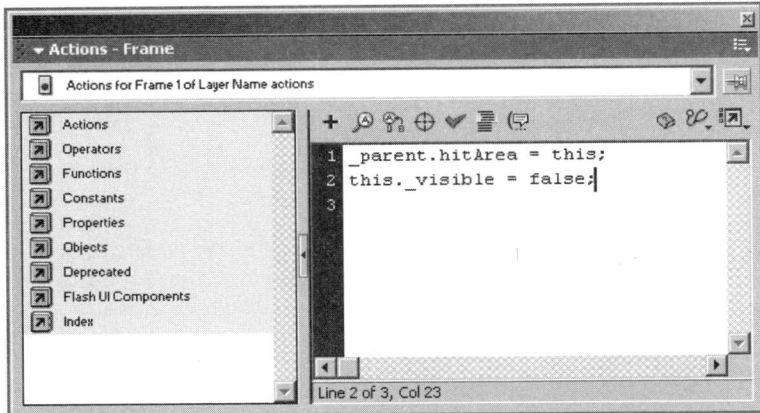

So what does this code do? Well, the first line tells Flash that this movie clip is the hit area for the movie clip it lives inside (that is, _parent). We don't want to see the hit area, and the second line makes it invisible by making the _visible movie clip property false (that is, make this not visible).

Although this may seem like a long-winded struggle just to define a hit area, here's the payback – the hit area movie clip you have just created can be used in *any* button movie clip. Simply drag it into a clip that you want to use as a button, resize and position to make the required hit area, and you are done.

11. Our button movie clip is almost complete; there is only one thing left to consider. Although we are creating a button movie clip, it differs from a 'conventional' button in that it has a timeline and timelines always play unless you tell them to stop. We therefore need a stop() action at frame 1 of the mc.button timeline.

12. Click on mc.button to get you back to the button movie clip:

13. Select frame 1 of the actions layer and attach the following action to it:

```
stop();
```

We have now created our button movie clip. We'll see an example of the usage of this framework shortly.

Advantages of the button movie clip

Now that we know how to build a button movie clip, let's take a look at some of its advantages over the standard type of button. It will work exactly like a normal button, but it has some useful features that make it a *super-button*, which we'll discuss in the next few sections.

Animated buttons

The timeline for a standard button looks like this:

You have only one keyframe for each state. If you want to add animations to the Up, Over, or Down states, you have to add a movie clip that contains your animation onto the button timeline. A button movie clip doesn't have this constraint. You can add keyframes in between the _up, _over, or _down keyframes if you want. For example, the button timeline shown below is completely acceptable:

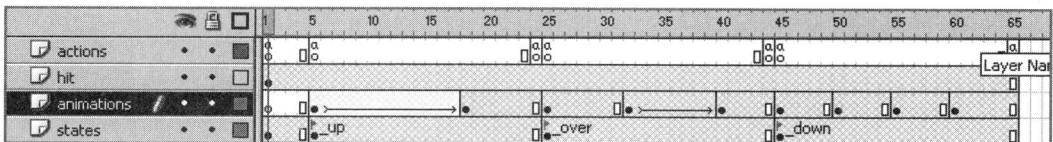

In this case, the animations layer contains animations as required by our button. The only feature of a button movie clip to watch out for is that when it sees a button event, the timeline will receive a gotoAndStop(); to _up, _over, or _down. To make the timeline play you have to:

- Add a play() on the same frame as each of the button labels. In our timeline above, the actions layer has play() actions on frames 5, 25 and 45.

- Code either a gotoAndPlay() or a stop() that prevents the timeline going on to the next button label. For example, the Up animation ends at frame 24. If we do nothing, the timeline will keep playing through the Over state. To stop this we can either add a gotoAndPlay("_up") at frame 24 (to make the button animation cycle), or add a stop() action (to make the animation play once and then stop).

Animated hit areas

Because the hit area of the button movie clip is itself a movie clip, it can be dynamically controlled, and made to change size or move. This may not be something you want to happen all the time, but it does have relevance in certain types of FLA, particularly games or advanced interface elements.

A real timeline

The fact that a button movie clip has a timeline means that you can make it go to a particular button state without that state actually occurring. For example, a normal button will not show its Down state unless you actually press the button. A button movie clip can be made to show its Down (or any other state) simply by performing a line of script from the main timeline. Here's an example:

```
myMovieClipButton.gotoAndPlay("_down");
```

This allows you to make the button appear as if it is being pressed without the user actually pressing the button.

It also means that you can add extra states that a real button doesn't have simply by adding additional keyframes (such as `disabled`) for a button that only becomes enabled once certain conditions are met. You might make the button appear grayed out for the `disabled` state in the same way Flash does for options that cannot be selected under the current circumstances, for example:

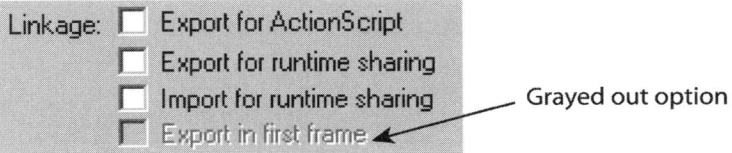
— Grayed out option

By adding **listeners** (a new kind of event that we will look at in Chapter 13), you can add totally new events that are based not only on what the user is doing to the button, but other stuff internal to the site logic as well. This allows you to add all sorts of intelligent features such as contextual help text.

Another attribute of timelines is that they can have variables associated with them. By making the text inside a button movie clip dynamic rather than static, and associating it with a variable `buttonTitle`, you can change the text displayed per instance, as follows:

```
myMovieClipButton.buttonTitle = "hello";
myMovieClipButton2.buttonTitle = "bye";
```

Because each button movie clip has its own timeline and therefore its own local variables, you can set each individual button instance with different variables and, ultimately, different attributes. This is something you could not do directly with standard buttons (as we saw earlier when we looked at text objects) because they don't have a timeline.

Now that we understand the movie clip button's advantages over the standard button, let's take a look at a simple application of the button movie clip we've just created.

Button movie clips as navigation elements

In the following example we will use movie clip buttons to create a simple navigation that harnesses the movie clip button's ability to include extra states. Have a look at `navigation.fla` in the download package.

The first thing to notice is that I have used four instances of the same movie clip button. Unlike a normal button though, the movie clip button has *its own timeline,* and this allows me to create variables inside it. I have created a variable `buttonLabel` in each instance, and this has been equated to "home", "about", "links" and "contact" to give me the standard 4-page navigation shown below:

When you click on one of the buttons, it becomes highlighted as any normal button would, but when you roll off the button after clicking, not only does it stay highlighted, but it stops being a button (you can no longer click on it):

This allows the user to know where they are in the navigation because the current page title remains highlighted. It also stops the user clicking on the same button and the navigation 'going to where you are already' (for example, if you were already at *links* and clicked on it again, the navigation would take you there again, which has the unfortunate result of resetting the page animations).

If you have a look at the stage of this FLA, you will see the four movie clip buttons that make up the navigation strip:

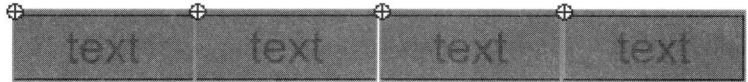

Inside a movie clip button

Each movie clip button timeline in the FLA looks like this:

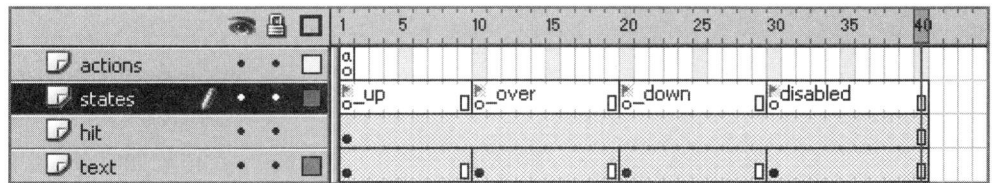

The actions layer contains a simple `stop()` at frame 1 to prevent the timeline running through all the button states.

The states layer contains a number of labels: _up, _over and _down are the standard button states, and the hit area is defined in layer hit. There is an additional label, disabled, which we will look at in a moment.

Finally, layer text contains the button text. It displays a variable buttonLabel on all keyframes.

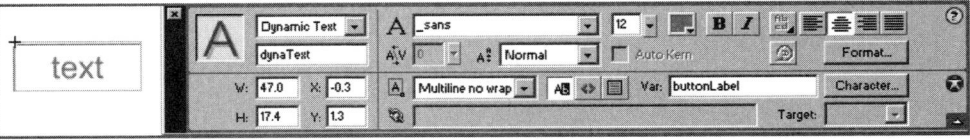

The main timeline

Back on the main stage, frame 1 of layer actions contains the script to get the whole thing working.

1. Function reset enables all the movie clip buttons with the enabled method (that is common to both buttons and movie clips), and returns them all to the _up button state:

```
function reset() {
  home.enabled = true;
  about.enabled = true;
  links.enabled = true;
  contact.enabled = true;
  home.gotoAndStop("_up");
  about.gotoAndStop("_up");
  links.gotoAndStop("_up");
  contact.gotoAndStop("_up");
}
```

Each button then has an onLoad event to initialize it, and an onRelease event to define the button release action.

2. The onLoad event sets the variable buttonLabel to the string we want the button to display:

```
// home button
home.onLoad = function() {
  this.buttonLabel = "home";
};
```

3. The `onRelease` function resets all buttons with the `reset()` function, and then makes the home button `goto` its own `release` label (`disabled`), which gives our movie clip buttons their 'latching' ability to stay highlighted. The second `goto` provides the navigation by making the main timeline go to a `home` label on the main timeline:

```
home.onRelease = function() {
  reset();
  this.gotoAndStop("disabled");
  _root.gotoAndStop("home")
  this.enabled = false;
};
```

4. The rest of the buttons do exactly the same thing as `home`, except they define different button `buttonLabels` and provide navigation to different labels on `_root`:

```
//
// about button
about.onLoad = function() {
  this.buttonLabel = "about";
};
about.onRelease = function() {
  reset();
  this.gotoAndStop("disabled");
  _root.gotoAndStop("about")
  this.enabled = false;
};
//
// links button
links.onLoad = function() {
  this.buttonLabel = "links";
};
links.onRelease = function() {
  reset();
  this.gotoAndStop("disabled");
  _root.gotoAndStop("links")
  this.enabled = false;
};
//
// contact button
contact.onLoad = function() {
  this.buttonLabel = "contact";
};
contact.onRelease = function() {
  reset();
  this.gotoAndStop("disabled");
  _root.gotoAndStop("contact")
  this.enabled = false;
};
```

> *Observant readers will have noticed that the only thing that changes between buttons is the button text and the place each button navigates to, and this string is something we already know; it's the instance name of each individual button:* home, about, links *and* contact. *By writing* onLoad *and* onRelease *event scripts that refer to the* _name *property, you can make a general set of scripts that work with any of the buttons. Unfortunately, the ability to implement this shortcut (using either the* apply() *method of the* Function *object or the Object Orientated and/or Component creation route via* prototype *and* registerClass()*) is not something we know about at this stage of the book, but you may want to revisit this FLA once you have finished Chapter 15.*

5. Finally, we stop the main timeline...

    ```
    stop();
    ```

Finished! A clean and simple navigation that has an uncluttered low bandwidth feel to it that would make even Jakob smile.

The switch action

Before summarizing this chapter, it's worth taking a moment to look at a really useful scripting tool for enhancing your overall scripting style. The switch action is a new logic action that is closely related to the *if... else* construction. In fact, like JavaScript, the switch action is converted to a corresponding *if... else* construction upon compilation, so the Flash player only thinks in terms of *if... else* anyway.

Have a look at the file case01.fla. This includes a simple input scheme:

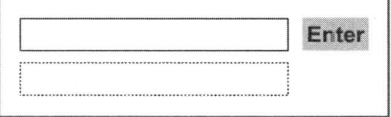

The top text field is an input field with variable inputText, the bottom text field is a dynamic text field set up to display variable outputText, and the button is called button01.

The script shown below will display "entered 1" if you enter 1, "entered 2" if you enter 2, and will display "entered something else" if you enter anything else (no points for imagination then!):

```
button01.onRelease = function() {
  switch (Number(inputText)) {
  case 1 :
    outputText = "entered 1";
    break;
  case 2 :
    outputText = "entered 2";
    break;
  default :
    outputText = "entered something else";
  }
};
```

Note our use of the switch action in the above code; this is equivalent to the following:

```
button01.onRelease = function() {
  inputText = Number(inputText);
  if (inputText==1) {
    outputText = "entered 1";
  } else if (inputText==2) {
    outputText = "entered 2";
  } else {
    outputText = "entered something else";
  }
};
```

Each case leg of the switch construct is the same as an *if... else if*, and the default is the same as the last else (that is, it runs if *all* the previous comparisons are *not true*).

> *Look on the switch as a short hand way of writing the longer if... else if else, and not as a totally new action. There is a good reason for doing so – if you want to optimize a section of code, you are much better off using the if... else if... else construction. Although it is longer in code, it is actually closer to the compiled code, and therefore gives you more flexibility to optimize critical loops in your ActionScript.*

The only real difference is that the switch is a little neater and therefore easier to read and understand.

The break action is not new (although its use within a switch is), and simply means 'don't look at subsequent *case* conditions if the current one is true". For example, if inputText was equal to 1, the case 2 and default test would be skipped. Not adding the first break action would be the same as doing this:

```
button01.onRelease = function() {
  inputText = Number(inputText);
  if (inputText==1) {
    outputText = "entered 1";
  }
if (inputText==2) {
    outputText = "entered 2";
  } else {
    outputText = "entered something else";
  }
};
```

Using switch with motion graphics

When animating motion graphics, you are always checking for boundary conditions. For example, if you are moving something around the screen via property-based animation, you will be constantly checking that the animated clip hasn't gone outside the screen area with code a little like this (see rangeCase01.fla):

```
ball.speed = 10;
ball.onEnterFrame = function() {
  if (ball._x<0) {
    ball.speed = 10;
  } else if (ball._x>400) {
    ball.speed = -10;
  }
  ball._x += ball.speed;
};
```

The following switch construct will do exactly the same job:

```
ball.speed = 10
ball.onEnterFrame = function() {
  switch (true) {
  case (ball._x<0) :
    ball.speed = 10;
    break;
  case (ball._x>400) :
    ball.speed = -10;
  }
  ball._x+=ball.speed
};
```

This will execute the first case that results in true (or neither if none of them do), and it is a good way of performing range checking.

You can also check for the `false` or *inverse* condition like this (see `rangeCase02.fla`):

```
ball.speed = 10
ball.onEnterFrame = function() {
  switch (false) {
  case (ball._x>0) :
    ball.speed = 10;
    break;
  case (ball._x<400) :
    ball.speed = -10;
  }
  ball._x+=ball.speed
};
```

This is cool, because `if` can only check for `true` (you *can* check for 'not true', with `!true`, in an `if` statememt, but not `false` directly), whereas you can in fact check for `false` directly in a `switch`, which can make your code much more readable.

Summary

As you can see from this quick trip through the Flash MX building blocks, there are numerous new ways to use Flash MX. As you have by now gathered, these new ways are never explicit – there are all sorts of little features that make life easier or allow you to take old Flash 5 techniques to new heights. The trouble is, you have to know they are there!

The button movie clip example that we looked at in this chapter shows the real power of Flash MX; Macromedia have opened up all the stuff that was previously inaccessible in Flash 5, allowing a large degree of flexibility in design techniques. This lets us dig deep into the interior of Flash and change the basic environment to suit our needs...and this in turn allows us to use the most powerful building block of all – imagination. In the next two chapters we'll be introducing some of the new Flash objects implemented in Flash MX. Remember, in Flash 5 we only had one graphic object – the movie clip. Now we have significantly more graphic objects, including buttons and text. The major benefits of using graphic objects are that they can be easily controlled by ActionScript, and that they have methods that allow us to perform standard actions on objects directly. We'll be studying the use of such objects through specifically targeted examples.

Chapter 7

Introducing Flash Objects:
Buttons and Text

Macromedia Flash MX has significantly expanded the number of graphic elements that function as **objects**. Flash 5 had only one graphical object: the movie clip. This meant that if you wanted to use ActionScript to animate something on screen, that something either had to *be* a movie clip, or be *inside* a movie clip. Macromedia Flash MX has many more graphic objects, including *buttons* and *text* (which includes a *text field* object as well as a *text format* object). This means that buttons and text don't have to be embedded in a movie clip before we can do anything cool with them. In fact, as we'll see in this chapter, both of these objects have not only cut the umbilical from the movie clip, they have evolved, and are now fully fledged entities in their own right, with a set of properties and events that allow them to fend for themselves on the stage.

What's the big deal with objects?

Put simply, *graphic objects can be easily controlled by ActionScript*. The more predefined graphic objects there are available within Flash, the greater the level of control that can be implemented.

Additionally, objects have *methods*. At their simplest level, methods provide standard actions that allow you to do stuff with objects directly. The movie clip object has loads of these already, such as a method to duplicate a clip (duplicateMovieClip), and so on. The new objects come with methods of their own, making the ActionScript features that allow you to control the graphic environment much more rich.

You also need to learn a new way of attaching events to some of the new Macromedia Flash MX objects. Not all of them have timelines, meaning that you cannot attach a script to all of them. This would cause problems with a Flash 5-centric view of scripting, but don't worry, the solution is not only easy, but also has hidden advantages...

> This chapter will look at some of the predefined Flash objects. Flash MX makes it much easier to create new objects and methods to extend these standard objects or create custom objects of your own. We'll come to the Flash MX movie clip object in Chapter 8, and in Chapter 15 we'll look at creating custom objects.
>
> Furthermore, Flash allows you to control interactive animations via a new event model using a new ActionScript feature called listeners - you can read more about this exciting new addition in Chapter 13.

The button object

The button has now become a fully-fledged object. This has the following advantages:

- You can now apply property-based animations directly to a button.

- You can dynamically change certain attributes of a button that were previously fixed in Flash 5, such as x, y, visible, and so on.

- The button object has new functionality that was not previously available, such as the ability to dynamically disable/enable a button.

Setting up a Flash MX button

Setting up a Flash MX button is identical to the old Flash 5 way of doing things:

You still have the same old Up, Over, Down, and Hit states to play with when you're creating the button graphics. You also have the same basic button events that you can attach to the button, so if you're used to Flash 5 buttons, you can simply carry on the tradition in Flash MX if you wish...but you'll be missing all sorts of cool new stuff!

There is one *big* difference to the way you attach events to buttons. In Flash 5, you attached event scripts directly to each button. For example, you may have created a home button that went to frame label home when released by attaching the following onRelease script to your button:

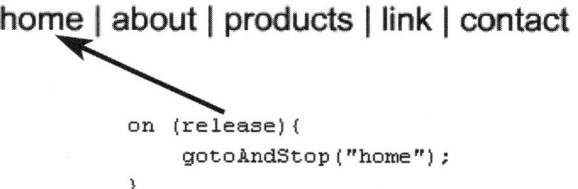

```
on (release){
    gotoAndStop("home");
}
```

You can still do this in Flash MX, but there's a better way for the ActionScripters who long for a more structured FLA. Attaching the event scripts to buttons is all very well, but it causes all sorts of readability issues when you want to see your scripts; because the scripts are attached to individual buttons, they may be all over the place within the FLA. Instead, you can attach the following script to the timeline that the button sits on (usually _root):

```
button01.onRelease = function() {
    gotoAndStop("home");
}
```

This is using the *method*-based version of the onRelease button event, and refers to the button by using its **instance name** (button01) rather than being attached directly to the physical instance.

We'll call this way of writing a button script a **remote button script**, to differentiate it from the old Flash 5 way of attaching a script directly to a button itself (which we will call an **attached button script**).

> *This feature of Macromedia Flash MX, whereby scripts don't have to be attached to symbols, is another of those fundamental changes that aren't immediately obvious. It allows you to separate out your code from the graphics that it controls. Unlike attached scripts, a remote script can be changed part way through a SWF simply by redefining it at a later frame. This allows you to have large centralized scripts that are easy to manage and modify, and is a style that many designers will doubtless want to adopt for their core site navigation scripts.*

It's a good idea to get used to the new way of attaching scripts to instances without actually attaching them directly to *the instance on the stage*, because there is at least one common new Flash MX object (*text* – which we'll look at later in this chapter) that *doesn't* allow you to use the old way.

There are some major advantages in using remote button scripts:

- All your scripts are in one place – usually in frame 1 of the scene, making it easy to see what is going on in terms of scripting. You will see a few good examples of this later in this chapter. Obviously, it also makes it easier to find scripts!

- The new Actions panel search/replace text-editing options work on a script attached to a single frame. By attaching all your button scripts to a single frame, you can edit them all globally using search/replace if you decide to change an instance name or whatever. You would have to edit each script separately if they were attached to the individual buttons.

- Because you're attaching events via ActionScript, rather than by manually attaching them to the graphic itself *you can dynamically change them all part way through your FLA*. For example, in a basic site page, by changing the scripts attached to each graphic object (buttons, text, clips), you could change the look and functionality of that page to effectively create a new page. You're no longer moving to a new web page in this scheme, but instead *repopulating or reprogramming the template* by changing all the object properties and event scripts. This is a new design basis that was not previously possible in Flash, and one that's used in other user interface (UI) design arenas. It has a number of cool features, the main one being that not only can you change the template to present new information, the user can too, customizing the UI in much the same way as your scripts automatically change the template – *the users can personalize their own pages!*

- You can remove an event by either setting the event to **null** or explicitly deleting the event. Either of the following will work:

```
button01.onRelease = null;
delete button01.onRelease;
```

This means that you can dynamically remove/add features to each graphic object (buttons, clips, and so on) in response to the user interaction. You can make small changes to the way the page works, allowing for more organic and subtle UIs that can change depending on what the user is doing.

An important point to realize is that Flash will allow you to add many movie clip events to a button instance without raising any errors during authoring, but these events may not necessarily work (they will fail silently). For example, the following script will obviously not work because onMouseMove is a movie clip event:

```
button01.onMouseMove = function() {
  //do some stuff...
};
```

It is important to refer to an ActionScript reference guide to make sure you know which events are button events and which are movie clip events, because Flash itself won't always tell you! Because both movie clip and button events will work on a movie clip button, this is yet another good reason to use movie clip buttons all the time in new Flash MX sites.

New button-related techniques

This section will present a few of the new techniques that can be applied to buttons. We haven't included them all, but just enough to allow you to see the general way to use buttons in Macromedia Flash MX.

Enabling and disabling a button

You can now enable/disable a button with the enabled property of the button object. For example, assuming we are still using our button instance button01:

```
//disable button
button01.enabled = false;

//enable button
button01.enabled = true;
```

Setting enabled to true will make the button work as normal. Setting it to false will mean that the button will not show the 'hand' mouse icon when you roll over its hit area, and neither will it animate to the Over or Down states. You do of course also have the option of disabling specific events by deleting the event, allowing you to have 'one shot' buttons for instance.

> *When changing a button's events or any attributes that inhibit its normal button operation, you may still see the button hand cursor. This doesn't mean that the change has not been recognized, but rather that Flash will not change the cursor to be consistent with your change until another event occurs (usually rollout or press).*

Where you have a menu-strip that stays the same wherever you are in the site, you may want to disable buttons that are no longer needed. For example, you may wish to disable the home button if you're already at the frame home:

home | about | products | link | contact

To do this you could use the following remote button script, in which we have assumed that the home button has instance name button01, and the others are button02, button03, and so on:

```
button01.onRelease = function() {
  gotoAndStop("home");
  // Disable 'home' button
  button01.enabled = false;
  // Enable all the other buttons
  button02.enabled = button03.enabled = button04.enabled =
  ➡button05.enabled = true;
};
```

To make it obvious that the button is disabled, you might also consider giving a disabled button a reduced alpha setting:

```
button01.onRelease = function(){
  gotoAndStop("home");
  // Disable 'home' button
  button01.enabled = false;
  button01._alpha = 50;
  // Enable all the other buttons
  button02.enabled = button03.enabled = button04.enabled =
  ➡button05.enabled = true;
  button02._alpha = button03._alpha = button04._alpha =
  ➡button05._alpha = 100;
};
```

Alternatively, if you were using attached scripts, you would use:

```
on (release){
  gotoAndStop("home");
  // Disable 'home' button
  button01.enabled = false;
  button01._alpha = 50;
  // Enable all the other buttons
  button02.enabled = button03.enabled = button04.enabled =
  ➡button05.enabled = true;
  button02._alpha = button03._alpha = button04._alpha =
  ➡button05._alpha = 100;
}
```

You should note from this that the following script would not work:

```
on (release){
  gotoAndStop("home");
  this.enabled = false;
}
```

Why? Well, with references to the last line: `this.enabled = false;`, in a button `this` refers to the timeline the button is on and not the button itself. This is not what we have in mind when we refer to `this` *button,* and `this` is not even a button, so the action will fail. You should use this format instead:

```
on (release){
  gotoAndStop("home");
  myButtonInstanceName.enabled = false;
}
```

Most scripters will be crying their eyes out over this; you have to know the instance name of the button whether you use remote or attached scripts, and that means you can't use general scripts that refer to `this`. Don't worry though, because there are a number of ways around this. Most of them involve using the button *movie clip* again – you can use one instead because it can implement the 'this' syntax. We will look at this in the next chapter.

Button over cursor

Flash MX allows you to decide on whether or not the user will see the hand cursor when they are over the button hit area. Sometimes you don't want the user to know they are over a button, especially when you're actually using a button as a 'mouse detection' device. To enable/disable the hand cursor, we can use the same kind of approach that we did for the `enabled` method:

```
// Sets hand cursor off for instance button01
button01.useHandCursor = false;
// Sets hand cursor back on
button01.useHandCursor = true;
```

Here, the button on the left has its hand cursor enabled, while the one on the right has it *disabled*:

Although the hand cursor is a standard browser action for web page links, many Flash buttons are not related to browser URL navigation, and for these buttons you may consider turning the hand cursor functionality off, relying instead on the button *over* and *down* states for user feedback. We will use this feature later in this chapter to create help text pop-ups.

Button visibility

The Flash 5 movie clip had a `_visible` property, and indeed the Flash MX button `_visible` property works in exactly the same way. Setting it to `true` results in normal button appearance and operation; setting it to `false` will make the button disappear and not function. There are several useful applications of an invisible button:

- If you wanted each button to be pressed only once, making it invisible on the first press

- If you wanted certain buttons to appear only when certain conditions have been met, such as other buttons being pressed

- If you wanted buttons to be pressed in a sequence, each button only appearing when it is next up in the sequence

These different possibilities are implemented in a similar way, so we'll use the last option as an example here.

Buttons in sequence

1. Create a button-sized circle. Select it, hit F8 and make it a button (you don't need to edit the button states).

2. In the main timeline, add three instances of the button in a line and call them `button01`, `button02`, and `button03`:

  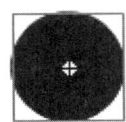 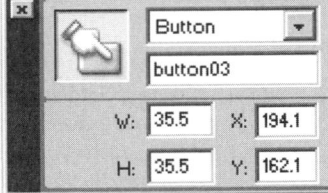

3. Rename the current layer buttons and add two new layers, text and actions:

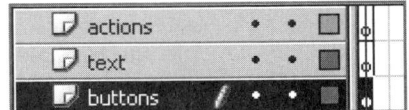

4. In layer text, add the static text '1', '2', and '3' over the three buttons. Make the text the same color as the background. The reason for this is that when the buttons disappear, the text will still be there, but white text on a white background looks like it's disappeared. This is an old trick from Flash 5 – it saves having to create three different text button symbols because the buttons are not the text but the *background*. Is that sneaky or what?

   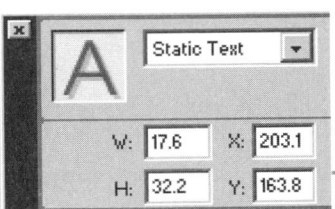

5. Finally, attach the following remote button script to the first frame in the actions layer:

```
// hide buttons 2 and 3...
button02._visible = button03._visible = false;
// button01...
button01.onRelease = function() {
  button01._visible = false;
  button02._visible = true;
};
// button02...
button02.onRelease = function() {
  button02._visible = false;
  button03._visible = true;
};
//button03...
button03.onRelease = function() {
  button03._visible = false;
};
```

When you test the FLA, the buttons will be presented following their numeric order.

ActionScript-based button animations

In Flash MX we can use ActionScript to create button animations. One possibility is an animation triggered by a simple button event. We'll take a look at this first and then move on to examine how we can extend the effect to work on a frame event as well as the simple object event.

Button event animation

1. Create a circular button shape. With the circle selected, hit F8 and make it a button symbol - call it bu.button. You'll have only the Up state defined so far, but that's OK; Flash will take the Over and Down states to be the same. It will also take the Hit state to be the same circle shape, which is fine because we have no pixel gaps (as we would do if the hit area was text).

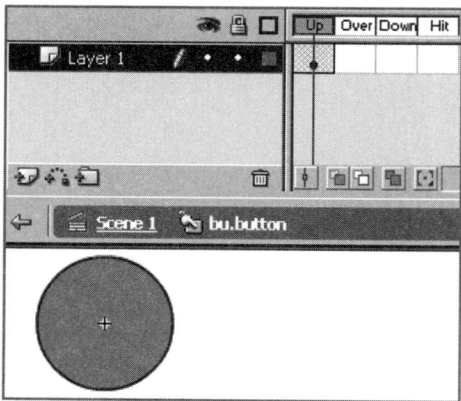

If you test this button you will see that no animation occurs if you roll onto or press the button, because all the states are the same. We can alter that by dynamically changing the properties that are made available to us now that the button is an object.

2. In Scene 1, the button will be on Layer 1. Rename this to graphics and add a new layer called actions. The button needs to be given an instance name before we can reference it via scripting. Using the Property inspector, give it the instance name myButton:

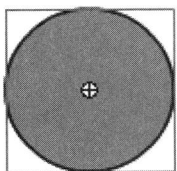 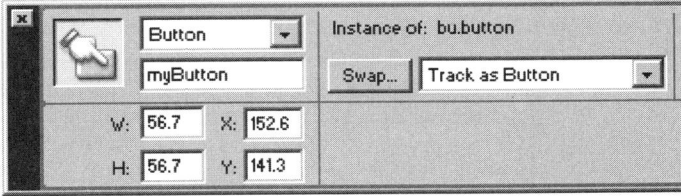

3. Attach the following script to frame 1 of actions:

```
function resize(me, value) {
  _root[me]._xscale = _root[me]._yscale=value;
}
myButton.onRollOver = function() {
  resize("myButton", 120);
};
myButton.onRollOut = function() {
  resize("myButton", 100);
};
myButton.onPress = function() {
  resize("myButton", 50);
};
myButton.onRelease = function() {
  resize("myButton", 100);
};
```

The function resize will resize symbol me by the percentage value (note that me can actually be a movie clip, button, or text field instance – we'll look at text fields in the second half of this chapter). The subsequent lines attach functions to the *over, out, press* and *release* events of our button. Each of these uses resize to animate the button per event. Also, more complex scripts could involve color or alpha changes (and so on) as well.

> *If you actually wanted the button to do something as well as look pretty as it animates, you would of course need to add some additional lines to the release event, such as:*
> ```
> myButton.onRelease = function() {
>   resize("myButton", 100);
>   gotoAndPlay("myLabel");
> };
> ```

The animations can only run when a button event has occurred. Most ActionScript site interfaces require all sorts of menus popping up or side-scrolling to their final position; this sort of animation requires the clip to fire off on an `enterFrame` event. The only way to do this with standard buttons is demonstrated in the next example.

Button and frame event animation

1. Using the same movie as in the last example, create a new empty movie clip and name it `mc.dummy`. Because we can't have a movie clip event equivalent to `enterFrame`, we must attach it to a movie clip – we'll use `mc.dummy` for this task.

2. Place `mc.dummy` in layer graphics, and put it somewhere off stage (I always place empty movie clips in the top left corner off stage so I know where they are):

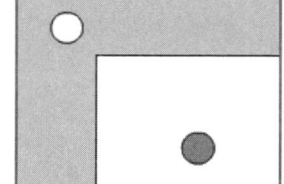

3. Attach the following script to it:

```
onClipEvent (enterFrame){
   _root.myButton._x = _root._xmouse;
}
```

This will make the button stay in line with the mouse's x position. You could also place the button inside the dummy movie clip (a way of implementing button animations that was used widely in Flash 5). That's fine, but it required a new movie clip for each dynamically animated button. Using a single movie clip allows you to control the property-based animation of all your buttons from one place. This adheres to the 'keep all your scripts together' paradigm that Flash MX seems to be leaning towards.

> *We are limited in the way scripting can interact with buttons to run methods or property-based animations because we cannot perform anonymous targeting of buttons; we cannot use* this *or* _parent *from a button.*

Flash 5-style buttons are really only useful for two purposes now:

- They allow a quick and easy way to create *simple* navigation buttons

- They maintain backwards compatibility with previous versions of Flash

The new button methods and properties are somewhat limited by the button symbol itself. We will see how to circumvent this issue when we come to look at movie clips.

By now you might be suspecting the truth about standard buttons: there are limited opportunities to apply method or property-based animation to them for more advanced scripters because the required events are not available for buttons. There are better ways to do this than the standard button object, and we will look at these in the next chapter when we come to study movie clips in depth.

The text object

Macromedia Flash 5 treated text as a simple graphic symbol. You could use it to display a literal string of characters (static text fields), the value of a variable (dynamic or input text), or assign a value entered into a text field to a variable (input text).

All this has changed in Flash MX. Although static text is still the dumb graphic it always was, input and dynamic text are now *objects*. This means that, like the button and movie clip objects, you can apply property-based animation to the text field using many of the old movie clip properties. More importantly, there are now text field-specific events available.

There are actually two objects used in controlling text:

1. You can alter the parameters of the basic text field itself via the text field object

2. You can set attributes of the text displayed in the text field via the text format object

We'll look at each of these in turn.

The text field object

The text field object can be a little confusing. In Flash 5, the only graphic object (the movie clip) lived in the library as well as on the stage. A text field, however, does **not** appear in the library. Because the text object doesn't have a timeline, you can't use attached scripts and must therefore use *remote* scripts.

Again, we will not look at all the text field properties, but instead just a sample of each type of property and event so that you'll know enough to use them all.

Using text field properties

1. Create an input text field, make it a single line, selectable, and give it a border. Give it an instance name of myText and make its input variable (Var) myVar, as shown below:

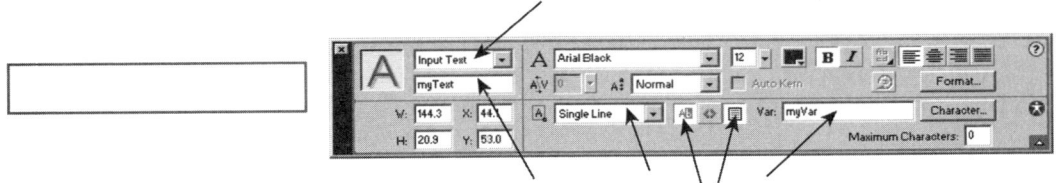

By placing the text on the stage, you have now created a text field *object* with instance name myText. We can now control this text field, changing the properties it inherits via the Property inspector settings you gave it (and by virtue of where on the stage you placed it for _x and _y).

2. Rename the layer you have the text on (Layer 1) to text, and add a new layer called actions.

   We will now make a few changes to the text field during run-time. The first things you can implement are the standard movie clip style animations by changing the _x, _y, _xscale, _yscale, and _visible properties. These property changes are similar to those we made to the button object earlier, but there's an important additional thing you need to know about text fields: you **must** embed the font outlines of all the text that the field is likely to contain, otherwise Flash will not animate it correctly.

   You embed outlines by hitting the Character... button on the Property inspector and selecting the outlines you want to embed in the Character Options window. Remember that embedding outlines can add a massive amount of bulk to the final SWF, so be careful. For example, if you knew that the field would only be used to accept numbers, you might select the options shown below (note that I have added the decimal point in the And these characters: field). If you know that the text field would never be animated in this way, it's better to use a system font (such as _sans, _serif, or _typewriter) and embed nothing (check the No Characters button):

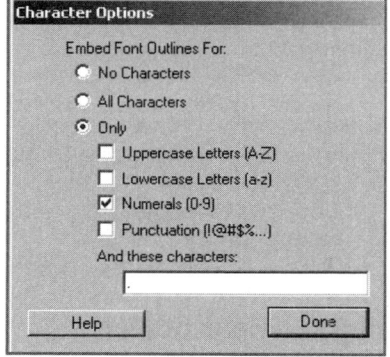

   For now though, select All Characters so we can move quickly through the example.

3. Adding the following code to the actions layer will move your text field, set it at an angle, and give it a 50% alpha:

```
myText._x = 200;
myText._y = 200;
myText._rotation = 45;
myText._alpha = 50;
```

   Not the most useful functionality perhaps, but an example of what's possible if you want your interface to have cool text input fields that whiz in and out of the screen.

   If you wanted to animate the text field in every frame (through an enterFrame event), you would have to attach the event to a movie clip and refer out to the text instance as we did to the button earlier.

The new **properties** that relate to the text field itself are perhaps even more useful...

Password style

If you wanted to use your input text field as a password entry field, you can make it hide the letters entered by removing the previous script and adding this in its place:

```
myText.password = true;
```

This code uses the text field object's built-in `password` property to render the user's input secret.

Background color

You can also change the background and border colors of the text field:

```
myText.background = true;
myText.backgroundColor = 0xFFFF00;
```

This will add a yellow background to your text field.

Text events

Color changes and password styles are all very well, but for ActionScript to be useful, it has to be able to respond to user interactions. The text field object allows you to respond to all the text field events, including:

- Text field selected (`onSetFocus`)

- Text field unselected (`onKillFocus`)

- Text field changes (`onChanged`)

- Text field scrolls down or across (`onScroller`)

> *The last event allows you to capture an ENTER, that is, to detect a 'new line' entered, although it can also mean that the current line has run over to a new line (for multiline text fields), so be careful of using it to signify the user telling you 'I've finished entering my text'.*

Using events to control the appearance of text fields allows you to enhance the usability of Flash forms. Let's add an `onChanged` script to the end of our password script:

```
myText.password = true;
myText.onChanged = function(){
  if(myVar =="pass"){
    trace ("correct password!");
  }
};
```

When you enter pass, you will see the trace window appear, signifying that Flash has seen the correct input, and the user doesn't have to press ENTER to do this; Flash knows what it's waiting to see, and responds to it as soon as it recognizes it. This is a hallmark of good interface design – if you know what the user will do next (hit ENTER), do it for them!

If this was the first frame in a restricted site area, you would do this:

```
myText.password = true;
myText.onChanged = function(){
  if(myVar =="pass"){
    play();
  }
}
stop();
```

The function is defined (but not executed), and then the timeline is stopped. As soon as the correct password is seen, the timeline is restarted, allowing Flash to continue through into the restricted (password protected) area.

Adding text events is perhaps the most useful feature that the text field object gives us: it allows us to respond to text inputs in an immediate and processor-efficient way. We are so used to using the mouse in point and click interfaces that we sometimes forget that there is only so much that can be done with a mouse-click. More complex functionality always requires your interface to be able to respond to text, and text field events will allow you to create advanced UI features that can interact with text:

- You can auto-complete or auto-correct a user's text input while they are inputting it

- You can quickly validate user inputs once they are complete

- You can make the display of text both context sensitive and dynamic when you tie it to events, allowing you to quickly build effective help systems for your UI

In the following example, we'll create a simple form using the new text field object events.

Creating a simple text field form

1. In a new movie, create the actions and text layers again. Create two new input fields in the text layer, giving the first an instance name of mytext and variable ageInput, and the second the instance name of mytext2 and variable name heightInput. Make both fields single line with a font of your choice, and give both of them borders:

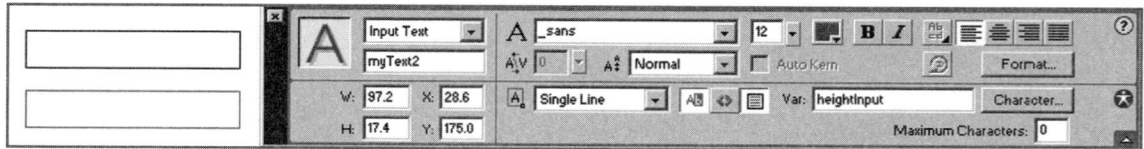

2. Label the two text fields with the respective static text age and height:

Our form will take two values; the user's age and height (you will be able to add more fields once you have completed this example). We will use text field event handling to control our fields, and then add some pop-up dynamic help text using a standard button.

First, we will add some scripting to highlight the active text field, and add some simple input validation.

3. Add the script we detail below to the actions layer. Note that we haven't added any comments in the script to keep it small, but the final file (which you will find as `textObject.fla`) has comments added. Additionally, a commented version of the finished script is included at the end of this example.

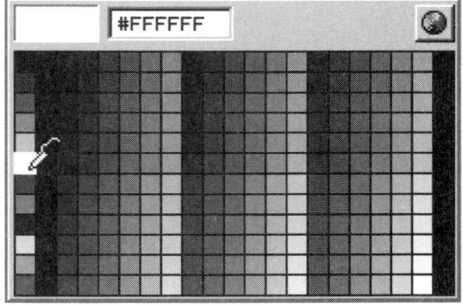

The first four lines define some color Hex values we'll be using. Any number preceded by `0x` means that it is in hexadecimal. The color values can be found on the color picker (which appears if you click on a color on the Tools panel):

```
white = 0xFFFFFF;
yellow = 0xFFFF00;
red = 0xFF0000;
green = 0x00FF00;
```

White will be our unselected color, and we also have yellow (selected), red (invalid input), and green (valid input). The next couple of lines give each text field a background color and define this color as white:

```
myText.background = myText2.background = true;
myText.backgroundColor = myText2.backgroundColor = white;
```

The `onSetFocus` event sets the background color of the field to yellow when the user selects the text field. This highlights the currently selected text field – a useful feature in large forms:

```
myText.onSetFocus = function() {
  myText.backgroundColor = yellow;
};
```

The next event is onKillFocus: this occurs when the user deselects the text field. This is an important event because it signifies that the user has finished their input. You would use this event to attach the individual *validation* script for each text field. For our age field, we'll specify that the user must be over 18. This is done via the if/else statements. If the age is over 18, then we color the text field green, else we color it red to signify an error:

```
myText.onKillFocus = function() {
  age = Number(ageInput);
  if (age>18) {
    myText.backgroundColor = green;
  } else {
    myText.backgroundColor = red;
  }
};
```

Note that we have had to convert our variable ageInput into a ***number***. *This is normal for text inputs where you want a number input. Since Macromedia Flash 5, Flash has always assumed any variable received from a text field is a* ***string*** *unless you explicitly convert it or apply an equation to it that results in a non-string result.*

You can add your own error detection for height, but for now, we'll only add the highlighting functionality (which works in exactly the same way as mytext):

```
myText2.onSetFocus = function() {
  myText2.backgroundColor = yellow;
};
myText2.onKillFocus = function() {
  myText2.backgroundColor = white;
};
```

4. Test the FLA. You will initially see two input fields. Click on the age input – it will become highlighted:

5. Enter 12, and then click on the height field. The height text entry field will now become highlighted, and the age field will go red, because the age has been incorrectly entered:

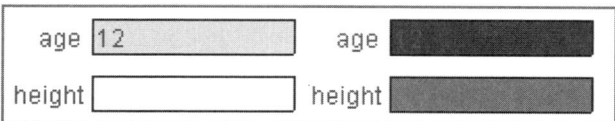

6. Go back to the age field; as soon as you do this, height will turn white (unselected) and age will become highlighted in yellow. This time enter 24 for the age and reselect height. The age field will this time become green when it's deselected, signifying a correctly entered value:

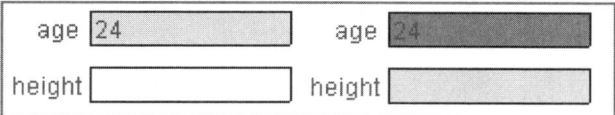

That might seem a little complicated when described on paper, but if you actually run the FLA, it feels totally intuitive; the coloring always gives appropriate feedback. So far, so good! We have added some neat new highlighting and error feedback features to our text. We still have problems though. For example, how does the user know what the correct age range is? Time for some additional help...

7. We'll now add a help box that appears over the static text if the user cares to roll over it. This will be based on an old friend – the Flash 5 invisible button. Create a new symbol from the library window, making it a button and calling it bu.invisible. Add a simple square as shown (no stroke is necessary) in the Hit state only, leaving the other states empty:

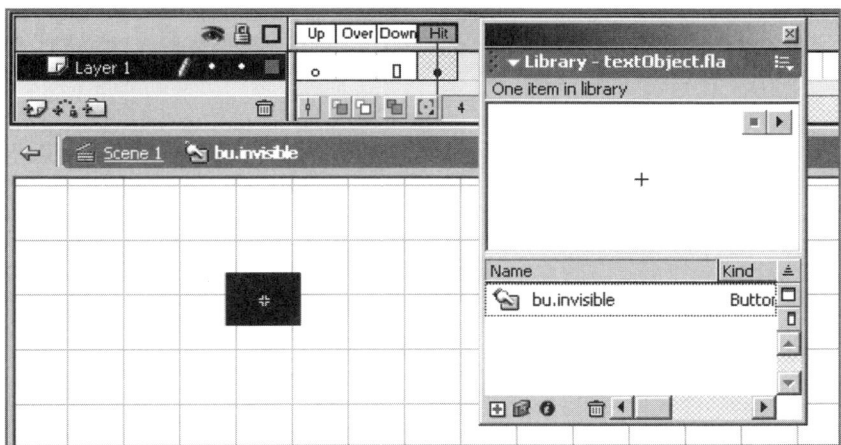

Although we have been maligning the old Flash 5 style button in this chapter, it does still have uses in Flash MX for basic functionality, and one of these is the simple invisible button.

8. In the main timeline, create a new layer called buttons:

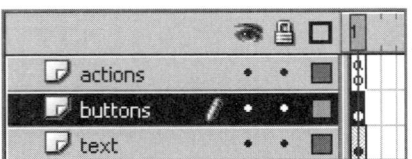

In the buttons layer, drag an instance of bu.invisible onto the stage and size it so that it fits neatly over the static 'age' text as shown. Give it an instance name ageRollOver:

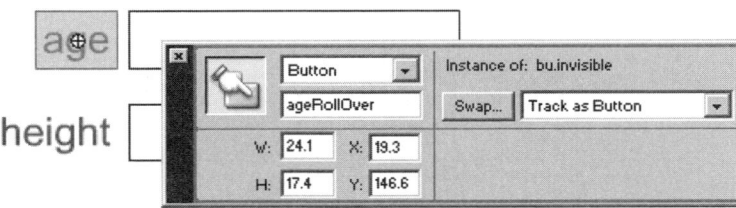

9. Next, we will add our help text field. Create a dynamic text field, placing it *off the main stage* (I have placed mine just above the top left corner of the stage). Give it an instance name of helpText and a variable helpMessage. Make sure Multiline is selected:

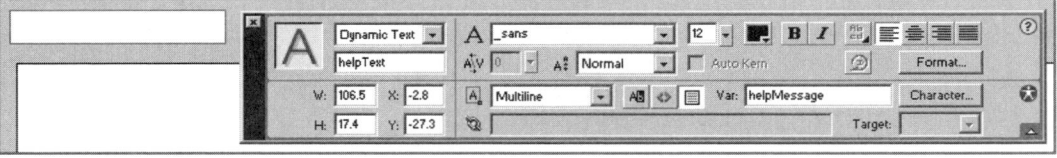

Next we will animate this text field, making it appear whenever the user rolls into the invisible button over the age static text.

10. OK, time for the scripts – we're going to add some new variables and a couple of functions to the beginning of our script. The additions are highlighted below:

```
white = 0xFFFFFF;
yellow = 0xFFFF00;
red = 0xFF0000;
green = 0x00FF00;
cream = 0xFFFFCC;
myText.background = myText2.background = true;
myText.backgroundColor = myText2.backgroundColor = white;
helpText.backgroundColor = cream;
helpText.background = true;
helpText.autoSize = true;
```

```
helpText._visible = false;
ageRollover.useHandCursor = false;
function showHelp(textString) {
  helpText._visible = true;
  helpText._x = _xmouse;
  helpText._y = _ymouse+20;
  helpMessage = textString;
}
function hideHelp() {
  helpText._visible = false;
}
```

Firstly, we have added a new color, cream. This will be the background color of our help text:

```
cream = 0xFFFFCC;
```

Next, we have defined some properties for our new text instance helpText. These make sure it has a background color of cream, and resize it to accommodate any text we place in it. Finally, we have made it invisible:

```
helpText.backgroundColor = cream;
helpText.background = true;
helpText.autoSize = true;
helpText._visible = false;
```

> *Some designers favor using* _alpha = 0 *to make things invisible. Using* _visible = false *is preferable in this case because, with the former method, the instance is drawn at zero visibility, whereas with the latter technique it is not even drawn – this is more processor-friendly.*

Our invisible button is going to be used as a rollover area, so we don't want the user to realize they are over a button when they 'mouseover' it. We have done this by disabling the hand cursor with this line:

```
ageRollOver.useHandCursor = false;
```

Finally, I have defined two new functions to show and hide the help text. The help text will pop up when the function showHelp is called, which looks like this:

```
function showHelp(textString) {
  helpText._visible = true;
  helpText._x = _xmouse;
  helpText._y = _ymouse+20;
  helpMessage = textString;
}
```

This makes `helpText` visible just below the mouse position, and equates the text field variable `helpMessage` to the argument `textString`.

We also need to hide the help text when it is no longer needed, and this is performed by the function `hideHelp`:

```
function hideHelp() {
  helpText._visible = false;
}
```

This simply hides `helpText`. Note that we don't care that it has been left onscreen because it is no longer being drawn.

11. That's our initialization over with. Now to add the actual function calls. This is simply a case of invoking a call to `showHelp` when `ageRollOver` is rolled over, and a corresponding call to `hideHelp` when we rollout again (note that the new code here is in bold text):

```
myText.onSetFocus = function() {
  myText.backgroundColor = yellow;
};
myText.onKillFocus = function() {
  age = Number(ageInput);
  if (age>18) {
    myText.backgroundColor = green;
  } else {
    myText.backgroundColor = red;
  }
};
myText2.onSetFocus = function() {
  myText2.backgroundColor = yellow;
};
myText2.onKillFocus = function() {
  myText2.backgroundColor = white;
};
ageRollOver.onRollOver = function() {
  showHelp("Enter age.  You must be over 18 to participate.");
};
ageRollOver.onRollOut = function() {
  hideHelp();
};
```

12. Test the FLA. You will see that our help text is now operational. Rollover the age text to see it:

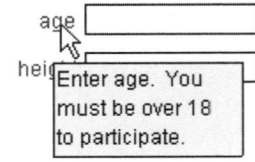

An important point to notice is that the *tab* order has now changed; the invisible button is now part of the tab order. The tab order is determined by:

- The order in which we placed the fields and text on stage

- The fact that Flash includes all text and all buttons on the stage in the tab order *unless you specify otherwise*

13. We can override the tab ordering via ActionScript by adding the following code in the initialization part of your code in the last example (immediately before the showHelp function definition):

```
ageRollOver.tabEnabled = false;
helpText.tabEnabled = false;
myText.tabIndex = 10;
myText2.tabIndex = 20;
```

We only want the *input* fields to be part of the tab order, so we have disabled the rollover button and help text from being part of the ordering by setting the tabIndex property to false. The two input fields have been given tab orders of 10 and 20 by setting the tabIndex property accordingly.

> *The tab index can be any integer from 0 upwards. You would be well advised to not choose the most logical ordering (0, 1, 2, 3, 4...) because it is the least practical when you (or rather, the client) come to change the form by specifying additional fields between the existing ones. By going up in tens, you are avoiding setting yourself up for misery later. Take it from a man who knows!*

That's it, we're finished!

Notice that the full script for this form is on Frame 1 of the actions layer. In Macromedia Flash 5, this script would be spread out all over the place, but in MX we have a single script, something that C++, JavaScript, and HTML coders will be much more at home with, and the rest of us will like because it makes for a more readable (and therefore easier to understand and update) FLA.

The help text on a typical operating system has a slight delay before it appears. Although this is easy to implement, it requires an understanding of more advanced ActionScript functionality that we will look at in a later chapter.

For the record, the full script as it appears in our final, fully commented version of this exercise, textObject.fla, is as follows:

```
// INITIALIZE
//
// Initialize colors...
white = 0xFFFFFF;
yellow = 0xFFFF00;
red = 0xFF0000;
green = 0x00FF00;
cream = 0xFFFFCC;
//
// Set properties for the two
// form text fields myText and myText2...
myText.background = myText2.background=true;
myText.backgroundColor = myText2.backgroundColor=white;
//
// Set properties for the help text helpText...
helpText.backgroundColor = cream;
helpText.background = true;
helpText.autoSize = true;
helpText._visible = false;
//
// Hide the handcursor for our invisible button ageRollOver
ageRollOver.useHandCursor = false;
//
// Set the TAB form ordering...
ageRollOver.tabEnabled = false;
helpText.tabEnabled = false;
myText.tabIndex = 10;
myText2.tabIndex = 20;
//
// Define functions...
function showHelp(textString) {
  // PURPOSE; to show helpText at the mouse position,
  // populating it with textString.
  helpText._visible = true;
  helpText._x = _xmouse;
  helpText._y = _ymouse+20;
  helpMessage = textString;
}
function hideHelp() {
  // PURPOSE; to hide helpText.
  helpText._visible = false;
}
// END INITIALIZE
//
//
// EVENT HANDLERS
//
```

```
// myText event handlers...
myText.onSetFocus = function() {
  // paint background in yellow when in focus
  myText.backgroundColor = yellow;
};
myText.onKillFocus = function() {
  // paint background color (red or green) when focus lost
  //   green - age in range (greater than 18)
  // red - age out of range (less than or equal to 18)
  age = Number(ageInput);
  if (age>18) {
    myText.backgroundColor = green;
  } else {
    myText.backgroundColor = red;
  }
};
// myText2 event handlers...
myText2.onSetFocus = function() {
  // paint background in yellow when in focus
  myText2.backgroundColor = yellow;
};
myText2.onKillFocus = function() {
  // Paint background in white when not in focus
  // (example only; in a full form would have a
  //data validation script here)
  myText2.backgroundColor = white;
};
// ageRollOver button event scripts...
ageRollOver.onRollOver = function() {
  // show help text on roll over
  showHelp("Enter age. You must be over 18 to participate.");
};
ageRollover.onRollOut = function() {
  // hide help text on roll out
  hideHelp();
};
// END EVENT HANDLERS
```

Although this may appear rather long-winded, remember that much of the functionality for *any* standard form is included in this script. The only other things you would normally use in a form are available as Flash MX **components**, which are hugely enhanced versions of Flash 5 smart clips. We'll look at components in Chapter 9, but for now all you need to know is that they are ready-built UI components that you can more or less drag and drop onto stage and then customize by setting a few properties.

Using the code above, plus component-based drop-down menus and/or radio button selections is really all you need to build complex user forms that would otherwise take forever in JavaScript. And don't forget that in Flash you have the beauty of a graphic authoring environment while you build up your UI elements, rather than the relative sterility of an HTML text editor.

Of course, there's no reason to stop at forms. Flash can create stand-alone *applications*. Flash 5 was good for point and click interfaces, which is cool for web pages, but not so cool for desktop applications that usually require substantial text entry. Macromedia Flash MX is now up to the task, so watch out Visual Basic!

The text format object

The text format object doesn't act on the text *field* itself, but instead affects the formatting of text that is displayed *within* the text field. Using the text format object is a little different to the text field object. There is one text field instance per text field graphic. The text format object is not related to any single text field, and you can apply it to *any* text field. It is best to visualize the text format object not as something that is attached to a physical graphic, but as a *setting* that can be applied to text in a given text field.

If that all seems a little ethereal and vague, you may already know of such an object from Flash 5: the *color object*. This was not a graphic object in its own right but an object that fixed the color of a movie clip. It was an object that acted as a *setting* to the movie clip's *color appearance*. In the same way, the text format object is a *setting* to a text field's *text appearance*.

If you did not create a color object for a movie clip, then that clip would still *have* color – the color you gave its various lines and fills when you created the movie clip. We can call these the movie clip **default colors**. As soon as you created a color object and linked it to a movie clip, you could then modify these defaults.

The text format object is much the same. All text fields have a default format (which is actually the old Flash 5 display style). So, even though you don't define a text format, the text fields within your FLA *still have formatting applied to their text* – it's just that you cannot alter it away from the defaults you specified (in the Property inspector) when you created the text field. Creating a text format object allows you to alter these defaults under the control of ActionScript at run-time.

This is how it works:

- As soon as you create a text format object, it is populated with a full set of formatting attributes, and these are all set to the default (standard) text field appearance.

- You can change any, all, or none of these attributes to create a new text format. At this point, the format has been created but not applied to anything.

- You can now apply the format to a text field. This field will reflect the new formatting attributes. Unlike the color object, the text format is not *linked* to the text field, and you can apply it to another text field if you so choose. You can also apply multiple text format objects to the same text field one after another, and the text field will show the formatting attributes of the most recent one.

As well as making text look pretty, text formatting has a number of advantages, not least that it allows your information to be more expressive. As a writer, I keep in mind that print is not all dull and unexpressive fixed text – I can add all sorts of voices to my text. I can **talk loudly** or quietly. I can highlight or *emphasize* what I am saying. If I wanted to graphically reflect a style, I could do so by using an APPROPRIATE FONT.

I can even do some **strange things** to get your attention**!**

The text format object has a number of formatting options, but its general operation is actually the same whichever formatting options you use.

In the previous example we added titles for each field via static text. We also added separate help text. However, a more efficient use of text fields is possible - we can have all our text, whether it is a title, help text, or users' input, all living side by side *in the same text field*. This is a feature that is not used often in UI design because it is so difficult to do properly, but with Flash MX it is actually very easy to do now. So let's do it!

The way to do this effectively is to give each different type of text a different **format**. We will use three different text formats to define three different uses of text:

- Help text will be green and centered

- Alert text will be red, bold, and centered

- Normal text will be the default Flash text

> *Notice that each of my text format styles has a certain voice as described above; the normal text has a neutral voice, the alert text is strident and brash, whereas the help text is eye-catching but not as in your face as the alert text.*

Using text format options

You can see our final FLA for this example in the download file `textFormat.fla`.

1. Create two layers (as before) called `text` and `actions`:

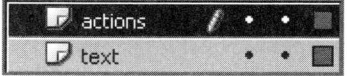

2. In the `text` layer add two input text fields, both single line. Name the top one `userField` and give it a variable `userInput`. Give the second one an instance name of `passField` and a variable `passInput`:

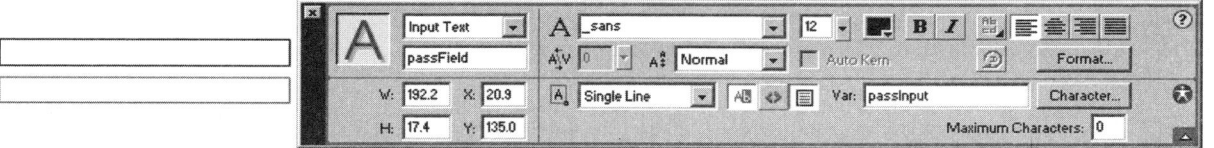

3.   In layer actions add the following script. We'll be slowly adding to this script, and the full script is at the end of the exercise in case you get lost:

```
// INITIALIZE
red = 0xFF0000;
green = 0x00FF00;
```

This simply defines the colors we will be using – same as the last exercise so far.

4.   Next, add the following to the end of the script:

```
infoText = new TextFormat();
infoText.color = green;
infoText.align = "center";
```

This defines our **information text** (or 'help' text) format. The first line defines our text object infoText. So far, it is populated with a full set of formatting options, all of which are at the standard default for Flash MX text. We want the text to be green and centered, and the next two lines do this.

5.   We need to do the same sort of thing for our **alert text**. To do this, we will define another text format object alertText. The code below will do this; it should again be appended to the bottom of the existing script:

```
alertText = new TextFormat();
alertText.color = red;
alertText.bold = true;
alertText.align = "center";
```

6.   Our final text format is the standard default, which we'll use as our **user text**. Because we don't want to change anything, we can simply create the text format object and leave it at that, safe in the knowledge it is populated with the defaults by default... I guess this is why they're called defaults!

```
normalText = new TextFormat();
```

Let's take a moment to have a quick look at the purpose of our file before we continue building it. In this example we're creating a standard login page, requiring a login and password of foed and flash, respectively.

UserField is the user name field and passField is the password field. When the screen first comes up, we want some help text in both fields to tell the user which field is which:

<Enter Username>
<Enter Password>

If the user clicks in the user field, we want the help text to disappear, the text field to clear and be ready to accept user inputs, and the text to be formatted as normal:

hello
<Enter Password>

Similarly, if the user clicks in the password field we want the text to be formatted as normal, but additionally we want it to be hidden as password text:

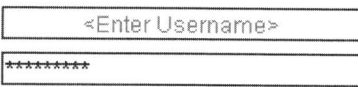

If the user enters an incorrect user name or password, we want the relevant window to show alert text flagging up the problem:

```
<Invalid user name. Re-enter>
<Invalid Pass>
```

Finally, if the user enters a correct user name (foed) and password (flash), then the login page should automatically detect this without the user having to do anything.

Although this design is simple in theory, and offers potentially huge benefits in terms of the clean interface and high level of usability, we should pause for a moment and consider how we would have had to do this in Flash 5. Yep, it's a nightmare in terms of the coding. The simplest ideas are sometimes the hardest to implement!

Not to worry, because using all that we have learned so far about the text field events, plus liberal use of our text formatting objects, we have everything we need to do it off the top of our heads (or at least you will when you've been playing with Flash MX for a few weeks).

Let's get back to building the file.

7. When we first initialize our text fields, we want our help text. Add this to the bottom of the script you've created so far:

    ```
    userInput = "<Enter Username>";
    PassInput = "<Enter Password>";
    userField.setTextFormat(infoText);
    passField.setTextFormat(infoText);
    ```

    We have set our input text variables to the text strings we want to appear as green help text, and the last two lines of this snippet set the formatting in each of the two text fields to info text.

8. We have now initialized all our text objects and set up all our initial conditions. We now need to animate the fields based on the text field events that capture what the user enters, read/write to the text fields accordingly, and set the text formatting to suit. Here is the full event scripting for the user field:

```
userField.onSetFocus = function() {
  userInput = "";
  userField.setTextFormat(normalText);
};
userField.onKillFocus = function() {
  if (userInput != "foed") {
    userInput = "<Invalid user name. Re-enter>";
    userField.setTextFormat(alertText);
  }
};
userField.onChanged = function() {
  if ((userInput == "foed") && (passInput == "flash")) {
    trace("enter main site");
  }
};
```

When the user first clicks on this field, their input has started. This is captured by our onSetFocus event. We can therefore clear the text field (by setting userInput to "") and then setting formatting to normal.

If the user leaves the text field, we can detect this by onKillFocus. This is when we do our input validation. We want to display our alert text, formatted in the alert style if the user name is *not* foed.

The final event, onChanged, checks to see if we have completed both the user name and password correctly on every change detected in the text field. As you will soon see, there is a similar event at work in the password field. This means that we are checking for any change in either field, and the user name and password can be entered in any order.

9. The password text field is a little more complicated. We need to make the change from hidden to viewable text so that the password is never actually displayed, and we also want to check for completion of the fields with the correct data:

```
passField.onSetFocus = function() {
  passInput = "";
  passField.setTextFormat(normalText);
  passField.password = true;
};
passField.onKillFocus = function() {
  if (passInput != "flash") {
    passInput = "<Invalid Pass>";
    passField.setTextFormat(alertText);
    passfield.password = false;
  }
```

```
  };
  passField.onChanged = function() {
    if ((userInput == "foed") && (passInput == "flash")) {
      trace("enter main site");
    }
  };
```

The onSetFocus and onKillFocus events are actually very similar to the user name field. The only difference is that when the user is inputting text (onSetFocus) we want to make the text field show password text. This feature is *not* a text format feature, but a property of the text field, and the line passField.password = true; puts us into password-enabled normal text. When we lose focus (onKillFocus) we know that any text in the field will be written by Flash, so we have to disable password text via passField.password = false;.

That's everything. Have a look at our version of this example (textFormat.fla) if you get stuck, and as promised, here's the full script:

```
// INITIALIZE
red = 0xFF0000;
green = 0x00FF00;
//
infoText = new TextFormat();
infoText.color = green;
infoText.align = "center";
alertText = new TextFormat();
alertText.color = red;
alertText.bold = true;
alertText.align = "center";
normalText = new TextFormat();
userInput = "<Enter Username>";
PassInput = "<Enter Password>";
userField.setTextFormat(infoText);
passField.setTextFormat(infoText);
// END INITIALIZE
//
// DEFINE EVENT HANDLERS
userField.onSetFocus = function() {
  userInput = "";
  userField.setTextFormat(normalText);
};
userField.onKillFocus = function() {
  if (userInput != "foed") {
    userInput = "<Invalid user name. Re-enter>";
    userField.setTextFormat(alertText);
  }
};
userField.onChanged = function() {
  if ((userInput == "foed") && (passInput == "flash")) {
    trace("enter main site");
```

```
      }
    };
    passField.onSetFocus = function() {
      passInput = "";
      passField.setTextFormat(normalText);
      passfield.password = true;
    };
    passField.onKillFocus = function() {
      if (passInput != "flash") {
        passInput = "<Invalid Pass>";
        passField.setTextFormat(alertText);
        passfield.password = false;
      }
    };
    passField.onChanged = function() {
      if ((userInput == "foed") && (passInput == "flash")) {
        trace("enter main site");
      }
    };
    // END DEFINE EVENT HANDLERS
```

There are a couple of additional points to consider when using text formatting:

- If you want to format some static text, consider using HTML formatting instead of the text format object. You can change text formatting partway through a document using this feature more easily than you can with the text format object. In general, you would use the text format object when you want to dynamically format text based on user interaction events, and HTML when you want to change the formatting at fixed points in a single chunk of text.

- The order of the actions *does* have an effect on which piece of text gets formatted. For example, reversing the order of the first use of text formatting in the example we just completed would result in info text formatting occurring in a different way:

```
    userField.setTextFormat(infoText);
    passField.setTextFormat(infoText);
    userInput = "<Enter Username>";
    passInput = "<Enter Password>";
```

Summary

We have had a close look at the new button and text objects included with Macromedia Flash MX. Between them, they give us a much richer set of basic input and output tools to use in our interface designs. We have a whole new palette of properties and events to use, and these allow us to create fairly complex interactions very easily.

The fun has just begun though, because there is an old friend that we haven't considered at all yet, and this mystery object is the most powerful graphic object by far – and always has been. No prizes for guessing what it is: the movie clip – and all will be revealed in the next chapter.

Chapter 8

MX Objects: Movie Clips and Sketches

In this chapter we'll continue our analysis of Macromedia Flash MX objects by studying the **movie clip** object. Moreover, we'll combine this topic with some (seemingly) diverse, but (ultimately) very important, discussions about the new drawing API in scripts. It will become evident along the way that the **scope** of a function is crucial to an understanding of advanced control of the Macromedia Flash MX movie clip object – and real-world examples are the best way to demonstrate this. First though, let's see what's new with movie clips.

Introducing the Macromedia Flash MX movie clip

The Flash MX movie clip is identical to the Flash 5 version if you look at it from the perspective of a designer or animator. The only apparent changes are:

- The replacement of smart clips with **Components** - we'll look at these in Chapter 9.

- The ability to use a movie clip as a button – we introduced the button movie clip in Chapter 6, and will delve deeper into this important new building block in this chapter.

- The ability to have a movie clip as a mask – version 5 allowed you to use a movie clip as a mask but it would only use the first frame and ignore any scripting attached to the clip. As we have seen in Chapter 6, MX allows you to use movie clip masks almost without limitations.

There are, however, additional features that the Macromedia Flash MX movie clip gives us. Unfortunately, these features are only accessible via ActionScript. We'll try our best to soften the impact of this to the design-based readers without dragging our feet for the ActionScript addicts.

We'll start from the bottom up. You may or may not already know that a *level* is really just a special case of the general movie clip object. We will therefore look at timelines first, and an all-pervading new level called **global**. Although this is not part of a movie clip symbol, it is closely related. The global level will radically affect the way you communicate between timelines and load levels. Then we'll look at additions to the movie clip itself, in particular:

- The movie clip has inherited many of the button events and properties. We'll delve deeper into the implications of this programmer-orientated feature of the Flash MX movie clip.

- It's now possible to draw lines, curves, and fills *at run-time*. This is an exciting new graphic-orientated feature of the MX movie clip, and designers will probably love it, even though it does require a little scripting.

The global level

The first fundamental change is that there is now a **global level**. Unlike most of the other new movie clip related features, the new global level seems at first to be a little...well, *boring*. It doesn't do anything obvious, and you can't even see it – but trust me, it's a cool feature, and we'll spend a while talking about it, because it can be *extremely* powerful. This is not to say that it's for advanced programmers only though; it actually makes ActionScripting *easier* for beginners as well because it totally obviates having to use paths.

> *Global variables are a bit like the remote scripts we looked at in the last chapter, in that they are one of many subtle features that totally change the way you will work in MX. They finally allow you to build truly structured code in Flash. Together, remote scripts and a global level make for a coder's paradise - Flash ActionScript can finally implement programming structures that other high-level languages use all the time.*
>
> *It also makes scripting more accessible to beginners because global variables are easier to understand than local variables (which, unlike globals, have all the complexity of scope and paths associated with them), but this will only occur if you take the time to get to know how to define them and how to differentiate globals from locals.*

In Flash 5, *global* had no real meaning. Although global could be taken to mean _root, this is not strictly valid in programming. For example, _root.myVariable will not exist at all on the _root.myClip timeline, so in Flash 5 even variables on the root timeline were only local to that timeline. The *true* global level is where all the Flash standard objects live. They can be accessed *anywhere* and exist on *all* timelines at the same time. A good example of this is the Math object.

If you were using the Math object to assign the variable x with the value of PI from a script on the main timeline, you would so like this:

```
x = Math.PI;
```

Similarly, if we were to do the same thing from movie clip myClip we would do this:

```
y = Math.PI;
```

If we now wanted to access x and y from the main timeline we would use this:

```
a = x;
b = myClip.y;
```

The next graphic summarizes the locations/scope of these elements:

Because x is local to where we are already (_root), we can simply call it x. The variable y however, doesn't exist on _root, and to access it, we have to use the path to the timeline it exists on: myClip.y or _root.myClip.y, (or even _level0.myClip.y if we want to be totally accurate).

Similarly, we have to use the path _root.x (or alternatively, we can also use _parent.x) to access x from myClip.

In both cases though, you don't need a path to specify the location of the Math object *because it exists everywhere* - this is what global really means in programming languages; *you never need to add a path to access a global object.* Although the global level *did* exist in Flash 5, and was where all the ActionScript actions and objects lived, you could not access it to put your own stuff there. Guess what - you can now!

To create a global variable x you simply do this:

```
_global.x = Math.PI;
```

You can now access this directly as x from *any* timeline, in the same way that you can access the Pi variable with Math.PI in your ActionScript, irrespective of which level, timeline, or function you are in when you access it.

There *is* a problem, though. What will happen to the two *local* variables also called x (_root.x and _root.myClip.x) when we define a global variable, also called x? Calling global and local variables the same thing is fatal. For example, if you say _global.x = anything; you should never have a variable called x defined anywhere else. Flash will allow you to do it, but take it from me, *you don't want to do it.* Don't create a variable x on the main timeline, on the timeline of movie clip anyClip, or even as a local variable in a function.

Doing any of these is fatal because you will end up with the same variable defined twice. This will result in one of the two variables being undefined, or getting yourself totally confused, and probably both. The best way to get round this issue is to make sure you use a consistent naming convention:

```
_global.globalx = anything;
```

Always name your global variables so that they are clearly differentiated from local variables, *even if you know there is no local variable of the same name.* For example, you could prefix all of your global variables with the letter g, so that you instantly know that gSpeed, gCreditRating, and gNewBalance are global variables, whereas staminaLevel and moneyLeft are both local. This way, you will never have a global and local variable that have the same name. You don't even want a chance of this happening because it can be a very difficult error to debug in a large FLA. Mixing global and local variable names is usually a recipe for disaster because it will cause a run-time error that the Actions panel's Check Syntax button will *not* show up during authoring, and it will also cause all sorts of vague and unhelpful errors in the debugger during run-time.

When to use globals

So, when would you use globals?

The answer to this question is: *Whenever you are creating a variable that you want every other timeline to be able to access.* If you are using load levels, global levels are also global across levels; if you want a variable to be available across levels it is probably a good candidate for a global variable (and avoids having to use one of those ugly long paths such as _level0.menubar.location = "home" if you wanted to access the local variable home in movie clip _level0.menubar from _level3).

Paths and scope can get a little hairy when you are talking about movie clips embedded even only a couple of levels deep.

The following script defines four variables and shows how you would access each from the three timelines _root, _root.myClip and _root.myClip.embedClip:

```
// globalx is global...
_global.globalx = something;

// x is local to the main timeline...
_root.x = anything;

// y is local to myClip, a movie clip on the main timeline...
_root.myClip.y = anything;

// z is local to embedClip, a movie inside myClip...
_root.myClip.embedClip.z = anything;
```

As you can see from the following diagram, the variable globalx is always easy to access because of its global scope, whereas accessing the local variables soon becomes a muddle of tricky relative and absolute path names:

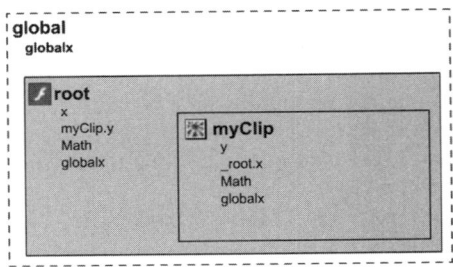

Of course, we have only really scratched the surface of globals. Variables are not the only thing that can live in the global level: functions and objects can as well. We'll turn to the use of global objects in Chapter 15 (the scripting divas will no doubt be licking their lips in anticipation!), but for the moment we will have a quick look at creating global **functions**.

Global functions

The trouble with functions is that you usually create them in the first few frames of the root, and then want to access them from all over the place. In Flash 5, you might have created a function double in frame 1 of _root like this:

```
function double (myVariable){
  return 2*myVariable;
}
```

To use it from a clip `anyClip` on root, you would have to do this:

```
x = _root.double(34);
```

You gain a couple of advantages by using the following function definition instead - one obvious, and one much more subtle:

```
_global.function gDouble(myVariable){
  return 2*myVariable;
}
```

The obvious advantage is of course that the function is now global. You can call it from anywhere in the FLA simply with:

```
x = gDouble(34);
```

This looks and feels more like other programming languages, as well as looking like what it actually does, rather than the more obscure `_root.double(34)`. You no longer have to worry about timelines and getting paths correct when calling global functions. Indeed, the lack of path names improves the readability, assuming your function names are meaningful.

The more subtle advantage is that, as well as calling the function from anywhere, you can also *define it from anywhere*. If you created a movie clip called `mc.functionLibrary` with the global function definition of our simple `double` routine defined within it, and dragged it into or imported it to *any* other FLA, the function `double` can be called *without having to know the path to* `mc.functionLibrary`, because `double` is defined as a global. You could, of course, have done the same thing in Flash 5 by using references to `_root`, but that is really only a workaround to get over the lack of globals – we have the real thing now! Using general global libraries allows you to create truly general, position-independent code, which is really a long way round to saying **modular** code, and modular programming.

> *Because it is not normally meaningful to have the same function defined in two places (the whole point of having functions is that you can define a function in one place and call it from several places in your code), you can get away with not having a global/local function naming scheme as we recommended with variables earlier. Programming purists may disagree, but I prefer not to use global names for functions (such as* `globalDouble` *or* `gDouble`*) because it affects the readability of the simpler and friendlier 'I do what my name suggests' function name* `double`*.*

Global depth

A good example of a global function would be one that assigns you a movie clip stacking level, or **depth**. As you may already know, methods such as `duplicateMovieClip` use depth. If you place two movie clips at the same depth, irrespective of which timeline they are on, the existing movie clip will be overwritten. Depth is a *global* or *FLA-wide* concept because it affects all timelines equally. We could therefore create a global function to manage depth.

The depth relates to the stacking order of symbols on stage. When an FLA is converted to a SWF, layer information is converted to stacking order (remember, layers do not exist in a SWF and are only there in the FLA as an authoring tool). The symbol that is furthest back has a stacking order of zero and the *n*th symbol forward has a stacking order of *n-1*. As any content in a depth position that already has something in it will be deleted, it's always a good idea to start with a level you know is not occupied, such as 100 or 1000, and increment the level you place a new clip in by 1 every time, so that each one is created in a unique level:

```
// define a global depth variable...
_global.globalDepth = 1000;
//
// define the global function...
_global.setDepth = function() {
  globalDepth++;
  return (globalDepth);
};
```

Every time you call setDepth(), you will get a new and unique depth, thus making sure that you never overwrite an existing movie clip when duplicating (or as we shall soon see, when *creating*) movie clips. You can see the current depth of a clip that was placed on stage via ActionScript by using the new Flash MX actions button.getDepth() or movieClip.getDepth().

> *Here I've created the* setDepth() *function because I could see that there was a* getDepth() *method for buttons and movie clips already in Flash MX ActionScript, but no corresponding* setDepth(). *I wanted the* setDepth() *functionality to be there in a particular FLA I was creating, and creating the function* _global.setDepth() *gives me the action I was looking for. Note that* setDepth *isn't actually a method of the button and movie clip objects though - it's a distinct, albeit global, function, rather than a method. But we could make it a method, as we shall see in Chapter 15.*

With global functions, we are already well on our way to being able to not only create things with ActionScript, but to also define ActionScript itself! Just pop all your global definitions in a template, alter the environment XML documents so that the Actions editor shows setDepth() in blue and knows what it is, and you would be hard-pressed to recognize that it wasn't a part of Macromedia ActionScript. See what I mean when I told you _global was powerful?

What global is, and what it isn't!

An important point to emphasize about _global before we complete this discussion is to differentiate between what *is* and *is not* global. Programmers will already have a good idea of what it is because it appears in so many other languages, but this may not extend to people who have learned scripting only in Flash and are used to a timeline-centric coding environment.

- The global level is the place where all predefined Flash actions and methods live.

- It is a level that sits *around* the timeline hierarchy, and is therefore accessible from any timeline without needing a path.

- It is *not* a timeline *above* _root. Many non-programmers may logically visualize a place called global as some sort of 'super system-timeline' sitting above the root. *You will only get confused if you apply the global level concept on the assumption that it is a timeline.*

- You cannot attach or duplicate movie clips into it in the same way you can with localized levels such as _root, _level45, or _root.invader. This of course is a consequence of the previous point – *a global is not a timeline.*

With the background and definition of the global level behind us, we can now move on to the more universally exciting things, starting with a look at the MX movie clip object.

The movie clip object

The movie clip has undergone a large number of enhancements in Flash MX. None of these will be apparent initially because they are all *additions* rather than changes to Flash 5 functionality. In fact, you could carry on using the movie clip as you did in Flash 5 with few or no problems – but you'd miss out on the fun!

The new stuff comes in two parts:

- The new events and properties

- The new methods

In Flash 5, you could change the appearance of a movie clip via property-based animations or by moving it along its own timeline so that it takes on the appearance of the graphics on that frame. The latter way of changing appearance can only select between frames that were created at authoring time. The former can *transform* the appearance of the movie clip *based on the original in the library* (for example by scaling and rotating it) but it cannot actually *change* it into something new. This is rather like the controls on a TV – you can alter the brightness and contrast properties of the screen, but you cannot change the content of the program you are viewing.

The **drawing API** (**A**pplication **P**rogramming **I**nterface) is a sexy new feature that allows you to create *totally new content* within your movie clips, on the fly, at run-time. You can tell Flash to create new content by creating new lines, fills and curves within a movie clip. This is like calling up the TV station during a showing of Star Wars and asking for Luke Skywalker to get killed and the Dark Side to prevail! You are effectively *changing the content*.

We have already covered using a movie clip as a mask in Chapter 6, but there is another new feature: creating totally *new* movie clips (ones that have not come from the library). Although we'll soon see that this is actually a crucial feature of the drawing API (you can create an empty movie clip and then create the graphics in it at run-time, as mentioned above), it also has applications *outside* the drawing API, and which we'll cover separately.

Finally, the movie clip now has a large number of added properties and events, plus a few new methods. These are not actually *new* – they were previously part of the button symbol. We have already seen how this can be used to create a button movie clip and we'll delve even deeper into this concept to show how you can actually *extend* the basic functionality of both the movie clip and button to create custom MX objects that are a mixture of the two. This makes the movie clip much more versatile and, as advanced users will realize, it makes the standard Flash 5 button pretty much redundant.

Creating new movie clips

Remember in the previous chapter where we had to create a dummy movie clip in the library to animate a button? We first created a dummy movie clip mc.dummy in the library, and dragged an instance of it to the top left corner just off the stage, before adding an onClipEvent event to it as follows:

```
onClipEvent (enterFrame) {
  _root.myButton._x = _root._xmouse;
}
```

We can do the same thing automatically with the new movie clip method createEmptyMovieClip. Rather like its related method duplicateMovieClip, you'll see that createEmptyMovieClip is easy to use once we show an example.

> Note that there's also another way to do this without using a movie clip at all, but we'll save this until later in the chapter.

Instead of creating mc.dummy, dragging it to the stage and adding the event to it, we can simply add the following code to the script we created in the last chapter when we demonstrated button event animation. The new code for this example, which will be located in frame 1 of layer actions layer as usual, is highlighted below:

```
function resize (me, value) {
  _root[me]._xscale = _root[me]._yscale=value;
}
myButton.onRollOver = function() {
  resize ("myButton", 120);
};
myButton.onRollOut = function() {
  resize ("myButton", 100);
};
myButton.onPress = function() {
  resize ("myButton", 50);
};
myButton.onRelease = function() {
  resize ("myButton", 100);
```

```
};
// Create the dummy clip...
_root.createEmptyMovieClip("dummy", 100);
//
// attach the enterFrame event to it;
dummy.onEnterFrame = function() {
  _root.myButton._x = _root._xmouse;
};
```

The first action attaches a new empty movie clip with instance name dummy to the main timeline. If you wanted to attach it inside an existing movie clip, you would have to specify the path:

pathToTimelineIWantToCreateDummyIn.createEmptyMovieClip("dummy", 100);

The two arguments in the brackets are the instance name of the new clip and the depth you want the clip to be in. I have chosen 100 for the depth, a level that is unlikely to be already occupied.

There are a couple of advantages to using this technique:

- You can create blank movie clips to use as ActionScript placeholders *at will* (as we have done in the above example). Remember, using remote scripts also has the advantage over attached scripts that you can change the actual script itself dynamically (we discussed this feature of remote scripts earlier in the book).

- You can now create content to fit into your movie clip as well as creating the clip itself. We will look at this when we consider the drawing API later in this chapter.

Using new movie clip events and properties

There are a few new events and properties that the movie clip has inherited from the button. It actually has ***all*** the events that the button object has and, of course, the movie clip can still use all the movie clip events as well as button events. A movie clip can therefore give you all the advantages of a button and movie clip at the same time.

This means that there is no real reason to use the button object at all in most circumstances. However, here are some reasons you *may* still want to use it:

- The button object has its Up, Over, Down, and Hit frames already defined. In a movie clip acting as a button, you have to add the button states as standard keyframes labeled _up, _over, and _down. We have already considered the button movie clip timeline earlier in this book when we looked at the Flash MX building blocks (Chapter 6), so you should already know how to set this up.

- The movie clip button sometimes requires that another movie clip be defined as the hit area. Again, we have already looked at this, and even designed a standard Hit movie clip that defines itself as a button movie clip's hit area. Remember, button movie clips are a little more complicated, so if you really just want a simple button or if you have imported Flash 5 buttons into Flash MX, use the standard button object.

- You are updating a Flash 5 site - there is usually little reason to convert the standard buttons to movie clip buttons, unless you are actually going to use some of the new functionality they offer.

It's all really down to ease of authoring; the standard button object is easier to use if you are just creating simple navigation. For anyone looking to take full advantage of Flash MX movie clips to build a 'gee-whiz' new web site UI, you can safely forget Flash 5 buttons. Additionally, as mentioned before, the new button object methods and properties are themselves somewhat physically limited by the Flash 5 button itself, because they don't have a timeline. This lack of a timeline can be a problem for a number of reasons:

- The standard Flash 5 button can only have three graphical states: Up, Down, and Over. As we shall soon see, the movie clip button can have as many as you want because you can add as many key frames as you want.

- The standard Flash 5 button cannot have movie clip events attached to it because it is not a real timeline. This stops you from making an `onEnterFrame` animation directly in a button.

- The standard button cannot hold local variables because it has no timeline to store them on. Advanced button behaviors will often involve one or two variables. On a standard Flash 5 button, these would have to exist on the timeline that the button is on, which means that you cannot have two button instances with the same set of local variables.

- The standard Flash 5 button cannot refer to itself. As far as a button is concerned, the term `this` means 'the timeline I am on', so a button cannot easily access its own properties via `this.property`. It has to be given its own instance name before it can control itself because anonymous targeting just will not work without a timeline.

We have already shown how to create a standard Flash 5 button using a button movie clip in Chapter 6. We'll now extend the concept here by creating a button movie clip with more functionality than the standard Flash 5 button. Additionally, we'll look at a particular feature regarding **scope** that you have to be aware of when using movie clip buttons.

The button movie clip revisited for advanced users

You'll find the completed version of this example included in this book's source code package as `movieClipButton.fla`.

1. First we'll create our standard button hit area movie clip. Create a new movie clip called `mc.hitArea`, giving it two layers, actions and graphics:

2. In the graphics layer, create a strokeless square fill as shown. Make the fill color black with 50% alpha via the Color Mixer:

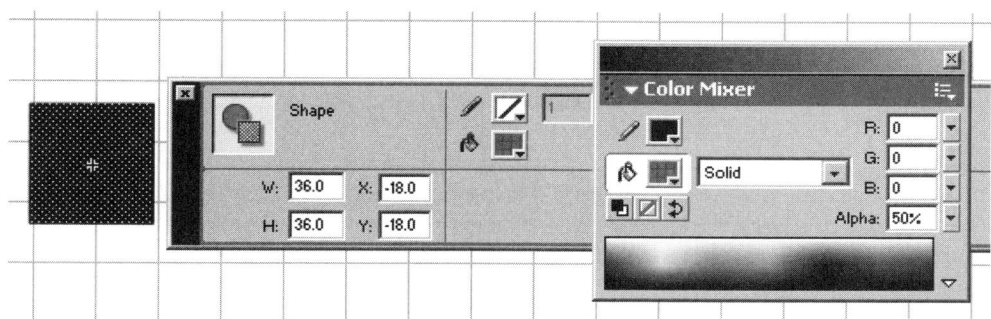

3. Next, add the following script to the actions layer:

```
_parent.hitArea = this;
this._visible = false;
```

Although the button hides itself with the action `this._visible = false` during run-time, the clip will still be visible in the authoring environment. To stop our hit area obscuring the movie clip button (which we will be creating next) during authoring, we gave it an alpha of 50% in step 2.

4. Create a new movie clip called `mc.movieButton` and give it three layers – actions, labels, and hitArea:

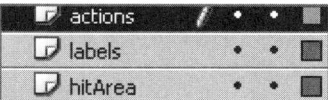

5. In frame 1 of layer actions add the following action:

```
stop();
```

This is to stop the movie clip button acting like a true movie clip and playing. Even though our movie clip will act like a button in terms of events, it will still *play* like a movie clip unless we stop it.

6. In the labels layer, add three button state labels, _up, _over, and _down at frames 10, 20, and 30 respectively, and make each of the layers 50 frames long:

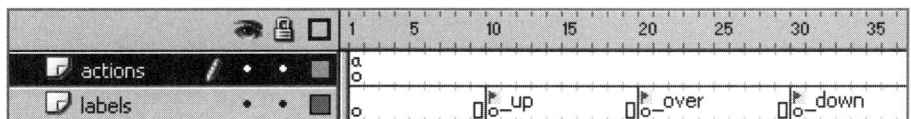

7. In the hitArea layer, add an instance of mc.hitArea in frame 1:

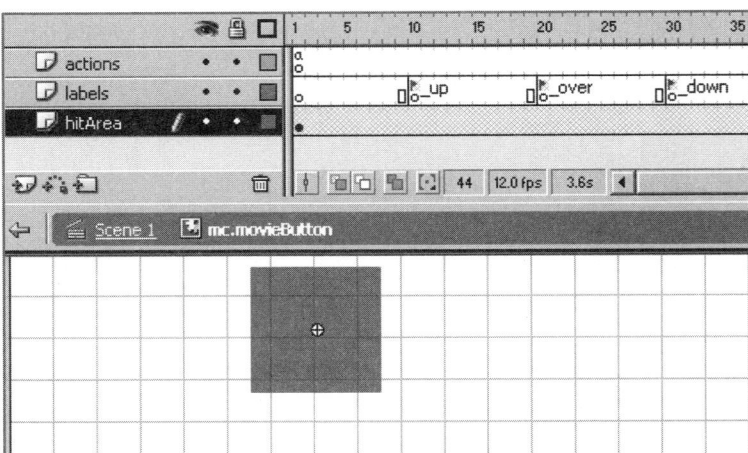

8. Add a new layer and call it graphics. Add some static text in this layer, making sure you *don't* use the _sans, _serif, or _typewriter fonts because they won't work when we try to animate them in a while (Flash doesn't save the font outlines for these system fonts, which makes them faster to draw and download, but prevents complex animation being applied to them because Flash doesn't have the point data). Now, scale and place the hit area over the text:

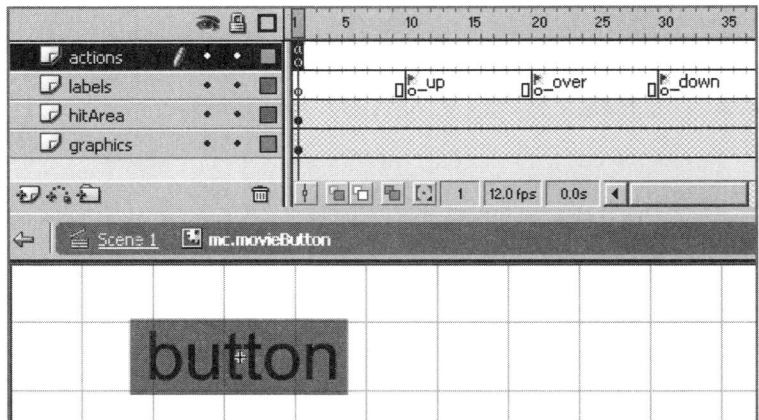

We now have our standard movie clip button. An advantage of this timeline is that not only can you add keyframes at frame 10, 20, and 30 of layer graphics to make the text appear different for each of the button states, you can do the same in layer hitArea and vary the hit area as well. This was sometimes a problem in Flash 5. If, for example, your Over state was bigger than the Up state, you might have had problems because it'd also be bigger than the hit area.

The following diagram shows this – the square is the hit area, and if the button becomes bigger than it in the Over state (right), the user may stray off the hit area because it is no longer implied by the button:

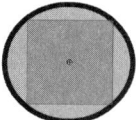

A small point perhaps, but it does make your site's tactile feedback less accurate and perhaps even a little shabby if your buttons are slightly out of touch with the hit areas. With Flash MX, however, you can now vary the hit area per button state.

9. Add keyframes at frames 10, 20, and 30 of layers hitArea and graphics. For each keyframe, give the button a different graphic, and size the hit area accordingly (the gray boxes around the text – we set the hitArea clips alpha to 50%, remember?):

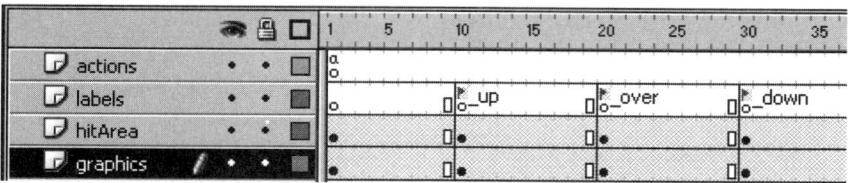

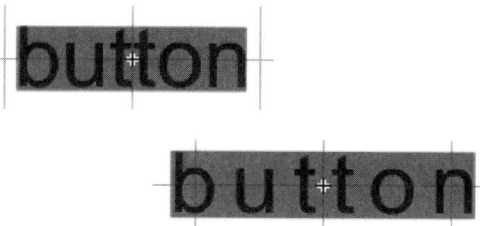

> You may have to temporarily lock the hitArea and graphics layers to make your selections, since the text and hitArea clip are right on top of each other.

Our Over state is larger than the Up state, but because we can resize the hit area, we retain a crisp, responsive active button area that is always directly related to the Over state (even if it does get bigger).

Notice also that we have not reduced the size of the hit area in the Down state. This is because the user might be on the edge of the hit area in the Over state, and making it smaller would mean you suddenly find yourself outside it in the Down state. To make sure you don't get odd effects from this, always make sure that your Down hit area is the same size as the *biggest* hit area in the other states (in our case this is our Over hit area).

10. But wait a moment... we have *another* button state lurking in our timeline. Frame 1 is not being used as a button state, but it is where the movie clip button stops when it first appears on stage. As soon as we click on it, the timeline will never go back to frame 1. Hmm, this sounds familiar...

    Browsers do the same sort of thing - they have *not visited* and *visited* colors for links. We can now do a lot better than that: we can have a different *appearance* to represent not visited and visited. In frame 1 of layers hitArea and graphics, add a new button graphic state for your unvisited button, and label frame 1 in layer labels as unclicked (implying 'unrolled-over' in this case):

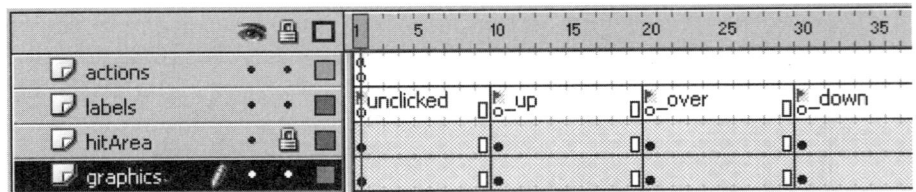

So now we have four states for our button instead of the normal three. However, we don't have to stop there!

11. Add a new label rollOut at frame 40 of layer labels. Add a keyframe at frame 40 of layers graphics and hitArea, and in this keyframe add the static text 'roll out' as shown below. At frame 50 add a keyframe to the actions layer and add the script:

    ```
    gotoAndStop("_up");
    ```

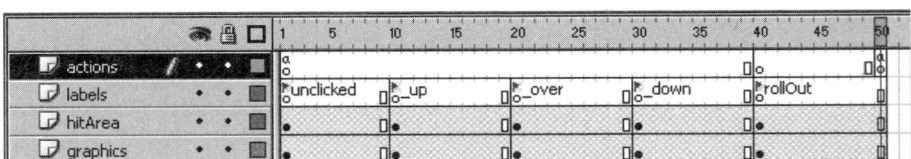

A button 'knows' about the Up, Over, and Down states, and we have a free unclicked state by being sneaky. However, we can't assume that the movie clip button will know what to do with our rollOut state - we have to use some scripting to define it.

> *The reason I haven't labeled the new* unclicked *and* rollOut *states as* _unclicked *and* _rollout *is for compatibility. There is a chance that Macromedia may actually add these states as standard in a later version of Flash, and they will probably be preceded with '_', so I have avoided doing the same.*

12. At the moment we have a stop() at frame 1 of layer actions. Change it to this:

```
onRollOut = function() {
  this.gotoAndPlay("rollOut");
}
stop();
```

Note that onRollOut will not appear in blue because the Actions editor is expecting syntax of the form movieClip.onRollOut. The way we have done it will not be seen as a valid method because there is no object. If the lack of blue recognition worries you, then you can add this if you want:

```
this.onRollOut = function() {
```

13. OK, here's a bonus sneaky (and really powerful) tip - this is not for a movie clip timeline only; you can attach an onEnterFrame (or any other event) to the main timeline as if it were a movie clip. Just create a new FLA and try attaching this to frame 1 of _root:

```
_root.onEnterFrame = function () {
  trace("hi");
};
```

Not only do you never need a dummy clip on which to attach your general event scripts, because you can use createEmptyMovieClip, but you don't even have to do even that - you could attach them directly to the root timeline!

This is of course another way of writing scripts in Flash MX. It's probably only for the diehard ActionScripters though, so we won't go any further down this avenue, other than to make you aware of it (I use this technique all the time, and so might you if you realize the implications of how useful it can be...).

14. If you drag an instance of this movie clip button onto the stage, you will see it show off its two new states. You can actually create a button with all manner of custom

graphic states using the standard button events to drive new states, in the same way we have done here with `onRollOut`.

15. We now have our movie clip button on the stage, and you will have seen the extra states. You can attach the normal button scripts to it as well as movie clip scripts, like:

```
on (rollOver){
  this.gotoAndPlay("myLabel");
  gotoAndPlay("myParentsLabel");
}
onClipEvent(enterFrame){
  _x = _root._xmouse;
}
```

16. There is one very important thing to note here; the scope is different for button and movie clip events. Because a standard Flash 5 button had no timeline, if you did this...

```
on (rollOver){
  gotoAndPlay("myLabel");
}
```

...the button would do a `gotoAndPlay` on the timeline that the button was on. A movie clip button will do the same.

If you did this instead in a standard version 5 button...

```
on (rollOver){
  this.gotoAndPlay("myLabel");
}
```

...you would see no difference since `this` still means `_parent` for a version 5 button. An MX movie clip button is fundamentally different because it recognizes `this`, and the script above will do a `gotoAndPlay` on its own timeline and not on `_parent`.

If you have a look at `movieClipButton.fla`, you will see two instances of our button. Both behave like buttons and react to the mouse in the standard manner. Unlike a button though, they also include the custom unclicked and rollOut graphic states that we created. One of the buttons is also acting like a movie clip due to the appropriate script – it will follow the mouse and at the same time, it can still act like a button.

These new movie clip buttons are Flash MX gold dust for cool site UI designers. Of course, you must be one of those – you've bought a friends of ED book after all. Go design!

The next step up in designing movie clips is to be able to modify them at both authoring time and at run-time – to do this we have to familiarize ourselves with the drawing API.

The drawing API

Manny Tan loves to draw lines - check out www.uncontrol.com. He makes spiders and all sorts of creations out of basic elements; it's cool to watch them and even more satisfying to see how they are put together. I remember reviewing a chapter for *New Masters Of Flash 2002 Annual* where he created a butterfly by dragging things from the library, all under the control of ActionScript during run-time. Eric Natzke loves doing the vector toy thing as well, as do Andries Odendaal and Gabriel Mulzer when they're creating that amazing 3D stuff with Flash.

The trouble is, even these top guys could only achieve this in Flash 5 by using little tricks and sleight of hand, or standard actions that can get a little obscure in their use. Sure, the Masters are well up to the level needed, but for us mere mortals, it can get a little intimidating.

Flash MX has done away with all the smoke and mirrors. We no longer have to duplicate movie clip lines and scale them (sneakily) to emulate real vector lines. We can now get straight to the engine room of the movie clip and produce new sketches *on the fly*. In fact, there are three things you can create:

1. Lines

2. Curves

3. Fills

Although you could emulate lines in Flash 5, you couldn't control the movie clip with clever scripting to create controlled curves or fills, so this feature is totally new. As we'll see in the next section, it all started with a turtle...

Turtle graphics

The drawing API of Flash is based around something called **turtle graphics**, so we will have a quick look at what that is before we get down to business, because it can get a little complicated.

Turtle graphics is an old graphics language they used way back to control a little robot with a pen attached to it. The turtle was the robot – it typically looked like a little upturned bowl on wheels, hence the name, and it could do a few basic things:

- Lift the pen up (*penUp*)

- Put the pen down (*penDown*)

- Rotate without moving forward

- Travel forward (but not at the same time as rotating, so it could only travel in a straight line)

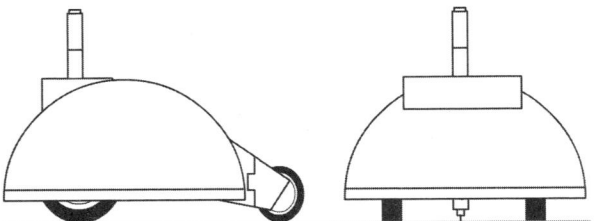

I can't swear on the details because I'm sketching from memory here (and I was young when I first saw one – I'm a lot older now), but I think it kind of looked like the one above. The pen fitted between the middle of two big wheels at the front, and the wheel at the back was like that of a shopping cart – it could twist on a hinge allowing the turtle to turn on the spot. Because the pen was situated at the center of rotation between the two front wheels, the turtle could rotate without moving the pen tip, and if the turtle moved forward with the pen down, it left a line describing its path.

You had two basic commands:

- *move (x, y)* – this was a *penUp* followed by a rotate until *(x, y)* was directly in front of you, and then move forward in a straight line as far as *(x, y)*. It didn't result in a line being drawn.

- *draw (x, y)* – this consisted of rotating until *(x, y)* was in front of you, followed by a *penDown* and move forward in a straight line as far as *(x, y)*. It resulted in a line being drawn from your *start point* to *(x, y)*.

Sometimes they put software on it that allowed you to enter angles and distances, so you could say 'rotate 90, move 5, rotate 45, move 6', and so on, but that was for the nursery kids! We used it with the Cartesian (x, y) scale. The deal was you put a piece of paper under the turtle and did stuff like working out how to draw a cube, or (even harder) an equilateral triangle. If you got that one, they even let you attempt to write your name with it. 'Sham' was the shortest name in class, so I aced it, but the surname was going nowhere!

Turtles were really cool in the early 8-bit computer days. Kids actually ran to math class to use them, and they only found out later that the turtle had fooled them into learning Cartesian geometry.

So anyway, what's this got to do with Flash? Well, Flash uses something that is recognizable as turtle graphics. In fact, most vector graphics actually *are* turtle graphics at the most basic level, and thinking in terms of the little turtle trundling around on cheap paper in real-time is easier than imagining the Flash graphics engine drawing stuff with scripts and events firing off, running at 12 fps. Indeed, the turtle makes it easy to visualize - they had kids doing Pythagorean theory at age 5 with these things, so it must be true!

Lines

Flash has a virtual turtle that controls the drawing API. It can move to a point (x, y) and then draw to a point (x, y). To draw a line from (50, 50) to (100, 100) you would:

  a. Move to (50, 50)

  b. Draw to (100, 100)

Easy huh? Let's get some practice by looking at an example.

Drawing lines

In a new movie we'll add a script on frame 1 of the timeline. You don't have to rename the layer or anything. We're going to do everything in ActionScript, and we only need that one layer and that one key frame. Some of the designers in the house may be a little reluctant to enter into anything that doesn't involve a full library of symbols that you actually place on stage yourself, and are already edging towards the door. If ActionScript puts you off, don't worry; it will only get difficult if you stop thinking about the turtle in the last section. There's no sneaky ActionScript voodoo in this section, and if you follow it through methodically, you'll see that it's actually very easy.

  1. The first thing we need is some paper. Let's create some virtual paper, a movie clip to be precise:

```
_root.createEmptyMovieClip("paper", 100);
```

This creates an empty movie clip called paper at depth 100. I chose 100 just in case you want to go and add some other stuff on screen later.

Where is this clip? Well, it's at (0,0) on the stage (because the _x and _y properties of a newly created clip are zero), which equates to the top left. Now here's an important point: *as long as you leave it there, the co-ordinate space of the main timeline is the same as the local co-ordinates of the movie clip.* As soon as you move it, however, the position of a turtle on the piece of paper called _root becomes different relative to a turtle on the piece of paper called paper, even if they head for the same point (x, y). As shown below, the internal co-ordinates of paper will show a different origin (0,0) to that of _root after being moved:

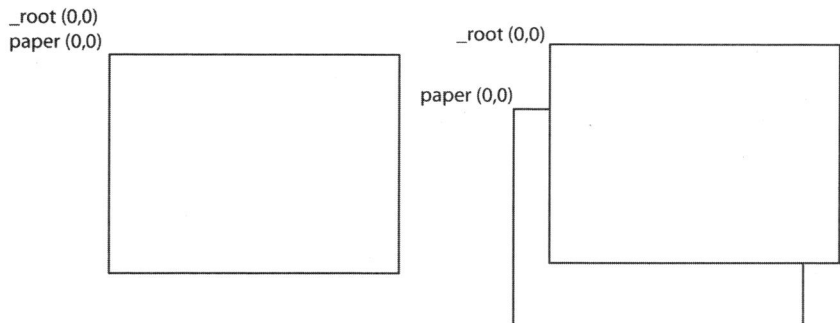

There are times when having the paper in a different place is a good thing, but not while we are getting to grips with the drawing API, so leave it where it is for now.

> *Don't forget that the y-axis is 'down' in Flash, not 'up' as it is in math. This is because web design is based around web pages, which is essentially an alternative to print, and they read from top to bottom.*

2. Next, we want to define our pen. A turtle could draw different lines depending on which pen you had in it, and the drawing API is no different. You select the `lineStyle` of the turtle on the movie clip `myClip` by doing this:

    ```
    myClip.lineStyle(thickness, color, alpha);
    ```

    We will have a thickness of 3, a color of red (0xFF0000), and an alpha value of 100% for our turtle on `paper`:

    ```
    paper.lineStyle(3, 0xFF0000, 100);
    ```

3. We now have to move to our start point. The method to do this is `moveTo(x, y)`. So if we wanted to move to (50, 50), we'd use this line:

    ```
    paper.moveTo(50, 50);
    ```

4. The turtle is in now position at the start of the line. It now needs to put the pen down and draw a line as it travels to (100, 100). The method we use to draw is `lineTo`:

    ```
    _root.createEmptyMovieClip("paper", 100);
    paper.lineStyle(3, 0xFF0000, 100);
    paper.moveTo(50, 50);
    paper.lineTo(100, 100);
    ```

5. On testing this code, you should now see your line, a short diagonal in the top left corner that points at the bottom right corner. That's fine, but there's not much happening after the initial elation. Time for a little interactivity. Instead of `moveTo` a fixed distance and then `lineTo` to another fixed distance, we will use `lineTo(_xmouse, _ymouse)`, and we will do this every time the mouse moves. Change your script to the one shown below (the second line is new, and the `moveTo` and `lineTo` arguments have changed), which you'll find in the source code folders as `lines1.fla`:

    ```
    _root.createEmptyMovieClip("paper", 100);
    paper.onMouseMove = function() {
      paper.lineStyle(3, 0xFF0000, 100);
      paper.moveTo(275, 200);
      paper.lineTo(_xmouse, _ymouse);
    };
    ```

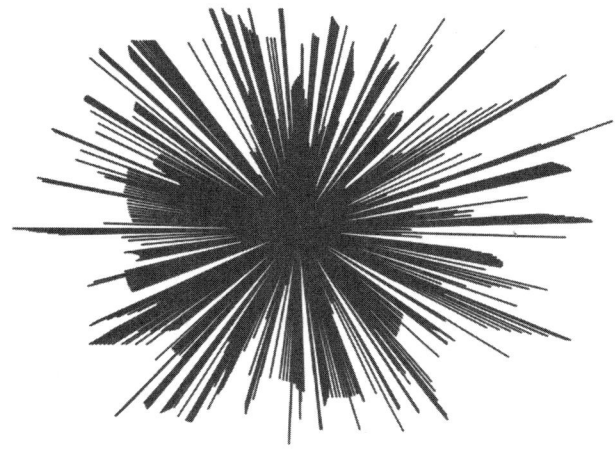

Wow, an explosion in a paint factory!

6. Notice that this script gets slow if you allow a large number of lines to be drawn. We should really clean up the excess lines every now and then. We can't *undraw* lines, but we can *clear* the whole movie clip with `myClip.clear()`. Try this (`lines2.fla`):

```
maxLines = 100;
lines = 0;
createEmptyMovieClip("paper", 100);
paper.onMouseMove = function () {
  lines++;
  if(lines<maxLines) {
    paper.lineStyle(3, 0xFF0000, 100);
    paper.moveTo(275, 200);
    paper.lineTo(_xmouse, _ymouse);
  } else {
    paper.clear();
    lines = 0;
  }
};
```

Here we are limiting ourselves to a `maxLines` of 100. As long as `lines<maxLines`, we do the original `moveTo/lineTo` actions in our clip `paper`. As soon as we see more than 100 lines, we clear our `paper` movie clip with `paper.clear()` and reset `lines` back to 0.

7. We can also make our lines into one continuous line simply by commenting out or removing the `moveTo` action. You'd then see something like this:

If you can't visualize what is happening here, think back to our turtle. Rather than go back to the center of the screen after every mouse move, the turtle just waits for us to move our mouse, and remains at the last position we moved to. It is effectively following us. If it does it fast enough, all our straight line segments get short and therefore start to look like curves.

You may see the path the turtle makes being rather blocky. This is a function of the frame rate; the mouse movement is only being sampled at 12fps. Try 18 or 24 fps if your machine is up to it (or reduce the stage size or quality if it isn't).

We almost have the beginnings of a drawing tool here, and we'll develop this idea in a while. First though, we need to think about curves.

Curves

The curve functionality of the drawing API is best described by demonstration - time for another script! Add the following script to the first frame of a new movie. We are only going to use ActionScript, so you just need this script and a single frame:

```
createEmptyMovieClip("paper", 100);
paper.onMouseMove = function() {
  paper.clear();
  paper.lineStyle(3, 0xFF0000, 100);
  paper.moveTo(100, 200);
  paper.curveTo(_xmouse, _ymouse, 400, 200);
};
```

You can find this script in the file curves1.fla. Note that we're now using a new method, curveTo, in place of our lineTo. We are moving our turtle to a point (100, 200) – center-left of the stage – and then drawing to (400, 200) – center-right of the stage. But something happens to the turtle in between. It's almost as if our mouse was some sort of turtle magnet; the turtle tries to get to the point (400, 200), but it is attracted to our magnet, and gets pulled away towards the mouse - the turtle's new path is a *curve*:

> *Notice that we are also clearing the paper every time. This means we delete the previous line and draw a new line every frame, and the resulting curve looks animated. Delete the* `paper.clear()` *command to see all the individual curves that are making up our animation. Isn't that pretty... I have a feeling that lots of geometrical screen savers and 'Please Wait... loading' screen eye-candy are on the cards!*

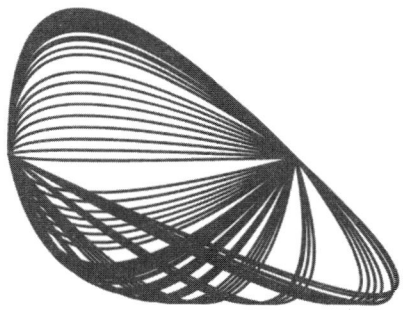

Looking at the difference between the `linetTo` and `curveTo` arguments we can kind of see what is going on:

```
moveTo(100, 200);
lineTo(400, 200);

moveTo(100, 200);
curveTo(_xmouse, _ymouse, 400, 200);
```

The first two lines of code will cause a line to be drawn. Our turtle moves to (100, 200) and then draws to (400, 200). The second pair of lines contain our `curveTo` action, which also has the (400, 200) point specified, but also has a new set of control points (_xmouse, _ymouse). That explains why the mouse is doing stuff to the curve – its position is being used somehow.

So we have:

```
curveTo(controlPointX, controlPointY, x, y);
```

The `curveTo` is just like a `lineTo` in that it causes the turtle to go to (x, y) with the pen down, drawing a line as it goes. Unlike the `lineTo`, however, `curveTo` has a control point made up of (controlPointX, controlPointY) that affects the path the turtle takes. The turtle seems to want to go through the control point, but doesn't do it, so it *tends towards* the control point. OK, that's fine, but we really need more information than that to know what the control point is well enough to actually create a curve we can predict.

There are two ways I can tell you about: one is to talk about quadratic Bezier curves and stuff like that for a couple of pages (and probably alienate half of my readership in doing so!), and the other is to tell you what it actually does in non-mathematical words and pictures. Well, the pretty pictures option wins hands-down every time for me - let's look at a quick example.

Create a fresh movie and attach this script to frame 1 of the main timeline (or just open up the file curves2.fla):

```
red = 0xFF0000;
blue = 0x0000FF;
createEmptyMovieClip("paper", 100);
paper.onMouseMove = function() {
  paper.clear();
  // draw curve...
  paper.lineStyle(3, red, 100);
  paper.moveTo(100, 200);
  paper.curveTo(_xmouse, _ymouse, 400, 200);
  // draw control point tangent...
  paper.LineStyle(0, blue, 100);
  paper.moveTo(100, 200);
  paper.lineTo(_xmouse, _ymouse);
};
```

This gives us the picture we want, and it's interactive as well! The thin line is the control line. It is a line joining the start point to the control point and the curve forms itself so that it is *tangential* to it:

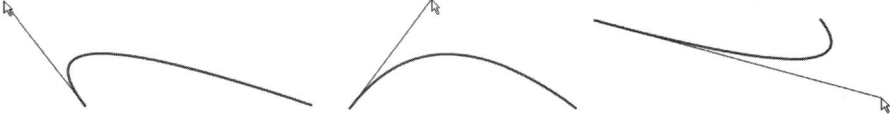

So, the control point is actually defining one end of a *bow tie*. It is very similar to the bow ties used by the Flash sub-select tool and the new envelope deform modifier that we looked at earlier in this book. Like bow ties, the control point is difficult to explain, but once you see what it is, its use becomes highly intuitive.

A simple tool for drawing lines and curves

We now have everything we need to construct a simple interactive drawing tool. I've been working on a few test scripts in my attempt to create an 'all-singing, all-dancing' Flash-based drawing application that uses drawing layers in the same way as PhotoShop, and has a floating toolbar, zoom in/out, snap, and a component driven UI. It will no doubt find its way into a later friends of ED book (unless one of you clever people create it first!), but as a starter, here's a beta script for the embryonic line/curve elastic band tool. You need to attach it to the first frame of a new movie as before, or just open up the file elasticBand.fla:

```
// INITIALIZE DATA
// Initialize Objects...
keyboard = new Object();
// Initialize variables...
endX = end2X=_xmouse;
endY = end2Y=_ymouse;
penToggle = false;
red = 0xFF0000;
blue = 0x0000FF;
black = 0x000000;
// END INITIALIZE DATA
//
//
// INITIALIZE GRAPHICS
// Create clips...
createEmptyMovieClip("paper", 100);
createEmptyMovieClip("pen", 101);
// END INITIALIZE CLIPS
//
//
// DEFINE EVENT HANDLERS
// keyboard listener and function...
keyboard.onKeyDown = function() {
  endX = end2X=_xmouse;
  endY = end2Y=_ymouse;
  penToggle = false;
};
Key.addListener(keyboard);
// pen events...
pen.onEnterFrame = function() {
  this.clear();
  if (!penToggle) {
    // if penToggle is false, use line pen...
    this.lineStyle(0, blue, 100);
    this.moveTo(endX, endY);
    this.lineTo(_xmouse, _ymouse);
  } else {
    // penToggle must be True, so use curve pen...
    this.lineStyle(0, red, 100);
    this.moveTo(endX, endY);
    this.curveTo(_xmouse, _ymouse, end2X, end2Y);
  }
};
//paper events...
paper.onMouseDown = function() {
  if (!penToggle) {
    //first press...
    // toggle to curve pen
    // and set second endpoints of curve...
    penToggle = true;
```

```
      end2X = _xmouse;
      end2Y = _ymouse;
  } else {
    // second press...
    // Draw the curve to the paper...
    this.lineStyle(0, black, 100);
    this.moveTo(endX, endY);
    this.curveTo(_xmouse, _ymouse, end2X, end2Y);
    // reset pen back to line pen...
    penToggle = false;
    endX = end2X;
    endY = end2Y;
  }
};
// END DEFINE EVENT HANDLERS
```

There are two movie clips: paper and pen. The pen clip is where the cursor lines sit, that is, where curves and lines in progress are drawn. When you are ready to fix a curve, it is transferred to the movie clip paper. We have to do this because to animate our lines in progress (our 'pen') we have to constantly clear the pen movie clip. This means that we cannot draw anything permanent in it as well, so the movie clip paper is where we place our lines once we want them to be indelible.

> *Notice that if you were to split the paper into several movie clips* paper01, paper02, paper03, *and so on, you have the beginnings of drawing layers straight away with no fuss.*

To draw a line you move the blue line around to the first point you want to draw to. Click when you have your mouse at the right place:

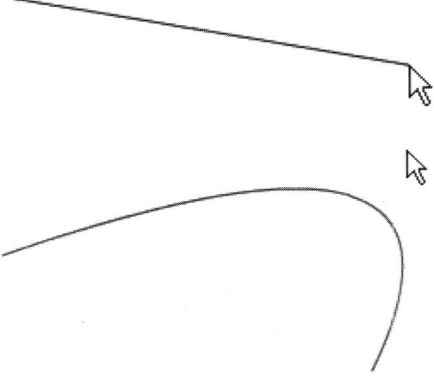

The line will then turn red. If you click again without moving the mouse, you will get a permanent black line. If you actually want a curve, move the cursor while the line is red to form a curve:

Once you are happy, simply click again and the red curve will become a permanent black curve.

So, double-click to make a straight line and single-click, bend the line, single-click again to make a curve. Also, to move your cursor without drawing, just press and hold any key while you move. By doing this you can easily make a simple drawing consisting of lines and curves:

Not quite enough to make Picasso jealous, but pretty neat anyway!

How does it work?

As it stands, the basic code works as follows: all lines are drawn from point endX, endY to either the mouse position (_xmouse, _ymouse) for a line, or to (end2X, end2y) with the mouse position as the control point for the curve:

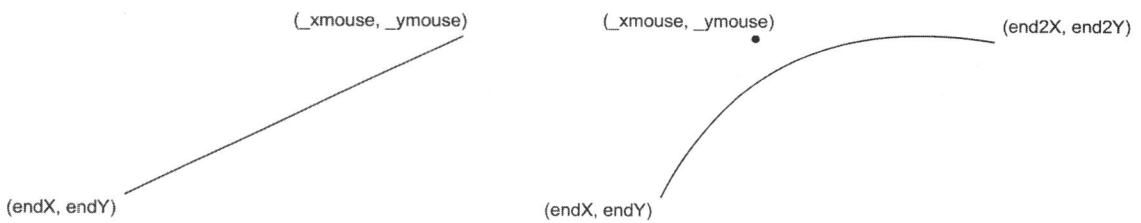

When drawing the current line style permanently to paper, the pen has two states: you've either clicked once (and the pen will draw a blue line) or twice (so the pen now needs to draw a red curve). This is controlled by the variable penToggle. If you have read and understood the stuff on events in Chapter 7 and the material on turtle graphics that we've just covered, there is not actually much else to note about this script; it is pretty straightforward except for the two points listed below:

- **Point 1 – hold any key to move without drawing**
  The only thing we haven't covered so far is the bit that monitors the keyboard for any key press:

```
// DEFINE EVENT HANDLERS
// keyboard listener and function...
keyboard.onKeyDown = function() {
  endX = end2X=_xmouse;
  endY = end2Y=_ymouse;
  penToggle = false;
};
Key.addListener(keyboard);
```

This is using a **listener** and, for the moment, all you have to know is that the `keyboard.onKeyDown` function is executed every time you hit a key. It won't fire off until you click once on the SWF (to give it focus), so in a real drawing program you would make sure that the user clicks on the screen at least once before using the drawing tools.

● **Point 2 – function scope**
Notice that the functions have a scope of `_root` (the timeline they are defined on) *and not the timeline they are handling events for*. This is evident because variables like `red` and `blue` are defined in `_root` but used in the functions without a path *because the functions are also attached to `_root`*.

If you need to use local variables in a function, you should either use `Var` (a good option if you want to keep it all structured, but it can slow down critical loops that call the same function a lot, since ActionScript is an interpreted language), or attach your scripts to the local (movie clip) timeline that you are handling events for. The second option may appeal to you because you end up with the scripts attached to their associated movie clips (so that the scope is the same as Flash 5 scripts attached directly to the movie clips), while keeping all your script definitions on the same frame.

> *An understanding of the scope of a function (point 2 above) is crucial to an advanced understanding of Flash MX Actionscript because the method-based way of using events (assigning callbacks to object events) is fundamental to Flash MX.*

Scope experiment

In the following little experiment on scope we will show how to define an event script in the main timeline but attach it to the movie clip (thus giving you the best of both Flash 5 and Flash MX coding practice).

1. In frame 1 of _root add this script:

```
apple = "rootApple";
```

2. Create a movie clip, place it on stage, and give it the instance name `myClip`. In frame 1 of its timeline add this script:

```
apple = "clipApple";
```

Now run the debugger. You will see two versions of `apple`:

```
_level0.apple = "rootApple"
_level0.myClip.apple = "clipApple"
```

3. Change the script in frame 1 of _root to:

```
apple = "rootApple";
myClip.onEnterFrame = function() {
  trace(apple);
};
```

You see the function pick up the version of apple on _root (which is the same as _level0 in a SWF without load levels) or *the version of apple on the timeline that the function was created in.*

4. Now add a with around the function definition, as shown below:

```
apple = "rootApple";
with (myClip) {
  myClip.onEnterFrame = function() {
    trace(apple);
  };
}
```

You should now see that the function is scoped to the timeline myClip, and is picking up the version of apple that exists in myClip (clipApple).

We would add the with if we wanted our functions to do the following:

■   Modify the properties of the movie clip that is causing the events without having to keep adding the full path to the properties. The script below will animate myClip. If you don't use with in the function definition, you will animate with root._x:

```
with (myClip) {
  myClip.onEnterFrame = function() {
    _x++
  };
```

■   Use local variables that exist on the myClip timeline. This is the same scope as the standard that you have attached to your movie clips back in Flash 5, like this:

```
onClipEvent(enterFrame){
  // do stuff
}
```

Fills

OK, we're on to the final bit of the drawing API now - fills. Obviously, our poor virtual Flash turtle can only draw lines, so how do we visualize it drawing a fill? The answer is that it trundles around the *perimeter* of the area we want to fill and then politely asks the drawing API to fill the area it just defined. This perimeter is called the fill path, or just **path**.

Although the detail of the fill part of the drawing API is a little hairy, the fundamental principle is easy - as usual; we'll dive into an example to show how to use it.

Filling shapes

1. The first thing to do is create a movie clip object to draw into. In a new FLA, attach the following script to frame 1:

```
createEmptyMovieClip("paper", 100);
```

2. Now that we have something to draw into, we want to draw round the edge of our shape. Here, we'll draw the square shown below:

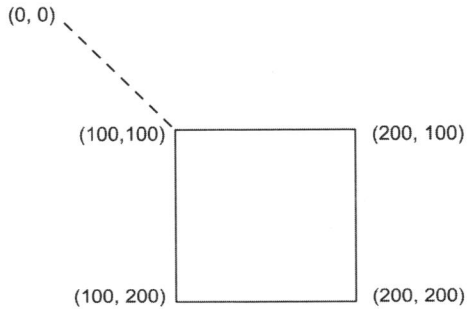

We have to move from the origin (0, 0) and draw out our square path. To do this, add the following lines:

```
paper.lineStyle(3, 0x000000, 100);
paper.moveTo(100, 100);
paper.lineTo(200, 100);
paper.lineTo(200, 200);
paper.lineTo(100, 200);
paper.lineTo(100, 100);
```

We have given our turtle a pen of thickness 3, black color (0x000000), and alpha 100%. Our turtle then moves from the start position to (100,100) and proceeds to draw round our perimeter in a clockwise direction. If you run the movie you will see the finished path drawn:

An important point to notice is that you must get the order of the corner points that you make the turtle visit correct. If they are out of sequence it will draw incorrectly, as the script below demonstrates:

```
createEmptyMovieClip("paper", 100);
paper.lineStyle(3, 0x000000, 100);
paper.moveTo(100, 100);
paper.lineTo(200, 200);
paper.lineTo(200, 100);
paper.lineTo(100, 200);
paper.lineTo(100, 100);
```

This looks like an hourglass or a rotated bow tie - clearly not what we want! Flash would still fill the path if we asked it to, but it would fill out the two enclosed triangles rather than the square we want filled.

3. To fill our square, we first need to define our fill color. This is done via the `beginFill` method.

```
myClip.beginFill(color, alpha);
```

The `color` refers to the color of the fill, and you can also set the `alpha`. The `beginFill` also tells Flash one other important thing: essentially it says to the drawing API 'I'm setting my turtle off on the path I want you to fill'. To tell Flash that the turtle is done, you simply include an `endFill(x, y);`. Enter the following code in now:

```
createEmptyMovieClip("paper", 100);
paper.lineStyle(3, 0x000000, 100);
paper.beginFill(0xFF0000, 100);
paper.moveTo(100, 100);
paper.lineTo(200, 100);
paper.lineTo(200, 200);
paper.lineTo(100, 200);
paper.endFill(100, 100);
```

This script tells Flash that we have started defining our path. It also tells Flash to fill with a red pen (0xFF0000) with 100% alpha. We then continue round our square as before (in the right order) to define the area to be filled. The last `lineTo` is now replaced by an `endFill`. This tells Flash to draw to the point (100, 100) and to fill the path defined by the turtle since the initial `beginFill`. You will see the red square with black border shown below if you run this FLA (or open up `fillSquare.fla`):

4. You can also make it out of curves instead of lines.

```
createEmptyMovieClip("paper", 100);
paper.lineStyle(3, 0x000000, 100);
paper.beginFill(0xFF0000, 100);
paper.moveTo(100, 100);
paper.lineTo(200, 100);
paper.lineTo(200, 200);
paper.lineTo(100, 200);
paper.curveTo(50, 150, 100, 100);
paper.endFill(100, 100);
```

This creates the shape you see here:

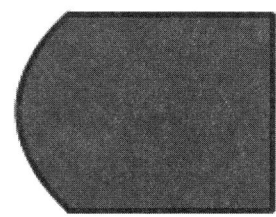

Notice that because we have to end our path definition with an `endFill`, and the line we want to end with is now a `curveTo`, we are a little stuck with the `endFill` since there are no more lines to create in our path. Instead, we simply `endFill` to the point we are already at (100, 100).

5. We can of course animate our filled shapes by using `clear()` and redrawing a transformed version of the same shape every frame. You'll find the following code within the file `fillCartoon.fla`:

```
createEmptyMovieClip("paper", 100);
vertexX = new Array(100, 200, 200, 100);
vertexY = new Array(100, 100, 200, 200);
//
paper.onEnterFrame = function() {
  for (i=0; i<4; i++) {
    vertexX[i] += (Math.random()*10)-5;
    vertexY[i] += (Math.random()*10)-5;
  }
  paper.clear();
  paper.lineStyle(3, 0x000000, 100);
  paper.beginFill(0xFF0000, 100);
  paper.moveTo(vertexX[0], vertexY[0]);
  paper.lineTo(vertexX[1], vertexY[1]);
  paper.lineTo(vertexX[2], vertexY[2]);
  paper.lineTo(vertexX[3], vertexY[3]);
  paper.endFill(vertexX[0], vertexY[0]);
};
```

This time we're assigning the four points of our square to a couple of arrays. Our points are now (vertexX[0], vertexY[0]) to (vertexX[3], vertexY[3]), and we are varying their positions by a small random value every enterFrame (try different random increments for vertexX and vertexY, and different frame rates to find a nice organic animation).

Flash also allows you to define gradient fills. We would recommend that you don't use this for dynamic animation until you are fully up to speed with the solid color fills. It uses a number of objects to define the gradient, and, as with gradient fills generally, is a little slow if you try to animate your shapes as we have just done with solid fills. This completes our tour of the Flash MX drawing API - as you can probably see, it's a pretty powerful addition to our box of tricks.

Summary

By now you should have an impression of the enhancements that the Flash MX movie clip object presents. The actual number of changes is small, but they totally change the way you will use movie clips in the future. More than ever, movie clips have become the standard Flash graphic object. You could do away with graphic symbols in Flash 5, and in Flash MX you will probably do away with most buttons as well, leaving only the movie clip and text graphic objects in the running.

The thing to be aware of is that getting the most out of the new Flash MX movie clip features will require a competent understanding of ActionScripting. If you haven't done so, we really recommend you get hold of a foundation scripting book and sit down with it for a while - this will really help you to get the most out of some of the new features we've discussed.

Later in this book, we'll have a look at a couple more major pieces in the Flash MX jigsaw: **listeners** and the updated **object model**. We'll be near the top of the Flash MX mountain by the time we get to that stuff and, as such, we will really start to use the movie clip object in powerful ways. That's enough teasers for later in the book; let's now move on to the next chapter where we'll start to examine the default **components** that are included with Flash MX.

Chapter 9

Introducing Components

Just before we look at the cool functionality offered by new Macromedia Flash MX **components**, we'll review some of the advantages and disadvantages or their earlier incarnation – *smart clips*. In Flash 5, smart clips were a great innovation, and they meant that you could:

- Build generic movie clips and share them with other designers, who could then configure them to their own specific needs.

- Use the same general movie clip design in several places in your own FLA, making each instance look or act slightly differently by configuring them individually.

- Build up a personal library of movie clips that you use often.

The trouble with smart clips, however, was that they were not really clever or self-contained enough:

- You could not, for example, drag a scrollbar onto a text field, and expect it to think, "I've been dropped onto a text field, so I'll configure myself to be the scrollbar for this text field!"

- You could pass a number of parameters to a smart clip, which could change either its appearance or the way it worked. The trouble here was that these changes in appearance did not take effect until run-time.

- One model for using smart clips was the scripter-designer pairing. The scripter writes general UI smart clips, encapsulating the clever voodoo scripting inside the clip. The designers would then use the smart clips as stand-alone, 'off-the-shelf' units for each web site. The problem was that each web site would typically require a different look and feel, and this would have to be reflected in the smart clip graphics. The changes you could make with smart clips to change their appearance were limited – for instance, you could not change one of Joshua Davis's minimalist gray sliders from Praystation (see www.praystation.com) into one that would fit well inside a Tomas Jankowski-style cyber-punk future world extravaganza (www.mondo.com.pl) just by varying a few smart clip parameters. This meant that designers nearly always had to go into the smart clip to change the graphics, and that smart clips rarely encapsulated their functionality successfully, since there was no real separation between graphics and scripting.

Despite their drawbacks, smart clips were a good idea in principle. The new Flash MX equivalents are called **components**. Note that they are *not* just newly repackaged smart clips – Macromedia have listened to user feedback and addressed all the big issues mentioned above. As we shall see, components are clever enough to respond to simple 'drag and drop' techniques (such as the slider example above) if their functionality allows it. Any changes you make to the smart clip properties are reflected at authoring time, so you don't have to keep running the SWF just to see if the checkbox titles in your checkbox component line up and don't detract from the overall design.

Finally, designers can change the graphics of a component without having to see all those ActionScript timelines and event scripts, via a process called **component skinning** which allows you to give the default components custom 'skins'.

New component functionality

Components don't just fix the stuff that was wrong with smart clips – they also take Flash in a new direction. As well as implementing generic movie clip-based components, Macromedia have made it easy for components to embed themselves into the Flash UI. Not only do components replace smart clips, in that they are pre-built, common building blocks that save time, they also introduce additional features. For instance, with components you can:

- Add more functionality to your clips, such as making your components animate while they are in the authoring environment. You can do this by representing them on stage as a SWF, which can include an animated version of the component in action, or even an instructional video! This feature is called **live preview**, and we'll take a look at it in Chapter 14.

- Create components that *don't have a physical appearance at all*. This may seem odd, but there are many reasons why you might want to do this. Consider, for example, building a 3D engine component. This would not be a UI component such as a scrollbar, but an ActionScript-based component that adds a new object and custom methods allowing the user to control a 3D environment through scripting. Now that *is* powerful!

> *As you will by now be realizing, components are much more flexible and clever than smart clips, but this comes at a cost – the components must be designed to be very general, and this means that they can often be rather complex inside. We must therefore briefly delay our look at creating complex components from scratch (complete with embedded instructional videos, true drag and drop usability, and a discussion on ActionScripting specific to Flash MX component design). This advanced stuff is in Chapter 14.*

This book is about transforming Flash 5 skills over to Flash MX, so we will also look at converting any Flash 5 smart clips you may have amassed into Flash MX components. This should demystify much of the process of creating simple components, allowing us to hit the ground running when we get to Chapter 14.

The component environment

Let's start our study of the new MX components by becoming familiar with their environment. Components have their own panel called...Components. If you can't already see this panel, you can bring it up with Window>Components, or by hitting F11:

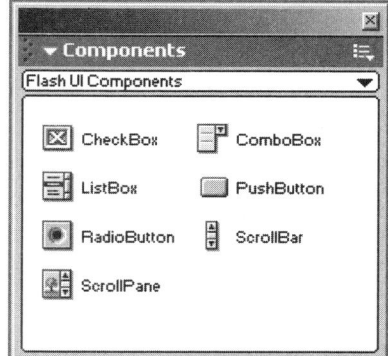

The default components are shown in the panel, and include all the basic Flash UI components you will need to build a standard Flash site or form. The panel will show further component sets (once they're installed) if you click on the down arrow on the top right.

> New panel sets are not included in the default Flash MX configuration, but you can add them as developers release them. Look out for stuff from Samuel Wan and Brandon Hall, two people who really went to town with components during the early testing stages of Flash MX.

Using components

Components are fundamentally different from Flash 5 smart clips. To ease you into the workflow used by components, we will first provide an overview before we get into the specifics of each component.

With both the Library and Components panels open, click-drag any component onto the stage. In the picture below, we have done this with the CheckBox component:

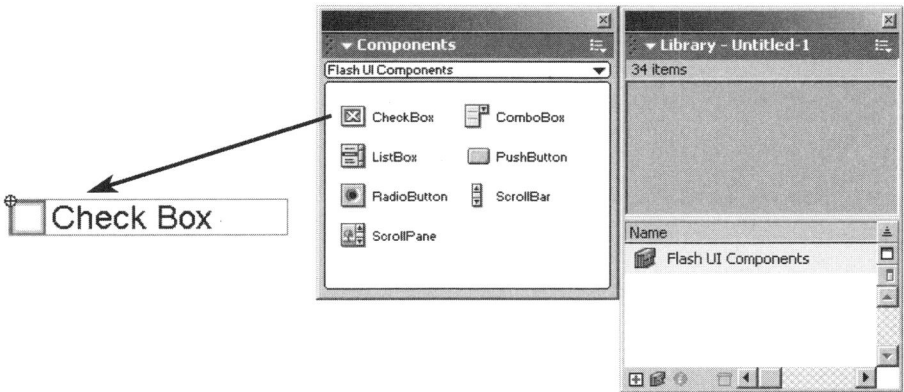

There are two things to notice here:

- As soon as you place the checkbox on the stage, a folder called Flash UI Components appears in the library to show that the required components will appear in your FLA. In other words, the components listed in the Components panel are those available to the Flash application itself, and you signify that you want to use one or more of them by dragging them from the panel onto the stage.

- Now try double-clicking on the component that you dragged onto the stage. Unlike smart clips, components really are self-contained building blocks – you can't go into them to do a sneaky edit (either on purpose or by mistake).

Once you have dragged a CheckBox onto the stage, you must use the version in the library if you want to add another one to your stage. Open the Flash UI Components folder to see where this is. The CheckBox component will be there, as highlighted in this diagram. If you want to add additional instances of this component, *this* is the version you should drag onto stage.

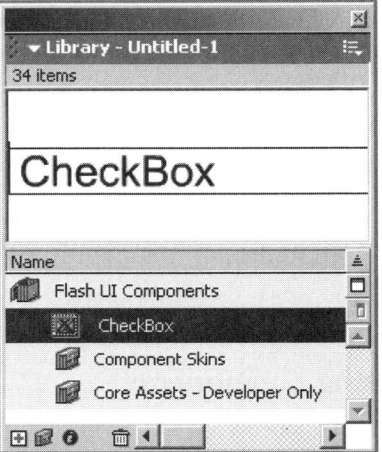

Macromedia Flash MX doesn't mind if you drag multiple identical components from the components panel; it's clever enough to know you already have a version of the checkbox in the library and will not create another one. It may, however, cause problems when you customize your components – the components you drag onto the stage are always uncustomized, and all the customization is applied to the version in your library. It's good practice to get into the habit of using the version in the library as soon as it appears there; this way, the component structures will work for you rather than against you.

While we're here, note that there are two other folders in the Flash UI Components folder: Component Skins and Core Assets – Developer Only. The Component Skins folder contains the skins we talked about earlier; a designer who wants to change the look of the component to fit in with the style of the site they are designing can do so by using the symbols in this folder:

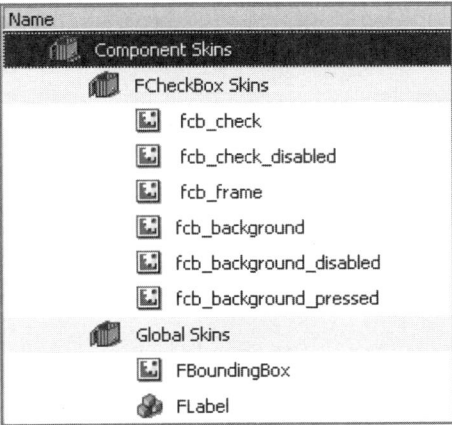

The individual movie clips that make up the look of our CheckBox are in the FCheckBox Skins folder. The designer can access these symbols, and edit or replace them.

What if you want to change the general appearance of the *complete* Flash UI component set? To change common elements that are used in the entire component set, you need to alter the symbols in the Global Skins folder. For example, changing the font of the text box will change the font used in the components globally.

Scripters can change component skins through ActionScript, something we will look at in the advanced chapter on components towards the end of this book.

> The way that additional third party components are set up may also affect other component sets. It's also worth noting that component skin changes are not reflected on the stage at author time – you have to run the FLA to see the new skins being used.

The final folder, Core Assets – Developer Only, is full of all the clever stuff that makes the component work. By incorporating all the ActionScript inside this one folder, designers know where they need to go to significantly alter the actual functionality of the component, or if they want an easy life, free from any ActionScript voodoo, they know which door never to open because something scary lives inside!

Returning to the discussion of the instance we just dragged onto the stage, if you look at the Property inspector (and assuming like me you used the checkbox), you will see this:

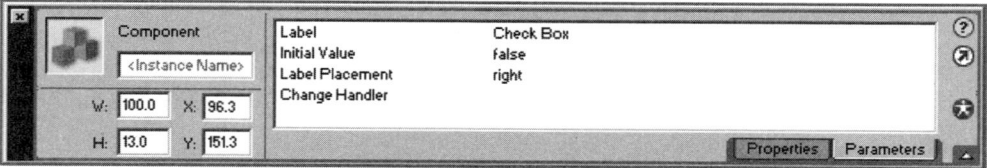

This information is also available from the Component Parameters panel (SHIFT+F11).

Supposing we wanted to change the text to Sound On for our web site. Simply click on Label and change Check Box to Sound On. Our component will automatically change to reflect this:

But wait, notice that the Initial Value is `false`. We want the sound *on* by default, so we actually want the Initial Value to be `true`. Change it to true by clicking on false or the little down arrow on the far right; either method will bring up the menu shown:

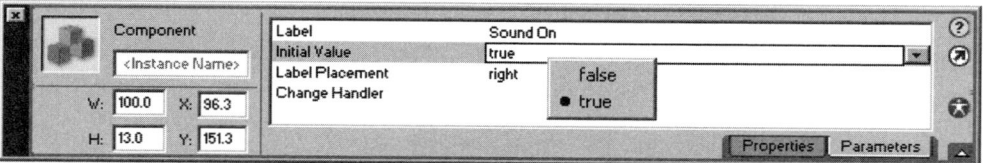

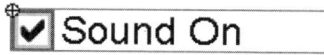

This change is again reflected in the component instance itself, and gives you immediate visual feedback of what the component settings will be initialized to at run-time, without you having to delve through parameter lists. This is particularly useful where you have a number of components on screen when your site opens; the initial conditions you set up via component parameters are important to the usability of your site.

Using the default components

As we stated earlier, the default components include all the standard UI building blocks that you might want to use to help you build up basic sites and forms. Some of them are very simple drag and drop affairs, while others may require you to add a few parameters. The more complex default components may even require you to add some ActionScript of your own to handle the component events. We will go through all three of these types in the following sections. You should of course note that we can change these basic UI elements to make altogether more interesting concoctions, something we will start doing in this chapter.

Drag and drop components

Drag and drop is just that: drag a component onto the stage, or onto the element you want it to be associated with, and the component will 'do its thing' automatically. This is really cool because you can immediately add stuff that would otherwise require a lot of coding to implement. Better still, drag and drop components have no parameters to enter!

The default components have only one drag and drop component – the scrollbar – but there are sure to be more in the future. Let's take a closer look at this simplest of components via some worked examples.

The Scrollbar

1. Open a new FLA and add an input text field with the properties shown below. Make sure that it is set to Multiline and that the text field has a border. Give the text field an instance name myText:

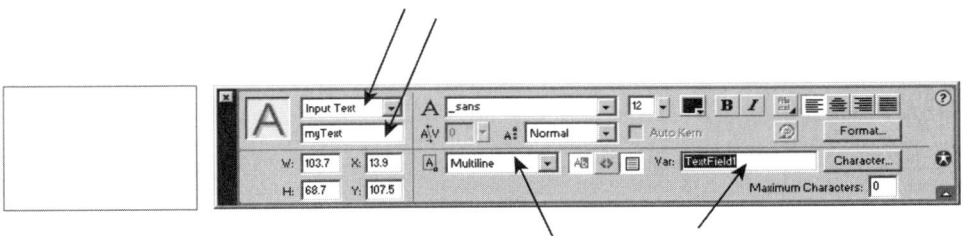

2. Now click-drag an instance of the ScrollBar from the Components panel onto the text box. Drop it over the text box, and close to the right edge of the text field. You will see that the scrollbar will automatically snap itself to the right edge of the text field (below left). If you now test the FLA, you will see the scrollbar work as you would expect; the scrollbar is grayed out until you add more text than the text field can display, at which point the scrollbar becomes active; you can then use it to navigate up and down through the field.

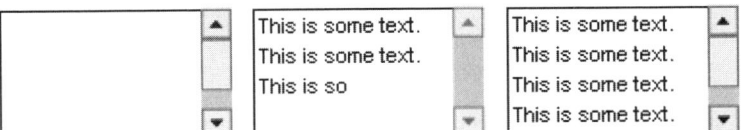

Flash has done a few things behind the scenes to make this totally intuitive feature work. Let's do that again in slow motion so that you see all the little bits of magic.

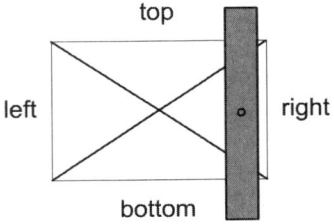

First off, how did Flash know we wanted a scrollbar on the right? Well, as far as the scrollbar is concerned the text field is actually split into four areas. The scrollbar will snap to the edge of the area that its center point is in when you release it. When we dropped it, it snapped to the right edge because it was in the 'right' zone:

Knowing this means that you can use the scrollbar to create many combinations of scroll functionality:

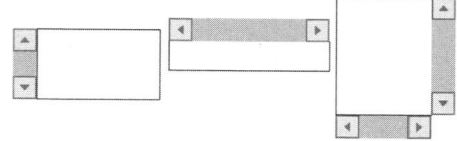

To make the scrollbars with the horizontal scroller work, you have to make them Multiline no wrap *otherwise the text field will change the text itself and never allow the scroll bars to get a look in.*

The parameters of the scrollbar look like this (you will find them either in the Property inspector or the Component parameters panel):

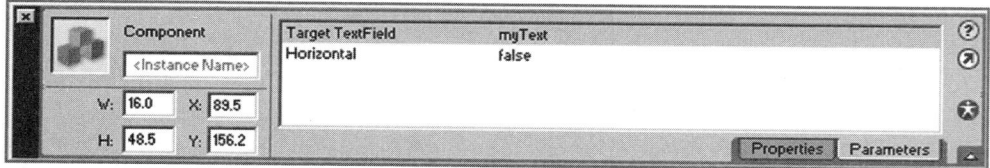

Unless you need to do anything non-standard, the drag and drop functionality has already got it worked out for you. The Target TextField is the name of the input text you are controlling (this is defined by the act of dragging the scrollbar on it) and the Horizontal true/false part defines whether your scrollbar is controlling horizontal or vertical scrolling (again, this is defined automatically – according to the edge you choose to drop the scrollbar on).

Although you can usually use either the Property inspector or the Component Parameters *panel, there is one piece of information that is not shown on the inspector – it's on the* Component Parameters *panel instead. Some components have help text defined, and this will usually tell you what the parameter settings do. To see this, select the component, and on the* Component Parameters *panel drop-down menu select* Help in this Component. *Note that this will be grayed out if there is no help text, which occurs on many of the default components.*

There are of course times that you may want to define the scrollbar's parameter values yourself:

- When you want the scrollbar to be some distance from the text field. You can actually achieve this by following a sneaky route and still use drag and drop – drop the scrollbar on the text field to give you your Target, then pick it up again and move it to the new location.

- When you don't want a scroller but a value slider (we'll explain what this is shortly).

A slider is cool for interface design. You can use it for all sorts of stuff:

- As the navigation slider on a side scroller UI (such as the *stun:design* site from the *Foundation ActionScript* book that you may be familiar with)

- To control values in a Flash particle effect toy

- As a slider to control the thickness of the lines in a paint Flash-application that uses the Drawing API

- To control zoom in/out functionality for a bitmap viewer

- To change the view angle of a 3D engine

- As the volume control for your site's sound

Setting up a slider is easy, but requires a bit of scripting, which is not a *bad* thing because it gives us the perfect opportunity to introduce the ActionScript associated with a component...

Slider

1. In a new FLA, create two layers called actions and graphics:

2. In layer graphics add a scrollbar. You can accept the default component values as we are not using the scrollbar to scroll anything. In the Property inspector, call the scrollbar scroller:

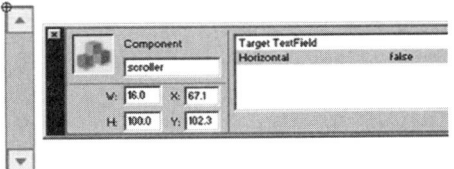

3. Add a dynamic text field above the scrollbar. Make it single line and give it a variable name scrollValue.

4. On frame 1 of the actions layer, add the following script:

```
scroller.setScrollProperties(99, 0, 100);
scroller.onEnterFrame = function() {
  scrollValue = scroller.getScrollPosition();
};
```

setScrollProperties takes three arguments:

```
setScrollProperties(pageSize, min, max)
```

Here, min and max are the minimum and maximum scrolled positions, and pageSize is the amount of the page you would see at any one time. Giving min and max values of 0 and 100 gives us a scale of 0 to 100, or a percentage.

Although we are not scrolling through a text field page, `pageSize` still tells the scroller the maximum size of the page we would see at a time, in this case, 99:

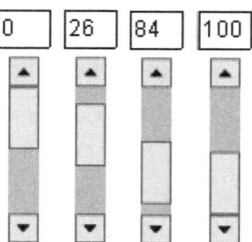

Although we are not scrolling through a text field page, `pageSize` still tells the scroller the maximum size of the page we would see at a time, in this case 99. By setting it to something smaller, you will get a smaller scrollbar handle. For example, this has a `pageSize` value of 10:

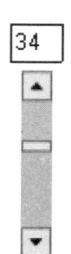

Because the size of the handle tells us the area we are viewing in relation to the whole document, a value of 100 might be expected to disable the scrollbar (because you can see the whole scrollable area), but doesn't (so we can actually set it to 100 in the script above if we wish). To disable the scrollbar, you have to disable the scrollbar explicitly via ActionScript.

You can make the scrollbar disabled (grayed out) with the following action:

```
scroller.setEnabled(false);
```

...and re-enable it with:

```
scroller.setEnabled(true);
```

This is actually better than the scrollbar disabling itself, because you have more options for re-purposing it (as we have done here in making it a slider).

Components that associate via linkage

Drag and drop is great for the web designer's workflow, but there are times when you want some other kind of component-target association. Like, for example, when the element you will be working with is either general or not even on stage during author time; rather, it might load in at run-time on the Web.

The scroll pane

The scroll pane is related to the scrollbar in that it is a scroll function, but it consists of two bars. In fact, the scroll pane is pretty much the same deal as the scrollbar except that it works with movie clips rather than text fields. This means that you can use the scroll pane with *anything*; you just have to embed your 'anything' into a movie clip first (if it is not already a movie clip). You can use bitmaps of large maps, animated content, video – whatever you want, really. A big plus is that you can load content into a movie clip at run-time dynamically or on demand as a load level, allowing you to stream all sorts of content into a scroll pane. You don't have to know the size of this content; the scroll pane will take care of that – it's the perfect view window!

Using the scroll pane

Let's examine how to use the scroll pane with a simple example.

1. Create a static text field with the letter 'a' in it. Using free transform, scale the text up so that it is huge - as big as the one shown here in relation to the whole stage area:

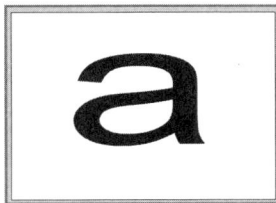

2. Break apart the text (CONTROL+B) and then hit F8 to make it a symbol. In the Convert to Symbol window, give the movie clip the name myClip. Check Export For ActionScript (whereupon Export in first frame will also become checked – you should generally keep this checked, otherwise your ActionScript may try to refer to an instance that has not yet loaded in, and your script will fail silently). Give the clip the identifier myClipID:

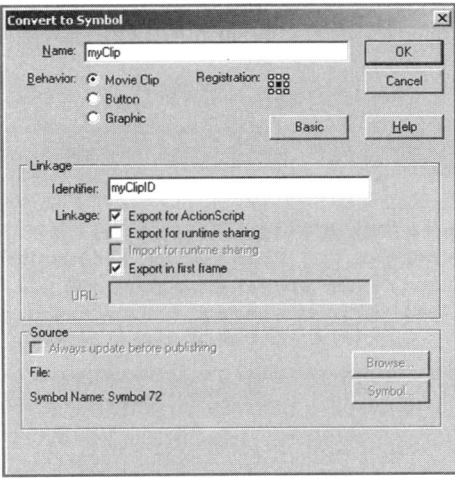

> *When you are loading content for ActionScript to place it on stage dynamically, you generally don't know which frame you want the content loaded by. If Flash doesn't see the content (movie clip, component) downloaded and in the library by the time the ActionScript is looking to place it on the stage, nothing will happen, because the content hasn't downloaded yet. If you load the content in frame 1 you know it will be there when ActionScript starts to look for it because it is available at the earliest conceivable time that a script can run. If you don't check* Export in first frame, *then the content will never be loaded in (because Flash assumes you never need it, given that it sees no instances of it placed on stage at SWF compilation time); unless, that is, you place at least one instance on the stage manually at authoring time (and if you do this, you can choose a particular frame other than frame 1). However, you do have to be certain that the ActionScript will not attempt to use* duplicateMovieClip *or* attachMovie *before everything's ready.*

3. The Identifier tells the scroll pane what its content is, and it will link to our movie in the library – so you can delete the version on the stage now.

4. Now drag a scroll pane instance onto the stage. In the Parameters tab of the Property inspector, make the Scroll Content equal to myClipID, and leave the other parameters at their default:

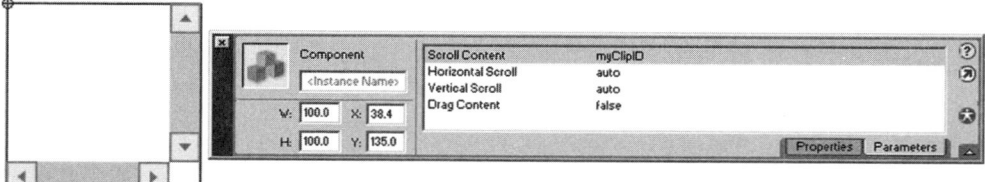

You can play about with the other parameters once you have got it working. The two scroll values are currently auto, meaning that the scrollbars only appear if the graphic is bigger than the available panel size. You can also make them true (*always* have scrollbar) or false (*never* have scrollbar). The Drag Content property allows you to drag the content by click-dragging on the actual pane as well as the scrollbars. Don't choose this option if the content has embedded buttons.

5. For the moment, let's test our basic scroll pane. When you test your movie (CONTROL+ENTER) you should see something like this:

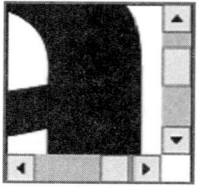

It's amazing how close you are to creating fully functional scrolling, resizable panels to load SWFs or movie clips into by using the scroll pane – allowing you to make up an interface designed around floating windows. This is something that was a real head-scratcher in Flash 5, but not now!

6. Have a look in the code download package for this chapter's bonus goodies – the files `0764_06_scrollPaneF5Style.fla` and `0764_06_scrollPaneFMXStyle.fla`, which demonstrate how to implement floating panels.

This effect forms a good example of the difference between Flash 5 and Flash MX scripting. We have actually created two files to show how you can define hard-to-locate little scripts distributed across/inside embedded movie clips (as was de rigueur in Flash 5), or how you can define everything in frame 1 of the highest-level movie clip (the new, easier to maintain and read Flash MX way).

For the Flash MX style scripting, each window instance has only one script definition inside itself, even though there are two clips to attach events to. I have coded it so that the events actually are attached to the target movie clips in both FLAs, but in the Flash MX version, the code is all in one place.

In a typical complex FLA, you may have several embedded clips to attach scripts to, which can be a nightmare to read and understand unless you actually read them in the order the original scripter wrote them!

Resize the windows by dragging the bottom right corner, and move the windows with the top drag bar. Of special note when you come to pore over the FLA is the way we have used the scroll pane's `setSize` method. This is the only way you can scale a scroll pane without distorting or magnifying the content it is showing (as would happen if you used `_height` and `_width`).

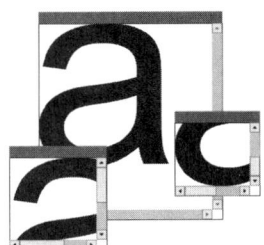

Don't forget you that you can also add titles to the windows – just give each main window an instance name that describes its content, and display the `_name` property of the main window clip in a dynamic text field over the title bar. You can of course change the `_name` every time new content is loaded in the window, because nothing external to a window needs to know anything about it; all references to each window are from inside the window itself and work via the anonymous `_parent` path.

Components that require event handlers

Some of the components require a script from you before they become useful. Those of you with more of a pure design focus (as opposed to scripting) might be thinking 'Well, that's just useless, why didn't Macromedia write the scripts as well?'

In fact, most UI devices (such as buttons) are actually designed to *'detect something'* rather then *'do something'*. You need a script to implement the actual *'do something'* part, because buttons are just inputs to a wider processing scheme.

In the following sections we'll look at the remainder of the default components that ship with Flash MX. These are:

- Checkbox
- Push button
- Radio button
- List box
- Combo box

With these components you'll need to write a script to utilize their associated functions, and this script is not actually a part of the component functionality. This is why Macromedia can't write it for you – *it's specific to your application.*

> *Think of all these components as normal Flash 5 buttons, with lots of extra features. Just like a Flash 5 button, you have to add a script to actually make something happen when the button is pressed.*

The checkbox

A button in the context of Flash is a bit like a doorbell – it changes state for as long as it is pressed, but if you release it, the button reverts to 'off'. A checkbox is a more advanced button in that it toggles, rather like a bathroom light switch. Pull the cord once and let go, and it's 'on'. It stays on until you pull it again, and then it is 'off'. The checkbox is generally used to make a *selection*, or to *enable* or *disable* something.

The basic checkbox

1. Like we've done previously, open a new FLA and create two layers as shown here:

2. Drag an instance of the checkbox onto the stage in the graphics layer. You will see the following:

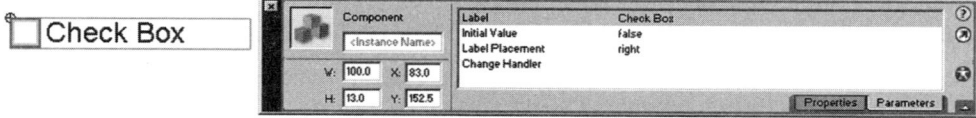

The Label is the text message you want to be written next to the checkbox. The Initial Value can be either true (checked) or false (un-checked). The Label Placement can be either left (text label on the left side of the checkbox) or right. The Change Handler is a function you can define (it is optional) that will run when the state of the checkbox changes. Think of it as the same as the standard Flash 5 onPress event handler.

> If you have followed the advice given in earlier chapters to use the remote scripting style of coding that Flash MX prefers, instead of the Flash 5 way of attaching event scripts directly to the button/movie clip, you will be at home with the use of functions to define event handlers. This is one reason why we pushed this method earlier (apart from greater readability of code). Many of the major new features of Flash MX require it, and you won't be able to use them if you don't have an understanding of how to do things in the new way.

3.   Name the instance myCheck1.

If you need to know the value of the checkbox at any point, you could use the following code:

```
myVariable = myCheckBoxInstance.getValue();
```

So for our checkbox, you would read the current value (true or false) with:

```
checkState = myCheck1.getValue();
```

This could be put in a loop on the same timeline as the checkbox. That's the simple and easy way, but you can also use the **change handler** to do stuff whenever the checkbox is changed by the user.

Using change handlers

The use of change handlers is the same for all components, so we'll spend some time on it with the checkbox as a typical example.

> What are change handlers? This is the Macromedia term for the standard programming term **event handlers**. In the construction of your code you start with the event (onPress, onLoad, etc.). The code that runs in response to the event is the **change handler**. You can use the change handler to define a function that you want to run every time the checkbox value changes.

Using a change handler is recommended when the checkboxes are being used to change something that is happening *now*; for example, if the checkbox is being used to toggle sound on or off.

If the checkbox is being used to make a selection (such as 'I want the car to have a sunroof'), you don't necessarily need to know this until the customer submits their order, and can use the simpler way we showed earlier using the checkState variable (which is called **polling**). (The checkState way of doing things is less efficient than the event-driven method of change handlers, because it revolves around the use of a loop constantly looking for changes in value.)

Even in a form-filling situation though, you might want a change handler for building in intelligence for logical forms or real-time validation. If a customer buying an auto asks for a sunroof, you may for example want to disable the 'I want a soft top model' option when 'sunroof' is checked. This can easily be done with change handlers.

In our next example we'll create a general event handler that sets a variable to the current state of the checkbox, and works for as many checkboxes as you have, so if you're stuck for a script to get these babies running, this should be the only one you need...

Applying change handlers to checkboxes

Use the FLA we've created for the basic checkbox example as our starting point in this next exercise.

1. Enter checkBox as the Change Handler, and attach the following script to frame 1 of the actions layer:

```
function checkBox(component) {
  _root[component._name+"value"] = component.getValue();
}
```

The component value indicates which component called the function. The component.getValue() therefore gives us the current value of myCheck1.getValue() if this function is invoked by our checkbox. The line _root[component._name+"value"] will assign the state of our checkbox instance to variable _root.myCheck1value. You can see this value by adding a dynamic text field next to our checkbox, and giving it the variable name myCheck1value:

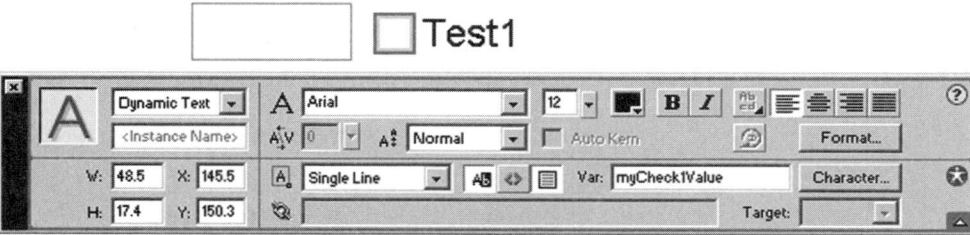

2. If you run this FLA you will see the value of myCheck1Value toggle between true and false for the two checkbox states, and it will do so as soon as we click on it:

The function above is just the bare bones. We would usually use the component name and its current state to do other stuff within the same function:

```
function checkBox(component) {
  if(_root[component._name] == "myCheck1"){
  // do this stuff
  }elseif (_root[component._name] == "myCheck2"){
    // do this stuff
  // etc...
}
```

You might have noticed that the value is not shown in the text field if you haven't clicked in the checkbox at all. To set checkBox1value equal to the initial state of the checkbox, you need to *initialize* it. The best way to do this is to use getValue() again:

```
// Initialize components...
myCheck1Value = myCheck1.getValue();
myCheck2Value = myCheck2.getValue();
// etc...
// component handlers...
function checkBox(component) {
  if(_root[component._name] == "myCheck1"){
  // do this stuff
  }elseif (_root[component._name] == "myCheck2"){
    // do this stuff
  // etc...
}
```

You can also have a separate 'on change' function for each checkbox:

```
function myCheck1Handler(component) {
  // Code you want to run when myCheck1 changes
}
function myCheck2Handler(component) {
  // Code you want to run when myCheck2 changes
}
```

This may be preferable because it is faster (there is no big if... logic involved).

Let's see how this theory works in practice with another quick example.

Have a look at soundCheck.fla. This shows how we can use the checkbox with a change handler to allow the user to select whether they want the site to have sound or not. We have a checkbox labeled Sound on the stage. Its change handler (in the Property inspector) is soundCheck. You can see soundCheck defined in the actions layer:

```
function soundCheck(component) {
  state = component.getValue();
  if (state) {
    loop.start(0, 999);
  } else {
    loop.stop();
  }
}
```

If the value of the calling component is true, then we start playing the sound loop, otherwise the checkbox value must be false, and we stop the sound loop. There are a few things to notice:

- It is critical that you begin with the correct checkbox value. We have set it to true (checkbox checked) via its Initial Value (as listed in the Property inspector) and started the sound object loop playing on start-up.

- The function soundCheck will run every time we click on the checkbox (on change). This is an efficient event-driven system; the change handler (the soundCheck function) only runs when it is needed.

- Although the function soundCheck has a component argument defined as the instance name of the calling checkbox, the FLA still works if the checkbox is not given an instance name. This is because Flash will give any instances you don't name a 'default' instance name (instance1, instance2, etc.). You can see this if you debug the FLA: the checkbox is given a name instance1.

The push button

The push button is just like a normal Flash 5 button. So why use it? We already know how to make buttons! Well, suppose you wanted to customize your components by changing the 'skins' folders or using ActionScript to set a particular component style (we'll look at this in Chapter 14). In this scenario *all* components would be affected by your changes automatically. If you use just components, all the UI elements can be tweaked globally just by changing a couple of minor things.

For example, if you wanted everything to be aquamarine in color, then you'd just need to set a few things up, and all UI components across your FLA will change to that color automatically. If you instead use components for 'the bits that are hard to do' and add your own buttons because you're familiar with them anyway, you are missing out on the global style changes you could have made.

Using just components for your UI effectively gives you a style sheet that the site will conform to automatically, and this can be really powerful. It means that you can create a standard template using components and then add skins and a global style to customize it per customer. Although the default components are a bit plain looking, there are many ways to make them look cool, so don't be afraid of using them in high end designs – you'll find they will go as far as you can push them! We'll look at this feature in detail in Chapter 14.

A button component only has two properties:

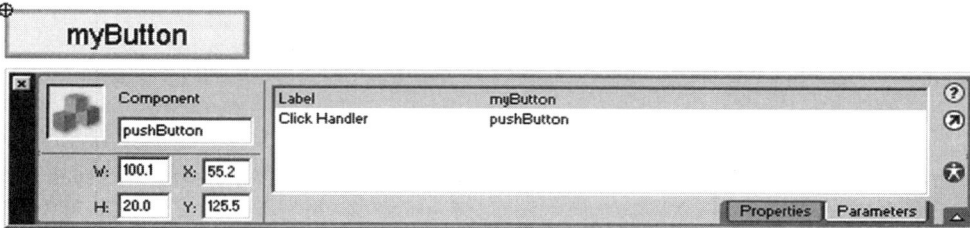

The Label is the text that will appear over it. You can of course leave this blank for no text. The Click Handler is the same deal as last time – it's the function that you want to execute as your event handler. The following code will set a variable push to true if the button above is pressed:

```
push = false;
function pushButton(component) {
  push = true;
}
```

Note that because the button state is fleeting (it exists only for the frame you click on the button), you always need a Click Handler. The checkbox we looked at earlier doesn't need a change handler because you don't always want to do things on the change event.

Normally though, you wouldn't want to set a variable in this way. A more common scenario would be adding a script that performs the button functionality, such as navigating to somewhere else on the timeline, opening a URL, or stopping the video. As we said before, just like a Flash 5 button!

As an example of how you could use the push button to navigate, the following code would send you to a frame labeled home:

```
stop();
function pushButton(component) {
  gotoAndPlay("home");
}
```

The radio button

The radio button allows you to make one choice from a set of available choices. You can see radio buttons at work in the Symbol Properties window. You can make your symbol *either* a movie clip, button or graphic, but not a combination of the three options:

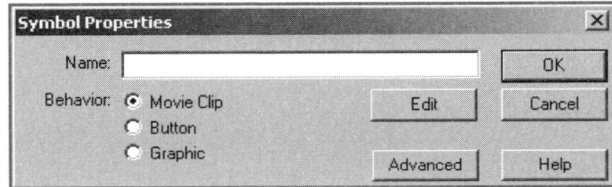

Setting up a radio button differs from normal push buttons because they are *grouped* such that you can only select one radio button from the group at any time. For example, the group above might well be called *behavior*.

Creating a radio button based animation

The completed FLA for this example is saved as radioControl.fla.

We will set up two radio button groups that control the appearance of a simple animation. One group, *color*, will set the color of the animated element, and another, *speed*, will set the speed of the animation.

1. In a new FLA, create three layers, actions (top layer), controls and animation. In layer controls we will add our controlling radio buttons. Add three buttons as shown here:

   ○ Radio Button
   ○ Radio Button
   ○ Radio Button

2. Give the top one:

   - An instance name of red

   - A Label of red

   - An Initial State of true

   - A Group Name of colorGroup

   - Data of 0xFF0000 (hexadecimal for red)

   - A Label Placement of right

■ A Change Handler of `colorHandler`

> *You have to scroll down the Property inspector display to see the* Change Handler *if you have the panel undocked.*

3. For the green and blue radio buttons, give them the same parameters as the red button, except:

   ■ Give them no instance names

   ■ Give them a Label of green and blue respectively

   ■ Give them both an Initial State of `false`

   ■ Give them Data of `0x00FF00` (hex for green) and `0x0000FF` (hex for blue)

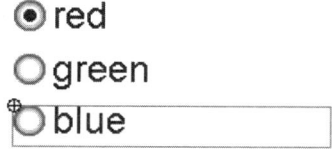 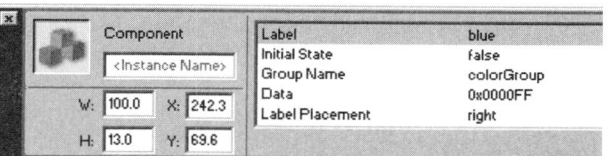

4. Still in layer controls, add a second group of three radio buttons as follows:

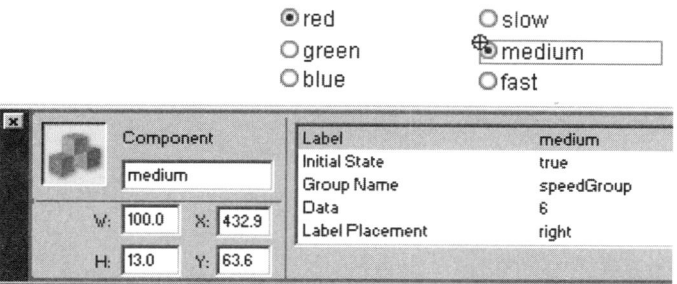

Give the middle one:

   ■ An instance name `medium`

   ■ A Label `medium`

   ■ An Initial State of `true`

- A Group Name of `speedGroup`

- A Data value of `6`.

- A Label Placement of `right`

- A Change Handler of `speedHandler`

For the top and bottom ones, give them the same as the middle, except:

- Give them no instance names

- Give them Label fields of `slow` and `fast`

- Give them Initial State values of `false`

- Given them a Data value of `2` and `12`

To recap, so far we have added two radio button groups: `colorGroup` and `speedGroup`. Only one radio button of each group can be selected at any time, and you can prove this by testing the FLA. The radio buttons won't do anything (we haven't defined the change handlers yet) but you will find that you can only ever select one color and one speed.

5. In layer animation, draw out a small square somewhere below the radio buttons (its color is irrelevant because we will change it dynamically later), convert the square to a movie clip and give it an instance name `square`:

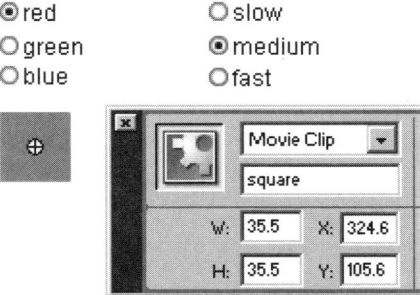

6. OK. You probably know where we have to go next: into the actions layer. Add the following script:

```
// define change handlers...
function colorHandler(component) {
  col = Number(component.getData());
}
function speedHandler(component) {
  speed = component.getData();
}
```

This defines our two change handlers:

- colorHandler equates a variable col to the Data value of the currently selected radio button instance component in group colorGroup. Well, it *actually* looks at the last radio button to have *changed*, but as that will be the one currently selected, it's the same thing. Because the data will be interpreted as a string (it has an 'x' in it), we have to use Number() for Flash to realize it will actually convert to a base 10 number (if we simply entered the numbers as base 10 instead of hex to start off with we wouldn't have to do this, but almost all web designers who dream in color express those colors in hex).

- speedHandler does the same thing for the group speedGroup, and the variable speed.

7. Below the script so far, add our animation scripts:

```
squareCol = new Color(square);
// define animation event...
square.onEnterFrame = function() {
  this._x += _root.speed;
  if (this._x>400) {
    this._x = 50;
  }
  _root.squareCol.setRGB(_root.col);
};
```

We have defined a color object squareCol to color the square, and then added a simple onenterFrame script to:

- Move the square from left to right at speed speed

- Color the square with color col

8. If you run this FLA you will notice that the color is zero and the square doesn't move *unless* you select one radio button from each group.

> *This is an important feature of change handlers; they won't run until they see a change! This means that nothing is initialized until you press something and cause a change.*

To fix this, we will initialize the FLA before we do anything else. Add the bold lines below to the existing script to do this:

```
// Initialize starting values...
col = red.getValue();
speed = medium.getValue();
square._x = 50;
//
// define change handlers...
function colorHandler(component) {
  col = Number(component.getData());
}
function speedHandler(component) {
  speed = component.getData();
}
squareCol = new Color(square);
// define animation event...
square.onEnterFrame = function() {
  this._x += _root.speed;
  if (this._x>400) {
    this._x = 50;
  }
  _root.squareCol.setRGB(_root.col);
};
```

You can now see why we gave only the red *and* medium *radio buttons instance names. They are the only ones we ever need to refer to directly. The others are named (or referred to) via the general change handler argument* component.

As a final point, in this example we explicitly set one of the radio buttons in each group to true. Sometimes you want to make 'select none' a valid option. There are two ways to do this:

- Make all the Initial States false. This means that at start up, none of the radio buttons are selected, but if the user selects a radio button in error, they can never unselect.

- Make one of the radio buttons correspond to a 'none' option, and make it the initially selected one. This is preferred because the user can change their mind to 'no selection'.

The list box

The list box allows you to select an item from a scrollable list. You don't *need* to have an event handler defined but, as with the checkbox, it can sometimes be useful if you want it to react intelligently to user selections by updating the list box (or related UI elements) dynamically.

> *JavaScript form builders tend to have a big* Submit *button at the end of their forms, because creating intelligent forms that update themselves interactively is such a pain. With ActionScript, Flash components (and a true graphic environment in which to develop our page layout and functionality) allow for a much easier life. So you don't have to just emulate 'standard' forms in Flash – you can make them far superior.*

How the list box works

1. Let's look at how to work with a list box. Again, create the actions and graphics layers as we've done in previous examples and drag an instance of the list box onto the graphics layer:

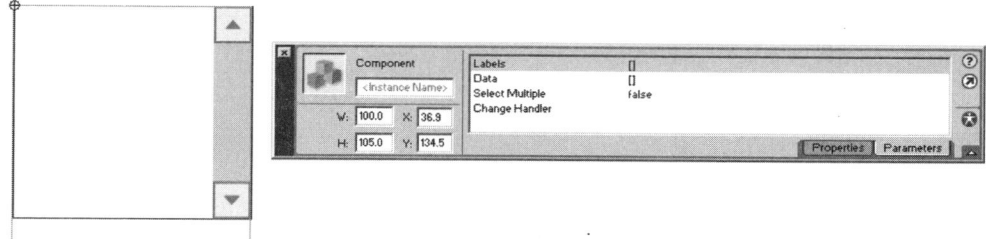

    There are surprisingly few things that you have to set for the list box...

2. The Labels field is where you define the text you want to appear in the list box. If you click on it, you will see a little magnifying glass icon appear.

3. Click again (either on the icon or anywhere on the labels field) and the Values window appears:

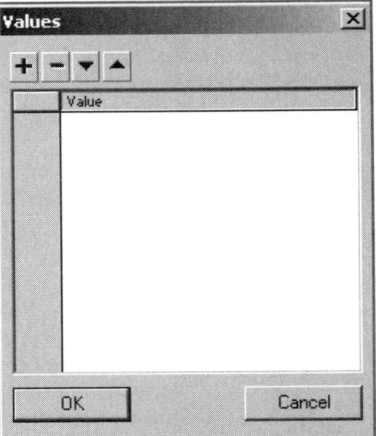

To add a label, simply hit the + button and add the text string that you want to show up in the list box. The entry will start off as defaultValue. Click on it to change the text, and press the + button again to add more. You can delete a text field you no longer want with the - key, and change the ordering with the UP and DOWN arrow keys:

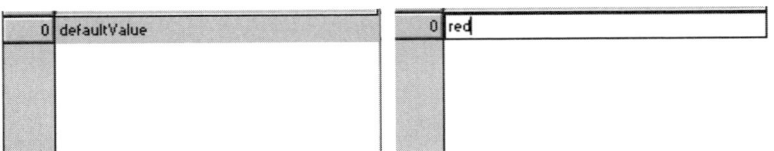

4. Add the colors shown below left for our example, and then test the FLA. You will see the list box appear as per the picture below:

5. Name your instance myList and enter listHandler as the Change Handler. Add the following function to the actions layer and see what the list box does:

```
function listHandler(component){
  trace(component.getValue());
}
```

As you press each color, the function will return the string value:

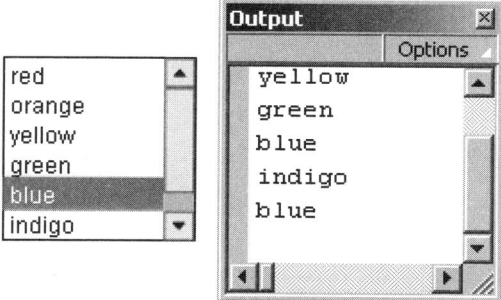

What if you didn't want to return the strings, but actually wanted to return a number 1-7, corresponding to the position of the color in the list? The list box will return the string value by default, but you can override this by adding values in the Data field of the list box.

6. In the same way as we added values in the Labels field, add the numbers 1 to 7 in the Data field:

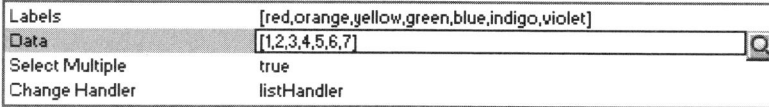

As expected, you now get the number values corresponding to each list item.

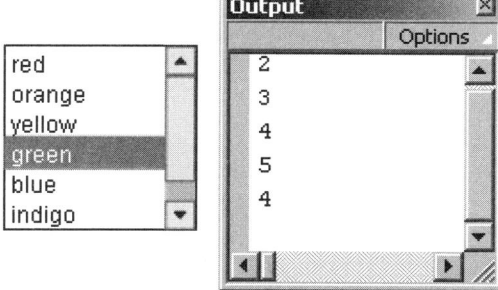

If you don't want to use an event handler, you can simply retrieve the current selection with `instanceName.getValue()`, but be prepared to get an undefined value if no selection has been made.

> *You would use this if you were sure the choices have been made. For example, if you used a* Submit *button, you know that the user has entered all their choices when they hit* Submit. *You can just read the values with* getValue() *after the button has been pressed (using the* Submit *buttons* onRelease*), and don't have to use separate* onchange *handlers for each component. Most JavaScript forms actually use a submit, so using it in this fashion is actually very common.*

You can allow the user to make multiple selections by making the Select Multiple field true. If you do this, the user is allowed to make multiple selections if they hold down CONTROL or SHIFT and then click. If you choose to do this, it is strongly recommended that you use a change handler, because a single getValue will only return one value.

The combo box

We should be getting good at this by now, and this is the last of the default components that we'll cover. In fact, it's actually one of the most useful because it can contain many user options in a very small area of screen real estate. It takes up much less room than the list box, although it doesn't directly allow you to make multiple selections as the list box does. The combo box is also useful for a quick navigation bar, and many old HTML sites used to have them.

Making a combo box

1. OK, let's get down to it - the usual two layers deal: actions and graphics. Drag an instance of the combo box onto the stage and add values so that your Property inspector looks like ours:

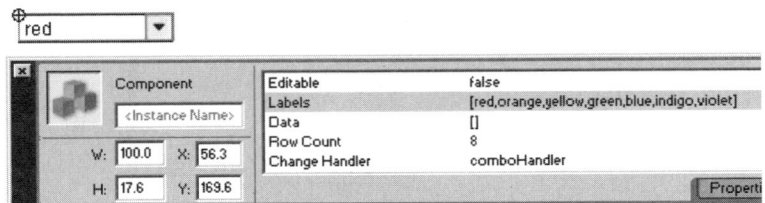

2. Add the following script in layer actions:

```
function comboHandler(component) {
  trace(component.getValue());
}
```

When you test the FLA, the first thing you will see is the picture on the left. When you have made a selection, the list box will look like the picture below right:

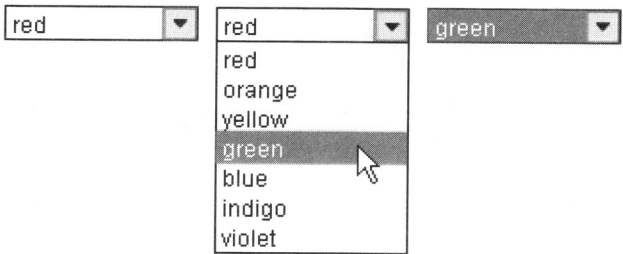

You can also make the combo box *editable*, which allows the user to enter text in the field. But be careful if you choose this method because incorrect strings (that is, strings not listed in the dropdown) can be entered, so you need to add some error checking before accepting inputs from an editable field.

> *A subtle problem with our combo box so far is that the user will get 'red' if they make no selection, making it the default. This is fine for some, but you don't want a default on a few types of form, because then you might get loads of returned red cars from customers who yell down the phone "I never asked for a red car!". The best way out is to make the first item in the list <color>, and make sure that the form validation script rejects any form containing strings that have a <> around them, and possibly also put some highlighting around any detected during form filling.*

The Row count specifies the maximum length of the dropdown. If you make it 4 for our color dropdown, you will now see a scrollbar as shown here, allowing you to see up to four items at a time:

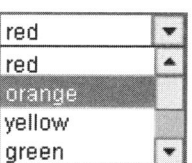

If the dropdown won't fit in the current window, the combo box is actually clever enough to make it 'dropup' as shown here, so there are very few occasions that you would want to limit the number of rows, unless you have a very large list.

It is also worth noting that you should avoid using the getValue() method outside a change handler, unless you are absolutely sure that the user has finished his input (for example, you can use the getValue() if you are doing it as soon as the user presses a Submit button). If the user has the drop-down open, the combo box will return the item currently under the cursor, and this may not be the same thing as the currently selected item in the combo box. This means that you should not use the combo box to alter something that is happening *now* (the list box or scrollbar value slider ·may be more appropriate).

Creating custom Flash MX components for Flash 5 users

So far we've concentrated on the default components that come with Macromedia Flash MX, and we've learned that they can be pretty powerful tools. However, there are a few people who bought into smart clips during Flash 5 and built up libraries of them. Those of you who have done this are potentially getting a little anxious about having to convert them all to components. Don't worry though, because MX will actually recognize smart clips as components. If you open a Flash 5 FLA containing smart clips they will show up as Flash MX components, as shown here:

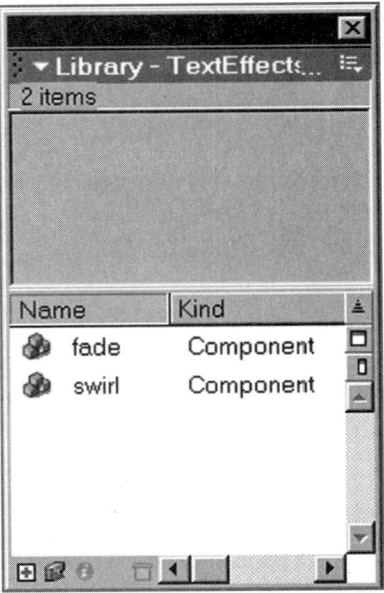

Although the old Flash 5 smart clip icon has now been changed to the Flash MX component icon, they will work just like smart clips in Flash MX except that if you double-click on an instance on the stage, you won't be able to edit it.

You can also make your old smart clip libraries part of the Components panel itself. This is an easy way to start off creating your own custom components, so we will explore it, and hopefully demystify components along the way. You might even be eager to create your own when we get to look at advanced components in Chapter 14.

Creating the Flash 5 file

The Flash component definition is just a normal FLA with the following characteristics:

- The name of the FLA is the name that appears on the Component Panel Group title.

- The individual components are all items in the library of the FLA that you have marked as 'to be included' in the Components panel.

The first thing is to create an FLA that includes all your smart clips that you want to use. Because these will be grouped under one heading in the Components panel, you should place related smart clips together in your FLA:

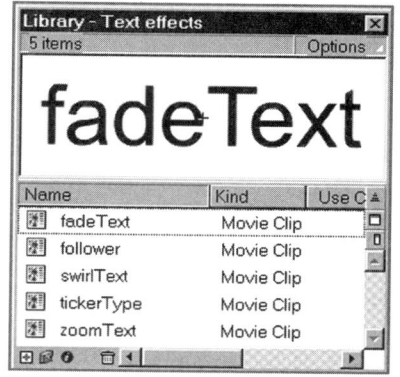

Save this FLA as a Flash 5 file and name it with the text that you want the group to be known as. I have called my FLA Text effects.fla.

Installing the components

Now open the FLA in Flash MX. This time all the smart clips will be shown as components in the library as before, but they are not yet seen as components that are marked for display in the Components panel.

For each component you want to show up in the Components panel (you don't have to select them all), change the name of the library version to the name you want to appear in the Components panel. Next, right-click on the component and on the drop-down menu select Component Definition.... You will see a window appear reminiscent of the old Flash 5 Define Clip Parameters window, but this time round it's called Component Definition. There are a few new features, but for now we will just look at enough to get your new components displayed as per the default UI components that we played with earlier.

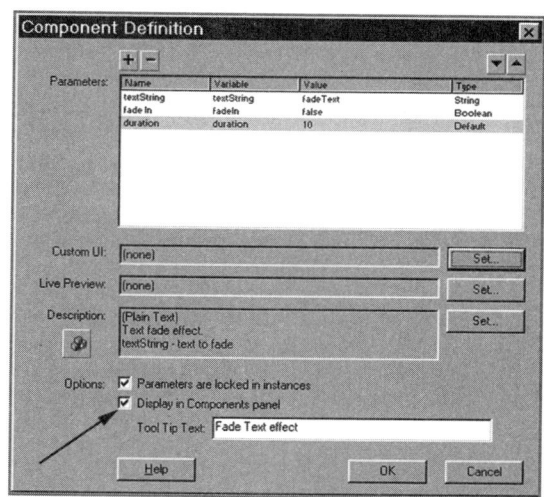

The Display in Components panel checkbox *must be* ticked if you want the component to display in the Components panel.

> *Those of you who have already used smart clips (which is probably everyone) will recognize the* Parameters *dialog as the old Flash 5 way of adding parameters to a movie clip, thus changing it into a smart clip. If you have no smart clips handy for this exercise, simply create a few Flash MX movie clips and add parameters as you would in Flash 5. When you have made your changes, the movie clip will appear as a component. Save the FLA as a name that you want to show up in the* Components *panel, then carry on following the text from this point down and you will end up with components created entirely in Flash MX.*

You can select the icon that the component will show up as in the Components panel and the Property inspector from a drop-down that will appear if you click on the icon to the left of the Description field.

Finally, set the Tool Tip Text to whatever tool tip text you want to appear when the user moves their mouse over the component, then hit OK to close the window.

It's worth noting that Macromedia have set a few other defaults for their standard components, so it would seem a good idea to do the same for ours. Right-click again on the component and select Linkage... In the Linkage Properties window, check Export for ActionScript. The Identifier will populate with the library name of the component, and the Export in first frame checkbox will become selectable and checked. Leave the options in this state and hit OK to close the window:

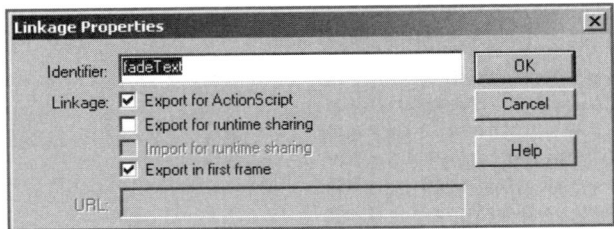

Repeat this process for all components that you want to appear in the Components panel.

Save your FLA and close down Flash at this point – we're almost done – the final thing to do is save the FLA in the folder where Flash looks for installed components every time it runs.

Within your Flash installation directory, look for the \Configuration folder. You should see a Configuration_ReadMe.htm README file. Open it up – this will refer you to a location of the Flash configuration folder for your particular system and operating system. For example, for my Windows 2000 machine, this location is:

```
C:\Documents and Settings\<user name>\Application Data\Macromedia\Flash MX
```

In the \Components folder of this location, you will find a FLA called Flash UI Components.fla. This is where the Flash default components are defined. The component set gets its name from the name of this FLA, and each separate component is simply a library symbol in this FLA that has been marked for display in the components panel.

To install your new components FLA, this is the location you need to copy it to. When you do this, you will see a new component set available in the Components panel the next time you run Flash (depending on what you called the component set, it may not appear straight away, in which case hit the little down arrow to the right of the component set title):

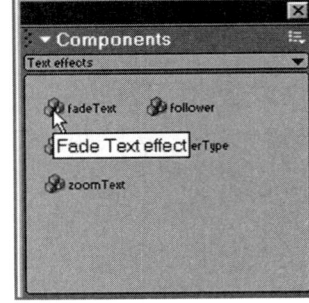

Notice that:

■ The title of our FLA, `Text effects.fla`, is reflected in the component group title

■ The title of each component is taken from the library name of the corresponding component in the library of `Text effects.fla`

■ For those components where you haven't defined the tool tip text, the tool tip still appears, but with the library name of the component

> Now that you know where the default components that ship with Flash are, 'sticky fingers' may well get in there and break them (not yours of course...), but Macromedia have allowed for this. Flash will look for the `Flash UI Components.fla` when it is run. If it can't find it, Flash is clever enough to re-install a new copy of the default file. It's perhaps better to copy the default file (or any subsequent third party component FLA that you may install later) to a new location if you want to open them and play.

Summary

We started this chapter with a look back to the smart clips of Macromedia Flash 5, and how their shortcomings have been addressed by the new component functionality offered by Flash MX. After introducing this new component environment, we jumped right into the deep end and learned how to use each of the new default components:

■ Scrollbar

■ Scroll panel

■ Checkbox

■ Push button

■ Radio button

■ List box

■ Combo box

You may have thought that the component set included by Macromedia was a little thin, but as you are probably already starting to realize, the choices are actually well thought out. You have all the common UI devices already there, and you can use them to create other UI features such as value sliders. Furthermore, you can add to the components' functions by using them with other stuff, adding a few scripts to tie it all together and repurpose the component, as we did with the scroll pane to create a floating resizable window.

This is only the start, of course, because you now have an introduction to creating your own components. Bring across all the old ones you used with Flash 5 and get ready to rework them so that they are all drag and drop wonders of UI engineering!

In the next chapter we're going to turn our attention to the publishing side of Flash design. Clearly, your finished sites will usually be accessed via a browser, so it is very important to become familiar with the browser control in order to present your SWFs exactly as you wish.

Chapter 10

Browser Control: Flash and the User

Almost all your SWFs will be viewed within the browser environment, so it's important that you make sure that the browser shows your presentation in exactly the way you expect.

In Flash 5, we had no real integrated way to do this, and instead had to rely almost totally on the underlying HTML that our SWF was embedded in, or use JavaScript functions to help us force our will on the browser.

We still have to do this to a certain extent, but Macromedia Flash MX does give us a number of features that allow us to do a few things from the ActionScript environment directly. MX now understands the Back button completely, which should keep our friend Jakob Nielsen happy, and also allows technologies that make the Web accessible to the visually impaired to read SWF content.

There are also some cool lower-level features that allow you to specify what happens when the browser window changes size. You can now also interrogate the browser to get it to tell you what it knows about the machine you are running on, important stuff that allows you to modify your content based on the browser configuration the user is viewing your site with.

Finally, you now have a cool new way to save information on the user's machine in the same way other web technologies already do. With *local shared objects* we now have the equivalent functionality of cookies, baked to a fresh new Macromedia recipe... you won't be able to resist taking a bite!

You and your user

The things that the browser can and can't do depend partly on the user's machine. The new system capabilities object lets you ascertain the configuration of the host system, where previously you had to use external calls to JavaScript to find out.

The system capabilities object itself is a little hard to find in the Actions panel since the objects and properties appear in two different places!

The object itself is in Objects>Movie>System>Capabilities, while the properties are in Objects>Movie>Capabilities>Properties:

The properties you can retrieve are shown below:

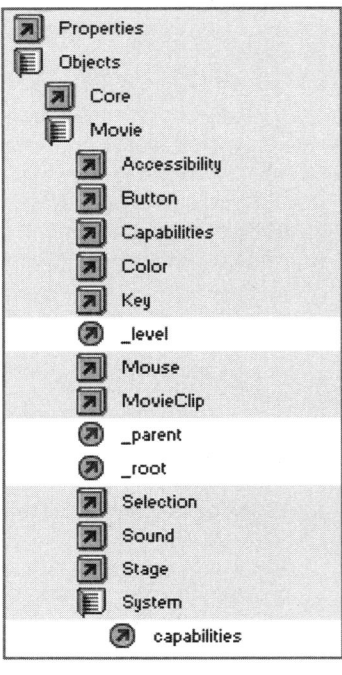

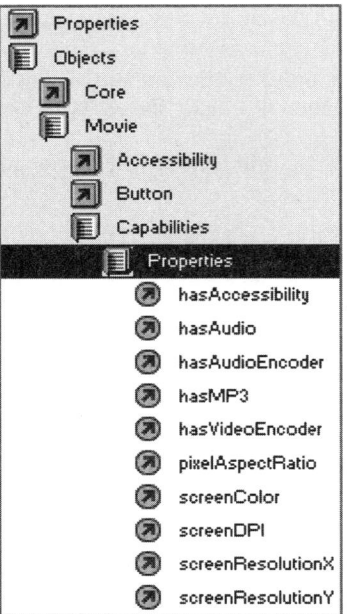

System capabilities are actually very easy to use, since they consist of a list of read-only properties. The following code will print out the screen resolution, and tell me whether my system has audio capability:

```
trace(System.capabilities.screenResolutionX);
trace(System.capabilities.screenResolutionY);
trace(System.capabilities.hasAudio);
```

For my system, this results in this output window when I test the FLA:

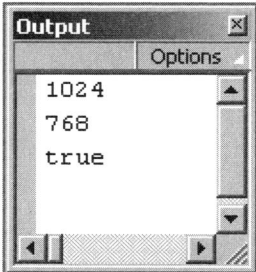

This tells me that my machine has a resolution of 1024x768, and that it has a sound card.

When looking at the system capabilities of the user's machine, you can deduce what type of machine the user is viewing your SWF on. A non-color screen resolution below 600x400 is probably not a desktop machine for example, and may be a PDA or wireless Internet device. Any computer that has a screen resolution of less than about 72dpi is probably not a traditional monitor-based machine, and any with a dpi much higher than this, (and with a large screen area), is probably a fast designer's machine. This object holds many clues to allow you visualize your user's environment. We will explore this concept a little further when we look at accessibility.

The Flash stage and browser window

In the Flash authoring environment, you are the ruler of all you survey. When you test or otherwise view the Flash SWF, you can control the way the stage is shown, how big your browser window is, and whether or not you resize the browser half way through the presentation. Out in the wild, anything goes, so it is a good idea to at least know what the audience has done to your stage.

The Stage object allows you to view the size of the stage in 'real pixels' (the size of the browser window in true pixels) or the Flash stage size (the internal Flash coordinate size, which is the same as 'real pixels' only when the SWF is viewed at 100% magnification). There are a number of features of the Stage object you can play with.

Using the stage object

1. This example is called stagesize.fla. Create two layers, actions and graphics. In the graphics layer, add two dynamic text fields with variables swfHeight and swfWidth:

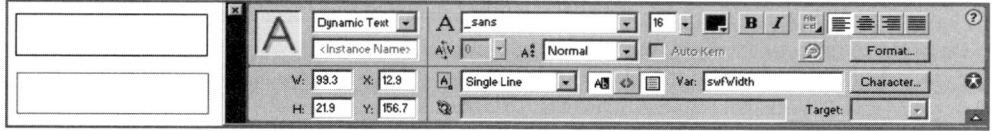

2. Now add the following script to frame 1 of layer actions:

```
_root.onEnterFrame = function(){
  swfHeight = Stage.height;
  swfWidth = Stage.width;
}
```

3. Go into File>Publish Settings>HTML and set the Scale to No scale, and the Dimensions to Percent (the next part will not work unless you do this). Now publish the FLA and open the HTML file created. You will see the text fields alter to reflect the current stage size within the browser (change the size of the window and see!):

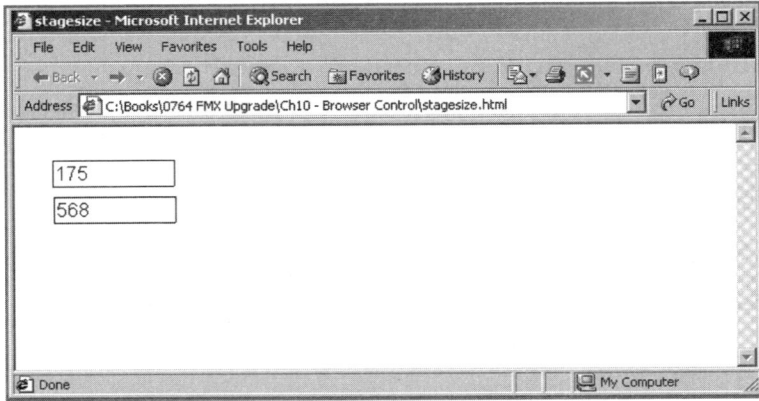

Since you must set the scale to No scale (although you now know the actual browser window size in pixels), Flash no longer auto-scales the SWF. To have any sort of scaling, you now have to do it yourself. Think of no scale as meaning that auto-scale via the Flash player has been disabled; we can take over that task now if we wish, and do it in a way that does more justice to our content.

There is a better way to implement this last FLA, but this involves the use of listeners. We will discuss the code to add a listener later in the book (Chapter 13), but here's a sneak preview of some listener code:

```
function stageResize() {
  trace("detected");
  // or add your own code here...
}
// Add listener for the Stage.onResize event…
myListener = new Object();
myListener.onResize = function() {
  stageResize();
};
Stage.addListener(myListener);
```

You won't see the trace output in a browser, but the script will work if you test the movie and resize the bandwidth profiler, or make the application window less than full screen and resize it.

Rather than using the `enterFrame` event, we have used the `Stage.onResize` listener event, which will be invoked whenever the user resizes the window. Obviously, it is more efficient than the `onEnterFrame` because it is only invoked when resize actually occurs.

The stage can only measure the browser window size if you use No scale. If you use any of the other scaled sizes (Show all, No border, Exact fit) in the Scale drop-down of the HTML Publish Settings window when you publish, the `Stage` object will give you the stage size values you see if you look in Modify>Document (or if you click on the stage and look at the stage size on the Property inspector). We will refer to these values as the **Flash stage size**. This can be useful in itself, because you now have a way to look at the size of the Flash stage directly. In fact, by setting the `scaleMode` property of the `Stage` object, which allows you to change the scale mode dynamically, you can retrieve both the browser window size, *and* the internal Flash stage:

```
// Get Flash stage size
Stage.scaleMode = "exactFit";
// NB - you could also have used
// "showAll" or "noBorder"
FlashStageX = Stage.width;
FlashStageY = Stage.height;
// Get Browser size
Stage.scaleMode = "noScale";
BrowserStageX = Stage.width;
BrowserStageY=Stage.height;
```

Since the screen will not update while the script above is running, nothing untoward will happen as you shift between scale modes.

You would normally put the last three lines in the function called by our `onListener.onResize` function, because these values will be updated every time the browser is resized.

> For this to work you must again set the movie dimensions to 'percent'. You don't have to set the scale, because we are now doing it dynamically. A word of warning though: the `Stage` object does not respond to the zoom in/out feature of the Flash player (as shown on the menu that pops up if you right-click on Flash content in a browser). If this will cause a problem, you may need to disable it.

Dynamically resizing the stage

You can see an example of all these techniques in action as resize.fla. This shows the advantage of doing away with Flash's auto-resize and taking control of this yourself; you can *choose which parts of the SWF get resized.*

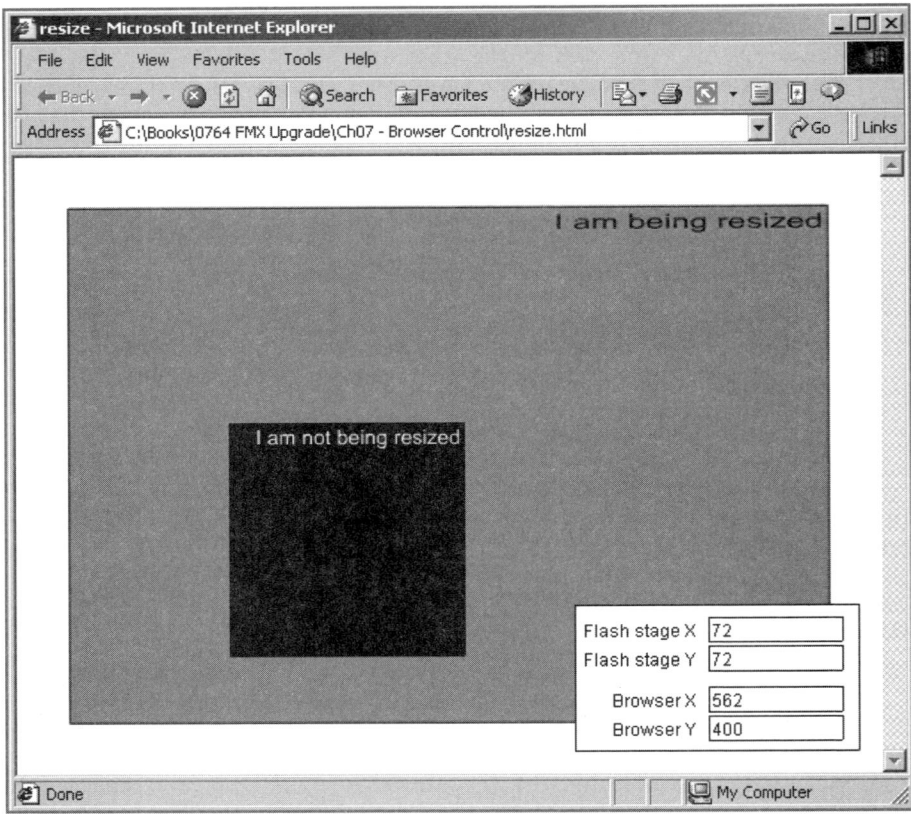

For example, if the black square was small text, we would not want to resize it and risk creating legibility issues, although we may be happy for all the motion graphics that are acting as a backdrop to resize with the browser (depicted via the gray square). The code for this FLA is shown below:

```
//Capture Flash stage dimensions...
//Stage.scaleMode = "exactFit";
FlashStageX = Stage.width;
FlashStageY = Stage.height;
//Move resizing box to center of the screen...
box._x = 275;
box._y = 200;
//
// Set noResize because we will handle
// resizing from now on...
```

```
Stage.scaleMode = "noScale";
//
// function to run when browser resized...
function stageResize() {
  browserX = Stage.width;
  browserY = Stage.height;
  box._width = browserX-40;
  box._height = browserY-40;
}
// Add listener for the Stage.onResize event...
myListener = new Object();
myListener.onResize = function() {
  stageResize();
};
Stage.addListener(myListener);
```

The four text fields are showing the Flash stage (FlashStageX, FlashStageY) and browser dimensions (BrowserX, BrowserY) respectively. The box that is being resized is a movie clip called box, and you can see the code that updates it whenever the browser is resized in the function stageResize. This function also updates the new browser dimensions in the browserX and browserY text fields. The lines below the function definition define our listener event, and you can ignore these for now (they define our function as the one to jump to when the onResize event occurs).

You can do some really cool things with the stage onResize function and the ability to swap between the browser dimensions and Flash stage dimensions. Imagine if you had written a space invaders game, and part way through it the user decided to make the browser area larger. Rather than simply allowing Flash to auto resize the stage, why not take the opportunity to make the invaders spread out across the new screen, or scurry into the smaller available space if the browser window becomes smaller. You could even go so far as to add in little screams for the invaders who fall off the edge of the browser and don't make it!

The back button and bookmarks

The browser *back* button can really irritate Flash users. HTML sites recognize it, and it is indeed a cool way of getting around, but Flash 5 didn't acknowledge it. If Jakob Neilsen thinks Flash is 99% useless, the lack of the back button probably contributed about three quarters of that, so we're down to 25% in one revision! Flash MX now fully supports the browser back button. It also now supports bookmarks, so the user can jump straight to a particular part of your SWF that you choose to make available for bookmarking.

The way both of these features work is via **anchors**, which are specific points on your timeline that you identify. The browser will act as if each anchor point is a new HTML page, so using the Back/Forward buttons allow you to move between anchors, and the browser also allows you to bookmark an anchor just like it would a standard HTML page.

Adding an anchor is easy; you simply create a keyframe and give it a label in the Property inspector. Any keyframe with a label will cause the Named Anchor checkbox to become selectable. Check it to create your anchor:

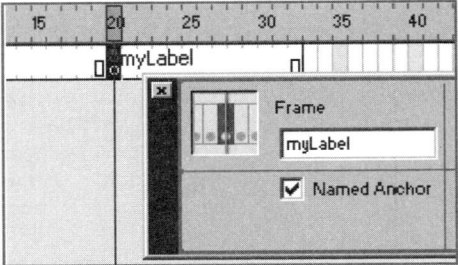

> *The name that you give your frame will appear in the address bar of the browser, and will suffix the HTML page name when appearing as a bookmark, so it's worth giving some consideration to your naming scheme and thinking about the user's perspective when using anchors.*

You can also get Flash to create anchors at the start of every scene. This is a reasonable thing to do, because a change of scene is usually an indication of a change of subject or a jump to a new site area. To enable this feature select Edit>Preferences…>General and check Named Anchor on Scene in the Timeline Options. Flash will now place an anchor called Scene_X on frame 1 of every scene (where 'X' is the scene number). It's worth noting that because the start of the page is already a bookmark in HTML (and always was), this option won't create an anchor in frame 1.

> *When you go to a Flash movie using a bookmark, it effectively executes a* gotoAndPlay() *action to the bookmarked frame, so even if you are using* gotoAndStop() *within your FLA file, it's still worth including a* stop() *if you're planning on using it as an anchor.*

For those ActionScripters who have not used scenes for a long time (and there are many of them!), remember that you create a new scene by clicking the little + button on the Scene panel:

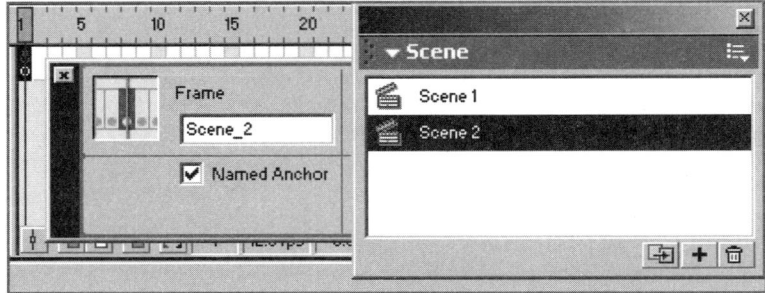

Another thing that many of you may have forgotten about scenes is that the order in which scenes are streamed in is the order shown in the Scene panel, and *not* their naming convention or the order that you created them in.

To allow the browser to see the anchors you *must* use Flash with Named Anchors as the Template in File>Publish settings>HTML. If you publish the SWF and view it in a browser, you will now see full browser bookmarking and back/forward button functionality (but note that anchors are only recognized by a version 4.x and above browser).

Direct loading of images and sounds

As a web designer, you will know that you can link to bitmaps from other sites as long as you know where they are on the server. Flash has always been different in that it could not do this; any external content usually needed to be a SWF, so you had to first embed the bitmaps in a SWF. This was not a big problem for most designers, but it *did* cause problems if the clients wanted to be able to update the Flash site themselves. With Flash 5, they would have needed the Flash 5 application, but not anymore, because Flash can now load content in *directly* without it being embedded in a SWF.

Although a minor technical point, this feature, together with the anchor functionality, now makes a Flash SWF look and smell a lot more like HTML, something that will no doubt make it a much better competitor to raw HTML sites, where there has previously been client resistance to using SWF-based content because it 'doesn't feel like or integrate well with HTML'.

The 'load image' functionality in MX will only accept standard JPEGs. If you are intending to create your JPEGs in Photoshop, note that Flash seems to recognize optimized JPEGs (Baseline Optimized in the PhotoShop JPEG Options window) as well as standard (Baseline Standard), so you could use optimized rather than just standard, because it does make file sizes smaller.

The best way by far to load a JPEG from the Flash designer's point of view is as follows:

1. Create a movie clip to hold the image using `createEmptyMovieClip()`

2. Make this clip invisible

3. Load the JPEG into it

4. After the JPEG has loaded, resize or move the empty clip to where you want the image to appear on the stage

5. Make the clip visible

You could also consider making the empty clip invisible with the `_visible` property until you have loaded the image. This allows you to resize the image so that it fits perfectly within the surrounding text and graphics by looking at the `_height` and `_width` of the clip once it has the JPEG inside it. You would then make the clip visible again once you have resized and moved your clip to fit.

This has the advantage of allowing you to dynamically resize, color, move, or otherwise control the movie clip containing the JPEG via standard movie clip methods. The following code will load a JPEG called `myPic.jpg` (which is in the same folder as the SWF file) into a specially created empty movie clip called `holder`, created at a depth of 1000 (to make sure I don't overwrite a depth of any other object). The top left corner is the registration point following loading of the image:

```
_root.createEmptyMovieClip("holder", 1000);
holder.loadMovie("myPic.jpg");
```

Before load   After load of *myPic.jpg*

o holder
(empty movie)

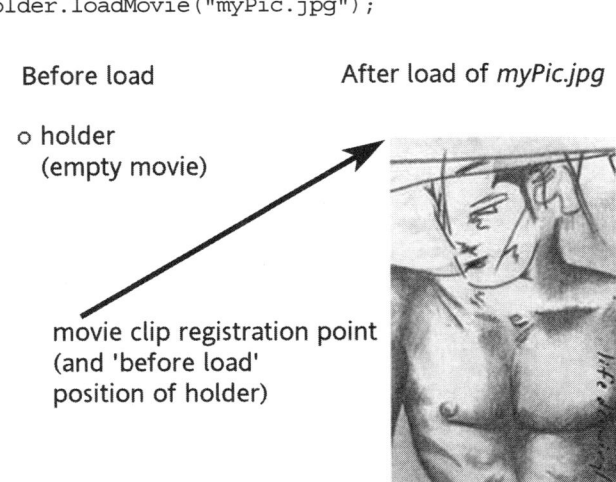

movie clip registration point
(and 'before load'
position of holder)

By default, `holder` will be created at coordinates (0,0) of the timeline you create it in (because we have created it in `_root`, in our case, this will be the top left corner of the stage), and the registration point of `holder` will be the top left corner of the image once loading has completed.

A disadvantage of SWFs that contain images has been that these images are usually loaded in automatically, even if the user never chooses to view them. Loading each image only when the user elects to view the page containing them would make for a much better image loading strategy, approaching that of images embedded in a set of HTML tables in download time (and of course, now making it just as easy for the client to update his images). Look out for a real world example demonstrating the direct loading of images in Chapter 16.

As the title of this section suggests, you can also do exactly the same with MP3s. Loaded sound can be configured as either a **streaming** sound or an **event** sound. The MP3 file must be configured as Constant Bit Rate (CBR).

Streaming sound

To load a streaming sound, simply use the `loadSound` action:

```
mySound.loadSound("url", soundType);
```

For example:

```
mySound = new Sound();
mySound.loadSound("mySound.mp3", true);
```

> Note that the second argument is `true` for a **streaming** sound, and `false` for an **event** sound.

This will load a streaming sound into the SWF. It will start playing once the sound buffer has the minimum specified duration of sound downloaded (this value can be changed via the global Flash player property `_soundbuftime`). It will actually synch the timeline with the sound, skipping frames if it needs to, so be careful using this type of sound if your timeline contains ActionScript - some of your scripts may not be executed, and this usually kills your presentation.

The `loadSound` method is, however, useful for MP3 players. The MP3 file itself is not made available to the user, and so this is a useful way of allowing the user to listen to a sound without them being able to retain the recording.

To load an event sound you use `loadSound` with the `soundType` set to `false`. Because event sounds are attached to a sound object, you need to both have a sound object defined, *and* use `loadSound` as a method of that sound object:

```
mySoundObject.loadSound("mySound.mp3", false);
```

Any ActionScript that tries to play an event sound before the sound has loaded will not play anything. You must of course define the sound object before you load the sound:

```
mySound = new Sound();
mySound.loadSound("mySound.mp3", false);
```

This in itself will not play the sound. To do that you have to use the object's `start` method:

```
mySound.start ();
```

Accessibility

The *Americans with Disabilities* Act enshrines the principle of equal rights in the workplace for the disabled, plus suitable provision for access in public places.

Recently, steps have been taken to include software and the provision of information within the remit of 'access', and this access will most likely, sooner or later, extend to include the Web. Consequently, it may soon be up to Web content providers to give the disabled community access to content as far as is practicable. At the moment the default is 'no provision' in many cases.

The Americans with Disabilities site is located at www.usdoj.gov/crt/ada/adahom1.htm. *You can also find a demo version of Window Eyes (the screen reader that Flash MX directly supports) at* www.gwmicro.co/ *(25Mb, but Windows only) if you wish to check your content for accessibility.*

Screen readers give blind and sight-impaired users the ability to use the Web, but this does of course depend on the sites being correctly formatted. For HTML sites, the readers will read the ALT text for each picture and button, plus any main text. Flash 5 did not support any similar functionality, so adding accessibility usually involved adding a separate HTML site or losing any client who specified accessibility requirements in the spec.

The accessibility functions in Macromedia Flash MX now support these important features within the Flash player itself. To decode this accessibility, you will need to get the *Window Eyes* screen reader. The screen reader can detect and read text (and text labels) on a site, allowing a practiced sight-impaired user to utilize the site.

Flash MX accessibility uses the Microsoft Active Accessibility (MSAA) model, as supported by Windows Internet Explorer. There is no support for any native operating system accessibility in the Mac at the time of writing. You can still create accessible content on the Mac (the full functionality is included in both versions of Flash), but only a Windows machine with IE is currently able to view it. The fact that Macs do not support accessibility is not an issue; people who need accessibility will have a machine that supports it, and at the moment, this is likely to be a PC.

Creating accessibility falls into three areas:

1. Accessibility that will be included by default if you enable it for the whole SWF - text areas can be read by the screen reader, and text that is placed close to a button will be associated with that button.

2. Accessibility that you have to define yourself. Graphic elements with no associated text must have accessibility information explicitly defined via the Accessibility panel if you want the screen reader to address them.

3. Additional design considerations when dealing with accessibility, such as:

   - Careful design of animated content so that it can be followed via the Flash sound track alone should be considered, but be aware that the screen reader produces its own audio stream, and you don't want to detract from it if you also have lots of embedded accessibility.

- The fashion of using small Flash buttons and miniscule UIs is definitely a bad idea when creating universally accessible sites.

- The appropriateness of animated interfaces with button elements that move of their own accord should be carefully considered.

Some of you will of course be saying 'well, I know this is a good cause, but it's crushing our scope for motion graphics design'. In fact, this is just not true! We can actually find out if the user's machine has accessibility from the system capabilities object:

```
accessibility = System.capabilities.hasAccessibility;
```

The accessibility value will be true if a reader that can view Flash accessibility content is installed on the user's machine. The temptation here is then to say, "Cool, I'll leave my main Flash site content as is, with an 'accessibility = true' redirection to a cut down scene at the end with the accessibility stuff". To me, that's just a case of the minimum design thought to meet a requirement.

Instead, there could be a single site that looks for capability access enabled, and dynamically throws off all the non machine-readable stuff to become accessible on the fly. Of course, the 'one site with dynamic accessibility' paradigm has other advantages:

- You can do the same thing for hardware. Drop the processor-intensive stuff if you see a wireless PDA rather than a 2 gb desktop with 20 inch TFT.

- You could load up higher quality sound files if you profile the site loading time and detect a high bandwidth, and a low quality or a reduced set if you see a 56k modem.

This is not simply a question of being socially aware, it's about the broader issues of knowing your audience and giving your site enough intelligence to adapt itself to be *accessible to everyone*. These are clearly universal design and accessibility issues.

> *Accessibility is not a design limitation or legislation requirement, it's another design consideration within a more aware Web environment. If you don't target content to the needs of all your Web users, you are part of yesterday's World Wide Web, not tomorrow's.*

The first thing you should do is set your global accessibility properties. Click on the stage, then bring up the Accessibility panel You can do this via the Accessibility icon 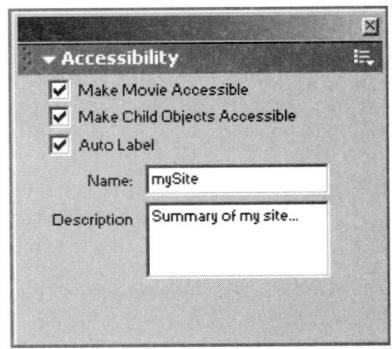 on the Property inspector, Window>Accessibility, or F9. The panel will have three checkboxes and two text entry areas, all of which are properties of the entire SWF:

If you want to make your SWF accessible, check Make Movie Accessible. Because Flash allows symbols to be embedded inside each other (for example, buttons embedded inside a movie clip), you may elect to make the embedded child objects readable by the screen reader with the second checkbox, Make Child Objects Accessible. This means that the movie clip that the buttons are embedded in (the parent) will then be ignored by the screen reader. The choice on whether you check or uncheck this is down to which option will allow the screen reader to read the descriptions for the core UI and text fields. You probably *don't* want to make movie clips that contain animated effects accessible.

Finally, Flash can associate text that is close to or touching a symbol (such as text near to a button) to the symbol itself. To do this, check Auto Label.

If you select a movie clip, you will see these accessibility options:

The reader will read back the name and description of the movie clip, plus the keyboard short cut (if the movie clip has been set up to recognize them). If you have embedded symbols inside the movie clip, then you should check Make Child Objects Accessible and not enter anything for this clip, instead placing all the accessibility on the child symbols.

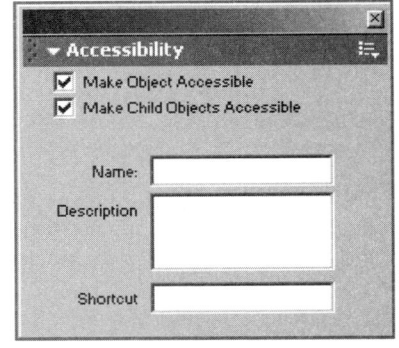

If your movie clip is providing animated information, consider replacing it with a text section. It may be a good idea to make all movie clips jump to a frame called *accessible* if an accessibility-enabled user is recognized. The keyframe would reconfigure the clip for machine readability and usability for a blind person. This may include stopping the clip if it is moving, or adding navigation to keyframes that tell the story of the animation via a series of text pages.

If you select a button, these options will be available:

The options are very much like the movie clip. Notice that you cannot make child objects to a button accessible. Many buttons will already have text associated with them if the text is in close proximity. In this case, it may only be necessary to specify a keyboard shortcut (you will also have to set up the button to actually detect the key press).

Although the Macromedia Flash MX side of the accessibility functionality is implemented, at the time of writing the only screen reader available that can decode this information is a Beta demo version of Window Eyes. As such, it's worth keeping an eye on www.friendsofed.com - when we hear anything further on this topic, and when appropriate screen reader software is released, we'll post up additional information alongside the code download package.

Local shared objects

The use of `FsCommand` to save data to a hard drive has been removed from Flash MX. It was a feature that perhaps should never have been there in the first place, since it allows the SWF to place things on a user's machine without either the user or the browser knowing it.

We now have a new object know as a **shared object** instead. This feature lets you store data on the user's hard drive in a controlled way. At their simplest level, shared objects are very much like cookies. You can store a user's profile so that they don't have to log into a restricted area every time, or you can present a custom page based on the client's previous buying habits for an e-commerce site. If we want to emulate what the browser and HTML/JavaScript can do, we can simply mimic the functionality of cookies, and because this is Flash we can go even further with them! Your Flash applications can be much more than just login pages or sites with simple preferences; they can be whole applications. You could use shared objects for saving any of the following:

- Data to represent artwork created by the user within a Flash paint application created with the drawing API

- The data required to re-create a sound mix created by an online Flash music mixing desk

- The user files for a desktop-based personal organizer, written in Flash and designed to work on both desktop and PDA screens

- An online Flash form that remembers previous responses the user made in the same domain and auto-completes the user's name, address, e-mail address, and so on

- The 'save game' data for an online Flash-based adventure game such as *Banja* (www.banja.com)

So it's pretty clear that shared objects are a cool new feature!

You should never underestimate the advantages of applications that save data over applications that can't or don't. It's like the difference between the old 8-bit arcade conversion games we used to play on home computers in the 1980s (with no save feature), and the games that appeared soon after, which had the ability to save the game progress to tape or onto 48kb floppies (remember those enormous disks that you never ever thought you'd be able to fill?). You can build up a much more interactive and complex environment, *even if your graphics and processing abilities stay the same.*

The Flash equivalent of the cookie is something we could easily call a *super*-cookie, because the Flash environment allows you to build *applications* rather than just web pages, and these can be both online or offline (or in the case of a personal organizer, both).

It is important to remember that shared objects are not part of the same system as standard browser cookies, and they don't conform to the same rules. If a user has opted out of saving regular cookies, this doesn't mean they have also disabled shared objects, and vice versa. Whether or not most users decide to allow Flash sites to save Flash cookies will be down to how responsibly they are used by Flash developers; the use of standard cookies was a little irresponsible in some early sites (the alert box saying 'Welcome back Sham B! Click OK to continue.' comes immediately to mind from the time when JavaScript and cookies first became widely supported).

It is also important that you **don't** call the shared object 'Flash cookies', 'super-cookies', or similar. This will only tend to confuse you about the relationship between cookies (controlled by the browser, all stored in a temporary internet folder on the system disk) and shared objects (controlled by the Flash player, stored in a local file different to the browser folders, with each file kept within a directory structure that shows which SWF created it).

The Flash Player 6 right-click menu now has a new Settings... option. Click it to see the new Macromedia Flash Player Settings window, and click on the second tab fom the left (the one with a folder icon on it) to see the Local Storage options:

The slider allows you to set the maximum amount of data that the current web domain can store in total (for all files created, not per file). In the picture shown, this domain is called local (Flash SWFs run from the local hard drives), but could in fact be a URL like www.friendsofed.com or www.macromedia.com. The slider value can be anything from None to Unlimited. If the user checks Never, then the feature is disabled, and the domain will not be able to save anything. If the user doesn't check Never, Flash is able to ask the user to increase the value if you need to save more than the user is currently allowing for your domain, so it's significant to distinguish between the user selecting None on the slider (Flash will ask the user for space if required) and the user checking Never (Flash will not ask for space, and your site will be blocked from saving a Flash shared object).

> *It's important to realize that the user can block you from saving Flash shared objects, and a Flash site that cannot continue because of this is bad news. Remember too that users will tend to check* Never *if your site keeps asking to save more data. This will most likely block your site from ever saving data on the user's machine again, so go easy!*

If any Flash SWF asks for more than its allocation, the user will be asked for confirmation with the following dialog window (the rest of the stage will go gray when this window appears):

In the following example we'll be using the new `SharedObject` object and its methods. This object is a little fiddly to use at first, but once you've done the basics once (saved data, and then loaded it back into Flash), it will all fall into place.

Creating and using a local shared object

In this example, we'll create a simple shared object and use it to store some data on the local hard drive. We will then find where that data is stored and confirm that the specific information we stored is actually in it.

To create a shared object and save some data with it, you need four things:

a. A local file created on the user's hard drive to store the data in

b. An indication of the amount of data you will be storing, so that Flash knows whether there is sufficient storage space allotted

c. A chunk of data inside the Flash player that you want to store in the file

d. A command to say 'retrieve the data and hand it over to the local file'

To create a local file, we notify Flash of a file name. We can also specify the `path` of the file, but for now we will allow Flash to decide that (and in doing so, we will soon find out where Flash stores all that data).

1. Create a new FLA and create two layers, actions and graphics:

2. At this point we should make sure that our preferences are set up appropriately to allow us to store things. Test the empty FLA and right-click to bring up the menu. Select Settings... (as we saw earlier) and in the Local Storage tab, make sure Never is unchecked and set the size slider to 10kb.

3. In layer actions, add the following line in the Actions panel:

```
localObject = SharedObject.getLocal("aardvark");
```

We have done a few things here:

- We have created a file `aardvark` that will store our data, and which we can find and check. (But why have I called it `aardvark`? Well, I wanted to create a file on your hard drive that is uniquely named. Failing that, how about `aardvark2`...?).

- We have defined our local data object `myLocalObject`. We have to populate this with the data we eventually want to send to the local file `aardvark`.

4. We now need to start populating our data object with data. Add the following lines:

```
sessionName = "sham";
sessionPass = "fred";
localObject.data.userName = sessionName;
localObject.data.pass = sessionPass;
```

We are using the `data` method to temporarily store data using the properties of our `localObject` object. This temporary data will be saved to the local file later. There are a few things to note here, because it is very easy to get this part wrong. The following code, for example, *won't* work:

```
localObject.data.userName = "sham";
localObject.data.pass = "fred";
```

You cannot assign literal values directly. This next code won't work either:

```
localObject.userName = sessionName;
localObject.pass = sessionPass;
```

This hasn't used the `data` method, so the properties wouldn't get sent to the local file. You *may* want to do this for some properties (because, for example, some of the properties are used in local calculations and not required for storage), but you must remember to include `data` for all the data elements that you *do* want to store.

5. OK. The final bit that says 'store the data' is as follows:

```
localObject = SharedObject.getLocal("aardvark");
sessionName = "sham";
sessionPass = "fred";
localObject.data.userName = sessionName;
localObject.data.pass = sessionPass;
localObject.flush(1000);
```

This is simply telling Flash to allocate 1000 bytes for storage in file `aardvark`, and store the properties of `localObject` (the two strings `sham`, `fred`) into it.

6. Test the FLA. Nothing will appear to happen, but the data *has* been saved. Time to find it! Search your computer for a file called `aardvark`. If you can't find it, a good clue is to look in the installation folder, open Configuration and read the Configuration_readme file. For instance, on my Win2K system I have the file `aardvark.sol` within `C:\Documents and Settings\<username>\Application Data\Macromedia\Flash Player\localhost`. If you use a simple text editor to view the contents, you will see that the values of our `username` (`sham`) and `pass` (`fred`) properties are inside `aardvark.sol`:

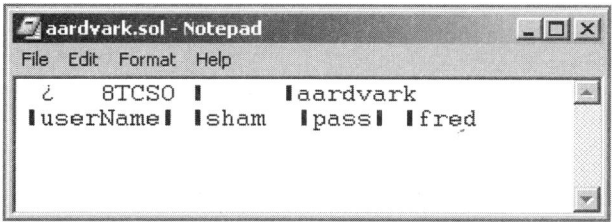

7. One final little test - change the last line so that we ask for more than the allotted 10K:

```
localObject.flush(20000);
```

If you test the FLA this time, you will see this dialog:

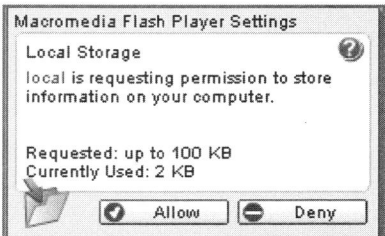

> *Remember that whether this warning is issued is determined by how much space you ask for, not how much you use. Typical Web users are actually very careful and cautious, and are likely to say no to anything they don't understand, so if you want more than the default amount, make sure the user is an informed user. They are also likely to say 'no' to anything that is not in their interests. Giving www.myFirstFlashsite.com any space on a hard drive is not likely to happen, and even www.bigHotShotFlashDesign.com is pushing it for more than 100K unless the user can see that they get some cool features by doing it. Knowledgeable users will certainly be reticent to give up 1MB to every site that asks for it, particularly as Flash's shared objects don't expire like cookies do.*

8. To avoid this kind of dilemma, we need to know the size of the data that we want to store. The way to do this is via the `getSize` method. Add the following line immediately before the `flush()`, and change the requested flush size back to 1000 bytes, as shown below:

```
localObject = SharedObject.getLocal("aardvark");
sessionName = "sham";
sessionPass = "fred";
localObject.data.userName = sessionName;
localObject.data.pass = sessionPass;
trace(localObject.getSize());
localObject.flush(1000);
```

When you run the FLA now, Flash will tell you the result of `getSize` in the output window (I get 62 bytes). This equates to my system's size property for `aardvark.sol`. But remember, the limit is the size of *all* files that you have saved from the domain, not just the current one.

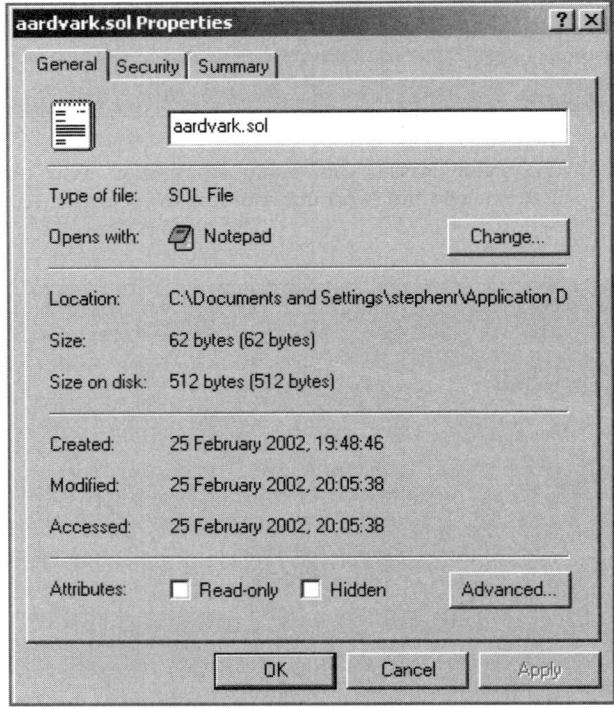

9. All we need now is to pull that data back. We actually already have everything we need. Once you run the FLA again, the object `localObject` will be repopulated with the last values. Comment out all the lines in your FLA except the first one, as shown on the next page:

```
localObject = SharedObject.getLocal("aardvark");
//sessionName = "sham";
//sessionPass = "fred";
//localObject.data.userName = sessionName;
//localObject.data.pass = sessionPass;
//trace(localObject.getSize());
//localObject.flush(1000);
```

If you run this FLA, there is nothing in it that tells it what values `localObject` had the last time round, right? To check this, debug the FLA, and in the debugger look for our data:

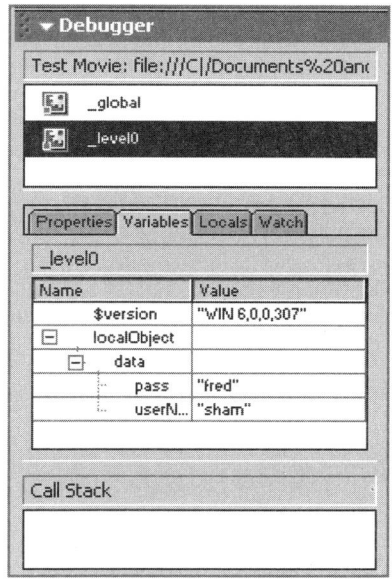

So, the only way it can exist is if our SWF looks in `aardvark.sol` - this is our local shared object in action.

Summary

Flash sites have traditionally behaved differently from HTML sites. Things like the Back button and lack of control on resize has always caused problems, primarily because they are some of the first things that a user notices. Although the Flash 5 SWF auto-resize feature was pretty cool, we designers sometimes want tables and text in Flash that behave just like their HTML counterparts, and the capacity to decide what happens when a browser is resized is indeed a good thing.

Macromedia have started the ball rolling on these issues in MX. Although they may not seem all that sexy at first, they do totally change the way Flash content is presented on the Web, making the transition from a HTML site to a Flash site less painful to the user.

Another concern for many designers has been that the links between the Flash SWF and the browser traditionally have to go through a rather longwinded route: Flash talks to JavaScript, and the JavaScript talks to the browser. JavaScript is now much less important, and MX integrates much more closely with the browser and the user's system, allowing the Flash SWF to *know* things, or to *do* things (like save data to the user's hard-drive) within an integrated system that doesn't use odd (or difficult) JavaScript conventions.

Finally, the lack of accessibility has started to become a problem for some big clients. The requirements for accessibility has made people start to ask the *scary* question, 'Should we even be using Flash if it doesn't do this?' Adding accessibility makes MX content just as accessible as HTML, and that can only be a good thing. Accessibility isn't just about taking care that disabled users can utilize your web content (although it is the biggest concern); it also relates to your web content being able to intelligently change itself to cater for *as many users as possible*. For example, can someone on a PDA access your content (something that even HTML has trouble with)? With the release of Macromedia Flash MX, these improvements to the flexibility of browser control mean that Flash has become a better overall design choice.

Although this book has been written in close association with Macromedia and following discussions with the Flash MX test team, it's likely that we'll see some further additions to the browser control features in the final release of Flash MX. Accordingly, for the sake of completeness, check out the source code download page for this book on www.friendsofed.com for an update, when information becomes available.

In the next chapter we're going to get to grips with the new debugging functionality that ships with Flash MX.

Chapter 11

Debugging

The debugger in Macromedia Flash 5 was seen as a big step forward for the typical ActionScripter, but it was still a little buggy itself - it didn't always work when you wanted to debug your movie. You would have to debug a few times (or in some cases many times!), which could often become as infuriating as finding you had bugs to debug in the first place!

All these teething problems with the debugger have been laid to rest in Macromedia Flash MX, and you get some cool new features on top of this, including **breakpoints** and the ability to step through any script line by line.

A breakpoint is a 'marked position' in your script where you want to pause its execution. Not only can you halt execution, you can also restart it as if it had never stopped. This allows you to set up one or more breakpoints around a piece of code where you think a bug is occurring and check the actual variable values against expected values. By setting up breakpoints, not only can you see the effects of a bug, but you can also see these effects developing, which helps you work back to the actual source of the problem. Think of a breakpoint as a temporary break in the code execution that allows you to look at a snapshot of what is going on.

Breakpoints are not just for debugging though; they're a great aid for learning new techniques, and for seeing how code is actually working behind the scenes.

In this chapter, we'll first look at the debugging environment, and show exactly what breakpoints are, not to mention how and why to use them. Then, to drive home some of the theory, we'll look at a few examples of specific debugging scenarios.

For complex scripts, the debugger is not a magic bullet that will kill all your bugs. An understanding of how scripting actually works is still required, so we will use the debugger itself to illustrate some important concepts regarding the *order of execution* - a knowledge of which will tend to make you a better scripter, as well as helping you understand the debugger!

Existing debug options outside the debugger

To set the scene, let's first take a look at some ways that you can debug *without* using the debugger.

First up, you can use the `trace` action to work out if variable and property actions are as you expect them to be:

```
x = "apple";
trace(x);
```

This will cause an Output window to display the value of `apple` when the trace is seen during testing of the SWF. You can also use `trace` to see if a particular script is actually being run, and the order of the execution. For example, the following `trace` will tell you if the `onPress` script is actually running, and you will see `mybutton pressed` appear in the Output window if the button is pressed:

```
myButton.onPress = function() {
  // add your code here...
  trace("mybutton pressed");
};
```

When you are expecting a number of events to run in a certain order or after certain real-time events, `trace` messages are very helpful for debugging a real-time environment. The debugger cannot easily do this because it can't handle real-time events in the same way.

The `typeof` action is also useful in verifying that particular objects are of the expected type. For example, the following script will tell you that `x` is a number:

```
x = 10;
trace(typeof (x));
```

If you had taken the value of `x` from a text field, and *assumed* it was a number, you would be surprised if you looked at its type, because it would be a *string*, and you would have to convert it to a number with `Number()`.

> Both `type` *and* `typeof` *include debugging features that you cannot always replicate with the debugger. The* Output *window may look a little less sexy, but it does have its uses for certain situations.*

Now that we have done our duty by making you aware of the other less glamorous debugging options, let's plow on and look at the debugger's environment.

The debugging environment

The debugger can step through your code while actually showing you the individual lines of ActionScript. This may be beneficial for you at authoring time, but if the debugger can list your code to step through it, then so can anyone else if you put the debug SWF on the Web and they look at the version in their Internet cache after loading your site. Letting people have free access to your code is cool if you like sharing your ideas with the Flash community (as many designers do in the spirit of knowledge sharing), but your *client* might not be too impressed if the SWF is from a commercial site.

To combat this, the debugger will contain all its run-time debug data, including your scripts and breakpoint data, in a separate file called the **SWD** (Shockwave debug) file.

The SWD file

If you debug an FLA, you will see an additional SWD file created alongside the SWF in the same location as the FLA:

webFairy	webFairy	webFairy
FLA	SWF	SWD

> You should not upload the SWD file to a server unless you want to debug online, and you should always remove it when you are done.

If you look inside a SWD file using a text editor (such as WordPad), you will see that it contains all the scripts from your FLA. The SWF contains **byte code**, which is not readable, or rather, not easily readable, especially if the SWF is also compressed (remember that anything on the Web that leaves traces of itself in the cache is never really 'secure'), so there's no need to worry about the debugger adding your scripting secrets into the SWF for all to see.

The debugger window

The Debugger window will appear if you test a movie via Control>Debug Movie (or CTRL+SHIFT+ENTER). The debugger will *not* appear if your FLA has no scripts in it; this is reasonable, because there is nothing to debug! So to get the debugger up for now to see how it works, just add a stop() action to frame 1, and you should be OK:

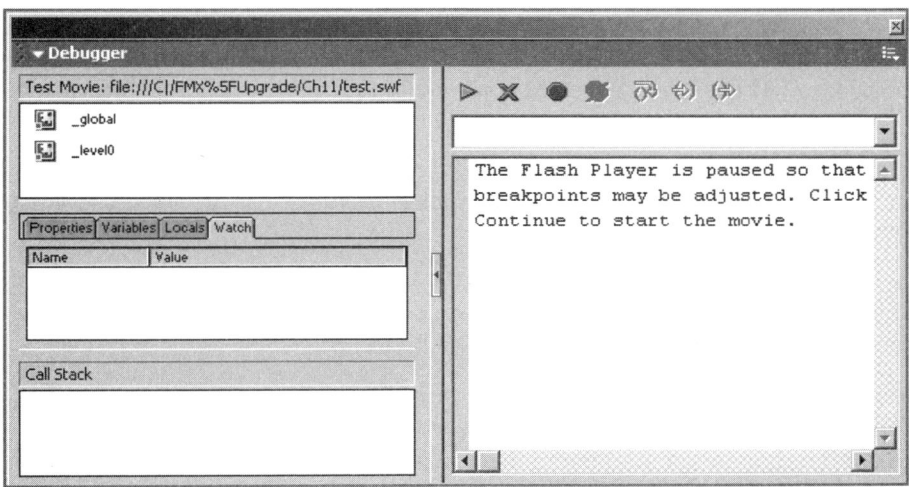

You will see the window appear as shown. As well as the display list pane (top left) that's retained from Flash 5, you also have the following:

- A new Locals tab in the tabs pane (center left) that allows you to see the values of local variables. Locals are variables that are created in function code blocks, and cease to exist when the block is completed. We'll look at examples of this later.

- The Call Stack pane tells you about nesting (or 'hierarchy') of calls to functions. For instance, if function A is called by function B from the main timeline, the stack allows you to see all this. This is a standard feature with many debuggers for more structured languages.

- A new **script** pane to the right - this is the 'meat' of the new debugger, and it is very useful, so we will spend some time with it here.

The script pane has a menu at the top as shown in close-up below:

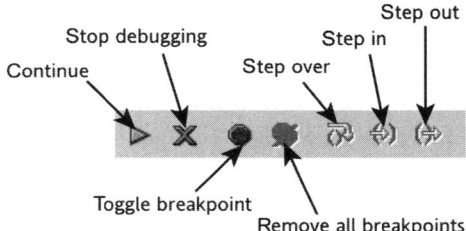

When you first debug a movie, the debugger will pause your movie. Flash 5 did *not* do this, so it's a change you need to be aware of. To actually begin the debug session (that is, play until the first breakpoint – or, if there are none seen, play indefinitely) you need to hit the *continue* icon. Hitting it a second time will make the SWF run until the next breakpoint is reached. If there *is* no next breakpoint, you will end up with real-time debugging (the same as the Flash 5 debugger).

The *stop debugging* icon does just what it says - it halts the debugger. So why would you want to do this rather than just quit? Well, remember that you can change the values of any variables in the tabbed area on the fly, so one reason to create a breakpoint may not be to check your code, but to insert test values of variables at a certain point. You might want to stop debugging if you have found the error, confirm this by setting the erroneous variable to the correct value, then confirm that correct program execution is seen from that point by exiting debug mode, allowing the SWF to continue.

Similarly obvious is the *toggle breakpoint* icon, which will toggle the selected breakpoint. To be useful, you do of course have to activate a breakpoint before the program execution gets to it. Likewise, *remove all breakpoints* does exactly what it says - it removes all the breakpoints.

The final three options allow you to step through the code one line at a time, and let you define what happens when the debugger comes across certain code structures:

- *Step Over* - executes the current line, and stops at the next line in the script. If the current line is a function, the debugger will execute the function without making you step through every line of it as well (the thing you are stepping over is the function). Sounds complicated, but it's actually very easy when you do it, which we soon will.

- *Step In* - executes the current line, and if that line is a function call, the debugger will let you step through every line of it by jumping across to the script that contains the function. If the current line is not a function call, then both 'step over' and 'step in' do the same thing: execute the current line and stop at the next one.

- *Step Out* - executes all lines up to the end of the current code block. For example, if you were in a long `for` loop that looped 100 times, you might just want to execute all the lines in the loop at once, and see what the variables were doing at the end of the loop.

Using the debugger

That's enough theory; it's time to use the debugger for real. The best way to learn to use breakpoints and single stepping is by example. Because debugging is a practical rather than theoretical exercise, in this chapter we'll treat it as such, with plenty of examples.

Linear scripts

In the following example, we will add a couple of breakpoints to a script and run it with **breakpoints** and **single stepping**.

1. In a new FLA, add the following script to frame 1 of Layer 1 (or open up `linear.fla`):

    ```
    fruit0 = "apple";
    fruit1 = "pear";
    fruit2 = "peach";
    fruit3 = "lemon";
    fruitEaten = new Array();
    for (i=0; i<4; i++) {
      fruitEaten[i] = _root["fruit"+i];
      _root["fruit"+i] = "gone!";
    }
    ```

    At the beginning of this script, we define `fruit0` to `fruit3` as strings that represent names of various fruits. We then use a loop to add each fruit to an array of fruit eaten. As each fruit is added to the array, we reassign the `fruit` variable as `gone!` (because I've eaten it!). If you debug the FLA (remember, CTRL+SHIFT+ENTER), you'll see the Debugger window appear in its paused state. Hit the *continue* icon to run the debugger. The script will run through to the end, and the Variables tab of the debugger will show you the end result, as you'll see on the next page.

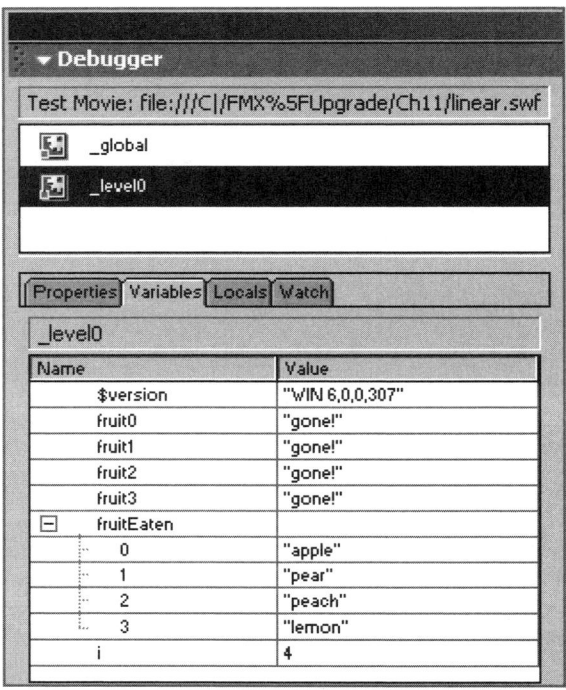

As you can see, all of my `fruit` variables have now `gone!` and I have placed them in my `fruitEaten` list, which is an array. That's fine when it works, but there's all sorts of things I could have done wrong, such as make the loop start with `i=1`, which would give me this:

Name		Value
	$version	"WIN 6,0,0,307"
	fruit0	"apple"
	fruit1	"gone!"
	fruit2	"gone!"
	fruit3	"gone!"
⊟	fruitEaten	
	1	"pear"
	2	"peach"
	3	"lemon"
	i	4

```
1  fruit0 = "apple";
2  fruit1 = "pear";
3  fruit2 = "peach";
4  fruit3 = "lemon";
5  fruitEaten = new Array();
6  for (i=1; i<4; i++) {
7      fruitEaten[i] = _root["fruit"+i];
8      _root["fruit"+i] = "gone!";
9  }
```

Although the line containing our error (i=1 instead of i=0) is highlighted in the listing above, the debugger is not that helpful in telling me this (unless I understand the nature of the error), because it doesn't let me see inside the loop; it only gives me a snapshot at the end of the script.

2. To see what is going on in our script, let's add some breakpoints. It would be nice to see that all my `fruit` are properly defined, and that the results at the end of each loop are correct. To do this, we want a snapshot at line 4 and one at the end of each loop, line 8.

Note that the end of the loop is not the brace. If you try to add a breakpoint on a line containing a brace, Flash will raise an error during the debug session, stating that 'One or more breakpoints have been removed because they are not on valid lines of code'. You cannot add a breakpoint to any line of script that will not compile to a byte of code in the final SWF (which leaves Flash nothing to attach the breakpoint to), and this includes:

- Braces

- Function definition heads (that is, the line with `something = myFunction(){` at the top of a function definition)

- Lines containing comments only

To add a breakpoint to a line, place the text cursor on the line and then either:

- Right-click anywhere on the Actions panel's script editing pane and select Set Breakpoint from the pop-up menu that appears, or...

- Click the Debug Options icon (top-right of Actions panel) and select Set Breakpoint

Add breakpoints to lines 4 and 8:

```
1 fruit0 = "apple";
2 fruit1 = "pear";
3 fruit2 = "peach";
4 fruit3 = "lemon";
5 fruitEaten = new Array();
6 for (i=1; i<4; i++) {
7     fruitEaten[i] = _root["fruit"+i];
8     _root["fruit"+i] = "gone!";
9 }
```

You can also add breakpoints while the debugger is actually running. We will not be looking at this feature, but will instead concentrate on getting up to speed with actually using breakpoints and single stepping.

3. Now start the debugger – it will initially appear paused; click the *continue* icon. You will see the script appear as shown. Select _level0 and click the Variables tab to see the current state of the variables on the main timeline:

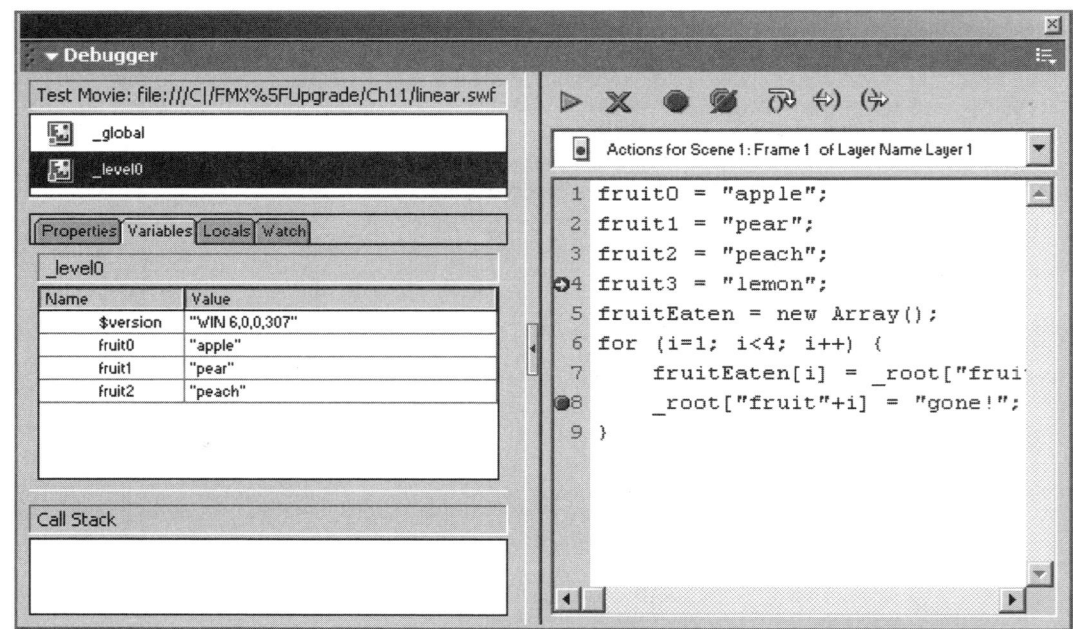

> *Notice that the debugger also allows you to see global values via the global timeline* _global. *Although it is shown as a movie clip, you should be aware that* _global *does not represent a timeline.*

4. The first breakpoint has a little arrow over it – this arrow will always point to the next line to be executed. The debugger has ran through all lines up to the breakpoint, executing lines 1, 2 and 3. You can see this in the Variables tab: fruit0, 1, and 2 have been defined, but there is no fruit3. To run the script up to the next breakpoint, hit *continue*:

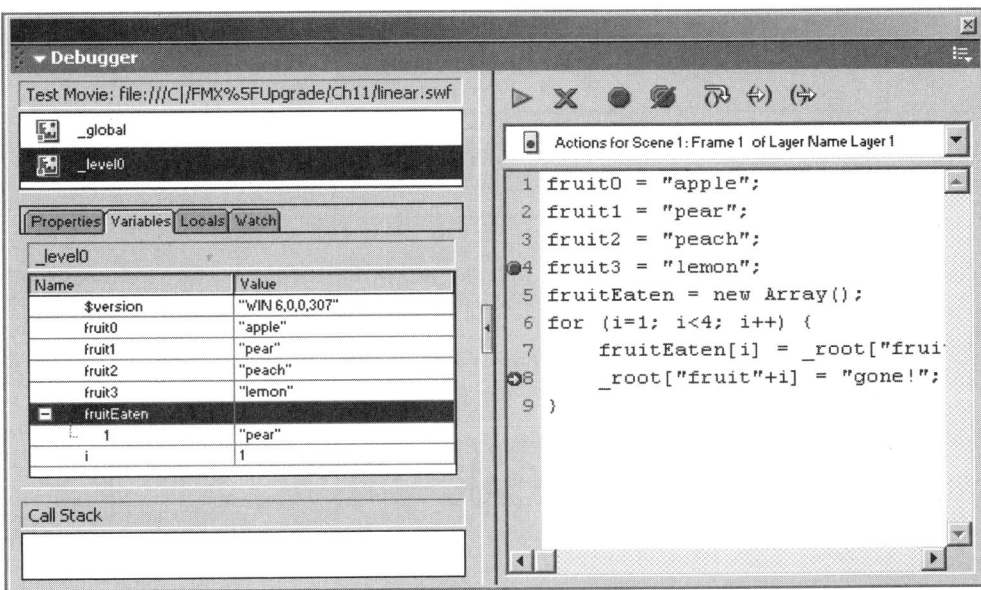

The script will now execute up to (but not including) line 8. This already shows us the error: the loop starts at 1, not 0, so the first fruitEaten is the pear, not the apple. Hit *continue*. You will see that nothing much changes - the arrow stays at line 8. This is because we are in a *loop*. Program execution has run the first loop, and the breakpoint stops execution on the next loop. You can continue looping round by hitting *continue*, and you will see the Variables tab update to reflect changes made per loop.

OK, we have found our error, but what if our error was a little more subtle? We might want to look at each line in turn, a process called **single stepping**. This is just like having a breakpoint on every line.

5. Quit the debugger and delete all the breakpoints by selecting Remove All Breakpoints from either of the two menus described earlier.

6. Fix the for loop so that it starts at i=0. Now, add a single breakpoint at line 1, and select Control>Debug Movie again. This time, the breakpoint will stop the script at line 1. No parts of the script have yet been executed.

7. Select _level0, hit the Variable tab, and click on the Continue icon once:

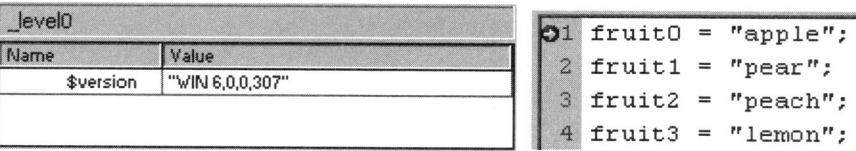

No variables have been defined, except for the system variable $version that tells you what version of the Flash player you are debugging with.

8. Now *single step* by hitting the *step in* icon. This will execute the current line, and stop at the next one:

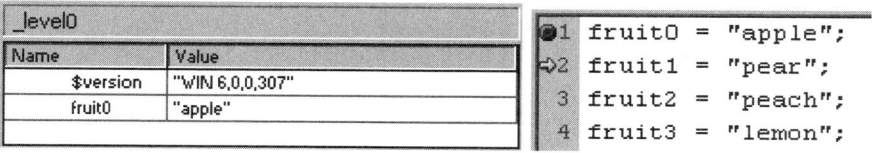

This causes line 1 to create `fruit0` and set it to a value `apple`. If you continue single stepping through to line 5 (again, using the *step in* icon), you will see this:

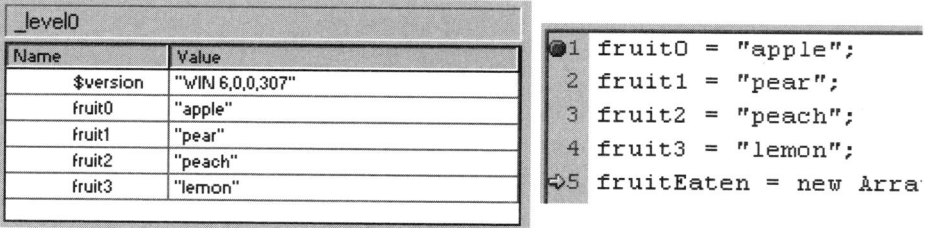

9. All the `fruit` have been defined, and we are just about to enter the loop. Hit *step in* once more – you will jump to line 6, and the `fruitEaten` array will now be defined. It doesn't have a value yet, because it is still `undefined`. Hit *step in* again:

$version	"WIN 6,0,0,307"
fruit0	"apple"
fruit1	"pear"
fruit2	"peach"
fruit3	"lemon"
fruitEaten	
i	0

```
6  for (i=0; i<4; i++) {
7      fruitEaten[i] = _root["fruit"+i];
8      _root["fruit"+i] = "gone!";
9  }
```

10. At line 7, we have our loop variable set to 0. Hit *step in* a few times to see the execution loop round the `for`, and you will see the effects of me eating the fruit; the `fruit` become `gone!`, and `fruitEaten` gets updated appropriately. You will also see the counter updating.

> *The process we are going through is actually a very powerful debugging technique. You are seeing snapshots of the Flash player at every single line, and can see everything that is changing. It is, however, only useful if you have a good idea of what you expect to happen, so it's a good idea to jot down a few notes before you start debugging at this low level, working out where you want the breakpoint (in large scripts you will want to start single stepping a few lines before the place you think the error is occurring – and you must know roughly where the error is for single stepping otherwise you are in for a long debugging session), and what you expect to happen to key variables involved with the error.*

11. We are looping only *four* times (0, 1, 2, 3), but what if I was a particularly hungry designer, and was eating a hundred pieces of fruit? Single stepping becomes a rather long process as soon as we hit a loop that big. We might have got all the usefulness of looking at individual loops by the third or fourth loop iteration. That's where the Step Out icon comes in. Hit it and the loop (or any block, such as a function or do... loop) will run through until it is finished:

Name		Value
	$version	"WIN 6,0,0,307"
	fruit0	"gone!"
	fruit1	"gone!"
	fruit2	"gone!"
	fruit3	"gone!"
⊟	fruitEaten	
	0	"apple"
	1	"pear"
	2	"peach"
	3	"lemon"
	i	4

> *You will know that the script has finished when you can no longer see the little arrow pointer.*

The script we have just looked at is fairly simple; all the action takes place in one script on a single frame. Where you have functions, however, you may be jumping all over the place in the timeline, so let's have a look at that next.

Scripts that call other scripts

When you call a function that you have defined earlier in the FLA, the debugger must jump backwards out of the current script and resume execution at the function. Once the function has finished, execution will resume at the call point. Let's have a look at this in action.

> *As we mentioned earlier, the debugger is not just for debugging. When you call many functions in a small script, you may not be aware of the total number of lines that may end up being executed. When you are writing code loops that are critical to performance (such as those within games, communication loops, or XML parsing), the debugger will show you how many lines are executed; in this context, the debugger is an aid to* **code optimization**.

1. In a new FLA, rename Layer 1 to scripts. Add the following script to frame 1 (or take a look at nonlinear.fla):

   ```
   function tax(value) {
     var taxPercent = 0.175;
     var taxAmount;
     taxAmount = value*taxPercent;
     return (taxAmount);
   }
   ```

   This function works out the amount of tax due on the argument value, and returns the amount of tax payable, calculated at 17.5% (for example). It uses var to define two local variables taxPercent and taxAmount.

2. In frame 2 of scripts, add this:

   ```
   salaryAmount = 1000;
   taxAmount = tax(salaryAmount);
   myTakeHome = salaryAmount-taxAmount;
   stop();
   ```

   This script uses the tax() function to work out the tax I have to pay (taxAmount) on my salary salaryAmount, and works out my take home pay myTakeHome. Notice that there is already a variable taxAmount in the function we just created in frame 1; we have a variable local to the function and another variable of the same name in our main script. So, as well as looking at how functions affect program execution, this simple bit of accounting will also tell us how Flash handles variables that are local to a function block.

3. Debug the script with CTRL+SHIFT+ENTER. By clicking on *continue* and going to the Variables tab of _level0 you will see the final results:

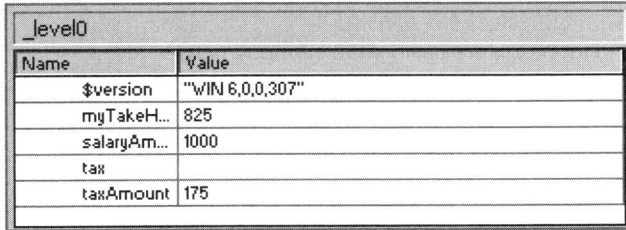

We have our function `tax` defined, as well as our variables `myTakeHome`, `taxAmount`, and `salaryAmount`. Although this tells that the scripts have worked (because we can see that the answers are correct), it does not tell us anything about the interactions that occurred within the code, *because it all occurs within the space of a single frame*. Let's have a look at that now.

4. Add a breakpoint at line 1 of the script at frame 2, and then debug the movie:

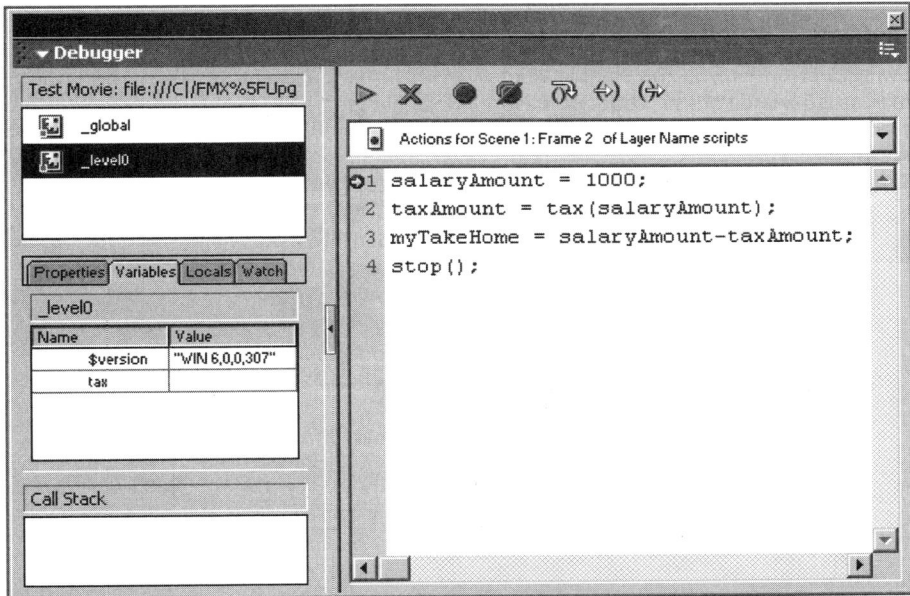

There are a couple of things to notice as soon as the script starts:

- The debugger has already run through the script at frame 1 and the function `tax` has been defined. When using functions it's always important to check that all functions are defined before you actually call them. Obvious, perhaps, but still a common mistake!

■ We are now looking at the script at frame 2 of the scripts layer; the title bar at the top of the script pane indicates this. If we want to recap what the function `tax` actually looks like, we can click on this title and select it from the dropdown of available scripts:

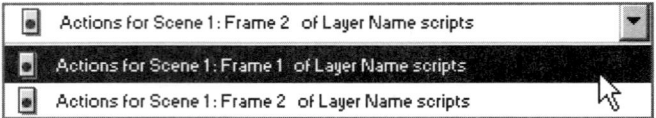

This is a very useful feature for FLAs that contain a large number of scripts; you may need to look at other scripts to help you deduce what has happened.

5. Hit *step in*. Irrespective of which script you are currently looking at, the debugger will jump to the script line that is currently about to be executed - line 2 of the script on frame 2:

```
1 salaryAmount = 1000;
2 taxAmount = tax(salaryAmount);
3 myTakeHome = salaryAmount-taxAmount;
4 stop();
```

To execute this frame, Flash has to jump to the function `tax`. We can do one of two things here: we can either watch Flash as it does this, or we can stay within the current script. We will do both to demonstrate, starting with the full deal.

6. Hit the *step in* icon again. You will see the function script appear, because that is where program execution has jumped to in order to evaluate `tax(salaryAmount)`.

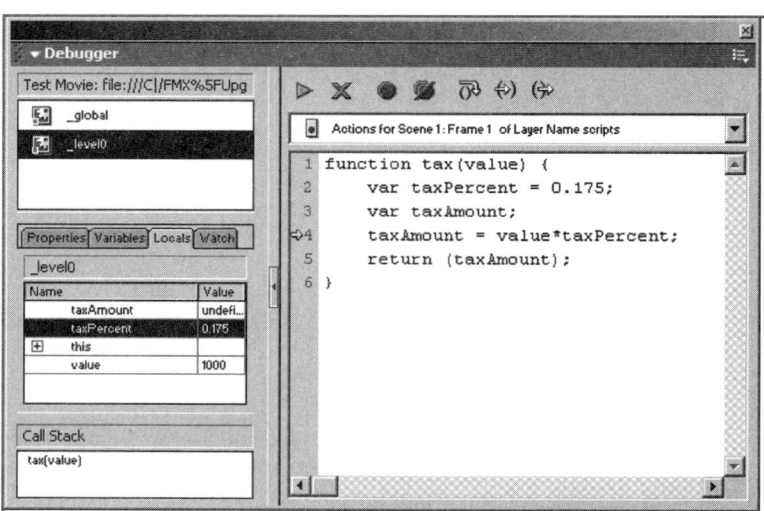

7. Use *step in* to step down to line 4 as shown on the previous page. We want to look at a different `taxPercent` here: the version that is local to our function. To do this, look at the Locals tab. Hit *step in* until you return to the main script, and *step in* to the end. Notice that when you return to the main script, the local variables disappear. This is to be expected - the variables defined with `var` have a lifetime only within the function block, and once program execution has moved out of the function, they cease to exist.

> Local values can only be defined in a function block. Using `var` in any other block (such as a `while` or `for`) does not create local variables.

We have not only proven that the script works by looking for the final result, we have also shown that the *route* to the result is correct.

- We have shown that the function executes as expected.

- We have shown that there are no collisions between the two versions of `taxAmount`.

- We now have a better understanding of the lines that are executed and their ordering, something that can only make us better scripters!

OK, so assuming we are meticulous scripters and we've fully tested our function, what if we know it works and don't want to jump to it, or don't want to run through all lines?

8. If we debug the FLA again, from line two of the main script we can:

- Hit *step over*. This will evaluate the value of the line `taxAmount = tax(salaryAmount);` without actually jumping to the function `tax` in the debugger. You would do this if you were sure that the function was running correctly, and that the main script was jumping to it correctly.

- Hit *step in* to jump to the function `tax`, but once you are there, hit *step out*. *step out* will evaluate all lines in the function in one go and jump back to the main script. This option is useful if you want to be sure that the function is actually being invoked by a line in the main script.

Although we have looked at a script that relies on another script to work, real FLAs contain much more complexity than this; they may use a large number of totally different scripts that all run on the same frame - we'll show this in the next example.

Distributed timelines

In the following example, `distributed.fla`, we'll look at how multiple scripts are actually executed by the Flash player. You need to know this before you can use breakpoints in most typical FLAs, because you normally have more than one script in more than one place, and it will also give you some insight of how scripts actually run.

1. In a new FLA, create three layers called fruit, islands, and graphics:

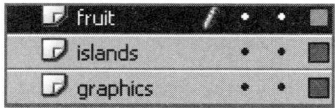

2. In frame 1 of fruit, attach this script:

```
x = "apple";
y = "pear";
```

We now have a script that gives our variables fruit-centric string values.

3. In frame 1 of layer islands, add the following script:

```
x = "Sumatra";
y = "Ireland";
```

This short script gives our variables values that correspond to names of islands.

4. In layer graphics, create a static text field with the text my movie clip in it. Hit F8 and make it a movie clip called myClip. Give the clip an instance name clip:

 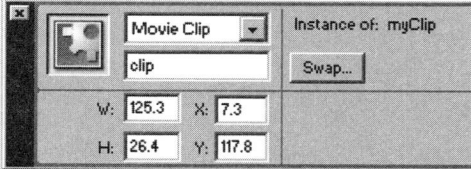

5. On this movie clip's timeline, add the following script to frame 1:

```
x = "cow";
y = "goat";
_root.x = "sheep";
_root.y = "pig";
```

This script makes our main timeline variables the names of some animals, and creates some versions local to myClip, which are also animals.

Now, the question is, when we run this FLA, *what will all the variables be equal to?* Go on, have a guess - we have three scripts, all three are on the same frame, but in different places. Which order are they executed in?

Well, we know all of them are executed by the end of the frame. It is, however, a whole different ball game when we are looking at the scripts line by line, because *there has to be a definite order.* Flash *doesn't execute them all at the same time,* it does something else, and we have to know what this is before we can understand how the debugger is used in single step or breakpoint mode.

> *The order of execution can cause problems during initialization, where one script will try to reference variables before they are created and defined.*

6. The first thing we have to do is add a breakpoint. In the Actions panel, bring up the script in layer fruit and add a breakpoint at line 1:

```
1  x = "apple";
2  y = "pear";
```

We have actually put the breakpoint on the first line of this script for a reason: *it is the first script to be run, so line 1 of this script is the first line to be executed.* Obviously, you will be able to make the same sort of decision with ease in a while (in fact, right after you have read this chapter), but for now, take it on trust that this is a good place to put a breakpoint if you want to do some in-depth debugging.

7. Test the FLA in debug mode, and press *continue* once to start the debugger, and again to run from the breakpoint to the end of the frame:

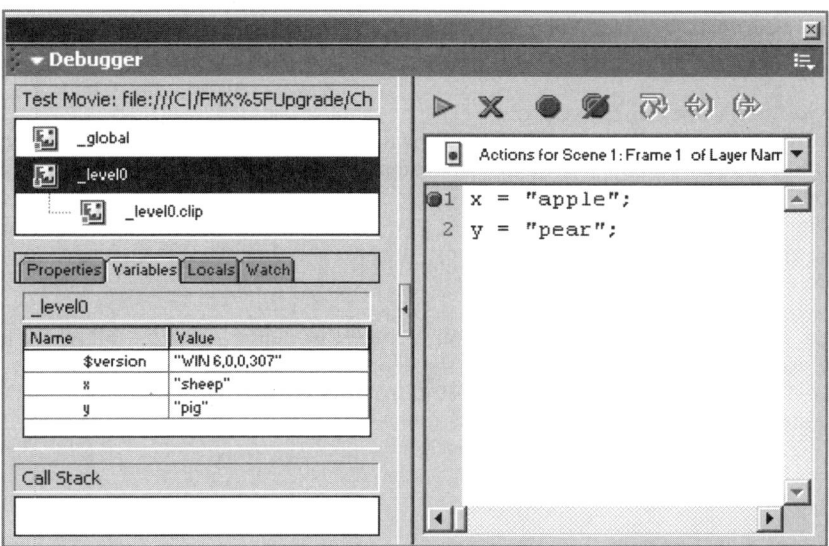

You will end up with the rather confusing display shown above. The script tells us that x = "apple", but the actual value is x = "sheep". This is because we have ignored the order of execution; if we want to debug frames with multiple scripts, we must place a breakpoint at the start of each script, because then the debugger will give us some important information, which includes:

- The order that each script executes in

- The variables that exist at the start of each script

- The variables that exist at the end of each script

If you now add a breakpoint at the start of the other two scripts, you will see the order of execution:

```
x = "apple";
y = "pear"
```

Then:

```
x = "Sumatra";
y = "Ireland";
```

And finally (from the timeline of the movie):

```
x = "cow";
y = "goat";
_root.x = "sheep";
_root.y = "pig";
```

The way Flash runs scripts is *related* to the layer order, but actually *equal* to the depth order. Layers only have meaning in FLA files; they do not exist in the SWF file, which runs scripts in depth order and runs the scripts lowest depth first.

If you don't use duplicateMovieClip or createEmptyMovieClip, the depth order is the layer order, and goes from top layer downwards. Any scripts that you place on the timelines at authoring time will be given a *negative* depth, which means they will always run before any scripts you define that are attached to clips you create at *run-time* (because they have positive depths). After all the scripts have been run in layer order, the first level of embedded timelines (such as the movie clip, which is embedded on _level0) are executed, and so on, moving deeper through the embedded timelines.

You can see how the layer order will change the depths, and therefore the execution order by re-ordering the layers, or by moving the clip to another layer, and then re-running the debugger to see the new order of execution. Although this is a trivial FLA, it is actually telling you some fundamental stuff about how Flash scripting works.

Summary

As you have probably gathered, single stepping and breakpoints in the Macromedia Flash MX debugger allow you to get deep within the Flash player, and see what is going on in your scripts at a very low level. Not only does it allow you to debug scripts, it allows you to do other things, such as gaining a better understanding of scripting in terms of scope, order of execution, performance, and number of lines executed to perform an operation, and it lets you fully optimize your code.

In the next chapter we'll take a look at some of the new options for importing video into Flash MX.

Chapter 12

Video

The big revolution in Macromedia Flash MX's multimedia capacity is the **video object.** We'll therefore dedicate this chapter to a study of the new video features. Let's start by looking at what the video object is, what it can do, and how you can expect it to behave.

The video object

With Flash 5 we saw a number of third party video-for-Flash applications. These used a series of JPEG images played together to fake a video stream. Such methods had the following limitations:

- You couldn't add sound easily. Third party solutions such as Wildform Flix did support sound in their import, but it came in as a separate MP3 channel, which can cause problems where close synch is required. Only combined audio/video codecs can give you really tight synching.

- JPEG compression was optimized for still images rather than video. Although there were options to combat this (such as splitting the JPEG into squares that did and didn't change between frames, thus giving you a delta video compression of sorts), it was all a little basic.

The new video object fixes all of these problems in a simple, almost script-free workflow (a real bonus!). There are, however, some limitations regarding what you can and can't do with it, as we shall see.

There are a number of issues to consider about the workflow of the video object:

- Acquiring and editing the video

- Getting it into the Flash environment

- Configuring the video content for the Flash player

We will look at the last two in detail later in this chapter, but will only briefly consider the first here.

Unlike the Flash 5 solutions for video, the Flash MX video object is a true **video codec** embedded within the Flash player. The codec used by the video object is **Sorenson Spark** – described in the next section.

Sorenson Spark and Sorenson Squeeze

Sorenson Spark is a *delta compression* codec, which means that it compresses the video based on the relative change between frames. Delta compression can be set to encode based on one of two things: maintaining a fixed bandwidth or maintaining a fixed quality. Flash maintains a fixed *quality* meaning that the exact bandwidth required depends on the amount of change between frames. A video with a relatively still (motionless) scene will take much less bandwidth than one that is full of action.

Likewise, a video with segments of high and low change between frames will have varying bandwidth requirements. Consequently, a video stream that *starts* with little initial movement will stream better.

The codec caters for both sound and video, although you can elect to have no sound (or stream it in separately as a sound object).

> *Technically speaking, Sorenson Spark is a Variable Bit Rate (VBR) codec – the bandwidth varies with the content.*

Sorenson have released a separate compression application that allows export of video as SWFs or FLV (video for Flash) format, both of which can be imported directly by Flash MX. This application, Sorenson Squeeze (www.sorenson.com/products/squeeze.asp), offers a lot more compression options than the Flash MX video import options do on their own – we will look at these shortly – and produces its own Flash-compatible format Sorenson Spark Pro.

You will end up with better quality video streams by using Squeeze and exporting directly to native Flash formats (SWF and the new FLV format) than by using Flash alone.

The Flash player and video

Irrespective of whether you use the native Flash video import or Sorenson Squeeze, the end result is a SWF with embedded video. There are two ways of loading video into the Flash player on the Web:

1. Video attached to _root will stream in, much like streaming sound. The stream is lost once it has played, and to continuously loop the video you have to be loading it in continuously, *or* load it in as a new level (such as _leveln, where n is above 0).

2. Video attached to a timeline within a movie clip will not begin playing until the full video file has streamed in. Once loaded, however, you can re-use it – much like *event sounds*.

Another issue to be aware of with video is that like MP3, Sorenson Spark takes a certain amount of processing power when it's in operation. *Unlike* sound though, video takes *much* more processing power, and if your video content is too big, you will see performance slowdowns.

> *Video content much larger than 320x240 pixels may cause problems on some machines. This is the pixel size of the original imported video – you can scale it up and down if you wish (more on this later).*

The final issue to take in account is the way the Flash player handles video internally. When you stream long video segments, the Flash player uses up system memory like there is no tomorrow, so limit your video clips to either short duration or small pixel sizes (and ideally both). A video clip of about four minutes is around the maximum, so if you want something longer, consider using a number of separate clips. Note that the movie clip method `clear()` allows you to delete unwanted video segments from the Flash player memory.

OK, that's our quick rundown of what video for Flash actually consists of. Now it's time to get some practical experience of it in action!

Video workflow

Let's get closely acquainted with the use of video in Macromedia Flash MX: starting with importing video; moving on to using video *without* scripting; and finishing with a look at the options for controlling the video content *with* ActionScript.

Importing video

The import options when working with video differ, based upon whether you are using Sorenson Squeeze or not. Here we will only look at the options available with Flash out-of-the-box.

> *Squeeze can, for example, produce SWFs with embedded video. Apart from the fact that the SWF has this embedded video, there is no real difference in how you would use this SWF over and above a standard SWF (that is, as a loaded level or loaded target).*

To import a piece of video, simply select File>Import and change the Files of type option in the selection window to All Video Formats.

You can import video in a number of formats:

1. Windows Media (.asf or .wmv)
2. Digital Video (.dvi or .dv)
3. MPEG (.mpeg or .mpg)
4. Video for Windows (.avi)
5. QuickTime (.mov)

Flash 5 supported QuickTime as an externally linked file, and you retain the option to do this for MOV files (note that Flash 5 only supported QuickTime when exporting to video and not to a SWF). Assuming you want to use the embedded Flash MX video object (which you would choose unless you were worried about Flash 5 compatibility), select Embed video in Macromedia Flash document if you see the Import Video requester dialog shown here:

Irrespective of which video format you import, you will then see the Import Video Settings window:

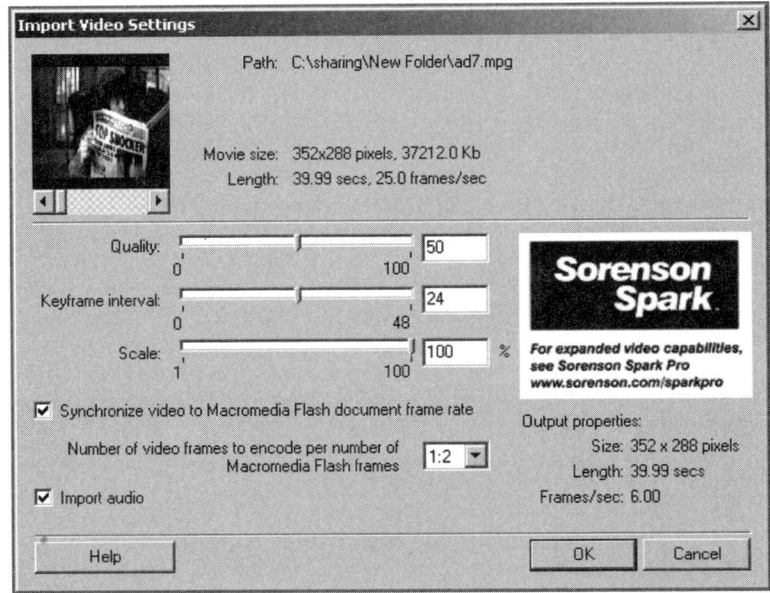

Note that these video settings *do not* allow you to do any of the following:

- Import only a section of a video

- Apply any filtering of the video that would allow more efficient compression or increase apparent video quality (such as de-speckle, de-interlace, or low level Gaussian blur)

- Resize the aspect ratio of the video

- Change the contrast, color, or brightness of the video

- Access the sound channel separately within the codec

> *Video is much like sound in that although you can apply post processing to the original video to clean it up, you should allow Flash (or Squeeze) to import the highest quality video source you have, as this will result in a better quality export to the final SWF or FLV.*

To do any of these, you have to post process the raw video in a suitable video application. Sorenson Spark, for instance, allows you to do many (but not all) of the above, and higher-end applications allow you to do the rest. Flash provides the *minimum control* when importing video, and for greater control you are advised to:

1. Do all your cropping and filtering in a dedicated video editing application.

2. Import this into Sorenson Squeeze to add compression suitable for video delivery.

3. Export the video from Squeeze as an FLV (Flash Video) or SWF (normal SWF file with embedded video).

4. Load the FLV in Flash MX as your starting point, complete with video already imported using the more advanced export features of Squeeze, or use the SWF containing the video at run-time as loaded content.

The top half of the Import Video Settings window shows you the properties of the original video file. The three sliders in the middle of the window have these effects:

- Quality - This controls the quality of the original source in relation to the final output. More specifically, it controls the *level of compression* applied. The lower the setting is, the greater the level of compression and thus file size reduction, but as usual, the trade-off is quality of the final output, which will start to appear blocky, especially with fast- changing video images or video with a lot of detailed items in it.

- Keyframe interval - This does not refer to Flash timelines, but the internal process of the codec delta compression. The compression takes the first video frame as the 'keyframe', and the next *n* frames (where *n* is the keyframe interval) are based on this frame, meaning that the compression will store only the changes between the subsequent *n* frames and the keyframe. After *n* frames, a new keyframe will be taken.

There are a number of issues to remember when selecting the value of the keyframe interval:

- Fast-changing video frames (such as a car chase) will suffer more if the keyframe interval is large, whereas relatively still objects (such as a head-and-shhoulders view of a person being interviewed) will be less affected.

- A keyframe interval of 1 will store every frame and will allow no inter-frame delta compression. Each frame will then be compressed individually. This is similar to using a series of JPEGs.

- Scale - The scale refers to the scaling of the final output in relation to the input. You would usually want to make the video smaller for large original video sizes. This would mitigate against performance issues related to the Flash player having to decompress a large amount of data.

Continuing with our study of the Import Video Settings dialog, the Synchronize video to Macromedia Flash document frame rate checkbox allows you to do exactly as it suggests. A point to notice is that the sound is always synched to the frame rate, so un-checking this option means that your sound will not be synched to the video. Not a problem if the sound is background music, but important if there are vocals and associated lip movements.

> *Why would you want to un-check this option? Well, because the results will be smoother. If you want it to synch to the soundtrack, then there is the possibility of low-end machines not being able to keep up, because to keep in synch there is a set speed the video has to play at (it has to keep in synch with the vocals). If the machine is not likely to keep up with the synch (or doesn't need to) then you should uncheck this option. You would uncheck it for videos that are graphics only (such as rotating logos) which are not 'live video'.*

Next up, you can select the number of video frames to encode per Flash frame. A ratio of 1:1 gives you one video frame per Flash frame, but 1:2 will give you one video frame per two Flash frames, and more importantly, will *halve* the file size of the video.

> *Once you have imported your video, avoid changing the frame rate of the FLA if you want the video to remain synched to the timeline.*

Finally, the Import audio checkbox will appear if the video source has audio associated with it. If you are using only Flash and you *do not* need close synch between the video and audio, consider using a separate sound object and an MP3 sound file.

This allows you more control of the sound because the video codec no longer handles it. If you need lip synch, you will most likely have to include the audio with the video.

As the video compression used in MX is based on fixed video quality and not fixed bandwidth, the import settings do not give you a file size for the imported video. Not only is the final file size dependent on the settings you use for import, it is also dependent on the video content. Although this will cause some head scratching to start off with, experience shows that you soon get a feel for what will result in a big file, and learn how to avoid it.

It's also worth noting that video import (and export to SWF where there is video involved) is a lengthy process even on a fast machine. Expect to go off and brew a coffee while you wait for video content to import! One way around this is to find a small section of video that is typical of your content, and play about with that small segment until you are happy. Once you have your import settings, load up the full video.

Once you have imported your video object, the first thing you will see is this information window:

The video object is not like a self-contained movie clip (a clip with 100 frames can live on a timeline that is much shorter than its own and still play out all 100 frames). In contrast, a video object requires a number of frames equal to its length. So unless you want the video cut short, hit Yes.

Now you'll see a new symbol for an **embedded video** in the library:

The embedded video object is a hybrid, having some features of movie clips, and some of imported sound files. Like the movie clip, it has an instance name and can be dragged to the stage. It also has properties such as _x and _y. Unlike the movie clip, however, it cannot be accessed internally; you cannot code a myVideoObject.gotoAndPlay(10) action for example. This is where the similarities to the movie clip and sound come in. If you simply place the embedded video on _root, it will stream in, and act like a streaming sound does. If you place it inside a movie clip (that is, on an embedded timeline), then it will take on the capabilities of the movie clip; you can have as many instances of it as you want on stage, but it will not now stream in; all the video content has to have been downloaded before the movie clip is seen on the timeline, otherwise the timeline will stop until the movie clip's content (the video) is fully loaded.

With the above points in mind, the best way to use embedded video is as follows:

- For long video segments, place it on the `_root` of an FLA, and export as a SWF. Load the SWF as a load level in the final site. Because there is no video equivalent to the sound object's `_soundbuftime`, you should make sure that the SWF allows the video content to buffer up in Flash's general buffer by adding some bandwidth-light content at the head of the SWF before the video starts – allow for approximately 10 to 30% of the total time of the video duration. (In sound, the `_soundbuftime` value is the amount of sound data the Flash player must load before streaming sounds are played. If you judge this right, you can fix things so that once the sound starts it will never stop and wait for more sound to stream in.)

- For short video segments, or if you want to use several instances of the video, just place it inside a movie clip.

So how do we control the video object? Well, since it has no timeline of its own, you have to control it *via the timeline it is on*. This will be either `_root` (or the corresponding `_level` once it is loaded in as a load level) or the timeline of the movie clip it is embedded into.

We recommend that you get hold of a few different video files (a quick search on your computer will probably reveal a few AVI or MOV files even if you don't think you have any!) and try importing them using different settings to get a feel for the effects of the various settings. You will soon find that:

- Video of live subjects with a static (or relatively static) camera compresses very well, especially if you set a high keyframe interval.

- Video with large areas of movement will compress poorly.

- Like JPEGs, you will gets lots of noise around sharp color changes (such as sudden change from black to white along an outline). A figure outlined against a blue sky will look bad. The same subject with the camera at a higher vantage point (so that the sky is no longer seen, and the background is darker) will show up less noise effects.

Adding video to Flash timelines

Let's have a look at the effect videos have on download times. I have produced a simple computer animation of a jet fighter and rendered it to an AVI for this example. To save download time and to make sure the lowest spec machines can handle the FLAs, I have already imported the video in the FLA files described below.

Streaming video

Have a look at `video01.fla`. This consists of a blank stage with our video, `plane`, in the library:

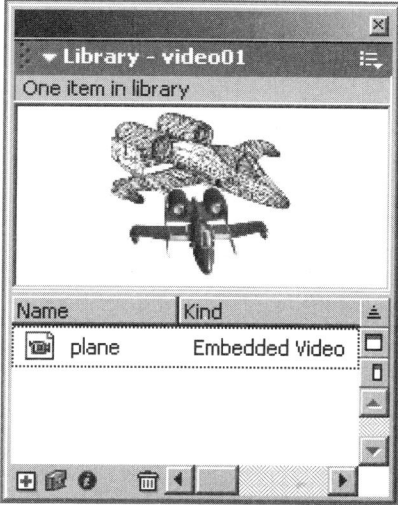

1. Drag an instance of the video onto the stage. You will see an alert pop-up asking if you want additional frames to be added to the timeline to fit the size of the video. Click Yes and test the movie:

The bandwidth profiler of this video will look something like this:

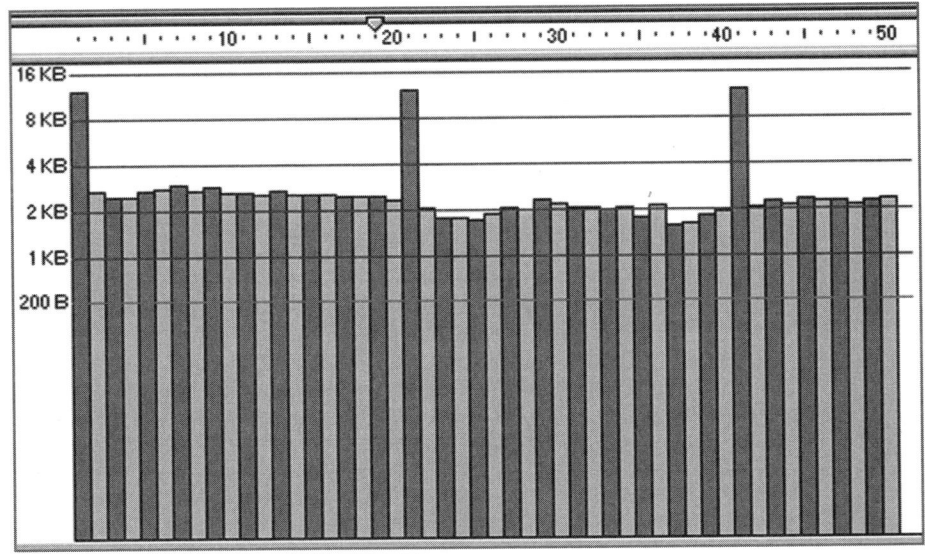

This tells us the following:

- Most frames take up 2k-3k per frame. This is about right for constant streaming using a 56k modem.

- The peaks at frames 1, 21 and 41 represent my *video keyframes*. My video keyframe interval is 20 (as set previously during my import via the Video Import Settings window. This is where the video codec loads in a new frame. In between, the 2-3k frames are just storing the changes between frames. That's cool, because without it, all the frames would take up as much bandwidth as the keyframes. It's not so cool because it kills my 56k constant-stream theory mentioned in the previous bullet point.

The way to combat this is to create a streaming buffer.

2. Back in the FLA, select frames 1 to 50 (double-click on the keyframe at frame 1 to do this), and then click-drag the frame block to the right, dropping them at around frame 80:

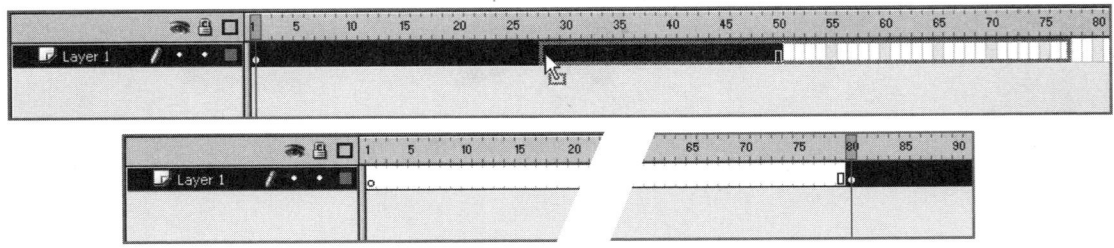

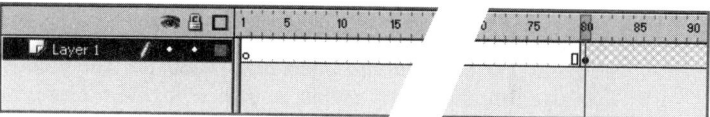

So you now have 80 blank frames to start preloading content, and then 50 frames of actual video content.

The profiler now shows that we have got rid of the first 16K spike, but we are still left with the other two:

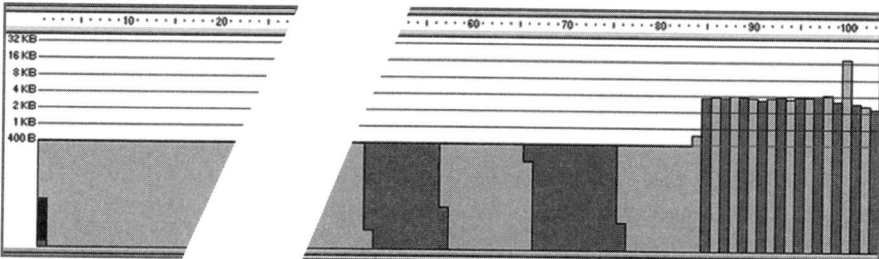

The problem here is that our content is just not designed for constant streaming on a 56k modem - the quality is essentially too high (I set it to 80%). Here, then, is the *Big Rule Of Using Video For Low Bandwidth Users*: to enable efficient streaming, you have to allow some space for preloading at the beginning, and for a 56k modem, you will have to have a fairly low video quality.

> *If you set the frame interval to the max setting (48) you would actually move the remaining two peaks farther apart, and would now have the profile you wanted.*

3. Add a second instance of the `plane` video on the stage (in a new layer to ease selection). Once again, move the clip to frame 80. Using the Free Transform tool, resize the new video object so that you have a smaller version of the video below the original as shown below right:

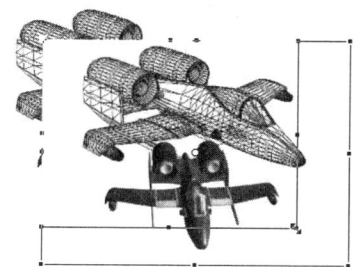
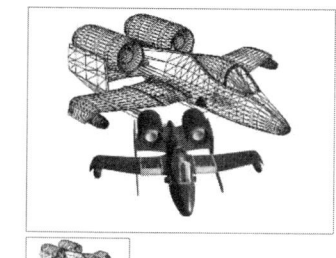

4. Now test the movie again. You will see two versions of the video playing. You will also see that the required bandwidth doubles! The video objects are not seen as *instances* but *streaming media,* and as such, Flash treats them in the same way as streaming sound.

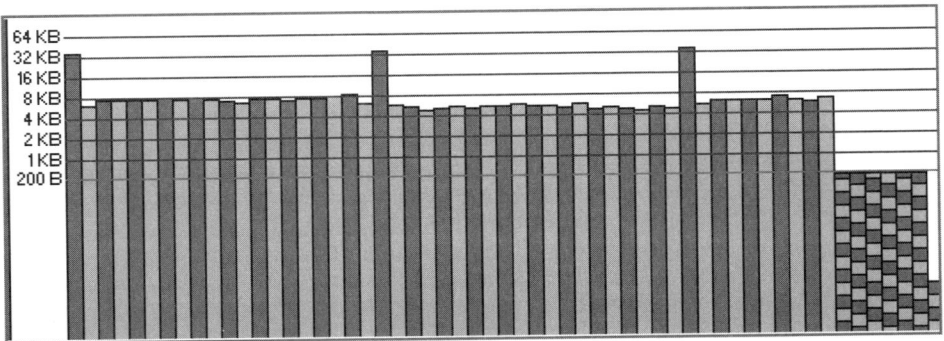

If you also have streaming sound channels, including streaming video with embedded sound, the sound channels will be added together in the final SWF.

Preloading video

The second way to add video to Flash is to ignore streaming and just preload it all. This has the advantage that you can use instances of the same video object to create 'video walls' or other effects, but the disadvantage of a potentially long preload for many users if your video assets are anything over a few tens of frames long. Let's look at the preload technique in this next example (the final effect in this exercise is saved as video02.fla in the download package).

1. Starting with video01.fla again, create a new movie clip called videoClip and place the plane video inside it at frame 1. You will be asked to allow Flash to extend the timeline to accommodate all the frames in the video again, so click Yes as before.

2. On the movie's _root timeline, create four layers called screen 1 to screen 4 and a fifth layer called actions, as shown below:

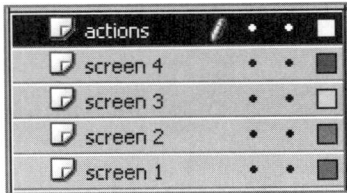

3. Add an instance of `videoClip` in the screen 1 layer and give it an instance name of `screen01`. Test the FLA. You will see that the whole SWF is loaded in on frame 1 – no streaming is now being used, and the SWF will not start until all the video assets are loaded in.

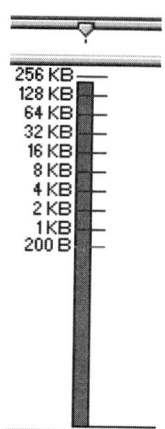

4. In layers screen 2 to screen 4, add one new instance of our `videoClip` on each layer (being careful not to use `plane` instead because they look the same on the stage) called screen02, screen03, and screen04, scaling them smaller using the Scale tool as shown here:

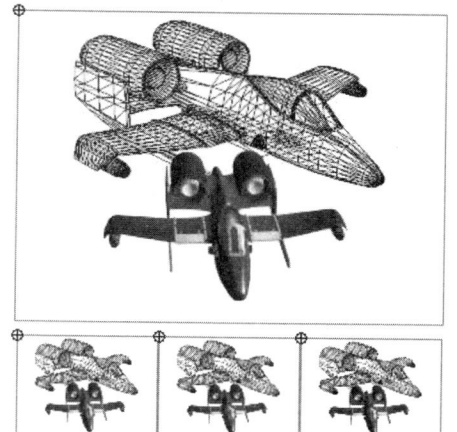

5. Finally, add the following script to the actions layer:

```
screen02.gotoAndPlay(10);
screen03.gotoAndPlay(20);
screen04.gotoAndPlay(30);
```

If you test the FLA, you will see two things:

- The bandwidth profiler has not gone up significantly. This is because we are now using *instances* of the video clip.

- The four video clips are playing out of synch (see image on next page), being 10 frames apart from each other.

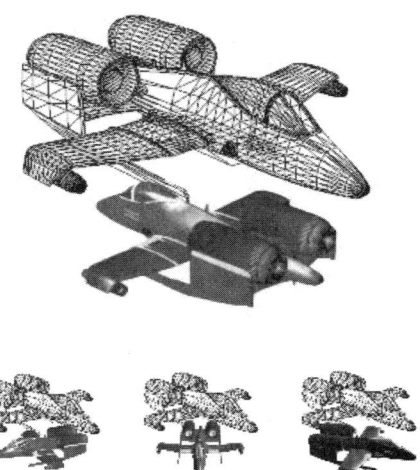

The way to control a video object is not immediately apparent, but you can see here how it is done. To go to a particular frame in a timeline *you refer to frames of the timeline that the video is on*. You have to do this because the video object does not have a timeline of its own.

> *Note that the Macromedia Flash player stores the video streams as compressed video, and has to decompress each video instance on the fly. There is obviously a big performance penalty in using too much video at once, and this may affect all the other non-video assets in your overall animation.*

A few additional points to note:

- Although you can also do this with a streaming video (one that is attached to _root) so that you have the standard *forward*, *back*, *play*, and *stop* video transport buttons, remember that you can't fast forward to a frame that hasn't streamed in yet!

- To allow the video to be controlled by the timeline it is on in this way, you must import it with the 'synch to Flash frame rate' option checked, otherwise going to a particular frame in the movie clip may result in different frames appearing for different users.

- There is nothing stopping you mixing vector graphics over the top of our video at this point. You can thus add titles, or even better, mix Flash vector animation with video animation. Don't forget the drawing API (discussed in Chapter 8) when considering this fact!

Because our video clips are now embedded in movie clips, we can apply any property-based animation we want on it. By tinting some of the movie clips in video02.fla, we reach our final effect (see next page). Try it yourself!

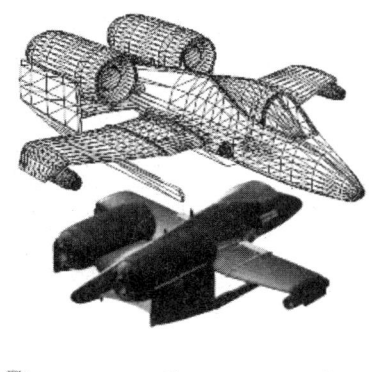

> *Although you can apply property-based animation to a video object that is not embedded inside a movie clip, this causes the video content to got back to its first frame and stop.*

I have added tint effects to screen02, '03, and '04 by choosing Color>Advanced in the Property inspector, and then selecting Settings... to tint the video clips red, green and blue:

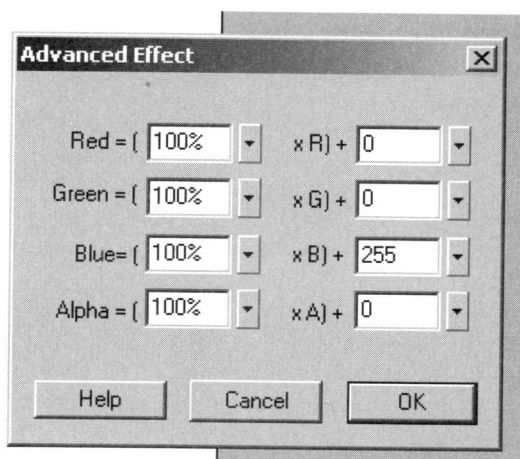

Summary

Although the video object has almost no methods of its own, it gets around this by using the movie clip timeline. This makes the video object very easy to use, and it requires almost no additional ActionScripting to use it well. The only real issue with using the video clip is *which timeline you place it on*. This affects how the video content loads into the Macromedia Flash player on the Web, and you should be aware of the differences between attaching a video asset to a _root level (streaming video) and an embedded movie clip timeline (non-streamed preloaded video). Choosing the latter as the delivery method for long video sequences may keep some of your users waiting for a *very* long time!

In the next chapter we're going to look at the new improved Macromedia Flash MX event model and learn how to get our Flash movies to react to real-time input using event-driven code.

Chapter 13

Events

The bedrock of interactive motion graphics is event-driven code. Without it, your Flash movies will not be able to respond to *real-time input*, a hallmark of any application that aims to provide real-time interaction.

Macromedia Flash MX has an enhanced event model, and in this chapter we'll look specifically at how events and 'event-like' functionality is used in Flash MX. We will also touch upon an important sub-topic in the event world: the use of events as **methods**; this is the direction that Flash seems to be heading in (and has been since Flash 5).

The more design-focused readers among you might find this chapter a little complicated in terms of scripting - event handling is after all a pretty non-trivial subject, and because we are looking at additions to the basic Flash 5 functionality, by definition it will get a little hairy at times! However, our emphasis on 'learning by example' will hopefully clarify any potentially confusing areas.

Event scripting techniques

It is good programming practice with Macromedia Flash MX to place all your code in one place - although we have already stated this earlier in the book, it's worth emphasizing here because it's a change that will take some getting used to for the typical Flash 5 scripter.

Instead of using **object scripts** (scripts that are attached to individual buttons and movie clips, or distributed throughout the timelines), it is much more efficient to define all your scripts early on, and if possible, on frame 1 of the _root timeline. To do this you should use **callbacks** instead of object scripts. Remember, callback functions have the same scope as the timeline that they are defined on.

Take a look at this code snippet:

```
myClip.onEnterFrame = function() {
  // code
};
```

As you are attaching the function to the *event* here, and not to myClip, this example has a scope of the timeline it is defined on, and *not* the timeline of myClip. If we were to additionally define a variable myVar inside the function it would exist as _root.myVar.

The following with structure gets around this potential problem:

```
with (myClip) {
  myClip.onEnterFrame = function() {
    // code
  };
  // other myClip events go here.
}
```

In this case, assuming our script is defined on frame 1 of _root, the event script is actually attached to _root.myClip, and any variable myVar we define inside the event handler will exist as _root.myClip.myVar. This is a useful technique because your scope will be the same as an object script, although you still end up with one long script on frame 1 of _root.

There is one occasion when you can't do this: when the movie clip you want to use is not on the timeline at initialization. There are two ways to solve this problem:

- Call a function directly from the movie clip you want to use:

```
onClipEvent (something) {
  _root.myfunction()
}
```

  This way, the function is still in a centralized script.

- Call a function that defines the event *when the clip is created*. Place this on frame 1 of _root:

```
function setEvents() {
  myClip.onSomeEvent = function() {
    // code
  };
  // other myclip events
}
```

  And then when you get to the keyframe where myClip first appears, simply do this:

```
setEvents();
```

There *are* other ways round this problem (and we'll look at one of the best ways in a moment - adding events to the object prototype chain), but the methods seen here should get you started on the road to centralizing your scripts.

Events as methods in Flash

You can also attach event handlers directly to the object prototype chain (instead of on the individual instances themselves). This is a much more elegant solution when you want to create multiple versions of an object, all with the same (or very similar) event handlers.

On a scripting level, we should really save this for Chapter 15. The reason we haven't is because to do so would ignore the real reason for going down this route to start off with; one of the things you usually want to use to customize a standard Flash object (such as the movie clip) is custom **event handling** that's specific to your application. OK, even I'm starting to lose the plot a little here - example time!

Creating intelligent particles

In this example we'll define a new object, a *particle*, by adding properties and events to the existing movie clip object. In this scenario a particle is something that could become the basis of numerous little Flash toys and games if you add some mouse interaction or a bit of AI (Artificial Intelligence), but we'll let you play around with that later. For now, we will look at how the particle can be made up from a collection of events defined as methods for a custom object.

The code for this example is in `objectEvents.fla`. The function `particle` defines our additional properties and methods. All the methods are actually event handlers, of which we have two:

1. The `onEnterFrame` event defines our particle movement. The particles in this script simply move in a straight line until they hit the stage boundary, whereupon they 'bounce' back towards the center of the screen. Observant readers will probably have already realized that we could use the `Stage` object here, and ensure that the particles will always remain the same size, and keep within the constraints of the browser window (irrespective of how big it becomes), via the little stage resize listener that we looked at in Chapter 10. Another concept for you to play with!

2. The `onPress` event stops the particle moving if we press on it with the mouse. Not the most useful feature at the moment, and hardly 'intelligent' as such, but this script is actually the basis of a little predator/prey simulation, where I have two kinds of particle: a virus, and the white blood cell that eats it. When clicking on a particular cell, you can change its parameters to make it act differently (mutate). If you like the sound of this little bio-simulation, why not try and create it yourself? First though, we'll cover the basics together to get started.

The use of `this` is again important. Because your scripts are remote from the actual objects that you are defining them for, **scope** becomes significant. In Flash 5, adding `this` was just a stylistic consideration: in many cases it was *implicit*, so you could put it in or leave it out because the default scope was invariably `this` anyway. In the script below, the default scope is the timeline that the function is defined on (`_root`). Adding `this` changes the scope, from `_root` to the instance's timeline (you can check this using the debugger). The properties of each particle are defined on the individual particle timelines. If you also try the script without `this`, you will see that the functions will create all the properties on `_root`, which is somewhat less than useful.

It goes without saying that an understanding of scope is not just applicable to *advanced* scripters in Flash MX (indeed, we emphasized this point in Chapter 8). It is a requirement if you want to do anything that involves a function or method, and this includes almost everything new in Flash to do with ActionScript. Creating objects and messing about with prototypes is no longer the black art it was in Flash 5, as long as you understand scope.

The `attachMovie` action takes a clip in the library with linkage name `ball` (we'll build this in a moment), and creates one hundred instances of it called `ball0` to `ball99`. We are creating *movie clips* when we do this, but the following line attaches our new functions and performs callbacks directly to each instance:

```
particle.apply(_root["ball"+i]);
```

The `apply` method takes one argument: the path and name of the target object. In our case, this is `_root.ball0` to `_root.ball99`, and `_root["ball"+i]` will resolve to the hundred paths we require. It is important to realize that it *does not* resolve to an instance name (such as `ball89`), which is a string (and therefore will not work).

Here's the full script:

```
particle = function () {
  // PURPOSE: defines the particle object
  //
  // initialize properties
  this.speedX = (Math.random()*8)-4;
  this.speedY = (Math.random()*8)-4;
  this.lowX = 0;
  this.lowY = 0;
  this.highX = 550;
  this.highY = 400;
  this._x = 200;
  this._y = 200;
  // END initialize properties
  //
  // Define events
  this.onEnterFrame = function() {
    if (this._x<this.lowX) {
      this.speedX = Math.random()*4;
    } else if (this._x>this.highX) {
      this.speedX = -Math.random()*4;
    }
    if (this._y<this.lowY) {
      this.speedY = Math.random()*4;
    } else if (this._y>this.highY) {
      this.speedY = -Math.random()*4;
    }
    this._x += this.speedX;
    this._y += this.speedY;
  };
  this.onPress = function() {
    this.speedX = 0;
    this.speedY = 0;
  };
  // END define events
};
//
// main code
for (i=0; i<100; i++) {
  _root.attachMovie("ball", "ball"+i, 1000+i);
  particle.apply(_root["ball"+i]);
}
// END main code
```

If you want to create custom event methods for a button, remember that a button has no timeline, so you may want to either use movie clips as buttons instead (recommended), or use the this._parent *path instead of* this. *The latter is really a non-starter (you can't have two buttons on the same timeline, otherwise the properties will overwrite each other), which is another reason why you can't use standard button objects if you want to use any advanced ActionScript with them.*

The final thing we have to do is to create the physical appearance of our particle, ball. Here's how:

3. Create a new movie clip called ball and go into its edit mode. With the pixel grid enabled (View>Snap to Pixels must be checked, then zoom in until the pixel grid appears), create a strokeless gray circle as shown here. We are keeping the particles small and basic to retain high redraw speeds (in spite of the fact that we will have a hundred instances onscreen):

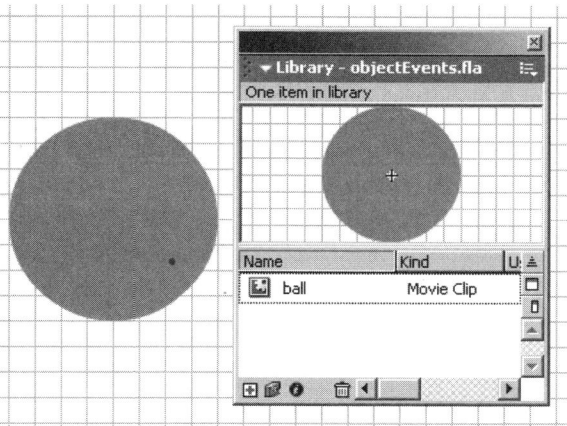

4. Open the Symbol Properties window (right-click on the ball symbol in the library and select Properties..., or select the same option from the Library window's pop-up menu).

With the Advanced options showing, check Export for ActionScript, leaving Export in first frame checked and Identifier as `ball` (both will appear with these settings as soon as you check Export for ActionScript):

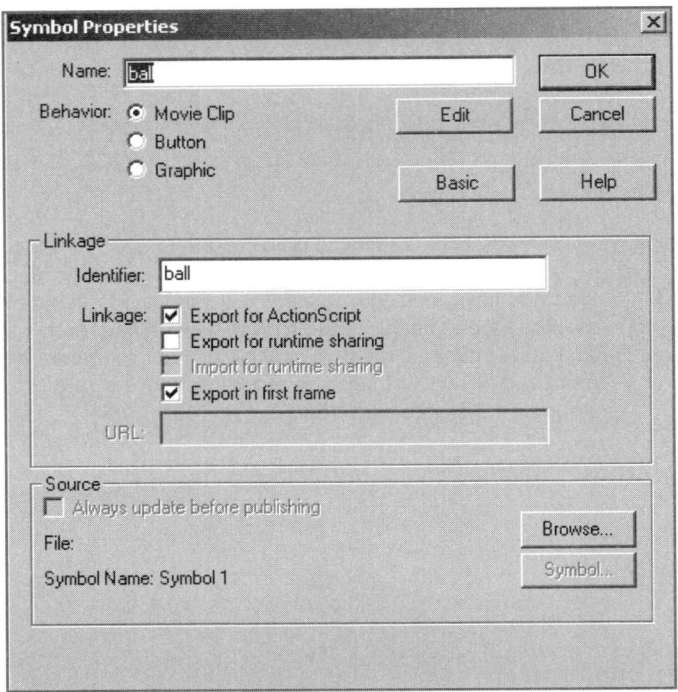

You are now all set. Test the FLA to see object-based event scripting in action!

This script is actually showing off a very potent Flash MX feature that power-scripters will relish; the ease with which you can now extend the standard Flash objects to create your own customized versions is extremely useful.

> *Notice that although we are creating a hundred separate objects, each with a set of events and properties, the script definition is still in the same place - frame 1 of the movie clip. If you have followed our recommendations to discard the old Flash 5 way of thinking (attaching events directly to the graphics on stage), you will have found the script above remarkably easy to digest - but near impossible if you haven't. There is one more advantage of writing scripts in the new way, and that will become apparent when we get stuck into creating our own components. If you haven't been converted yet, there is still time to make the break!*

The Macromedia Flash MX event model

OK, so far we have looked at activities that we could do in Flash 5. Flash MX simply makes these things more accessible, and allows us to do it all in a very structured and centralized way. Accordingly, the rest of this chapter will focus on some of the new features, including **listeners**, **timer events**, and **sound handling**.

Additionally Flash MX gives us **watchers**, a feature that allows you to assign a callback function to a state change. This lets you run event scripts based on changes *internal to the code itself*, enabling you to make all the internal interactions of your scripts (that result in changes to values) event-driven. We will save a study of watchers for Chapter 15, since they are part of Flash MX objects. However, functionally speaking you may want to treat them as a new type of event called an **internal script event**, because that is what you will mainly use them for (they can also be used within components to update live previews).

Returning to this chapter, let's take a look at what we mean by **listener** events.

Listeners

A listener is a special kind of event. It allows you to create event handler callback functions that respond to events raised by basic I/O objects other than standard button and movie clip instances. These objects include the **key**, **mouse**, **selection**, **stage**, and **text field**.

So what's the difference between a listener and a normal event? A listener event is attached to objects other than the one generating the event. A side effect of this is that the initiating event can affect more than one other object. This is reasonable, given the nature of the objects listed above; more than one object may want to react to a key press, and *all* movie clips on stage may want to react to a stage resize. Another special feature of listeners is that the initiating object is predefined and global; there is only one stage and one mouse.

The requirements for adding listeners is as follows:

- Your listener object must have at least one listener event/method defined for it (the available listener event/methods are listed below)

- The listener object must then be *registered* as a listener

Apart from that, the *listener* system is much the same as *events*. The list of available events/methods is as follows:

- **Key** - onKeyDown, onKeyUp

- **Mouse** - onMouseMove, onMouseDown

- **Selection** - onSetFocus

- **Stage** - onResize

- **TextField** - onChanged, onScroller

Let's look at examples of some of these events in action.

The Key object

In this example we will create an event-driven keyboard input-detection system for a video game using the onKeyDown listener. Rather than use key polling via Key.getCode, we will use the listener method to trigger events only if keys are actually being pressed.

You will find the finished FLA file for this exercise as keys01.fla in the download package. It includes a simple space ship graphic that moves left/right when you press the left/right arrow keys.

1. In a new FLA (stage size 550x400, 18fps), add two layers, actions and graphics:

2. Create your space ship graphic in the graphics layer and make it a movie clip with F8, ensuring that the registration point is at the centerline of the ship. Give it an instance name ship. You can leave the instance anywhere on the stage, since we will be placing it in the correct place via the script:

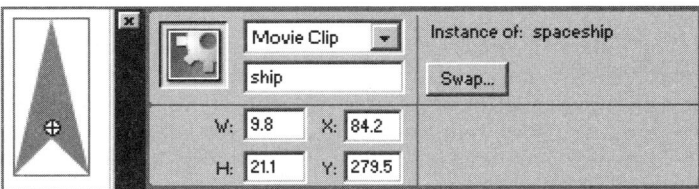

3. In the Actions layer, add the following script to initialize our FLA:

```
// initialize variables
speed = 8;
startPosX = 270;
startPosY = 350;
direction = 0;
//
// place ship at start position
ship._x = startPosX;
ship._y = startPosY;
```

This sets our ship speed at 8 pixels, and sets its initial (x, y) position.

4. There is a lot going on in most games, so it makes sense to have one centralized object to handle the general keyboard inputs. Add the following script to the existing one in frame 1:

```
// set up an object to handle key input,
// and make it a listener to the Key object...
keyDetect = new Object();
keyDetect.onKeyDown = function() {
  if (Key.isDown(Key.LEFT)) {
    direction = -speed;
  } else if (Key.isDown(Key.RIGHT)) {
    direction = speed;
  }else{
    direction = 0;
  }
};
```

Our keyDetect object has an event script set to run on the onKeyDown event. If the left arrow key is down, we set the movement direction to be –speed (move left), otherwise if the right arrow key is down, we will move right by equating direction to speed.

5. The last thing we have to do is register keyDetect as a listener to the Key object:

```
Key.addListener(keyDetect);
```

6. We now need to animate the ship. To move the ship in the correct direction, we simply need to add direction to the current value of ship._x. We only need to do this onKeyDown:

```
// set up the ship events and make it
// a listener to the Key object...
ship.onKeyDown = function() {
  this._x += direction;
};
Key.addListener(ship);
```

Notice that we have registered ship to the Key object as well. This means that keyDetect and ship are actually both responding to the same event, and this is another difference between a standard event and a Listener event; you can have multiple event handlers for the same event.

7. You will see two problems if you test this FLA. The first is that the SWF will not respond to key presses until it has focus, so click anywhere on the stage to give it focus (this isn't too big a problem as such - if this was part of a full game, you would make sure that the user clicked on the screen at least once before playing, usually via a Click to continue start screen).

The second problem is a bit more difficult. The key presses are coming through filtered by the computer hardware, and this adds a key press delay before the key press actually kicks in.

One way out of this is to add an inertia effect. The FLA with inertia is included as keys02.fla, and a fully amended listing is included below:

```
// initialize variables
speed = 8;
startPosX = 270;
startPosY = 350;
//
// place ship at start position
ship._x = ship.targetX = startPosX;
ship._y = ship.targetY= startPosY;
//
// set up an object to handle key input,
// and make it a listener to the Key object...
keyDetect = new Object();
keyDetect.onKeyDown = function() {
  if (Key.isDown(Key.LEFT)) {
    direction = -speed;
  } else if (Key.isDown(Key.RIGHT)) {
    direction = speed;
  } else {
    direction = 0;
  }
};
Key.addListener(keyDetect);
//
// set up the ship events and make it
// a listener to the Key object...
ship.onKeyDown = function() {
  this.targetX += direction;
};
ship.onEnterFrame = function() {
  this._x += (this.targetX-this._x)/4;
};
Key.addListener(ship);
```

We are constantly redrawing the ship via the `onEnterFrame` script at the bottom, but notice that we are only running the parts of the script that deal with keyboard inputs when a key is actually down, so *the code is using events to run only the scripts that are actually needed*.

The Selection object

The selection object is useful when used with text fields, although you can also use it with buttons (and movie clips that are acting as buttons). The selection listener allows you to detect when a new text field has just received focus. This will occur if the user has pressed the TAB key or clicked inside a new text field. Focus will change to *null*.

The `onSetFocus` selection listener event has two arguments: `oldFocus` and `newFocus`, which define the **variable path** to the text field that previously had focus, and the text field that has just *gained* focus. If no text field can be named as `oldFocus` or `newFocus`, that argument will instead be undefined.

OK, that's enough to put most people off - let's see if an example can shed more light on it! Suppose you had an online used automobile dealership. The user can specify a first and second choice of car color for the chosen model. For the current car, the color choices are the colors of the rainbow: red, orange, yellow, green, blue, indigo, and violet. The user can select a first and second choice by typing in two colors that comply with certain criteria:

- They must both be specified

- They must both be in the list of available colors

- They must not be the same

We could do this with components (using a list box or combo box), but let's suppose we want to stick to text fields because of the large number of available colors.

How do we implement this? There's a few simple ways of doing it, but they immediately become much more complicated if the user has the option of specifying two colors in any order. If we instead use the `onSetFocus` listener, we immediately gain one big advantage: *we know our script will only run when the user has entered one or both of the two choices*, so we don't have to mess about with `onEnterFrame` scripts that check after every key press.

Have a look at `selection.fla` - this has a simplified form with just the color options:

The text fields have instance names of `field01` and `field02`, and variables called `value01`, `value02`. There is a third dynamic text field at the bottom called `dynamicText` and it has a variable `message`. Let's study the scripting - as usual, you'll find this in the Actions layer.

1. The first thing we have done is set the array of available colors:

```
// set available colors...
cols = ["red", "orange", "yellow", "green", "blue", "indigo",
➡"violet"];
//
```

2. We then define an object `focusControl`, to which we have attached our listener `onSetFocus` event:

```
// define focus control object that will hold all our events
focusControl = new Object();
//
```

3. The `onSetFocus` callback function is defined next. This takes two arguments, `oldFocus` and `newFocus`. Remember that `oldFocus` is the name of the last text field selected. Possible values of `oldFocus` are:

   - `null` - no `oldFocus` defined because this is the first selection *or* the stage is selected

   - `_level0.field01` - the top text field was selected first

   - `_level0.field02` - the bottom text field was selected first

   Similarly, `newFocus` is the name of the text field currently selected, and it can be either:

   - `null` - no new selection or the stage was selected

   - `_level0.field02.field` - the bottom text field was selected second

   - `_level0.field01.field`

   To get to the value of either text entry field, we have to look at either of the following:

   - `_level0.field01.value01`

   - `_level0.field02.value02`

   We generally just want to look at the currently selected text field object's variable. The new method `textField.variable` almost gives us this because it returns the name of the variable as a text string (note that it doesn't give us the *value*, just the *variable name as a string literal*, so be careful!).

Once we have these two string literal inputs, the two loops check the two input values. Remember, if your scripts are expecting numbers, you need to enclose the whole path in Number().

The for-i loop checks that the oldFocus text field contains a valid color. If it does, the for-j loop checks that the newFocus text field contains a valid color *and* is not the same as the oldFocus color. Here's the code we add:

```
// set available colors...
cols = ["red", "orange", "yellow", "green", "blue", "indigo",
➡"violet"];
//
// define focus control object that will hold all our events
focusControl = new Object();
//
// define the onSetFocus event for the text control object
focusControl.onSetFocus = function(oldFocus, newFocus) {
  trace(oldfocus)
  lastInput = _root[oldFocus.variable];
  thisInput = _root[newFocus.variable];
  for (i=0; i<cols.length; i++) {
    // check last color is valid...
    if (lastInput == cols[i]) {
      // if so, check for valid second color...
      for (j=0; j<cols.length; j++) {
          // accept if  second color is valid and
          // not the same as the first...
          if ((thisInput == cols[j]) && (i != j)) {
                message = "accepted";
                break;
          }
      }
      break;
    }
  }
};
```

Notice that the two input values are in the form:

```
lastInput = _root[oldFocus.variable]
```

We have to form a path from oldFocus and textField.variable, both of which return string literals. This is the easiest way of doing this; the contents of the square brackets are evaluated, and the result is assumed to be a path.

4. Finally, we can add the focusControl object as a listener to the selection object:

```
selection.addListener(focusControl);
```

5. Test the FLA file (`selection.fla`) using the TAB key to switch between text fields:

select your color:

1st choice | blue |

2nd choice | red |

accepted

You may still be thinking that the components option would be much easier, but bear in mind that it's a fairly common function to require two text fields to be entered in any order, both of which must be correct at the same time. If you have a list of user IDs and passwords for a restricted area, you can't allow selection from a predefined list and so you must use text fields.

Also, when the user needs to enter two values where one value defines the allowed range of the other (such as the two figures that define the 'sell' range of an online share deal application - the minimum must obviously be less than the maximum), you can only do real-time error detection using the `onSetFocus` listener.

The other listeners work in much the same way, and it is only the detail of the listener events that change. We will therefore move on to the other new event-driven features - program timing and sound handling.

Timer events

Macromedia Flash is sometimes accused of being a little slow. Although vectors have the advantage of low file size and scalability, drawing via a vector engine always has a speed penalty, because you have to recalculate all those curves and fills in real time. It gets easier if you have dedicated hardware support (like an OpenGL or DirectX video card), but Flash *doesn't*.

For a bitmap-based system (such as Director), all you have to do is send the bitmap data to the video memory – something computers are much faster at doing – but that has the penalty of larger file sizes. You win some, you lose some!

In most cases, complaining about a lack of processing power always sounds too much like a spoilt child who wants it all; if Flash could replicate PlayStation visuals on the fly, we'd no doubt all be wailing about not being able to emulate PlayStation 2! It's always a case of looking at your performance limitations and being a little creative with the processing budget you have available. The early video game and computer UI designers had the same set of constraints and did OK, so why can't Flash web designers? The answer of course is that most of them *do* manage, and do so very well, but a bit of ActionScripting voodoo to help us will always be welcome - this is where timer events come in handy.

The setInterval event

The `setInterval` event is the advanced Flash game designer's dream. It is also beneficial to the design of performance-heavy web sites, because it allows you to run scripts based on a **timed event**.

We will build up to the significance of this slowly, because `setInterval` is far too cool for me to allow you to miss its implications for optimizing motion graphics for performance.

`setInterval` can be used in several ways, but the easiest implementation uses the following arguments:

```
setInterval(function, interval);
```

The function `function` will run every `interval` (in milliseconds). Let's see this in action - this next example is called `setInterval_event.fla`.

1. In a new FLA (550x400, 12fps), add two layers, actions and graphics. In layer graphics add two text fields as shown below. The two rectangles are un-selectable dynamic text fields, with associated variables `frame` and `event`. Static text has also been added to the left to denote the respective variables:

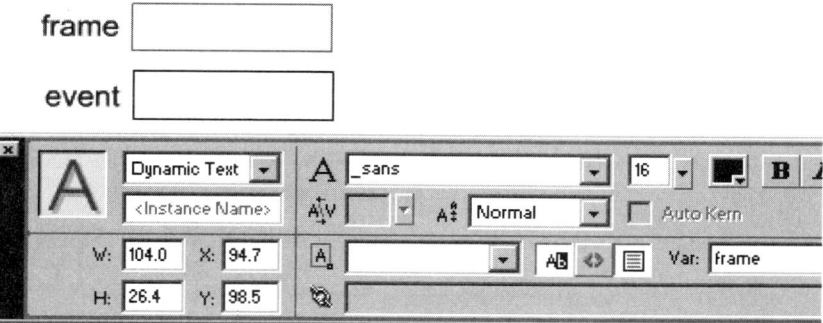

2. The variable `frame` will be the number of frames the SWF has stepped through, and `event` will be the number of `setInterval` event scripts we have executed in the same time.

3. Add the following script in the actions layer:

```
// set counters...
event = 0;
frame = 0;
//
// set up setInterval event to run
// every 40ms...
setInterval(update, 40);
function update() {
  event++;
}
//
// set up enterFrame event to run
// every frame (83ms)...
_root.onEnterFrame = function() {
  frame++;
};
```

The `update` function will run every 40ms, which is about twice as fast as the `enterframe` script below it, which will run 12 frames per second, or every 83 milliseconds (ms).

3. If you test the FLA, you should see the `event` field being updated approximately twice as fast as the `frame` one (this will depend on the exact version of the Flash player and the speed of your computer, as well as whether you are on a Mac or PC):

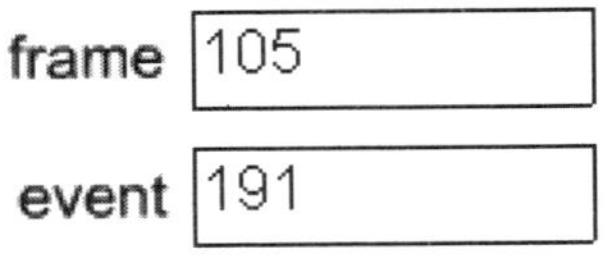

frame `105`

event `191`

Although the `update` event is running much more often than anything else in the SWF, the screen is still only updating at 12fps. You can see this by clicking anywhere on the stage and changing the Frame Rate in the Property inspector to 1fps. Although the event script is running thousands of times a minute, the screen is updating only once a second, and you only see the value of `event` at the end of every second. Obviously an event that runs much faster than the screen update is not much use for motion graphics, but don't worry, we can force the screen to change at the same rate (or as near to it as Flash can manage) by using `updateAfterEvent()`.

4. Change the `update` function so that it now looks like this:

```
setInterval(update, 40);
function update() {
  event++;
  updateAfterEvent();
}
```

If you run the SWF now, you will see the `event` display update itself as it increments.

So far, so good - but we really need to apply this all to *animation*.

Using setInterval for animation

The following example is saved in the downloadable source code package as `setInterval.fla`.

1. Open a new FLA (550x400, 12fps) and add the by now obligatory layers actions and graphics.

2. First of all, we need a ball. Create a movie clip called `ball`, and make a small filled circle in it. Add three instances of this symbol in the graphics layer, with instance names (from top to bottom) `ball01`, `ball02`, and `ball03`.

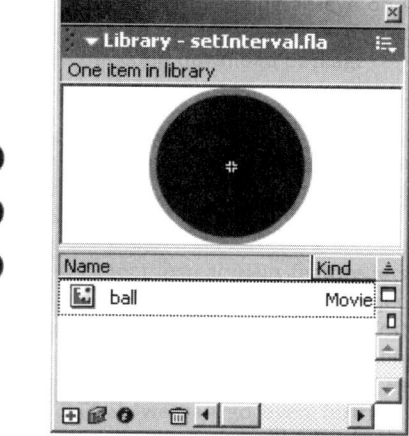

3. In layer actions add the following script:

```
speed01 = speed02 = speed03 = 4;
ball01._x = ball02._x = ball03._x = 200;
//
_root.onEnterFrame = function() {
  ball01._x += speed01;
  if ((ball01._x>300) || (ball01._x<100)) {
    speed01 = -speed01;
  }
};
```

The first two lines set up our initializations for this exercise. We have defined a speed variable for each ball and lined the three balls up at x = 200. The enterFrame script will animate our top ball at a sedate 12fps.

4. Now add a setInterval script to control ball02 via a timed event as shown. You can add it to the end of the existing script:

```
function updateBall02() {
  ball02._x += speed02;
  if ((ball02._x>300) || (ball02._x<100)) {
    speed02 = -speed02;
  }
  updateAfterEvent();
}
setInterval(updateBall02, 40);
```

This will animate the second ball every 40ms (or as close as your machine can make it to 40ms). You now have two levels of animation performance. The two scripts are animating stuff on screen at different speeds. If used wisely this can make your whole site more responsive.

- Those parts of the animation that are in the foreground or are interacting directly with the user can be made to run faster and therefore smoother than other elements in the overall animation by being updated from a faster timed event than the frame rate update.

- Those parts of the animation that are in the background, not moving much (or slowly), or not interacting directly with the user can be made to update on a slower timed event than the frame rate update.

A good example of this would be the ubiquitous space invader game:

- The player's ship would need to move in a responsive and smooth way, so you would make it move faster than the normal frame rate. In doing so, the user is focused on the most responsive element in the game, and *they will get the impression that everything is running this smoothly.*

- The space invaders are important in the game, but not the primary user focus, so you can make them update at the default frame fate.

- The background stars are just that - a background effect, and not the center of the user's experience. By updating them at a slower rate than the default fps, you can shift some performance across to the player's ship.

  If you are using timed events to make everything run faster, you are probably under the misconception that they will always run at the rate specified. This is not true; the events will run as fast as they can, and this may even end up being slower than the default frame rate. If, for instance, you are trying to redraw the whole screen every 5ms, the Flash player will certainly not achieve this. In general, the faster you want to animate something, the smaller it has to be and you have to animate something else at a slower rate to balance the performance budget.

  setInterval is about allowing you to deal out the performance budget in the most efficient manner, and not about trying to somehow conjure up a bigger budget. In many ways, a performance budget is like a cash budget: you can use it wisely or foolishly, but at the end of the day, the budget always has the same total starting value.

5. I know what you are thinking at this point, and yes, you can have more than one setInterval. Add the following lines to the end of the script so far:

```
function updateBall03() {
  ball03._x += speed03;
  if ((ball03._x>300) || (ball03._x<100)) {
    speed03 = -speed03;
  }
  updateAfterEvent();
}
setInterval(updateBall03, 1);
```

The final ball is running at a 1ms update. Well, not quite - it's actually running as fast as the Flash player can push it, but any spare capacity is being soaked up. Depending on whether you are running a lowly minimum-spec machine or a Giga-Hertz supercomputer (which probably doubles as a space heater!), you should see the last ball zip along faster than the other two balls.

If you want to really change the way the animation works, you can call the final function *twice*, thus giving the lion's share of the performance budget to ball03, but be aware that everything else will crawl along, so it's not recommended outside the occasional Flash toy implementation:

```
setInterval(updateBall03, 1);
setInterval(updateBall03, 1);
```

The sound completion event

The second timing event relates to sound, and is implemented via a new method of the sound object – *sound*.onSoundComplete. This method allows you to set up a script that will execute on completion of a sound. There are several reasons why this can be a really cool feature:

- Event sounds are not synchronized to the timeline, so in Flash 5, they were not really synchronized to *anything*. There was no real way to tell when they *started*, never mind *finished* (although there were a few good fixes to get round this, the best one being to fool Flash into thinking the event sound was a streaming sound via a 'kicker' – as documented in a number of friends of ED Flash 5 books).

- An event sound will not necessarily end at a frame border, so without events, you are severely limited to responding to sounds if you use frame-based scripts. Even if you *could* get an exact match, frame rate is not constant, so you could easily lose sound synchronization if the timeline slowed down because of some intensive animation.

- Most existing events are useless for sound because they are driven from either user interactions (which do not always relate to sound), or to frames (such as onEnterFrame, which may be an event but is tied down to the timeline, which as we saw in the previous bullet point is not useful for sound).

The onSoundComplete event fixes this by allowing you to run a script as soon as the current sound has finished. In this way, you can synchronize all sounds to each other, and this will occur largely independently of the timeline.

We say 'largely independently' because there is one interrelationship: **performance**. If you have a movie with a high frame rate or a lot happening on the timeline, then the onSoundComplete event will suffer by being less responsive. As with all event-driven structures, your events will respond immediately on a lightly loaded system, but as fast as they can in a heavily loaded system. This is a general feature of programming, and not a fault of Flash.

With other events, this loss of responsiveness is not normally noticeable to millisecond accuracy, but the human ear is much more sensitive to bad timing than the eye, so any glitches in sound due to performance issues will be picked up by the user.

Not only is Flash sensitive to its own loading, it has limited priority in the list of applications running on your computer, so any processes going on in your computer may affect onSoundComplete. Networked computers are always a problem here, because the background comms interaction can make an otherwise smooth SWF glitch every so often, and these glitches may affect onSoundComplete noticeably.

For the following examples, we will show how to use scripting to synchronize a sound to itself, and then we'll show how you can synchronize a number of sound loops together to form a composition. The latter example leads naturally to creating *interactive soundtracks* easily in Flash, because the synchronization is being handled on the fly by Flash.

You do, however, need sounds that can loop (that is to say the start and end of the loop is at the same point, so you can loop them without any gaps or glitches). The example files sound01.fla and sound02.fla provide some samples, but be aware that the sound files are large, and will take a long time to compile to SWFs on slower machines.

How to use onSoundComplete

1. To use onSoundComplete, you first need to create your sound object, and then link it to a sound file in the library:

   ```
   mySound = new Sound();
   mySound.attachSound("linkageName");
   ```

2. You then define a callback function to the onSoundComplete method of the sound object mySound:

   ```
   mySound.onSoundComplete = function() {
     // code to run on sound end
   };
   ```

3. Finally, you have to make the sound run at least once:

   ```
   mySound.start();
   ```

This will cause the sound to play through once. At the end of the sound, the onSoundComplete callback function will run. Assuming that this script contains a line to play mySound again, you will end up with continuous sound.

> *Note that if the callback starts another sound object* myOtherSound, *the callback above will not run on* myOtherSound *finishing. To do this, you need another call back listener registered to* myOtherSound. *There is of course nothing stopping you registering the same function to both sound objects, but as we shall see, there is a better way to do this by dynamically changing the linkage.*

Looping a single sound

The file sound01.fla has two sounds in the library set up for linkage to sound objects:

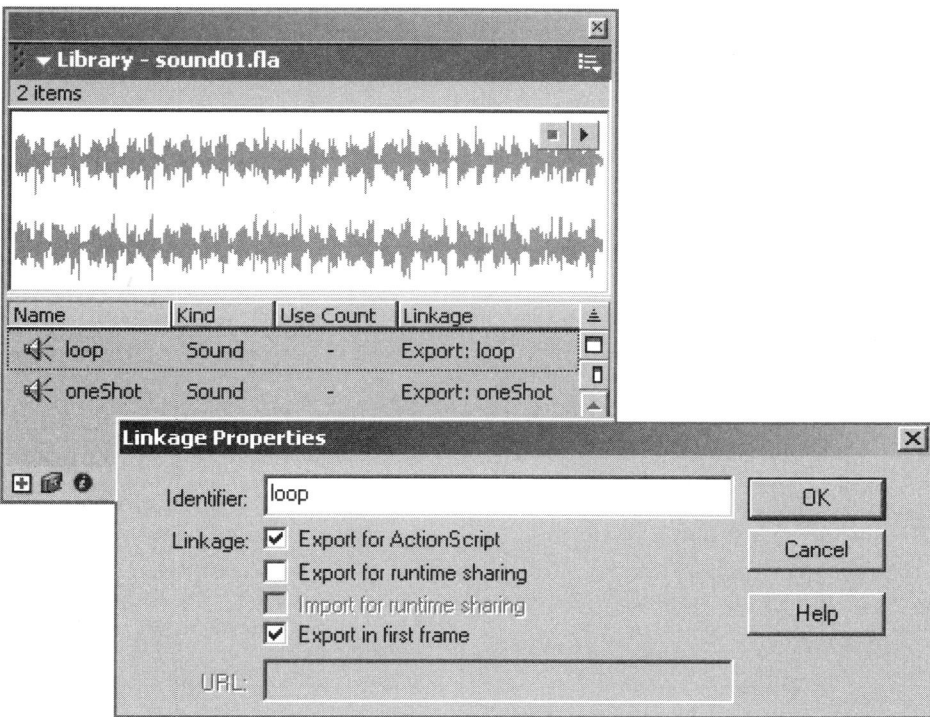

You must have the linkage options defined as above for each sound that you want to use in this way. To bring up the Linkage Properties window, you can select Linkage... from either the right-click menu or the Library's drop-down menu.

Our two sounds have linkage names of loop and oneShot. The former is a rhythm sound made to loop continuously, while the latter is a cymbal crash intended to be played only once. We will loop loop via an onSoundComplete listener, and cause the cymbal to sound on an onMouseDown event. There's a special feature of sound files played on user events that you need to know about, which is why we will also use a Mouse listener.

Have a look at the script attached to frame 1 of the timeline.

1.   This script begins by creating two sound objects, looper and cymbal:

```
// define sound objects and soundCompletion event...
looper = new Sound();
cymbal = new Sound();
```

2. We then define our onSoundComplete event and register it as a listener:

```
looper.onSoundComplete = function() {
  looper.start();
};
```

3. Next, we've added a mouse listener that will fire off the cymbal sound every time you click your mouse down on the stage (you have to be within the stage area if you view the SWF in a browser, and the first click may not result in a cymbal noise because Flash first needs browser focus):

```
// define mouse listener and fire off the
// cymbal sound whenever the mouse is
// down...
mouseSound = new Object();
mouseSound.onMouseDown = function() {
  cymbal.stop("oneShot");
  cymbal.start();
};
Mouse.addListener(mouseSound);
```

> Notice that we stop the cymbal noise before we start it. This is because Flash has only eight sound channels, and if you click more than seven times, you will overload them all (you can run the final FLA with the cymbal.stop("oneShot"); commented out to see what this does).

4. Finally, we have attached our sounds to the two objects, and started the loop running:

```
// start the sound at first loop...
looper.attachSound("loop");
cymbal.attachSound("oneShot");
looper.start();
```

That's fine, but we are not really using the onSoundComplete to do anything new or cool here. We can repeat a sound just by doing this:

```
mySound.start(0, 999);
```

This loops mySound nine hundred and ninety-nine times. What we really need is to be able to sequence *different* loops together...

Sequencing multiple sounds

The library of `sound02.fla` has five sounds in it, with linkage names `t1` to `t5`:

These are designed to be linked together (if you want to know how they were created, have a look in the Flash 5 book *Rich Media: Video and Sound in Flash*, also from friends of ED - the full dance track these loops were taken from is also there).

Let's take a look at the scripting for this example:

1. The script for the sequencing of the loops (a process known as **tracking**) is stored as an array called `tracker`. This stores the name of each sound we want to play in the composition order:

    ```
    //define tracker sequence...
    tracker = ["t1", "t1", "t1", "t1", "t2", "t2", "t2", "t2",
    ➥"t3", "t3", "t4", "t5", "t5"];
    ```

2. We then set two variables: `i` is the current position in the composition, and `j` is the length of the composition:

    ```
    // initialize tracker position and tracker length...
    i = 0;
    j = tracker.length-1;
    ```

3.   The sound object and the onSoundComplete event are defined next. At the end of each sound, the event dynamically attaches the next sound to be played onto the sound object loop1, and starts it off again:

```
// define sound object and soundCompletion event...
loop1 = new Sound();
loop1.onSoundComplete = function() {
  i++;
  if (i>j) {
    i = 0;
  }
  loop1.attachSound(tracker[i]);
  loop1.start();
};
// start the sound at first loop...
```

Note that the first time the loop is run, i is 1 rather than 0. This is because the first time we play a sound, it is started at the bottom of the script, and not by the event as tracker[0].

4.   Finally, we set the system going by attaching the first sound, t1, and starting loop1:

```
loop1.attachSound("t1");
loop1.start();
```

> *You may hear the odd glitch in the soundtrack. This is a function of how fast the* onSoundComplete *is responding. It is usually quick enough, although if something else is going on in the browser you sometimes get a slight space.*

The beauty of this system is of course that you don't have to use an array; you can allow the user to do it *dynamically*. To get rid of any slight glitches, the best way round is to have more than one sound playing (and remember that you can have up to eight tracks looping at any one time with this method!), and to arrange the timings such that the sounds do not start at the same instant:

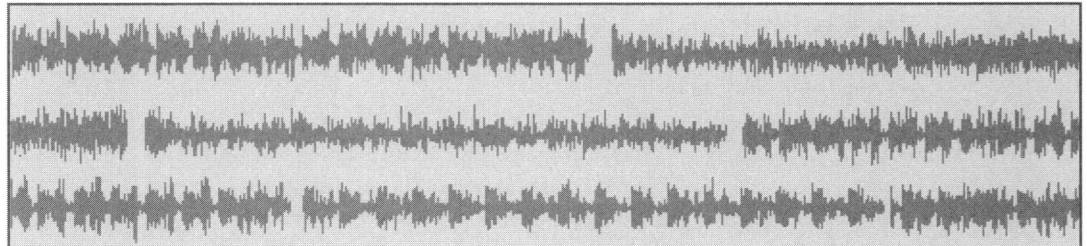

This hides glitches under other layers of continuous sound, and is actually a technique used in modern mixes that use numerous loops. You have to be careful that all your loops never start at the same instance otherwise the listener will see that you have used samples straight away by the noise created by all the initial splice points.

To do this sort of thing in Flash requires you to create at least one sound that is exactly half the length of all the others to stagger the loops, and it also requires that you know how to create loops that are still in beat synch when you do this. An understanding of the applications to allow you to do this (such as the rather sexy *ACID* sound editor from *Sonic Foundry* - www.sonicfoundry.com/) is beyond the scope of this book, but it certainly makes for fun learning if you are of a musical disposition.

Summary

As this book aims to get you into Flash MX techniques as fast as possible, we have not been able to allow ourselves to get side tracked by showing you all sorts of cool applications of the new event model. Instead, we have concentrated on demonstrating the general principles and bare bones of the scripts you need to use. After a brief review of some good practice for scripting with events, we looked at event handling and how an object can use events as methods. We then went on to describe some of the important new features in the Flash MX event model, namely:

- Listeners - demonstrating the *key* and *selection* objects

- Timer events - using the `setInterval` event

- The sound completion event - scripting with the `onSoundComplete` event

Everything is here to produce efficient event-driven video games and a cool interactive sound mixer. Just add a little imagination to your old scripts! Next stop - building advanced components in Flash MX.

Chapter 14

Advanced Components

Earlier in the book, we introduced the use of components in Macromedia Flash MX and noted that they form the general building blocks of Flash designs. Components encapsulate specific features, which you can fine-tune via various properties, or **parameters**, to create the tailored functionality you require.

We've looked at building simple components with the level of complexity of the old Flash 5 smart clips. With the basic concepts behind us, we can now learn how to install and use third party UI elements and other useful components without having to go to the trouble of 're-inventing the wheel'. We may even want to create our own intricate components that use all the new features. However, even if you never need to make your own from scratch, there is the strong possibility that you will need to modify third party components, and to do this you need some understanding of how components work.

We will look at a number of distinct tasks:

- **Adding styles and skins to the default components**
  The default components go a long way towards providing a large proportion of the stuff you need in normal Flash web design, but they still need to be integrated with your own web site design. This is achieved by adding a style or skin to the component, changing its appearance completely while keeping its functionality intact.

- **Using component UI features**
  The default components allow you to do a lot more than smart clips did. They allow true drag and drop, 'snap into place', and live preview functionality – among other things. We will look at the scripting behind such features, and show you how to use them to create everything from Director-style drag and drop behaviors to components that self-animate on the stage via live preview.

- **ActionScript for components**
  Components are unique in that they usually need to run scripts to register all sorts of stuff before they actually appear on the stage - we will look at why and how this is done. This material serves as a nice lead in to Chapter 15, where we will put our object-oriented programming hats on. The discussion towards the end of this chapter should cross over seamlessly into the next chapter.

Let's start with customization.

Customizing the default components

There are two ways to customize the default components in Flash MX: using the `FStyleFormat` object to define the component style, or **skinning** to define totally new graphics. In the following sections we'll look at both of these techniques.

Using the FStyleFormat object

This object works much like the `TextFormat` object we met in Chapter 7, except that it operates on all components that conform to `FStyleFormat`, rather than on text.

> *The letter 'F' in all the ActionScript involved with components simply means 'Flash'; it's not any complex programming convention to get worried about!*

`FStyleFormat` works using the listener event scheme that we came across in Chapter 13. The process of setting up a style format of your own is as follows:

1. Create a new `FStyleFormat` object.

2. Add listeners to all the components that you want it to act upon.

3. Change any style attributes as required by your new style.

The default style is called `globalStyleFormat`, and all default components are already registered to it. You can easily tell what the global style looks like; it's the style that all the default components appear in when you drag them onto the stage. You can change the appearance of all components by simply changing `globalStyleFormat`.

Changing the global style

The `globalStyleFormat` is already defined, so you don't have to set anything up beforehand. Merely change the `globalStyleFormat` properties you want to, and then make the changes with `applyChanges`.

> *The* `globalStyle` *is defined in the library folder* Core Assets – Developer Only *and it will only be included in a SWF that contains at least one of the default components.*

The following script will change the color of all default components to a shade of blue:

```
globalStyleFormat.face = 0x0099FF;
globalStyleFormat.applyChanges ();
```

Here, `face` sets the main color of the components, and we have set it to #0099FF. We then simply apply the change, and we're done. To see the effect of this, add some components to frame 1 of a new FLA, and then add the script in a layer above it.

Creating and defining a custom style

Changing the global style is useful when you want to change all components, but there may be occasions when you want to change only a subset of them. To do this, you need to set up one or more custom styles. Unlike the global format, no custom style is already configured, so you not only have to set up the style, but the listeners too. Don't worry though; this isn't so difficult!

As an example, suppose we were building a set of push buttons for an e-commerce store. We might want four push buttons, labeled Check Out, Review Order, Back to Shop and Cancel Order. We want the first three to be white text on a black button, and the fourth needs to have bold white text on a red background, where the red signifies 'Danger – you will delete your current order if you push this!' Let's make an example to demonstrate this effect.

Creating customized buttons

The FLA for this example is included in this book's source code as `FStyleFormat.fla`. Here we have two layers: graphics and actions, with actions the topmost layer, and a row of push buttons with instance names `bu01` to `bu04` in the graphics layer, as shown here:

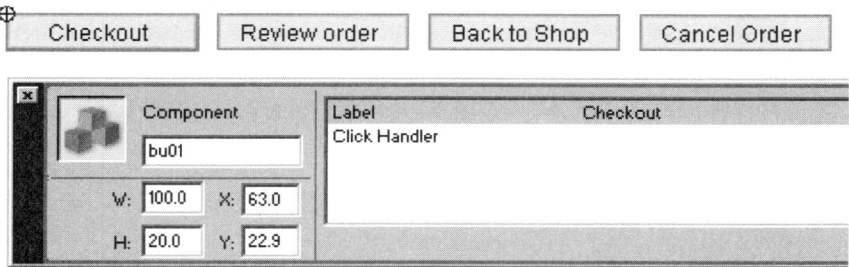

There are a number of changes we want to make to the button styles:

- Make all the text white

- Make the color of the first three buttons black

- Make the color of the fourth red

- Make the text on the fourth button bold

The first change is going to be applied to all the component text, so we might as well apply this change via the global style. The second alteration involves changing the color for only the first three buttons, so we will create a new style called `buttons` that does just that. With the final two changes, we want to change the color and text style of the fourth button only, so to do this we will create a new style called `alertButton`.

The code to achieve these modifications is attached to the actions layer:

1. First, we set the `globalStyleFormat` text color property `textColor` to `0xFFFFFF`, which corresponds to white in RGB hexadecimal:

```
globalStyleFormat.textColor = 0xFFFFFF;
```

2. Next, we define a new style – buttons. This will change the button color to black, and we want to apply it to instances bu01, bu02, and bu03. To do this, we simply register these instances as listeners to the style buttons. Whenever we invoke buttons.applyChanges, all registered listeners will update to the style buttons:

```
buttons = new FStyleFormat();
buttons.face = 0x000000;
buttons.addListener(bu01, bu02, bu03);
```

3. The process for the style alertButton is very much the same, except this time we only want to register one instance – bu04:

```
alertButton = new FStyleFormat();
alertButton.face = 0xFF0000;
alertButton.textBold = true;
alertButton.addListener(bu04);
```

4. Finally, we have to make the changes by using the applyChanges method on all our styles:

```
globalStyleFormat.applyChanges();
buttons.applyChanges();
alertButton.applyChanges();
```

The run-time appearance of the buttons is shown below:

If you later decide to change the appearance of a style, remember that you have to use applyChanges() before listeners will reflect the changes you have made.

We have applied our alertButton style to one instance only. This is fine, as we've assumed that this is only a small part of our final application, and we have a large number of other alert buttons.

If, however, we want to apply this style to bu04 only, we could use the setStyleProperty method. This is a method of the component itself, and all of the default components recognize it. It's useful if you only want to change one or two style properties for one instance only, and it doesn't require registering listeners or the creation of a style format. The following code would apply the face and textBold style changes to bu04 only:

```
bu04.setStyleProperty("face", 0xFF0000);
bu04.setStyleProperty("textBold", true);
```

This method, setStyleProperty, takes two arguments: the first is a string representing the property you want to change (remembering that as a string, it must be in "quotation" marks), and the second is the new value.

> If you want to make style changes to an individual instance dynamically (for example, the first time a button is pressed, you may want to change a button's face color to show that it has been visited at least once), you should use `setStyleProperty`. Not only is it easier, but using a style object instead would not only change the instance in question, but all other registered listeners as well – a nice effect, but something you may not actually want.

The ability to add styles is great, but you are limited to exactly how much you can change. For many design-based sites, complete with a wacky but clever UI, you want to give your components the same style as the rest of your graphics, and this means radically changing the component graphics themselves – a process known as **skinning**.

Skinning components

Skinning allows you to fundamentally change the look of a component. If you drag one or more components onto the stage of a new FLA, your library will look something like this:

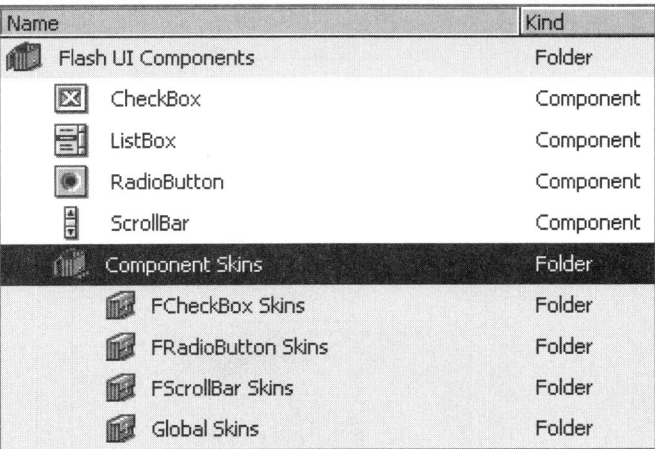

The Component Skins folder contains all the symbols that the components use. Have a look inside these folders to get a feel for what the standard skins look like.

Let's create a new skin for the scrollbar. The scrollbar is actually used in a number of other components, and changes in its skin are also reflected in the combo box, list box, and scroll pane components. The scrollbar is also perhaps the most difficult to get to grips with, so it represents maximum value for our time in this example: the hardest to work with and it lets us skin four for the price of one!

> *In practice, the only other component you really have to explicitly skin to form a new skin style is the push button, because the checkbox and radio button don't really contain that much to change, and you can probably get them close enough to your skins via tweaks with* FStyleFormat.

The first step is to get a good idea of how the default skins are put together. When creating new skins, you can choose whether or not to make them compatible with the FStyleFormat methods. Making a skin that is compatible is harder than one that isn't, so we will look at the easier option first. To make a skin that is not compatible with FStyleFormat is easier because you aren't building a general skin that has to allow for every possible change of style, as we shall see later.

> *By choosing to build your own custom skin in a commercial web design environment, you are most likely aiming to create a look and feel for your components that* can't *be achieved by using* FStyleFormat, *so you are unlikely to want to spend the time to create a generalized 100%* FStyleFormat *compliant skin.*

To create our skins, we have to simply replace all the graphics in the Component Skins **folder** with alternative ones with roughly the same attributes, but a custom style consistent with your overall final purpose for the components (so that they fit in with your web site design).

As ever, the best way to show this is by example. Have a look in the Window>Common Libraries>Buttons common library. If you search around in the Playback **folder**, you will see the gel series of buttons.

I've got a bit of a soft spot for these buttons – they're pretty, but maybe a bit too cheesy for a commercial web site, making them great for a book example! We'll base our scrollbar skin around them. The first thing we have to do is look at the skin set that makes up the standard scrollbar. In a new FLA, drag a scrollbar onto the stage and have a look in the library (look in the folder called Flash UI Components>Component Skins>FScrollBar Skins).

Alternatively, take a look at `defaultSkin.fla` in the source code files, in which we've taken all the skin components and laid them out on the stage so you can look at them all together in one place:

The `upArrow` and `downArrow` skins form the arrow heads at the top and bottom of the scrollbar `fsb_ScrollTrack`. The arrows have three variants each: `Arrow`, `Arrow_disabled`, and `Arrow_press`. The thumb wheel that moves up and down the scroll track comes in three parts: `top`, `middle`, and `bottom`. Note that because the thumb wheel has some small parts (`top` and `bottom`), I have enlarged them in relation to the other more regular skins (it's actually the same width as `fsb_ScrollTrack`).

Whenever you decide to skin a component, a printout like the screenshot above is by far the best starting point; it can be a little difficult to remember which elements comprise a scrollbar, and easy to leave one out. The next step is to apply your inspiration, the aim being to produce the same image, but in custom style. Don't worry too much about exact sizes and shapes; we'll soon sort that out.

Here's my gel version of the default skins, which you can find in the source code as `gelSkin.fla`. The library of this FLA is shown over the page, below right.

The gel symbols are actually made up of very few unique individual clips: the contents of folder parts and clip gel_ScrollTrack. Obviously, the fewer individual clips you combine to make the final set, the more bandwidth-friendly your design. Notice also that the graphics are not the same size as the default skins, although they are roughly in proportion.

The final task is to replace the default skins with gel; we have done this in gelSkin2.fla. The following technique is one of the quickest and most efficient ways of correctly changing the default skins over to your custom skin theme.

Changing default skins

1. Open a new FLA and drag the scrollbar onto the stage. The full set of scrollbar assets will appear in the library.

2. Delete the scrollbar from the stage. Now open gelSkin.fla as a library (File>Open as Library).

3. Drag all the gel graphics across from the new library into your original library. Note that all the gel assets were placed in a single folder, so all you have to do is drag this folder (CustomSkin: gel) across.

4. Close the library for gelSkin.fla. When you have done this, your remaining library will have two folders in it:

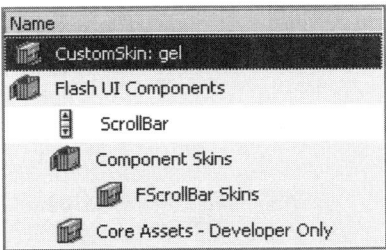

5. We have to replace the symbols embedded in the clips in the FScrollBar Skins folder with the ones in CustomSkin: gel. To do this without replacing the defaults with skins that are too big or too small, or have registration points in the wrong place, can be very fiddly – unless you do it accurately. The easiest way to achieve this is to:

   a. Convert the layers containing the original skins to guide layers. Not only are you then effectively deleting them from the final SWF, you can also see the original placements to help you when you add your new skins in their place.

   b. Create a new layer and copy the replacement skin into it.

   c. Rescale and reposition the replacement skin so that its bounding box is the same (or very similar) to the original skin.

> *We don't have to worry about getting the registration points right, because we are still using the registration point of the original clip.*

6. OK, that's probably too many words without anything practical to back it up — in your new FLA file, open the first component skin in the FScrollbar Skins directory, fsb_downArrow, by double-clicking on it. The graphic is in layer Skin Elements. There is also a README layer, which we will look at soon when we come to register parts of our new skin with FStyleFormat.

7. Now we need to make Skin Elements a guide layer, and add a new layer on which to place our replacement skin:

8. Next, drag across the replacement gel skin, which is called gel_downArrow in gelskin.fla. Resize it so that its bounding box is the same as that of the original skin, as shown below left. You may consider setting the guide layer to show 'outlines only' when doing this (below right), because superimposing the bounding boxes becomes easier to see in this view:

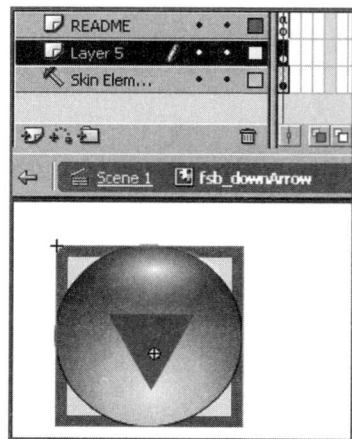
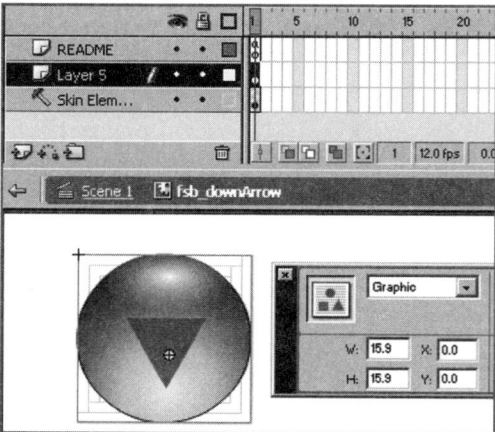

We will be making a lot of similar replacements, so it is also a good idea to make use of the Property inspector, which gives us the exact size and position to use when replacing the arrow skins.

You can see all the finished replacement buttons in gelSkin2.fla. The only changes we have made to the rule of keeping the bounding boxes the same is with fsb_thumb_bottom and fsb_thumb_middle (the skins for the bottom and top parts of the thumb wheel). We have made these bigger so that the curvature of our rounded gel skin shows up better for normal thumb wheel sizes. This will cause problems for extremely small thumb wheel sizes, but as long as you're happy that the skin works for the range of sizes you intend to use (and you should check the maximum/minimum sizes for all dynamic parts of your skin as you add them), you can safely flaunt the rules:

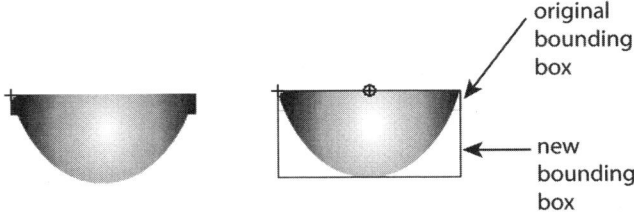

The other thing we have done is to round off the top and bottom edges of gel_ScrollTrack. Without this rounding, you can see the scroll track fouling the rounded edges of the gel buttons:

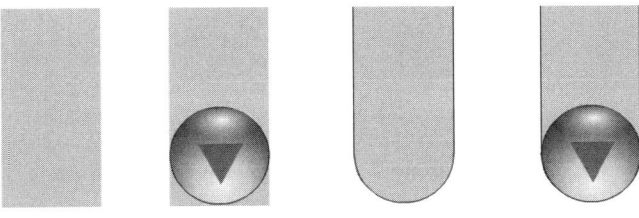

original scrollTrack   rounded scrollTrack

You may have noticed that we created graphic symbols to embed into the default skins, which are themselves movie clip symbols. The reason for the movie clips may have confused some, but is actually simple – the README layer can contain scripts, and these have to be in a movie clip otherwise they won't run. Our gel symbols are simply the raw graphics to insert into the existing skin clips over the top of the original graphics, and so don't have to be movie clips.

Once you have all your skins added (or you can have a look at our `gelSkin2.fla`), you can test the new scrollbar. We have set one up on the stage of `gelSkin2.fla`, and this is how ours looks:

Uh-oh, nothing's changed! Don't worry, only the default skin is shown in the authoring environment. We need to test the movie before we see the results of our work:

Secondly, MP3 in particular 'likes' maximized sound, and its compression algorithms work better with audio that

and its compression algorithms work better with audio that has been enhanced in this way because they can delete high bandwidth

are available for many shareware wave-editing programs like Cool Edit. Compression effects are included under

Secondly, MP3 in particular 'likes' maximized sound, and its compression algorithms work better with audio that has been enhanced

The first two effects are available for many shareware wave-editing programs like Cool Edit. Compression effects are included

The scrollbar will start off with the disabled skins, but as soon as we add enough text to cause a scroll (and of course we need to set our text field up with Multiline selected for this to happen), the gel scrollbar appears in all its luminous green glory! The scrollbar can be scrolled, and the up and down arrows change from their dark green to light gray when you click on them and select them.

Notice that in skinning our scrollbar, we have kept away from the ActionScript that defines all this cool functionality, and the process has allowed us to simply apply our artistic design only. This is a big plus point for designers: you can change the skin without having to consider the underlying (and complex) ActionScript. This was the major failing of smart clips – to change the graphics in the same way, you would have to open up the smart clip and navigate to the graphics you wanted to change, being careful not to tread on the fragile ActionScript all around you.

The fun doesn't stop yet – if you have a look at `gelSkin3.fla`, you will see the following:

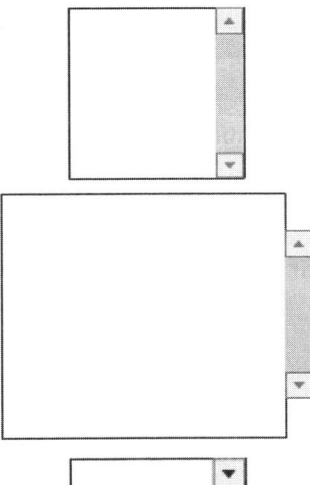

We have simply added a list box and a combo to the FLA. Both these components (and the scroll pane) use a scrollbar in their operation. When you drag such components into a FLA with a scrollbar already in it, you will see this alert:

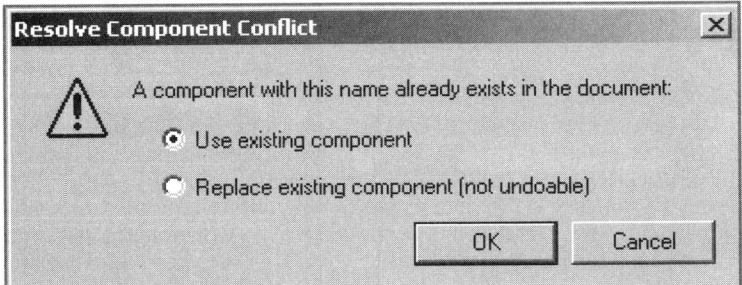

In simple terms, this is asking you, 'the components that you have just added use other stuff already in the FLA (that is, the scrollbar) – should I use the existing scrollbar in your FLA, or import the default version across?' If you select Use existing component, you will force Flash to use the existing FLA scrollbar, and any modifications in this scrollbar will be reflected in the additional components (be very careful not to click the other option if you don't want it – this will erase all your modifications!). Try it yourself, or use our version `gelSkin3.fla`.

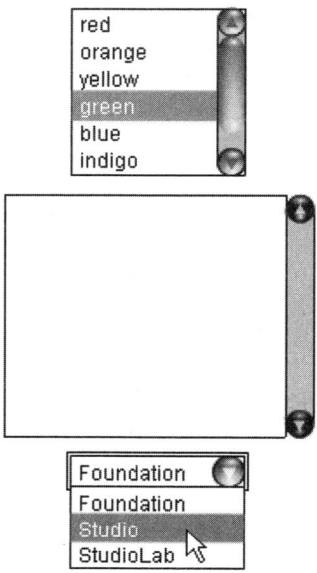

Notice that the text highlighting and text font is still using the default style. Since you haven't changed the component associated with this (it's in the Global Skins folder), you can use FStyleFormat to make the changes you want to complete your new skin.

So far we have avoided ActionScript, and we could safely continue to do so if the work so far is all you want to do. But for most of us, it's just not enough; we want to be able to customize and reuse our own skins for any and every occasion.

Customizing skins

If you're a cutting-edge designer creating award-winning sites one after another, you will probably only use this skin for one site, and create a totally new one for the next one, each a unique and individual shining light in your ever-growing portfolio... so you won't need to later customize the skin with FStyleFormat.

However, if you are just a little bit lazy like me (or, more politely, 'efficient'), you might want to reuse all that hard work in another site by sneaky tweaks to the style via FStyleFormat to make it look different. To do this, we have to look at the embedded clips that make up each individual default skin. These embedded clips are called **elements**, or sometimes **props**. You can see the next effect in gelSkin4.fla.

Open a new movie and drag the scrollbar onto the stage. Delete it and then go into the Flash UI Skins>Component Skins>FScrollBar Skins folder in the library window. Open the `fsb_downArrow` skin. It will initially look like the image below left. This looks like it consists of three elements: a dark border, a central lighter area, and finally the black down arrow. In fact, there are no less than six separate elements lurking in there. You can identify them all by looking at their instance names in the Property inspector as you click on each, but we have done it for you in the exploded view, below right:

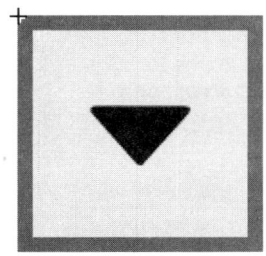
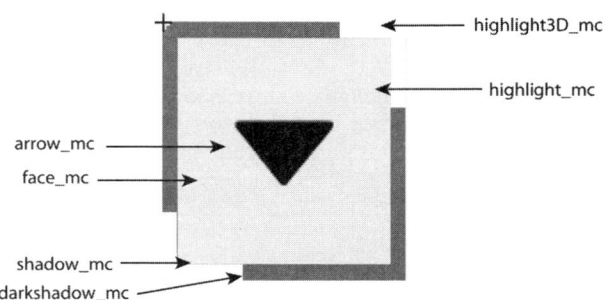

These six 'props' are registered to `FStyleFormat` in the script attached to the README layer:

```
var component = _parent._parent;

component.registerSkinElement(arrow_mc, "arrow");
component.registerSkinElement(face_mc, "face");
component.registerSkinElement(shadow_mc, "shadow");
component.registerSkinElement(darkshadow_mc, "darkshadow");
component.registerSkinElement(highlight_mc, "highlight");
component.registerSkinElement(highlight3D_mc, "highlight3D");
```

The last six lines are the important ones to look at. Each of the six elements' instance names is registered to a particular style property of `FStyleFormat`. For example, when you set a color to the `arrow` property, it's element `arrow_mc` that has the new color applied to it. Similarly, when you set a shadow color via the `shadow` `FStyleFormat` property, you are changing the color of the movie clip `shadow_mc`.

Let's cheat a bit here and skip ahead to see how we'll be creating our gel-style down arrow. For our gel shape, we don't really need all these properties listed above. We only really have a `face` (the color of the globe itself), the `arrow` color, and a 3D highlight, as you'll see on the next page.

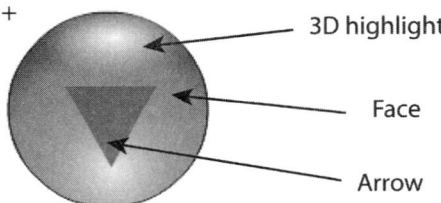

3D highlight

Face

Arrow

We actually have a second 3D highlight towards the bottom of the gel shape, but we will ignore this for the moment because it is actually formed as part of a color gradient of face.

To create our own elements, we have to split the gel globe into its constituent elements, and register them in the README script.

First we have created our separate elements as movie clips with instance names `gel_highlight3D`, `gel_face` and `gel_arrow`. Rather than the garish green, I have taken the 'base colors' that the elements will have (before any color changes are applied via `FStyleFormat`, that is) from the default elements that they are replacing. So for example, `face_mc` is color `0xE8E8E8` by default, so for my gel globe gradient (in `gel_face`) I have based the gradient around the same color:

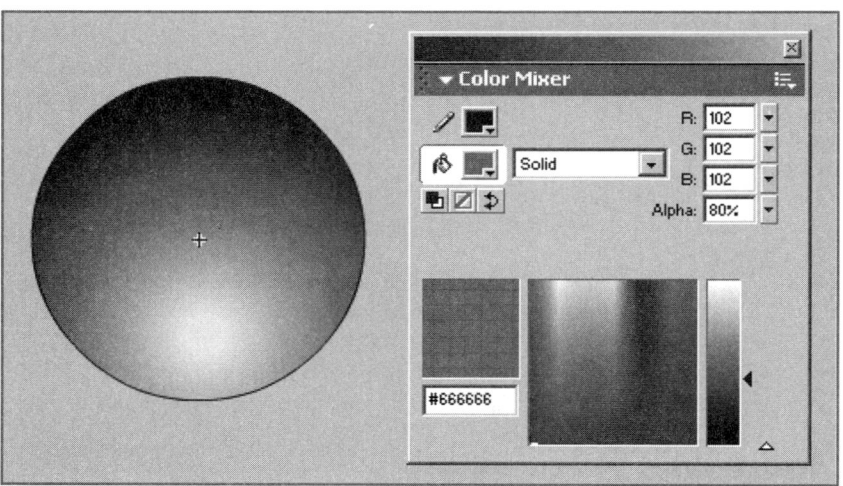

The 3D highlight is simply an alpha gradient, with a maximum of white at 100% alpha, and a minimum of (you guessed it) 0% alpha; this creates a 'shine halo' (I have also turned the background color to gray because a white halo doesn't show up well against a white background):

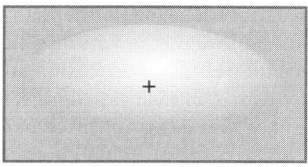

Finally, the arrow remains the same, but this time I have colored it black (0x000000) to tie in with the color of the default arrow element:

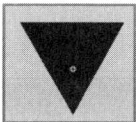

It doesn't really matter where we put the three component clips in the library (gel_highlight3D, gel_face, and gel_arrow), but for neatness you could put them in a folder called gelGraphics.

We now need to use the technique we used in the previous example to place our new clips into the default fsb_downArrow element. If you recall, we create a new layer and change the layer with the original graphic on it to a guide layer. We then place our three new movie clips into the new layer to form the new element.

The new fsb_downArrow is shown below assembled from my custom elements, with the instance names as labeled:

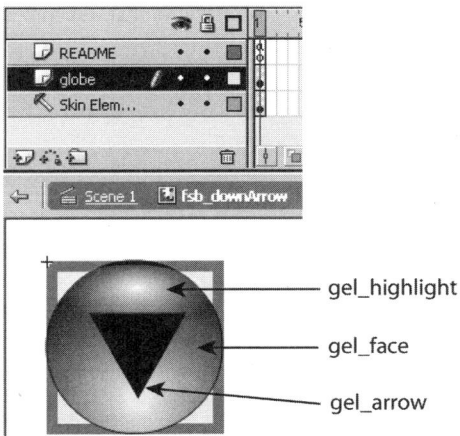

gel_highlight

gel_face

gel_arrow

All that remains is to register the instances:

```
var component = _parent._parent;

//component.registerSkinElement(arrow_mc, "arrow");
//component.registerSkinElement(face_mc, "face");
//component.registerSkinElement(shadow_mc, "shadow");
//component.registerSkinElement(darkshadow_mc, "darkshadow");
//component.registerSkinElement(highlight_mc, "highlight");
//component.registerSkinElement(highlight3D_mc, "highlight3D');

component.registerSkinElement(gel_arrow, "arrow");
component.registerSkinElement(gel_face, "face");
component.registerSkinElement(gel_highlight3D, "highlight3D");
```

Rather than delete the lines you don't want, it's probably a good idea just to comment them out (so you can reinstate them at a later date as you add more elements). The active lines are the last three; these register `gel_arrow` to the `arrow` property, and so on for `gel_face` and `gel_highlight3D`.

That's it; we're done! All that remains is to apply a style format. The following lines will change our custom `FStyleFormat`-compatible `downArrow` skin to one with a light gray highlight, a yellow arrow, and a blue globe face:

```
globalStyleFormat.highlight3D = 0xF0F0F0;
globalStyleFormat.arrow = 0xFFFF00;
globalStyleFormat.face = 0x0000FF;

globalStyleFormat.applyChanges();
```

> *You could of course use a custom style format here, but for simplicity we've just applied the changes globally.*

As you can see, creating an `FStyleFormat`-compatible skin is a little harder; rather than just build single movie clips, you have to decide which styles you want to register, and then define elements to support the style changes.

Although creating custom skins and `FStyleFormat`-compatible skins may seem like a diversion, it's always worth remembering that in commercial web design, using the software defaults or example files to create content is usually seen as a major faux pas; it's maybe even regarded as a distinguishing factor between the amateur and the professional. Of course, beginners do it to learn the techniques, but the rest of us have to make each site unique, and that will involve custom skinning rather than the use of `FStyleFormat` alone (or even worse, using the 'out of the box' default components) in all but standard form layouts.

Setting up advanced components

OK, so far we have shown how to add styles and skins to components. Hopefully, that should keep the designers happy for a while, but the ActionScripters might be asking questions like:

- When you drag and drop a scrollbar onto a text field, how does it just snap into place and bond so nicely?

- What's the voodoo driving live preview, and which doll do I need to stick pins into to get my components working with the same magic?

> *This section will expand on existing Flash 5 smart clips, and show how the additional features of components are set up. It therefore assumes a good working knowledge of smart clips.*

The steps involved in setting up the advanced features of components can be a little tricky, so to make it all as clear as possible, we will create a simple drag and drop function and concentrate more on the underlying setup of the component that encapsulates the functionality. There are already many components around (from early Flash MX testers) that seem to go for a high-level object-oriented programming approach as soon as they start working with components, but that can also hide the inherent simplicity of components, so we will not be going down that route. I'll use simple scripting, and then as soon as you have seen how powerful it all really is, you can get as high-end as you want in the next chapter.

We will look at three steps to make your components a bit more special than just smart clips with pretty icons:

1. Adding drag and drop

2. Adding the component script

3. Adding a live preview

We will create a function called bounce. You simply drag the bounce component onto a clip on the stage, which will make that clip bounce at run-time. A simple drag and drop component that sounds a lot like a behavior we might see in Director – something I've always wanted to be able to do in Flash!

Stage 1: Drag and drop

The thing that makes the scrollbar drag and drop is a component property called targetInstanceName. It takes on a string value equal to whatever you type in the Property inspector's Instance field for the item you drop the component over. It is not the path to the instance, but just the raw name. That might be a problem, but we can probably work out a simple path construction that gets us something like _root.dot instead of dot and _level23.menu34.ball instead of ball.

Of course, we need the path instead of the string because a path is required for us to add event handlers and apply property-based animation to the instance pointed to by `targetInstanceName`.

1. First, we will create an icon for our component; this will be the component's onstage representation. You can create a small graphic that implies 'I make things bounce', or you can use mine, which can be found in `component01.fla`. Assuming that we're still building the component from scratch, create it in a movie clip called `bounce`:

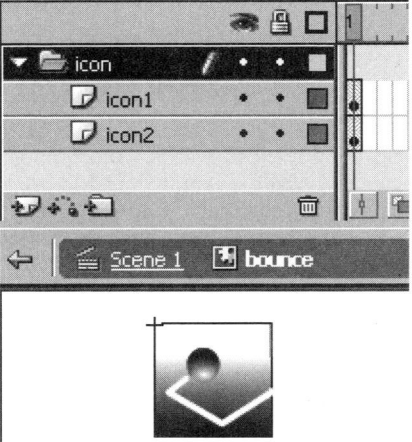

The graphic consists of (what I hope looks like) a bouncing ball, hitting the edges of the icon and bounding off it. It exists on two layers of the bounce movie clip, and to keep everything nice and neat, I've placed them in a layer folder called icon.

The next step is to add our drag and drop feature. You will be pleased to see that this involves no code whatsoever; it is simply a feature of how you define the component parameters.

2. In the library window, highlight the movie clip `bounce` and bring up the Component Definition window (right-click on the movie clip and select it from the drop-down menu, or select it from the library panel's drop-down menu). Hit the + icon as indicated over the page:

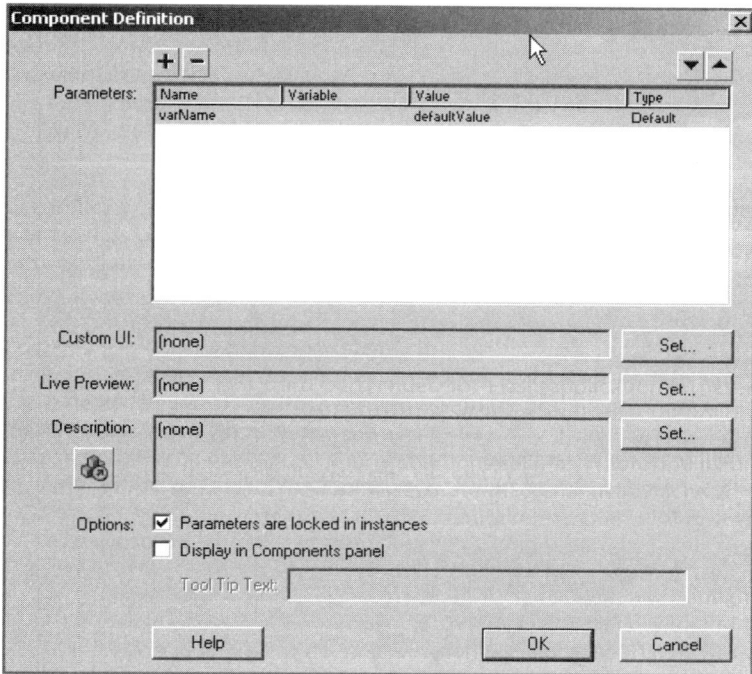

3. You will then get a new line with the name `varName`, value `defaultValue`, and type `Default`. Change `varName` to `bouncee` and add a variable value (previously blank) of `_targetInstanceName`:

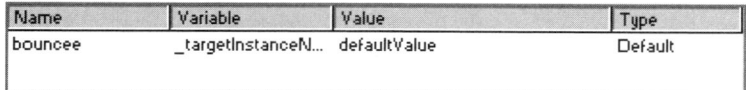

Name	Variable	Value	Type
bouncee	_targetInstanceN...	defaultValue	Default

4. Leave the other parameters as the default values. Next, we can also change the component icon (which is how it will appear in the Component panel and the library window). Click on the icon just below Description and select ActionScript Component Icon. Your icon will henceforth look like this:

5. Finally, check Display in Components panel; the Tool Tip Text entry box will become selectable, in which you can add a little description like 'drag and drop bounce behavior', as you'll see over the page.

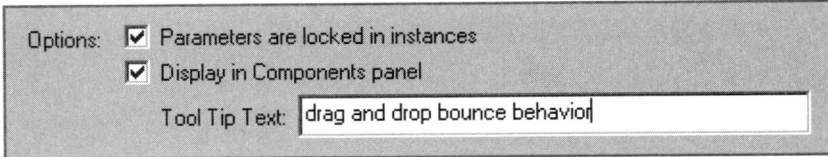

6. For the component to snap to the instance you drag it onto, you need to have View>Snap to Objects (CONTROL+SHIFT+/) selected. It also appears as the magnet icon on the toolbox as an option of the Arrow tool, and on the main toolbar (Window>Toolbars>Main).

7. To see the component snap to whatever you drag it onto, simply create a shape and make it a movie clip via F8. Do this for a circle shape and square shape; draw them on stage, convert them both to movie clips with instance names `circle` and `square`. Drop an instance of `bounce` over the top of both, and `bounce` will snap to the movie clip's top left corner. Better yet, have a look at the properties panel with either of the `bounce` instances selected. The component effectively knows what you have dropped it onto!

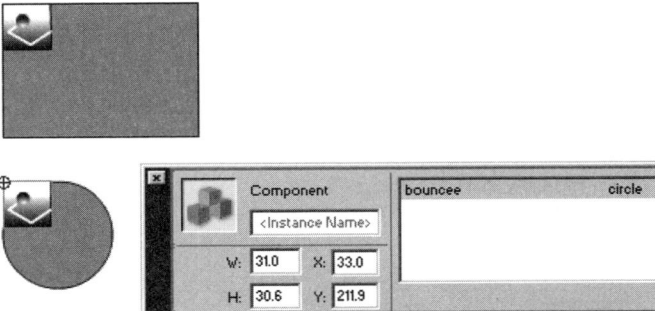

The `bouncee` parameter takes on the value of the instance you drop it onto. That means that any ActionScript we place within `bounce` can reference it and take control of it.

> *This is a very powerful authoring tool. Just dropping a component sprite onto a space invader will make the space invader inherit all the sprite's characteristics . Drop another component called* `fade` *on something you want to fade out, alter the component parameters to set the fade direction and duration, and you are done. Instant behaviors and effects!*

The next phase involves using the `targetInstanceName` to actually do something!

Stage 2: Adding the script

As we mentioned earlier, the script we use in our component is only limited by time and imagination. However, as we are looking to learn the technique of using components here, rather than showing off, we will keep it simple to avoid complicating the technique. The finished FLA for this section is included as `component02.fla`.

The bounce effect will cause any instance it is dropped on to bounce around the stage with a rate determined by the `speed` parameter. As soon as the instance goes off screen, it will bounce back into the screen by reversing the direction of `speed`:

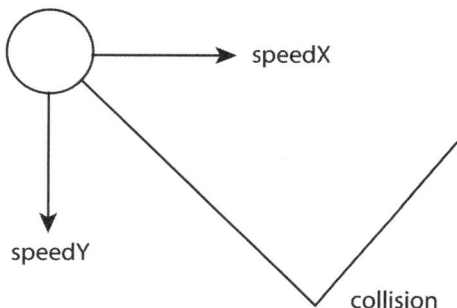

Let's give our bouncing object x and y speed components `speedX` and `speedY`, respectively; this means that as soon as the object hits the y-axis screen limits (top and bottom) we can simply reverse `speedY`, and bounce back in the trajectory shown (and similarly with the x-axis screen limits – left and right).

The first problem concerns the conversion of `_targetInstanceName` to a path. Assuming we drop bounce onto an instance `myInstance`, `_targetInstanceName` will return the string `myInstance`. So we have no idea of the path!

But wait, `bounce` does know most of the path because it will be on the same timeline. So wherever `bounce` is, the item it is dropped onto must be at `this._parent` relative to the timeline of `bounce`. If it is on `this._parent`, then to get the full path all we have to do is add the instance name, and we know that: `_targetInstanceName`!

So the full path from `bounce` to the thing we want to bounce, `bouncee` is:

```
bouncee = this._parent[this._targetInstanceName]
```

Or simply:

```
bouncee = _parent[_targetInstanceName]
```

And it will always be that whenever you use drag and drop.

The second problem is setting the speed of bounce. Well, that's easy; simply add it as a component parameter in the Component Definition window. I have added a new variable speed and given it a default of 20. I have also made it of the Number type:

Name	Variable	Value	Type
speed	speed	20	Number
bouncee	_targetInstanceN...	defaultValue	Default

In the component itself, you already have the icon timeline folder, but now add a new layer called actions:

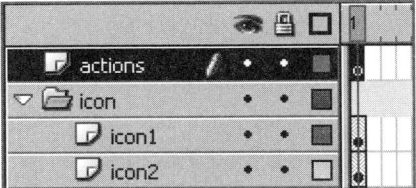

When the component first starts up, it needs to do two things:

- Derive the target to the object it is controlling, bouncee; it can do this by using its own path – this – and working back to find out where the instance it is controlling must be

- Turn itself invisible, because it isn't required to be shown during run-time

The following code does just this, so attach it to the actions layer you have just created:

```
// Set up path to bouncee and hide this
bouncee = _parent[_targetInstanceName];
_visible = false;
```

So we now have the path bouncee that is the absolute path to the target instance we want to control. The next thing is to set up the bouncee timeline by initializing the variables needed for our bounce action:

```
// Set up variables local to the bouncee
bouncee.speedX = bouncee.speedY=speed;
bouncee.minX = bouncee.minY=0;
bouncee.maxX = Stage.width;
bouncee.maxY = Stage.height;
```

This sets up the two speed components speedX and speedY, equating them both to our component parameter speed. The next few lines define our screen limits. Notice that we are using the Stage object to derive these. The component will therefore be able to tell the stage size without us having to tell it explicitly.

Finally, we have to add the script to control bouncee. The script is attached to the instance bouncee as an onEnterFrame event, as befits an animation that needs to run every frame:

```
// Set up onEnterFrame event for the bouncee
bouncee.onEnterFrame = function() {
  // If outside screen area, reverse direction
  if (this._x<0) {
    this.speedX = -this.speedX;
  } else if (this._x>this.maxX) {
    this.speedX = -this.speedX;
  }
  if (this._y<0) {
    this.speedY = -this.speedY;
  } else if (this._y>this.maxY) {
    this.speedY = -this.speedY;
  }
  // move...
  this._x += this.speedX;
  this._y += this.speedY;
};
```

Test your FLA, or `component02.fla` if you want to try our version. You can of course create more movie clips for it to control, and change the speed of the bounce using the Property inspector.

It's a good idea to use the debugger with this FLA, to familiarize yourself with where everything actually ends up in the final SWF during run-time. Although the script is attached to the `bounce` component, most of the variables and script actually end up on the `bouncee`.

> *In the next chapter, we will look at particular object-based techniques that are a little more elegant than this script. But for the moment this is a good base camp, and it is also quick and easy for those of us who just want something simple, portable, and fast (after all, many of us are trying to make money selling sites to clients!).*

We have already traveled far beyond smart clips, but there is further to go. We can also add a **live preview**.

Stage 3: Adding a live preview

The default components use live preview in the text options so that when you add a text title to a push button, it will update on the stage to reflect the change.

In general, live preview works like this:

■ You embed a SWF into the FLA, or define an external one (the choice of which one you choose is largely determined by whether you are angling to create a self-contained SWF or modifiable component library to be used by a design group).

- When you drag a component on to the stage it will appear as a running SWF rather than as a static symbol (provided that you have Control>Enable Live Preview checked). The live preview SWF will appear to be the same size as the bounding box of the original component graphic it is replacing. If you uncheck live preview, you will see the original component graphic.

- You can set up the SWF to reflect changes in the component parameters, giving a live preview of the effects of those changes in real-time during authoring. The parameter values are sent to the SWF as an object xch that sits on the root. For example, our parameter speed would appear in the SWF as _root.xch.speed.

There are a few caveats to this process. The first is that the live preview updates approximately once per second. Only one frame every second will be shown, so if you have your SWF set to run at 12fps, you will actually see only every 12th frame. It's therefore best to design your live preview SWF to run at 1fps. At least then you know how slowly it will eventually run on the stage! This means that you can't use live preview for an animation (or rather, you can, but it will be very slow), but you can use it to show the changes to properties that are configurable but static at run-time, such as our speed parameter.

The second limitation is that most users will be very sensitive to live previews that hog processor time and slow down the authoring environment. Sure, the embedded SWFs run at 1fps, but if there are twenty of them on stage, things start to get a little hairy. Keep live previews small and sweet, otherwise the user will simply turn live preview off.

As an example, we'll create a live preview of the speed parameter, plus a small animated icon representing the bounce effect. This will probably show you why it is a bad idea to attempt eye candy animation in the authoring environment, so you are never tempted to do it in real life (my good deed to the Flash community is done!).

The first thing we need to do is create our SWF. The FLA to do this is included as bounce_live.fla. You can actually call this FLA anything you want, but adding a '_live' extension at the end does make for better file management. Make the movie the same size as the component bounding box, in this case, 30x30 (via the Property inspector, or Modify>Document). Give it a frame rate of 1fps.

The timeline of bounce_live.fla looks like this:

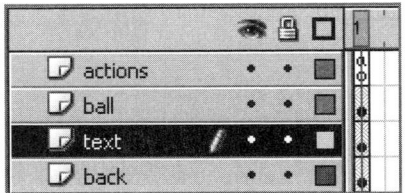

The back layer simply contains a solid background to make our live preview stand out; text includes a dynamic text field, whose important feature is that it has speed as a Var:

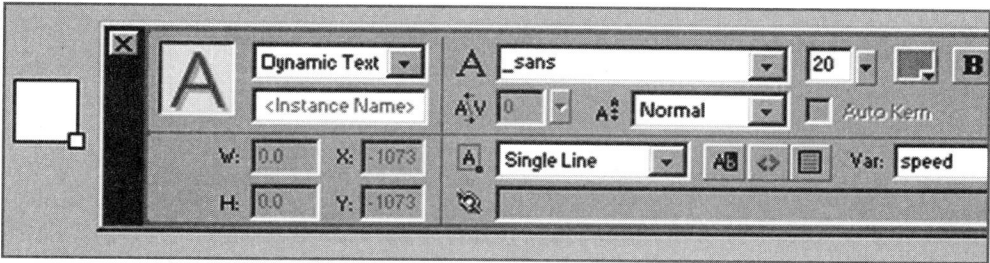

Layer ball contains a little ball movie clip. Actually, it's just a tiny little square, as shown below. It has an instance name ball:

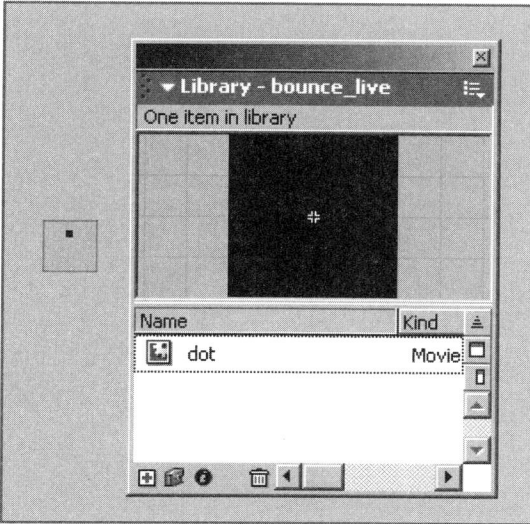

Finally, the actions layer contains the script to set it all in motion. Let's look into this code. First up, we set the speed of the ball, speedIcon, and use it to initialize the x, y components of the ball speed: speedX and speedY. The icon borders are set as 5 and 25. The ball will bounce back if its _x or _y value is greater than 25 or less than 5 (in much the same way our bounce component itself works):

```
speedIcon = 3;
speedX = speedY=speedIcon;
minX = minY=5;
maxX = maxY=25;
```

As you'll see on the next page, the onEnterFrame script for ball is identical to the script in the main component itself. The only thing we have done in addition is to get the speed value we display in the text field from _root.xch.speed.

```
// Set up onEnterFrame event for the ball
this.onEnterFrame = function () {
  // get speed from 'xch'
  speed = _root.xch.speed;
  // If outside icon area, reverse direction
  if (ball._x<minX) {
    speedX = -speedX;
  } else if (ball._x>maxX) {
    speedX = -speedX;
  }
  if (ball._y<minY) {
    speedY = -speedY;
  } else if (ball._y>maxY) {
    speedY = -speedY;
  }
  // move...
  ball._x += speedX;
  ball._y += speedY;
};
```

That's everything! Test the FLA at least once to create a SWF. When you do this, you won't see any text, because xch isn't being updated yet. All we have to do now is link it to our component.

Have a look at component03.fla. Remember, make sure Control>Enable Live Preview is checked – otherwise live preview won't be possible. Bring up the Component Definition window for our component bounce:

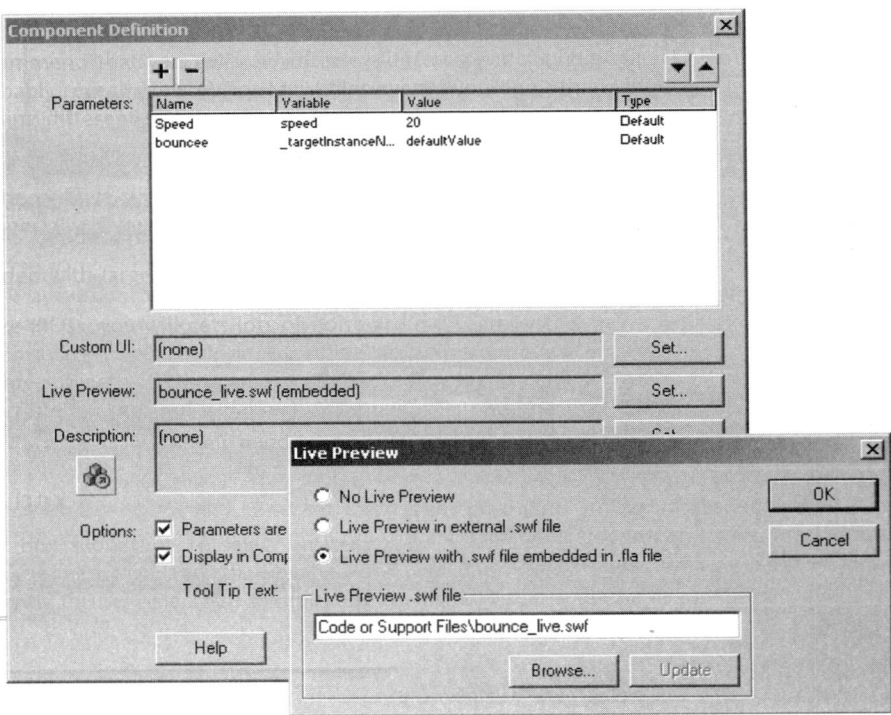

You have to link the SWF you have just created to the component. To do this, you would simply click on the Set... button for Live Preview. You'll notice that I've chosen to embed the live preview in the FLA file by selecting the Live Preview with .swf file embedded in .fla file. The other radio button options above this allow you to have no live preview, or simply link to the SWF without actually embedding it. The path selected when you first look at this FLA will be whatever the path is on my development machine, so hit Browse... to change it to the path on yours. Finally, click OK.

Now get back to the stage. You will see that the component icon has been replaced by the number 20 (the current value of the speed parameter) and there's a little bouncing ball animation showing what this component actually does (it's nice the first time you see an animated live preview, but can become rather distracting after twenty minutes or so!):

The really useful part is the 20, which tells you the current value of speed. If you had several bounce components on stage, you could see at a glance the values of each one's speed.

If you select the icon and change speed in the properties inspector, you will see the 20 change as well:

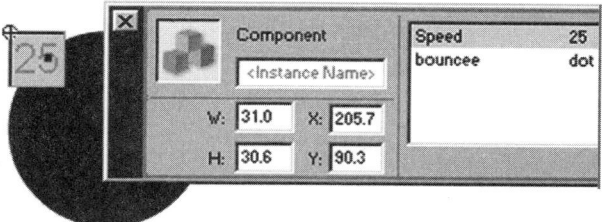

Supposing you have now tired of live preview, or have finished setting component parameters and want to do some other stuff; you can easily turn the live preview off (uncheck Control>Enable Live Preview...). You would then see the static icon return as shown below:

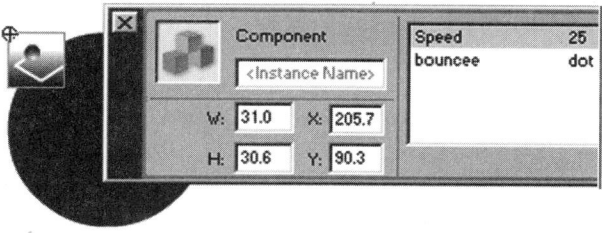

As mentioned when we started this example, the bounce component function is trivial in itself, but you can probably see the potential power of this already. We now have the extensibility to build custom components that encapsulate all the nasty code and timelines hidden within them, and have the simplest operating instructions of all: 'Drag and drop on to the target, set up the parameters... and that's it!' You can have the most complex object-based scripting embedded within one of these things, but all the user will see is a Components panel full of useful looking graphic icons.

Summary

We've covered a lot of new functionality in this chapter:

- Customizing the Flash MX default components with new styles and skins

- Using the `FStyleFormat` object to make both global and individual style changes

- Using component UI features

- Building advanced components with ActionScript, incorporating 'drag and drop' and live preview functionality

We've seen directly that components not only allow us to separate out the graphic skin from the 'nuts and bolts' of the code, they also make using the components a simple graphic process, allowing for easy workflows that let the user treat a component as a self-contained 'black box' – you never have to look inside it and see all that code that actually runs the thing.

Now that we've covered the main features of components, there's one final feature of Macromedia Flash MX that follows on quite naturally. Of course, we're talking about objects and object-oriented programming. The concepts are closely related to components, and are reminiscent of their encapsulated nature. This will be the penultimate chapter of the book – and potentially one of the most important for the advanced Flash MX user. Hold on to your hats...

Chapter 15

Advanced Objects

Many designers get totally confused when they read about objects and how 'you really need to get up to speed with object-oriented programming (OOP) before you can do anything *really* cool with Flash'. Perhaps the first thing we should do is dispel this myth.

> *A really good understanding of OOP is not the apex of Flash design. Creating compelling motion graphics for the web is what Flash is all about. Although there are moves towards Flash being an application builder rather than a motion graphics delivery system, in its normal mode of use, ActionScript coding does not require the sort of programming structures found in true application builders such as C++ and Java. When it does, we'll let you know!*

A reasonable understanding of 'dot notation' was all you really needed to keep up in Flash 5. Dot notation is associated with objects, but you *don't* need to know about OOP to understand it. As we'll see in this chapter, there is a world of difference between using `object.method` structures to form code lines, such as `myMovieclip.gotoAndPlay("home")`, and actual object-oriented programming.

Flash and object-oriented design

In Macromedia Flash MX, dot notation and a good understanding of functions and scope will allow you to use most of the new features. Where it doesn't, you can quite happily use object-oriented code to utilize the object-based Flash stuff, but once you have got what you want from it all, you can revert to any coding style you choose. Obviously, it's better if that style happens to be well structured, but if it *isn't*, and it *works*, and you like it, you're the boss!

In this chapter we'll present some really useful techniques for the motion graphics designer who simply wants to tweak the inbuilt objects of Flash, but then carry on programming using their own quirky style of coding – more generally known as 'getting the spec fulfilled on time' or 'doing it in a way I understand because I never learnt advanced programming at college'. That's what Flash is all about, and that's the stance we will be taking; so keep reading, even if words like prototype and inheritance make you head for the exit.

The advantages of the OOP approach only really start to kick in when:

- You want to build something on a fairly large scale (like a Flash-based drawing program, for example).

- You're using specific Flash functionality that talks to other object-oriented pieces of code (like XML and server-side applications).

■   You want to build general and encapsulated code (when building components, for instance)

> *I anticipate that the most common place for object-oriented coding in a 'Flash motion graphics for the web' design role will be the coding of components. When you do this, you are using the OOP advantages of generalization and abstraction within the component, but the external code that anyone using the components can use is of the 'any style that fits' variety.*

There is one other object-related concept that you can implement with the new Flash MX object/class structures:

■   Extend the default Flash objects to customize them for the task in hand

This is a cool thing to do if you have a load of little movie clips flying around all doing the same thing, such as in advanced UI design or Flash games. By extending the movie clip and creating a new 'movie clip-like' object class with the extra stuff bolted on, you can simplify it all into a two-stage process:

1.   Create the new movie clip class

2.   Use it as if it were a movie clip

Accordingly, in this chapter we will look at the new object-based features of Macromedia Flash MX, showing:

■   How you can register new classes and use the prototype chain to extend the default Flash movie clip object (although you can also do it with other objects).

■   The use of #initclip and #endinitclip to register objects and classes before run-time.

■   The object watch/unwatch methods, and its usefulness as a new kind of internal ActionScript event.

■   Function.apply as a structured alternative to the object-based approach.

■   The global level and its usefulness to extending ActionScript, and good programming techniques when using global scopes, including namespaces and avoiding conflicts with local variables.

> *Many of the features discussed in this chapter were available in Flash 5 using third party schemes (FLEM, ACK, and so on). Now that this sort of functionality is hard-coded into Flash, expect it to become much more prevalent.*

What we *won't* do in this chapter is show you all the irrelevant stuff that the OOP approach allows; such an exhaustive survey of OOP would be beyond the scope of this chapter – and you'd instantly forget it anyway because you'll never use it in motion graphics.

Extending classes

Flash doesn't really support totally new classes in the same way that true object-oriented (OO) languages such as C++ do. This is to be expected; ActionScript is essentially a derivative of JavaScript, and JavaScript itself is only *object-based*, rather than OO. In any case, you don't really want to create new classes in Flash; rather, you want to somehow *extend* the default functionality of some of the standard objects, particularly the movie clip. There is a way you can extend the movie clip (or any other object), and that is via the object `prototype`. We will pause for a moment to see what the prototype actually is, before using it to create new objects with `registerClass` and all sorts of other tomfoolery!

Prototypes

Suppose we were in the auto industry and wanted to create a new car. How would we go about it? Well, first off we'd design all the parts. We'd get them all working on paper and in software simulations, and then go ahead and build a first version. This would be our test car, and we would use it to check our design and confirm our simulations. Engineers call this test car a **prototype**.

Once we were happy that all our parts were good-to-go, we would use this prototype as the template for all further vehicles built to that model. To be sure, they would not all be identical; some would be green, or have a smaller engine, or a soft-top, but those are just the details, or properties, of the individual cars. You can tell that all the automobiles are in the same range, whether they are the sports model or family version, because they are built to the same prototype.

Objects are the same – a prototype defines the way the object fits together, and describes the properties and methods that make up our object (in the same way the prototype car is the *template* used to build many *instances* of the production models). Once you have created a Flash prototype, you can apply it to particular instances to make copies of the prototype object, in the same way the prototype auto is used.

There is one big difference between our auto prototype analogy and the Flash prototype though:

> Objects have **inheritance**. *If you apply a prototype to an existing object, such as the movie clip, not only do the instances have properties and methods of the prototype, they also inherit the properties and instances of the movie clip. This is a major feature of using prototypes, because it allows you to extend the predefined objects.*

Inheritance

Inheritance is something that cars do not have, so another example might clarify this term; a quick look at family lineage demonstrates the principles of inheritance quite nicely.

Consider a scenario in which John Doe, who has Bob and Sue in his family tree, gets married to Jane Jones, who has Bill and Clare in her lineage. The family trees of both individuals will merge such that their children will have all four individuals as relatives. The children may retain the Doe name, but in fact they contain the genes of both the Doe and Jones families.

Inheritance works in much the same way with objects, and the following figure shows the analogy to lineage:

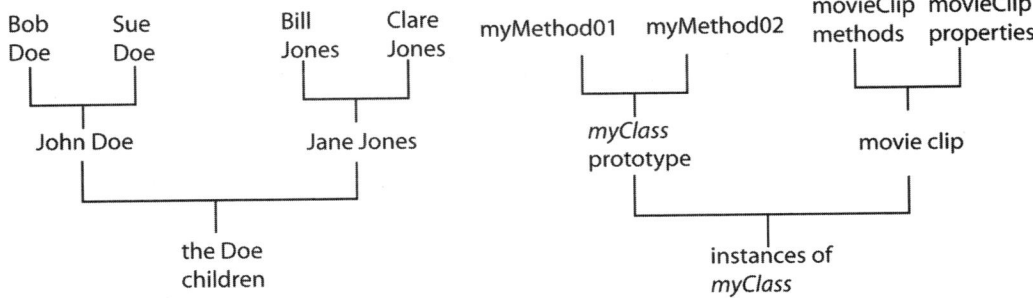

Your prototype *myClass* and the movie clip will 'marry' to form new child instances with the methods (and properties) of *myClass* as well as the existing methods and properties of the movie clip class.

A major point to notice for users with previous experience of OOP is that the prototype is *not the same as class*. It is a heavily cut-down version of it, and in our auto analogy, it works like this: we can build general car prototypes using our object-based methods, but we can't build totally different classes of things, such as aircraft or coffee makers. In the auto industry, all our prototypes must have headlights, four wheels, and a steering wheel. In the Flash world, if we are intending to register new classes with `registerClass` (which we'll look at next), the classes can only be based around the movie clip.

> *In real OOP languages (such as C++ and Java), you can create much richer structures (following our auto analogy again, you could build anything from speed boats to cell phones, not just autos), but in object-based languages (such as JavaScript and ActionScript) you don't really need true classes. ActionScript is intended for a fairly specific purpose (motion graphics and client-side scripting, and some application building), and the small size of the plug-in means that the high-end structures required to build 'anything objects' can't really be justified.*

So now we have a view of what prototypes actually are, where does that leave us in creating motion graphics with Flash MX? Well, the `Object` object has been updated, and it allows us to add the objects and methods of a `prototype` to the movie clip via inheritance, thus creating a 'super movie clip' object.

Using prototypes to create custom classes

We first need to create our new methods. Like JavaScript, ActionScript uses functions to create the methods of our prototype. The format is like this:

```
myObject = function () {

  this.myMethod1 = function(){
    // code that defines myMethod1
    this.myProperty01 = something;
    this.myProperty02 = something;
  };

  this.myMethod2 = function(){
    // code that defines myMethod2
  };

};
```

This code is called the **constructor** for myObject. Using it, myObject will have a prototype that includes:

- **Methods** – myObject.myMethod1() and myObject.myMethod2()

- **Properties** – including myObject.myProperty01 and myObject.myProperty02

> *The properties are variables that are defined in the various functions that construct the methods. If you need to use variables that you don't want to appear as properties, you should make them local to the function with var.*

The next thing we need to do is add the movie clip object to the **prototype chain** we've built so far, then myObject will also inherit the properties of the movie clip, and it will be able to apply movie clip methods such as myObjectInstance.hitTest, and so on:

```
myObject.prototype = new MovieClip();
```

Finally, we can create instances of the new object myObject, but before we can do that, we need to register myObject to one or more plain old 'vanilla-flavored' movie clip objects residing in the library. To do this, you use the new method of the Object object, registerClass:

```
Object.registerClass("mylinkageID", myObject);
```

Note that the particular movie clip that the new object, myObject, is applied to is identified by its linkage identifier, myLinkageID. OK, too much explanation! I feel like a working example coming on...

Independent motion simulation: fun with skaters

Skaters are those little critters that run around on the surface of a pond. They flit around without sinking relying on the magic of surface tension. Here we present an ActionScript-based simulation of their movement. The following FLA is included as skater.fla.

1. The first thing to do is create our skater. In the final version of this FLA, I'd probably create little bugs that always face the direction that they are currently flitting towards, but that introduces some trigonometry that confuses the way the movie clips are set up. Instead, just create a new movie clip symbol that is a simple unfilled circle (give it a hairline stroke, no fill), and call it ball:

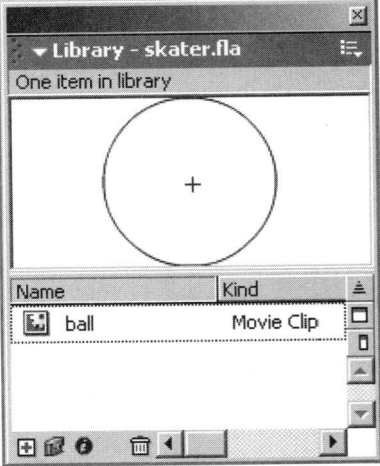

2. Pull up the Linkage Properties window (by right-clicking on the ball symbol in the library and selecting Linkage.... Check Export for ActionScript and the window will look like the one below, with an Identifier of ball and Export in first frame checked:

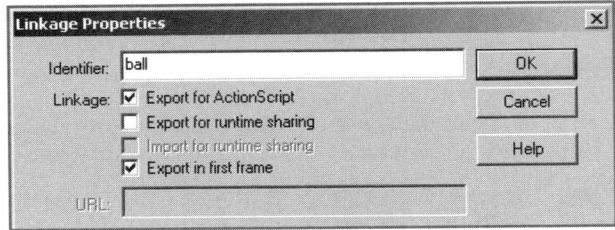

3. OK, we now need to add our constructor. Add the following script In Layer 1 of _root:

```
skater = function () {
  this.makeTarget = function() {
    this.xTarget = Math.random()*400;
    this.yTarget = Math.random()*400;
  };
  this.onLoad = function() {
    this.makeTarget();
  };
```

```
this.onEnterFrame = function() {
  this.distanceX = this._x-this.xTarget;
  this.distanceY = this._y-this.yTarget;
  this._x = this._x-this.distanceX/8;
  this._y = this._y-this.distanceY/8;
  if (Math.abs(this.distanceX)<1) {
    if (Math.abs(this.distanceY)<1) {
        this.makeTarget();
    }
  }
};
};
```

Our object is called `skater`, as defined by the name of the constructor. We have three functions within the constructor, `makeTarget`, the `onLoad` callback function, and an `onEnterFrame` callback function.

I won't go into how each function works, but the skater effect is essentially the old inertia movement that we have been using since way back in Flash 4.

Notice that our `skater` constructor includes event scripts! This is because the event callback functions act like any other function, and the constructor uses them to define our custom methods just like it would any other function, even though the callbacks happen to be anonymous (they don't have a name) and are attached to events.

This is part of the payoff for using callback functions instead of directly attached event scripts in the old Flash 5 fashion; the complex scripting suddenly becomes that little bit more accessible because it is just a step on from the stuff we have been playing with all along.

4.   We now need to attach our prototype to the movie clip object and register it to a particular movie clip in the library. To do this we need to cause our existing prototype, as defined by the constructor function `skater`, to be extended to include another object, the movie clip:

```
skater.prototype = new MovieClip();
```

5.   To make our object definition complete, we need to define which movie clip we want `skater` to become the object for. We want the movie clip `ball`, with linkage identifier `ball` to be the one we select (good thing too, because it's the only clip in the library!):

```
Object.registerClass("ball", skater);
```

Every `ball` movie clip that is placed on stage following this script now becomes a `skater`.

> *Because the script that defines this transition of* `ball` *from movie clip to skater does not run at authoring time, it will not be applied to the instances of* `ball` *we drag onto the stage while working in the FLA. It will only affect those instances that are placed on stage after the frame containing the* `skater` *definition during run-time, which limits us to creating instances of* `skater` *in only one way:* `attachMovie`. *There is a way around this, and we will look at it shortly when we discuss using* `#initclip` *to define the prototype and class before the first frame.*

6. Add the following actions to generate our skaters:

```
for (i=0; i<30; i++) {
  _root.attachMovie("ball", "ball"+i, 1000+i);
}
```

On testing this FLA, you will see it generate thirty skater objects. Look at them go!

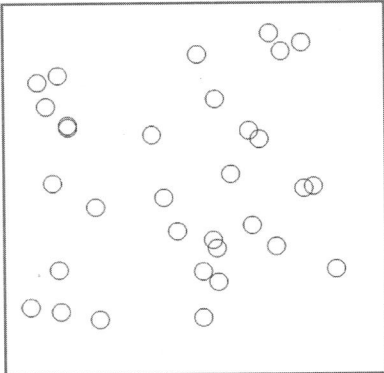

Using functions without OOP

As we mentioned earlier, OOP is not the be all and end all of Flash coding. There are several ways to do the same thing. The old Flash 5 way of doing it would be to attach the event scripts to one `ball` instance on the stage, and duplicate it twenty-nine times to make thirty in total. The most efficient non-OOP Flash MX way of doing it would use the same `skater` constructor to begin with, but replace the following script...

```
skater.prototype = new MovieClip();
Object.registerClass("ball", skater);
for (i=0; i<30; i++) {
  _root.attachMovie("ball", "ball"+i, 1000+i);
}
```

...with this:

```
for (i=0; i<30; i++) {
  _root.attachMovie("ball", "ball"+i, 1000+i);
  skater.apply(_root["ball"+i]);
}
```

Here we are using the new functional method `apply` to attach the `skater` constructor *as a function* to each `ball` instance as soon as we create it on the stage.

The object-based way is more flexible, and will probably save time and be of more use as your code gets bigger (it's easier to change as your code spirals in size). However, using `apply` is much easier on the brain, and probably more attractive to the busy web designer who isn't worried about elegant programming, but just wants something coded up quickly and working for the client meeting in three hours time.

There is, however, an important advantage in run-time file size terms when you use the OO constructions. If you look at the debugger for any of the skater instances using `registerClass`, you will notice that the functions are not attached to the individual instances (see left-hand screenshot below), whereas when using the non-OO `apply()` technique, each instance has a full set of the scripts attached to it (as shown on the right):

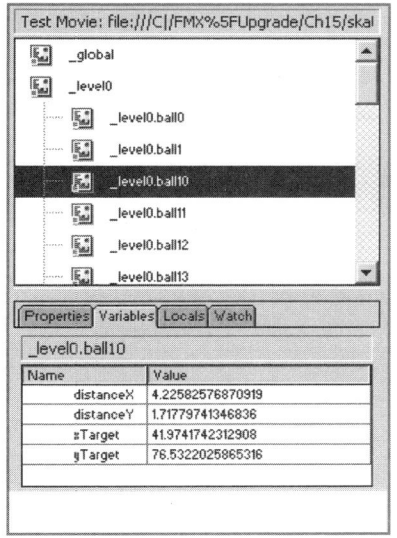
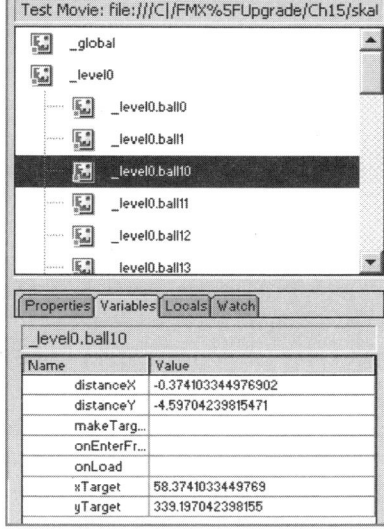

This means that although the OO version is a little more complicated, the non-OO version forces the Flash player to create many more scripts.

This difference refers to the amount of code the Flash player creates internally during run-time, rather than the file size of the SWF (which is more or less the same between versions).

The Flash player is not really designed to handle large amounts of data, and it becomes unstable if you make it do so. The OO version will probably therefore run better when using lots of instances or data. This again points to the use of OOP in large Flash applications.

OOP and components

One of the big bonuses of OOP is that it allows you to build *modular code*. For example, we could create all our generic low-level class constructors as soon as the SWF starts up, and then use the methods of objects like skater as if they had always been there (in much the same way that the movie clip is). This allows us to define our initial low-level objects in one component, and then build components (or non-component-based ActionScript), over the top of it, which can assume the basic framework is already there.

This layered approach is one of the hallmarks of OOP, and allows you to build up applications in a modular and structured way. It also allows you to implement something else: **abstraction**. The low-level objects allow you to assemble basic building blocks that add objects and methods which, for example, would allow you to create things like 3D worlds. Subsequent higher-level code can assume that it is running on a dedicated 3D system, thus *abstracting away* from what your environment *is* to what you would *like it to be* (by 'abstracting away' here, I mean that we are essentially *hiding away* the core characteristics).

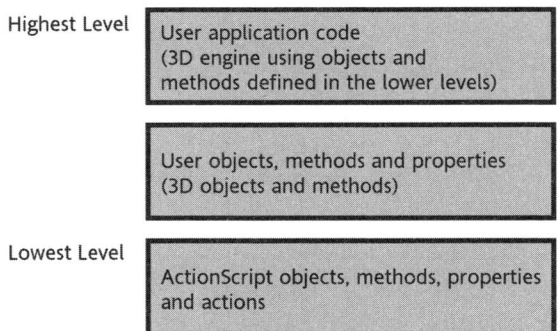

Highest Level — User application code (3D engine using objects and methods defined in the lower levels)

User objects, methods and properties (3D objects and methods)

Lowest Level — ActionScript objects, methods, properties and actions

There is one problem, though, concerning the *order of execution*. You want your low-level constructors and classes to be available *before* frame 1, when the main code on frame 1 of any timeline starts to use it. The way to do this is via #initclip and #endinitclip. It works as follows.

You can only place #initclip / #endinitclip on frame 1 of a movie clip. Any code included between the two actions is marked to run before anything else:

```
#initclip;
// script
#endinitclip;
```

This would cause //script to run before anything else in the SWF.

Before Flash starts to run the timelines in a SWF, it looks to see if there are any #initclip / #endinitclip actions. If there are, then the code between the two will be run *before the movie clip is placed on the stage*. Effectively, it runs when the movie clip is loaded into the library during run-time. Because the movie clip timeline is not yet defined at this point, (there are not yet any instances on the stage), the scope of the code within #initclip / #endinitclip is _root and not the movie clip timeline.

> *It is important to realize that* #initclip / #endinitclip *is not there to initialize the movie clip in the same way that the* onLoad *event is. When* #initclip *is invoked, the movie clip does not yet exist. Rather,* #initclip *is there to create the basic object building blocks (classes, prototypes, and so on) that subsequent code will require once the timelines are started. This allows you to do much more than* onLoad, *as we shall see below.*

You can also define an order value like this:

```
#initclip 10
// script
# endinitclip
//
#initclip 20
// more script
# endinitclip
```

In this case, script will have priority over more script as it has a higher order. Note that the highest order is 0, and an order of 0 is assumed if you do not specify an order.

If there is more than one #initclip / #endinitclip of the same order number, then the order between all affected clips will be defined by Flash itself. This would happen if the SWF was using components or clips from more than one author, each using #initclip numbering starting with 0. This is actually less serious than may at first appear; all you are bothered about is that your order 0 clip runs before your order 1 clip, which runs before your order 2 clip, and so on. If there were other clips running in between, you wouldn't care. It's probably time for another example...

The skater component

Consider a scenario where our skater from the previous example has become a new Flash phenomenon. Like the side scroller before it, the skater effect has become *the* thing to include in a Flash design, at least until it becomes an object of overuse and indifference six months down the line...

Anyway, everyone wants one, and they want one *now*, and what better way to feed the baying masses of expectant designers than implementing it as a component. To package the component we'll create a new action, makeSkater(). This has one argument, the linkage ID of the movie clip that you want to make a skater – linkageID. To use the makeSkater action that we'll create shortly, you simply do this:

```
makeSkater("myClipID");
```

From that moment on, all instances of myClipID will act like the skater while retaining all the other objects and methods of the *movie clip object*. You can call makeSkater() from anywhere in your FLA, irrespective of which timeline you are on.

The rules of using the skater component are simple: you just include it in the library of any FLA that wants to use it.

Cool! Um... well, sort of. It *would* be cool if we used an effect that was more useful than skater. That's where *you* come in when you have finished this chapter. For now, we will stick with the skater to show the basic principles. The following example is included as skaterComponent.fla.

1. In a new FLA, create a new movie clip called skaterDefinition. We'll take the functions we used in skater.fla and put them in this clip. The additional bits I have added to make *skater* a component are highlighted. Add the following script to frame 1 of skaterDefinition:

```
#initclip
_global.skater = function() {
  this.makeTarget = function() {
    this.xTarget = Math.random()*400;
    this.yTarget = Math.random()*400;
  };
  this.onLoad = function() {
    this.makeTarget();
  };
  this.onEnterFrame = function() {
    this.distanceX = this._x-this.xTarget;
    this.distanceY = this._y-this.yTarget;
    this._x = this._x-this.distanceX/8;
    this._y = this._y-this.distanceY/8;
    if (Math.abs(this.distanceX)<1) {
      if (Math.abs(this.distanceY)<1) {
          this.makeTarget();
      }
    }
  };
};
```

```
// Use prototype to create a movie clip that inherits the
// skater object
skater.prototype = new MovieClip();
// Create the action "makeSkater()"
_global.makeSkater = function(linkageID) {
  Object.registerClass(linkageID, skater);
};
#endinitclip
this._visible = false;
```

So what have we added here?

- To make sure that the skater object is registered as a class before any code starts to use it, we have included our definition of the skater prototype and its registering to the movie clip class within an #initclip / #endinitclip block. It will be defined before any standard ActionScript (all scripts that are not in an #initclip / #endinitclip block) is run, and before any other component that has an #initclip of 1 or more.

- To make the skater prototype available from anywhere in the FLA, we have made it global by renaming the constructor from skater to _global.skater. Instead of _root, the scope of *skater* is now _global.

- The skater prototype is now added to the movie clip object via the line skater.prototype = new MovieClip();.

- We have a new function _global.makeSkater() defined at the end of the script that looks like this:

```
_global.makeSkater = function(linkageID) {
Object.registerClass(linkageID, skater);
};
```

All this does is create a function that executes the line:

```
Object.registerClass("LinkageID", skater);
```

This registers the skater object to the movie clip with a library linkage ID of LinkageID.

For the next part, we need to:

- Make skaterDefinition a component.

- Make sure its linkage options ensure it is included in the SWF of any FLA it is included in, even if it is only placed in the library.

- Give the component some kind of graphical stage appearance.

2. To make skaterDefinition a component simply right-click on it, or use the library drop-down menu, to open the Component Definition window. Since this component is not actually doing anything configurable (it is creating a predefined class, and adding the configurable part as a new ActionScript action), we don't need any parameters. Give it an ActionScript Component Icon (by clicking on the icon just below Description and selecting the new icon type). Make sure you check the Parameters are locked in instances (so the user can't mess about with them) and Display in Components panel options (just in case the user wants to include it in their Components panel). You may also give it a tool tip message (I've added the text 'skater object definition' to mine):

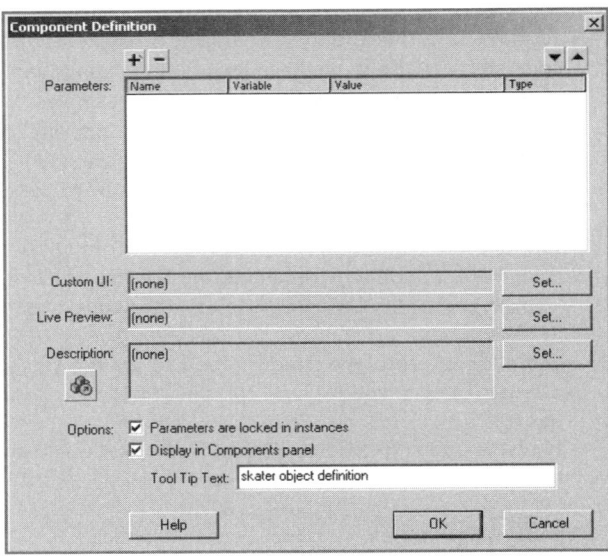

3. Next stop, linkage. From the same menu that you selected the Component Definition window, select the Linkage... option to bring up the Linkage Properties window. Check Export for ActionScript and accept the defaults for Identifier (skaterDefinition) and Export in first frame (checked):

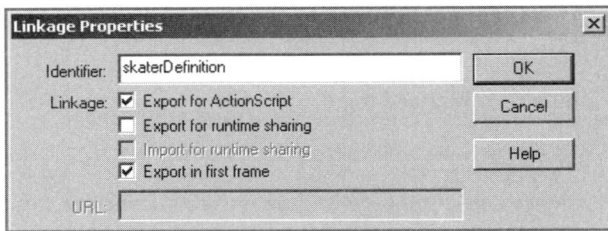

4. Finally, we need to give our component some kind of icon on its timeline. This isn't absolutely necessary, but it's a pretty good idea. You need to create this on the

timeline of skaterDefinition. I prefer to limit myself to a small 30x30 icon (as we saw with the bounce component in the previous chapter), and here's mine – a simple representation of a pond skater:

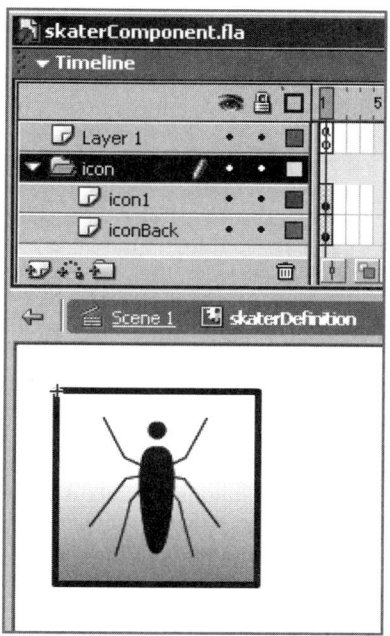

> Remember, the icon is only intended for the authoring environment, but it will also be exported into the final SWF, so don't go creating a 20k masterpiece!

5. We have now created our component. If you run the SWF, not a lot will happen graphically, but running it with the debugger will show you that the makeSkater action and skater object are all ready and waiting to be used in _global. The final FLA, skaterComponent02.fla, shows them being used. If you open this FLA you will see this script attached to frame 1 of _root:

```
makeSkater("alphaSphere");
for (i=0; i<30; i++) {
  _root.attachMovie("alphaSphere", "sphere"+i, 1000+i);
}
```

This turns a library movie clip with linkage ID alphaSphere into a *skater clip*. Notice that to do this, the user does not have to look inside the component. The nuts and bolts of the makeSkater is hidden and encapsulated within the component, and the only interface is the makeSkater() action.

The for loop simply uses the attachMovie method of skater (which it has inherited from the movie clip) to create thirty instances of skater clips onto the stage.

Run the FLA to see the skaters in action:

Now think beyond this simple and slightly dated (not to mention cheesy!) effect, and think about what we have *really done*. We have modified the movie clip to create a new graphic object. We have hidden all the code to do this in a generalized component that can be used *in any FLA*. To use the `skater` object, the user simply puts the `skaterComponent` in the library of the FLA they want to use it in. They can drag the component onto the stage if they wish, but the export options place it on the stage anyway, so it doesn't really matter.

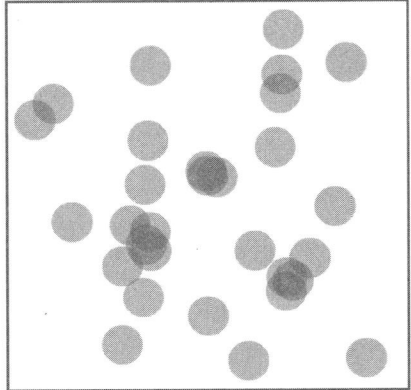

This seems slightly less exciting than the bounce drag-and-drop effect we looked at in Chapter 14, but it is in fact *much* more powerful. Here, although we are only creating a bit of eye candy, the *way* we have implemented it is truly modular and hides all the OOP behind a component where it belongs, allowing the coders to write the voodoo scripting, and leaving the designers to use it in their designs via the simple `makeSkater()` action.

Using this newfound knowledge, you could go on to create other basic objects, for example:

- Create a set of modified movie clip objects that support sprites as used in games, via a single component that defines all the classes and methods needed to achieve this and keeps them carefully hidden away inside, but accessible through a new set of actions.

- Create a set of 3D actions such as `define3Dshape` that takes a set of 3D points (x, y, z) and builds up a 3D shape based on it using the drawing API. Additional actions `move3D()` and `rotate3D()`, and even `collide3D()` can then be used to animate the 3D shapes from ActionScript, without ever having to look at the underlying trigonometry and optimized 3D code.

- Open up an FLA containing some default components, and see how they work by registering their own classes, and how the Flash UI component class tree works (in the Core Assets – Developers only folder – hey, you're a developer now!), and how it's based around the same sort of structures as our simple *skater*. Then you can make your name in the Flash community by building your own in the Macromedia style.

Before we leave the idea of registering classes and modified objects through prototypes, there is one final trick we can do to make life easier. In the examples so far, we took a new object and gave it the properties of the movie clip. We can also alter the movie clip (or any other object) itself.

Modifying the default object prototypes

The skater component did something to the movie clip that we don't want *all* movie clips to do. We don't want all our clips to move about, so we create a new class and apply it only to the particular library clip type that we want to skate. Sometimes though, we are happy to let *all* movie clips have additional methods.

What sort of methods would we want to add? Well, to perform property-based animation, we usually have to use event-based ActionScript, usually onEnterFrame. What if we could add the standard property-based animations such as rotate, move, and fade as *methods?* That would be cool, because not only do we save ourselves from having to set up enterFrame scripts, the non-scripting designer can have access to property-based animation using events without having to think about setting them up!

So how do we make this work? It's actually easy once you understand how we created skater; we simply give additional functions to the object we want to modify:

```
MovieClip.prototype.myMethod = myfunction();
```

> *You can of course extend any other default object that you want in this way, and are not limited to the movie clip. Beware of doing it to the* Object *object though, because you will find all objects inheriting the new methods, which is not usually something you want or expect!*

This will add a method myMethod to the movie clip object prototype, and this method is defined in myfunction. Easy! Let's see an example.

Creating a rotation component

Let's construct a component that gives us a rotation effect. Have a look at rotateMeComponent.fla. We will add a new method rotateMe(step,state) to the movie clip object. The MovieClip.rotateMe method has two arguments, step and state. The first is the amount we want to rotate by each frame: the second determines whether we want to start rotating by this amount (state = true), or if we have previously started rotating the movie clip via (for example)...

```
mySkaterClip.rotateMe(5, true);
```

...and now want to *stop* the rotation. To do this, we simply use the rotateMe method with state = false (the step is then not important, because we will no longer be rotating).

Because the actual packaging of the code into the component rotateMe is so similar to skater, we will move quickly through it.

1. The timeline of our component `rotateMe` is almost identical to `skaterDefinition`, in that I have added an icon graphic and there is also an actions layer at the top:

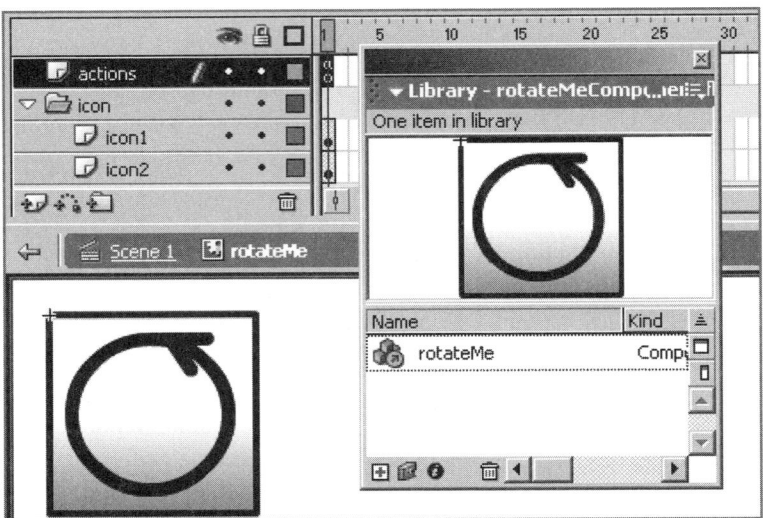

2. This is the script attached to the actions layer:

```
#initclip
MovieClip.prototype.rotateMe = function(step, state) {
  if (state) {
    this.onEnterFrame = function() {
      this._rotation += step;
    };
  } else {
    this.onEnterFrame = undefined;
  }
};
#endinitclip
```

The script implements an #initclip / #endinitclip block so that our object changes are defined before the timelines start to run in the final SWF. If state is true, we add an onEnterFrame callback function that causes this to rotate by step every frame. If state is false, we delete the onEnterFrame by setting it to undefined (which, incidentally, is a good way of deleting callback functions from events).

The linkage and component parameter options are identical to those specified earlier when we made skater.

3. To use this new method, simply call it like you would any other movie clip method from the main timeline. As long as rotateMe is in the library, it will be there

waiting to be used. In `rotateMeComponent.fla`, it is used in `_root` to rotate a movie clip with the instance name `box`:

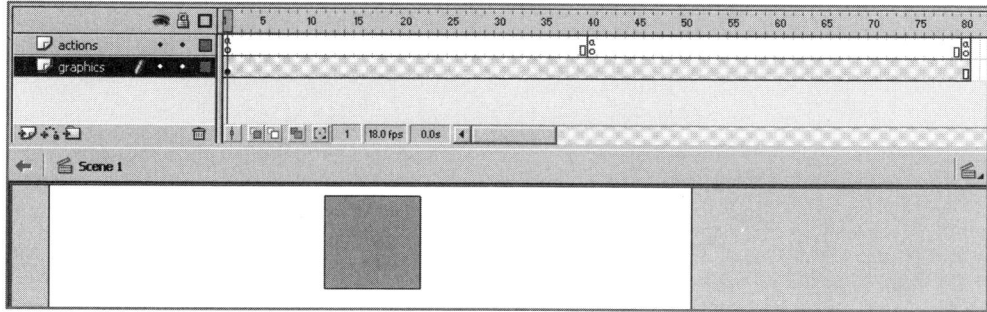

In frame 1 of the actions layer, we have:

```
box.rotateMe(5, true);
```

This starts rotating it by 5 degrees every frame. At frame 40, we use:

```
box.rotateMe(-5, true);
```

Which starts rotating it the other way. Finally, at frame 80, we stop the effect with:

```
box.rotateMe(0, false);
stop ();
```

Now the moment of truth: the script used here to define `rotateMe` is an exercise in how *not* to write components. It has a big problem in that it is not transparent to the other unrelated scripts that may already be in the FLA. For example, what if `box` already had an `onEnterFrame` event attached to it? By defining another one, we delete anything that is already there! A component should *never* be so bold. It should be written to perform its functionality and let any other scripts in the FLA do their own thing.

So we're stuck, right? We can't use event scripts, so we can't add animation methods directly to our movie clip... Well, that's all true, but we *can* add event scripts to *another* movie clip that we create ourselves. Since we create it ourselves, we can do whatever we want to it, including deleting its event scripts, or even deleting the movie clip itself – do you feel another example coming on?

Extending the rotation movie clip

Have a look at `movieExtenderComponent.fla`. This extends the movie clip by adding not one, but *two* new methods. Because each method is transparent to anything else, you can use either method with an existing `onEnterFrame`, and you can also use them both *together* – their effects become additive. As well as the `movieClip.rotateMe(step,state)` method, I have also added `movieClip.fadeMe(step,state)`. This works in exactly the same way, but fades our movie clips instead of rotating them.

Here's the new script inside the component (which is now called `movieClipExtender`):

```
#initclip
MovieClip.prototype.rotateMe = function(step, state) {
  var step, state;
  if (state) {
    this.createEmptyMovieClip("dummy01", 1000);
    this.dummy01.onEnterFrame = function() {
      this._parent._rotation += step;
    };
  } else {
    this.dummy01.removeMovieClip();
  }
};
MovieClip.prototype.fadeMe = function(step, state) {
  var step, state;
  if (state) {
    this.createEmptyMovieClip("dummy02", 1001);
    this.dummy02.onEnterFrame = function() {
      this._parent._alpha += step;
      if (this._parent._alpha>100) {
          this._parent._alpha = 100;
          state = false;
      } else if (this._parent._alpha<0) {
          this._parent._alpha = 0;
          state = false;
      }
    };
  }
  if (!state)          {
    this.dummy02.removeMovieClip();
  }
};
#endinitclip
```

Our first method, `rotateMe`, gets round the fact that we can't mess about with any `enterFrame` script that is already on `this` by creating `this.dummy01` and adding the event script on *that*. The only thing we have to do now is make sure that the rotate effect works on `dummy01`'s parent (the original `this` that the method is applied to), rather than `dummy01` itself. That's just a case of using the `this._parent` path rather than `this`.

Rather than leave `dummy01` there at the end and just delete the event script, we tidy things up by deleting `dummy01` itself.

The second method, `fadeMe`, works in much the same way. This time, we have to be careful not to mess up any existing `onEnterFrame` actions acting on `this`, and also not mess up `dummy01`, so I am now working with `dummy02`, which is also on another depth.

You can see it all working in the example included in the FLA. Not only are we applying fade and/or rotation effects to the instances, we are doing this in parallel with event scripts that might already be acting on the target movie clips and doing other stuff. This is good news, because by adding all these little animation methods, we can slowly build up the final effect.

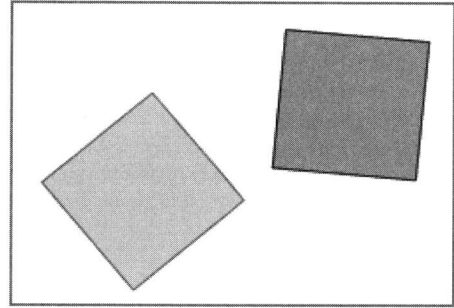

There is, of course, nothing stopping you adding more methods if you wish!

The use of prototypes in the way we have just seen has a number of distinct advantages:

- Firstly, you can take all your best techniques and place them all into a component as new methods. Non-coders can then make use of your expertise without knowing exactly what makes it tick. They will just see these features as a simple action or method that they use (by adding the new methods in the Actions panel's XML files, you can even make them appear the correct color in the scripting window).

- Secondly, changing the prototype of the base objects has a number of advantages over simply adding the base objects to new objects (as we did with skater). The methods become more general because they are not part of a new specialized object like skater, but general methods of existing objects. However, you need to take more care in writing them. They have to have an 'off' switch as well as an 'on' switch, and they have to be transparent to everything else, and well-behaved.

- Thirdly, you can redefine existing methods directly. For example, if you wanted to change gotoAndPlay(), you could do this within our component #initclip / #endinitclip block:

```
MovieClip.prototype.gotoAndPlay = function() {
  trace("you have been replaced");
};
```

This will replace the normal anyclip.gotoAndPlay() functionality with a message in the output window. A trivial example, but it shows a very powerful technique. If you don't like the way hitTest works, and you want something that is more in keeping with collision detection in video games, simply write the new method and replace it!

> *Before we move on from prototypes and inheritance, it is worth pointing out that* prototype *is preferred over* _proto_. *The latter is not part of the ECMA definition that ActionScript is based upon. The fact that it is not part of the specification means that it is always open to change, so you use it at your risk!*

As you can see, components and objects go well together. Sure, we have nice benefits like drag and drop and live preview, but here in the deep end we are well beyond nice one-trick effects, and moving towards some truly advanced techniques: *redefining ActionScript to suit our personal needs so that it does exactly what we want it to do.*

That would be a good point to end the book, because it shows how far removed Flash MX is from Flash 5, but there's more... We have only one final topic to look at and then we will have completed our tour of the Flash MX upgrades – we'll look at **watchers** in the next section.

Watchers

A watcher allows you to respond to an update in a variable or property that is updated through ActionScript. This means that you can respond to stuff like:

- User actions that change a continuous input value from things like UI sliders and spinners (in the same way that you can respond to button events). For example, if a slider value was currently 45.67, and the user changed it to 56.32, then you could use a watcher event script that takes the new value and, say, change the site master volume based on it. Because you are 'on-change' event-driven, your processes can only run when something needs to be done, a far better solution than having to do it every frame on an onEnterFrame.

- Internal logic states of your script. For example, if you had a Boolean out, which was set to true when a movie clip was outside the visible screen area, you could fire off an event on the change. This event would take steps to bring it back on screen.

- Filtering or processing values on change. For example, if a variable changes to a value that is too high, the watcher can look out for this, and run a script to get it back to an in-range value.

- Updating live previews on the change of the associated component parameters.

As always, there is a catch. For the watcher to see the change, the value must be explicit and require no additional evaluation. Some values, particularly properties of the standard objects, such as _x, _y, do not exist internally in the form we use them. The Flash player uses optimized versions of the values (that are probably expressed in actual pixels). When we read them, they have to be converted via a function (which scales the pixel values to take account of the current stage size, for example). The watcher doesn't use this function, and the change may therefore be masked from it *until our*

ActionScript causes a re-evaluation of the calculated values _x, _y by reading them explicitly with a line such as:

```
myPosX = myClip._x;
```

These functions are called **getter/setters**, and can hide the real value of a property. I'll explain briefly here how they work, and how the problem occurs.

> *The evaluation of high level properties that are not included in the optimized routines that the Flash player uses must be calculated on demand using the low level values that Flash actually uses. This occurs through functions called either getters or setters. A **getter** is evaluated by a function that takes no input parameters every time you read the value:*
>
> ```
> myGetter = function () {
>   return getTimer();
> };
> x = myGetter();
> trace(x);
> ```
>
> *This returns a value x that is derived by a getter evaluation. The returned value is based on a low level and changing quantity (the internal Flash timer), and the returned value x is only equal to the internal value when it is evaluated. After the evaluation, x remains the same but the timer continues to change. A watcher would not see the change in the timer because it is only looking at x, and will only see the next change when we read x again.*
>
> *A **setter** is evaluated by a function that uses input parameters (the 'settings') that help define the returned value:*
>
> ```
> mySetter = function (value, multiplier) {
>   return (value*multiplier);
> };
> x = mySetter(8,2);
> trace(x);
> ```
>
> *This returns a value x that is derived by a setter evaluation. The changes in value and multiplier will not be tracked by a watcher looking at x, because the changes in them only feed through to x when your code actually looks at x again via the function.*
>
> *The act of only seeing changes in values if the change is explicit and doesn't require you to re-evaluate anything is called **lazy evaluation**. It leads to greater efficiency in the Flash player, but masks changes to the watch method.*
>
> *Although your watcher will usually see changes in getter/setter properties if your ActionScript is reading it often enough, you should be aware that watching such values is not supported, and an unsupported feature is open to changes that may break any SWF that uses watchers directly on getter/setter properties.*

To set up a watch on a property you use the `Object.watch` method as follows:

```
myObject.watch("myProperty", function(id, oldval, newval){
  // call-back function code goes here...
});
```

This adds a watch to property `myObject.myProperty`. The function parameters are:

- `id` – the property identifier that will be sent as `myProperty`

- `oldval` – the last value that `myProperty` has the last time it changed

- `newval` – the new `myProperty` value that caused the watch event to trigger

An important point to notice is that the watch will trigger the callback function on update of `myObject.myProperty` and this will occur *even if the value has not changed*. An example of an update *and* change is:

```
myObject.myProperty ++
```

Whereas an update with no change is:

```
myObject.myProperty = myObject.myProperty
```

This means that if your watched property is being constantly updated (for example in an `onEnterFrame` script), it will trigger the watch callback constantly even if it never changes.

OK, we will now look at two examples: a standard piece of scripting to create a temperature conversion program, and a more 'Flashy' version that creates an animation.

Building a temperature converter using watchers

The following script sets up a temperature converter that converts degrees Celsius to degrees Fahrenheit and degrees Kelvin. You can see our version as `watcher.fla`.

1. In a new FLA with actions and graphics layers, add the script described below to frame 1 of the actions layer.

    First, define the property called `temperature.degC`. I have also added a counter `i`, which will increment to show us how many times the watch detects a change:

    ```
    temperature.degC = 0;
    i = 0;
    ```

2. Next, add the watch definition as shown below. Because `temperature.degC` will be a user input (Flash will assume that it's a string), the callback first makes sure it is converted to a number with `Number()`. The next few lines define our conversions for the other temperature systems. Finally, we update our counter, `i`:

```
temperature.watch("degC", function (id, oldval, newval) {
  newval = Number(newval);
  degF=(1.8*newval)+32;
  degK = newval+273.16;
  i++;
});
```

> *Because the function definition is part of the command line, the final ')'*
> *does not appear until the very end of the script. This will cause the tabs*
> *to go wrong, but if you hit* Auto Format *once the whole script is entered,*
> *it will correct itself.*

3. Add the following to the graphics layer:

    a. Static text labels degC, degF, degK, and updates.

    b. A bordered input text field with Var `temperature.degC` and Character Options set to accept numerals and the decimal point ('.') only.

    c. A borderless dynamic text field with Var `degF`.

    d. A borderless dynamic text field with Var `degK`.

    e. A borderless dynamic text field with Var `i`.

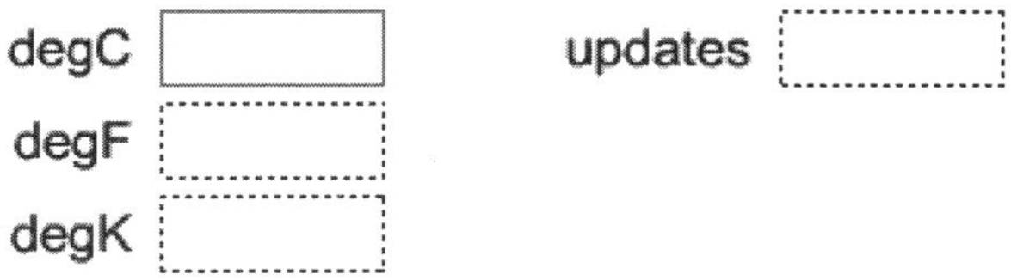

4. Now run the FLA. Start entering values in the degC input box and you will see the conversions taking place as you type, and the number of times the watch callback is triggered will appear on the right-hand side:

degC [28]   updates 2

degF 82.4

degK 301.16

The whole functionality of this conversion is event-driven, and that means that the conversion calculations only occur when they are required, increasing the overall efficiency of the code.

One thing to note is what happens when you put the same value in twice. For example, enter '30', and then continue to end up with '30.000'. The number of updates will continue to increase – the watch property is not actually changing, although it *is* being internally updated.

Animation with watch events

The problem with watch points is that we cannot use them to keep an eye on the movie clip properties that create animation because they are all getter/setters. We can, however, do something instead – we can constantly update a property of our own (that is not a getter/setter) to the movie clip properties of interest. We can then use the watch event to create the animated effect only when the property changes. Although our code is now only partially event-driven, the part that is the most computationally expensive (the actual animation) is event-driven and conditional on change, so we are almost where we want to be.

Have a look at spinnerWatcher.fla. Here, I have used two scrollbars as spinner inputs for an animation. The two scrollbars are being used to set the height and width of the clip on the top left (instance name square):

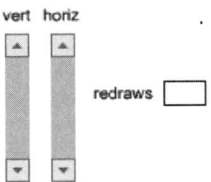

The script to run it all is built as follows.

1. Firstly, I have defined my object size with properties horizontal and vertical. I have again set up a counter, i, to show how many times the watch callbacks are run:

```
size = {horizontal:0, vertical:0};
i = 0;
//
```

> Note the different code convention we use here – the first line is equivalent to the following:
>
> ```
> size.horizontal = size.vertical = 0;
> ```

2. Next, I have set up the scrollbars to range between 10 and 400, with an initial position (value) of 200:

```
scroller1.setScrollProperties(200, 10, 400);
scroller1.setScrollPosition(200);
scroller2.setScrollProperties(200, 10, 400);
scroller2.setScrollPosition(200);
```

3. We have a problem straight away - the scrollbar positions are getter/setter properties because they can only be accessed through a method (function) getScrollPosition. To get around this, an onEnterFrame script makes the current values of these properties available as the non-getter/setter properties of size I have set up earlier.

```
_root.onEnterFrame = function() {
  size.horizontal = scroller1.getScrollPosition();
  size.vertical = scroller2.getScrollPosition();
};
```

4. The two watcher callbacks are set up next, one each for the horizontal and vertical spinners. Because the watch is firing constantly, the first thing we want to know is, has it been caused by an update (oldval = newval) or a real change in value (oldval != newval)? If it is the latter, we perform the property-based animation on square:

```
size.watch("horizontal", function (id, oldval, newval) {
  if (oldval != newval) {
    i++;
    square._width = newval;
  }
  return newval;
});
size.watch("vertical", function (id, oldval, newval) {
  if (oldval != newval) {
```

```
        i++;
        square._height = newval;
    }
    return newval;
});
```

We *could* just place these scripts in the onEnterFrame, but with the watch method we gain the use of oldval and newval, which is a quick way of telling us there has been a change. If you run this FLA, you will notice that:

    a.   I have used the scrollbar skins we created in Chapter 14 (sorry, I couldn't resist!).

    b.   The counter i starts off at 2 straight away. This is because the properties are initialized to 0, but immediately change to 200, causing both our watches to fire off once each.

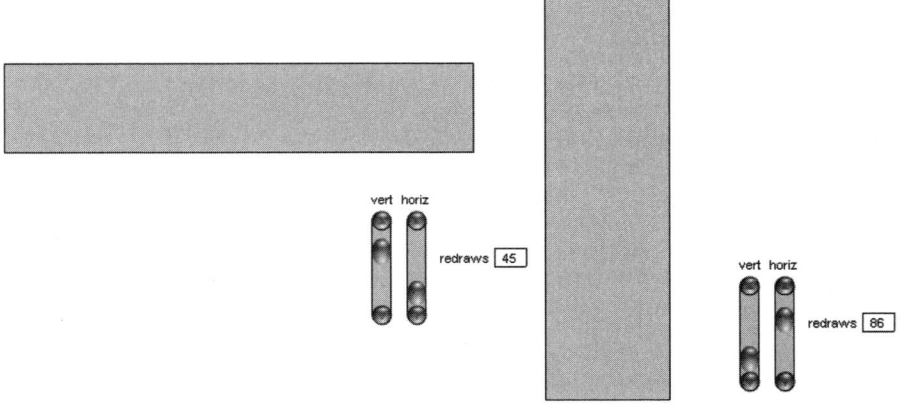

Well, that's cool, but it's all a bit jerky – how about making it little smoother via that filtering we mentioned at the beginning?

Have a look at spinnerWatchFilter.fla. This time we are filtering the horizontal and vertical input changes via a new value smooth. This uses oldval and newval to smooth of the spinner movements (it's our old friend inertia again). We run the animation only if we are more than 5 away from the desired size ((oldval-newval)>5). If we are, then we use the inertia equation to smooth any sudden movements in the input spinners. If we are less than 5 away from the desired size, we return oldval to allow oldval-newval to build up towards 5 (if we returned newval, oldval would always equal newval if the increments in the slider per frame were less than 5):

```
size.watch("horizontal", function (id, oldval, newval) {
  if (Math.abs(oldval-newval)>5) {
    i++;
    smooth = Math.round(oldval+(newval-oldval)/8);
    square._width = smooth;
    return smooth;
  } else {
    return oldval;
  }
});
```

Again, although we could have incorporated this script in the onEnterframe, we are using the oldval and newval values to tell us what is happening without having to set them up ourselves.

If you now run the FLA, you will see that the animation on square is smooth despite any jerkiness on the spinners. By looking for changes in the spinners and smoothing them out, we allow our UI to create an animation that looks like it has a higher frame rate:

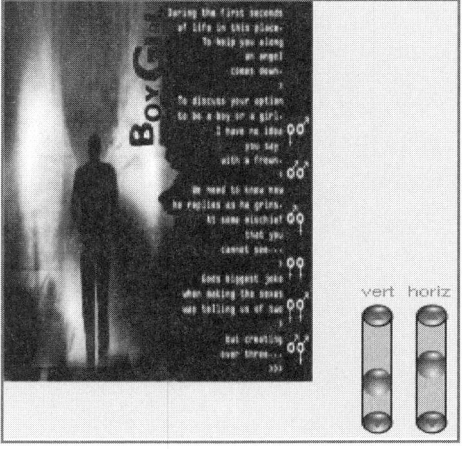

Additionally, we are animating a bitmap this time, and doing that on the fly is a very intensive process for Flash. If this UI was being used to navigate around a bitmap of a map, the scrolling and zoom in/out would stop as soon as the user reached the bit they were after, and we could then concentrate on animating overlays on the map. By using events to control our animation totally, we achieve efficient use of the Flash player's processing resources.

Summary

We have seen here how you can use Flash to extend the existing objects to create new custom objects and methods. This is the way to go if you want to move away from simple web design towards application building, where Flash is used to create code-heavy sites with lots going on under the hood.

As Flash has evolved from Flash 4 to 5, and now from 5 to MX, it is clear that Flash itself is starting to lean in this direction in its new functionality, and many of the more advanced new features require at least a basic understanding of the object model.

In the next chapter, we'll round off this book by presenting a couple of case studies of work designed using Flash MX with the aim of inspiring you to get out there and use this powerful piece of software in the real world.

Chapter 16

Departure Lounge

In the final chapter of this book we'll take a rather different approach to learning. We'll study some of the new features of Macromedia Flash MX by looking at the recent work of two designers who have been using Flash MX since its early trials. These 'real world' case studies will give us further insight to the creative potential that Flash MX offers. Throughout this chapter, we'll take a fairly high-level view of some of the technical concepts, concentrating on applying the MX-specific functionality that we've became familiar with over the course of this book to produce studio-quality creations.

With comments from the designers themselves, we'll be taking a look at the workflow, thought processes, and scripting techniques that they undertake during the creation process of two distinctly different projects:

- The Oracle, by aYo Binitie (www.ayobinitie.com) – a rather dramatic piece of work, which gives a very good impression of how a multimedia project can be built up from a single centralized main script.

- Spank the Monkey, by Hoss Gifford (www.h69.net) – a fun example that also serves to demonstrate how we can incorporate a couple of hot new MX features together – dynamic masking and the drawing API.

The Oracle, by aYo Binitie

My first encounter with the surreal was a print of Hieronymus Bosch's *Temptation of St. Anthony* in my father's library, and I've been fascinated by extraordinary art ever since. In art school I discovered a host of artists – Dali, Turner, Nelson-Cole, Kiefer, Wyeth, and so on – whose flair, vision, and sheer audacity of aesthetic expression have driven my artistic ambitions ever since. In 1996, intrigued and excited by the Internet, I began to explore web design, which led me to multimedia art – another whole new world. Flash has been one of my major tools for the last five years, and it has been pivotal in the development of my art, allowing me to experiment with the fusion of line, form, color, motion, sound, and interactivity. Macromedia Flash MX is packed with updated features and brand new tools, and seems destined to remain a constant companion of mine for a while yet.

My postgraduate sub-thesis researched a religious group, the Ogun-Nomayisi-Olokun cult. Their arcane worship practice focused on an intriguing soothsayer deity that possessed a powerful oracle. I planned to do a painting exploring the spirit world of the oracle, but never got round to it until now. I felt that the piece would require a multimedia approach to play on as many senses as possible and incorporate constantly changing states. Here, I'll walk you through the creation of this motion painting, which uses some superb new Flash MX functionality to achieve its effect. The finished work can be found as Oracle.fla in the appropriate code download directory.

I developed and created the backdrop of the painting first:

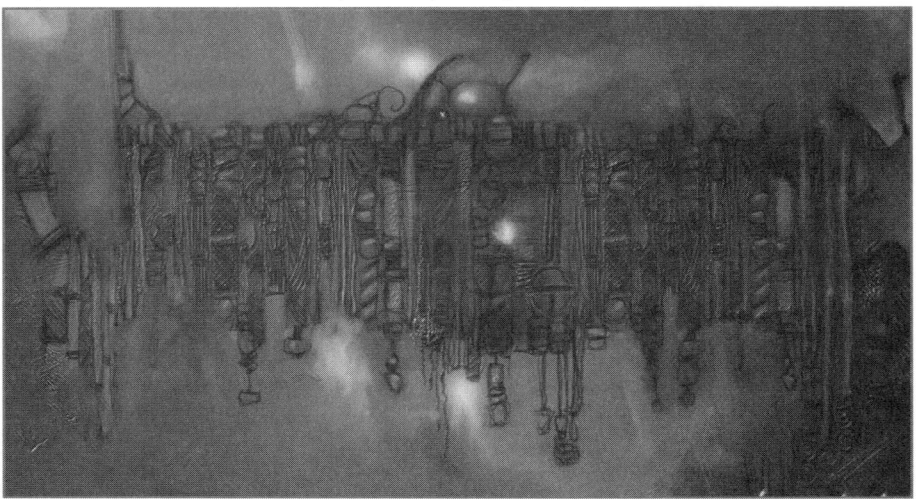

My idea was to fuse bioorganic forms with rune-carved wooden plaques to create a surreal mystical backdrop, with color, texture, and form merged to create a tangible yet vaporous feel. The working sketches and the painting were done using a cross-software combination of Painter, Fireworks and Photoshop, with the final image optimized in Fireworks ready for export to Flash. The brilliant optimization tools of Fireworks, and its seamless integration with Flash make it my finishing tool of choice.

Simultaneously, to structure the multimedia composition of the Flash painting, I tried to run through the various animation and media possibilities at my disposal, using notes scribbled on notepads and Post-it notes stuck to my desk and monitor. I must admit that most of those ideas were never used, but the useful ones never get forgotten...

When I felt the evolving concept had achieved a satisfactory feel and balance of form, I moved on to Flash MX.

Creation

To start, I created a new document called `Oracle.fla`, 900 by 500 pixels, gray background, 20 fps. Using the new Import to Library option, I imported all the pre-prepared images into an imports folder in the library. I then arranged all the possible visual elements on stage, layer by layer, like a collage – it's vital for me to see the form and structure of the painting and be comfortable with it.

> *I've discovered that my modes of thought while painting or creating art are very different from when I'm writing ActionScript. To cater for this, I try to do most of the creative work first, in 'artist' mode, then switch to 'logic' mode for the scripting part.*

When the tentative structure is satisfactory, I begin to orchestrate the animation and manipulate the various elements of the painting – we'll take a look at the individual elements in the subsections that follow.

Ray of energy

The revolving ray emitted from the energy core of the oracle was the first object I worked on: I created a rounded rectangle with a corner radius of 6 with the rectangle tool, then applied a linear gradient fill to it before adjusting the shape to its final form. The opacity was set to 0 at one end to create a dispersion effect, and then the faded rectangle was saved as a movie clip called `ray`. I then placed an instance of it (named `ray0` just in case I needed to create multiple instances) on the stage with its registration point at the core of the oracle. In the main movie I initialized a spin speed variable (`sVel`) in the code frame of the `code` layer. `sVel` was set to 8.

I attached the following code to `_root` to rotate the ray of energy:

```
ray0.onEnterFrame = function() {
  this._rotation += sVel;
};
```

I also needed an 'energy signature' at the end of the ray. To do this I typed in the desired parameters for the `beginGradientFill` method (color, alpha, ratio, and matrix). I then used the new `moveto` and `lineto` methods to draw the shape I needed:

```
ray0.colors = [0x6BD812, 0xDE650C];
ray0.alphas = [30, 30];
ray0.ratios = [0, 0x00];
ray0.matrix = {a:300, b:0, c:0, d:0, e:200, f:0, g:100, h:100,
➥i:1};
ray0.beginGradientFill("linear", ray0.colors, ray0.alphas,
➥ray0.ratios, ray0.matrix);
ray0.moveto(-10, 200);
ray0.lineto(10, 200);
ray0.lineto(25, 550);
ray0.lineto(-25, 550);
ray0.lineto(-10, 200);
ray0.endFill();
```

Bugs

Inspired by memories of *Indiana Jones* and movies like *The Mummy*, I wanted bugs crawling up and down the walls of the oracle, so I used the oval tool and a radial fill to create a bug:

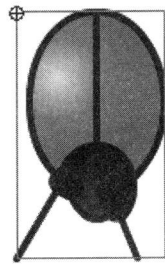
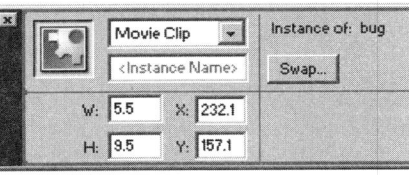

The resulting insect was saved as a movie clip (bug), and thirty instances of it created by attaching them to the stage (that is, to _root). Opening up the bug movie clip, I added two new key frames, rotating the bug slightly to left and right in each frame. The result, when played back, is the wiggly movement of a beetle or roach. In the main movie code frame I created a screen object that marked out the dimensions of the movie and specified the bug speed:

```
bugSpd=3;
screen = new Object();
screen = {top:0, left:0, bottom:500, right:900};
```

I initialized a local 'bug speed' variable localBugSpd and set it to the root bug speed, and also set the opacity of the bug to 60. The idea was for the bug to scuttle down the stage to the bottom of the screen, turn around, scuttle back up the panels, and disappear into its nest. To achieve this objective, as well as creating the stream of bugs, I attached the following code to onClipEvent handlers:

```
// duplicate bugs and add events to each copy...
for (b=0; b<30; b++) {
  // create bug clone...
  _root.attachMovie("bug", ["bug"+b], -b);
  _root["bug"+b]._x = 820+(Math.random()*20);
  _root["bug"+b]._y = 150+(Math.random()*150);
  // initialize bug clone...
  _root["bug"+b].localBugSpd =
Math.floor(Math.random()*5)+bugSpd;
  _root["bug"+b]._alpha = 60;
  // give bug clone an onEnterFrame call-back function...
  _root["bug"+b].onEnterFrame = function() {
    this._y += this.localbugSpd;
    if (this._y<(screen.top+100) || this._y>(screen.bottom)) {
      this.localbugSpd = -this.localbugSpd;
      this._rotation += 180;
    }
  };
}
```

Note the use of the Math.random functions applied to the x and y coordinates of the spawn bugs – this has the effect of positioning each bug uniquely on the screen.

Flies

The flying insects were developed in a similar fashion to the bug. The fly's body was sketched with the pencil tool set to free form, and the wings were linear gradient filled.

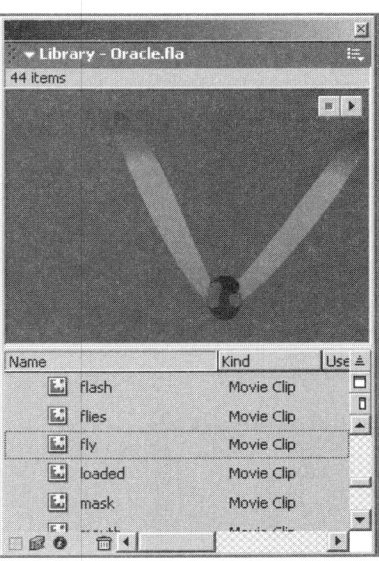

The drawing was then converted to a movie clip named flies, and its content animated to create the flapping motion of the insect's wings. Next I created a new movie clip called fly, where an instance of flies was tweened along a curved motion guide. Its x scale and y scale was reduced to 10% at the beginning of the motion path, and to 110% with an opacity of 10% at the *end* of the tween. As I planned to produce a *stream* of flies, I created an extra keyframe and attached a stop() action and a removeMovieClip(this) method to the frame. This was to make sure that each duplicated fly would remove itself when its 'performance' was over. This fly movie clip (instance name flying) had its rotation manipulated to give the fly a more erratic nature:

```
fly.onEnterFrame = function() {
  this._rotation = Math.random()*360;
  this._x = Math.random()*400;
};
```

The instance fly was saved as a movie clip called flyingEnvelope with an instance name fly and placed on the orb of the left mask: this mask had the instance name mask0. To duplicate fly and create the stream of flying insects, mask0 was given 'button' movie clip attributes with the onPress function, and the following script attached to it:

```
mask0.onMouseMove = function() {
  if (this.hitTest(_xmouse, _ymouse, true)) {
    fly.duplicateMovieClip(_root["fly"-i], i-40);
    --i;
  }
};
```

This action duplicates the fly movie clip whenever the mouse moves over it. The Math.random() function spreads the location of the flies over the required area of the stage.

The Oracle's 'being'

An oracle is both soothsayer and seer, so I decided to characterize the oracle with the organs of speech and sight. Once the sketches were satisfactory they were imported into the library of the Oracle Flash file:

The first of these sketches was placed on the stage and converted into a movie clip mouth, with an instance name mouth. The movie clip was then animated frame-by-frame to simulate a speaking mouth. The layer is labeled mouth. The first frame was cleared and had a stop() action attached. Frame 5 was labeled anime: the animation sequence starts here, with frames 5, 6, 7, and 8 all having different states of the animation. Frame 2 (which was to become the 'at rest' frame) contains an image of the mouth in the 'closed' position. Frame 8 of the movie clip controls the animation of the movie clip: a counter is initialized to count the required number of loops, and is initialized as lipcount. An if() conditional statement is then used to loop the animation, provided that the requested parameters are satisfactory. Here's the code:

```
lipcount++;
if (lipcount<20) {
  gotoAndPlay("anime");
} else {
  lipcount=0
  stop();
}
```

The mouth clip was then properly positioned on stage.

Next I wanted multiple instances of mouth (decreasing in scale and opacity) to cascade down, one after the other, from the main mouth clip if certain conditions were met. I created a new movie clip (oracleCtrl, instance name oCtrl) to do this job. The movie clip consists of four active key frames spread over 8 frames: frame 1 stops the movie, and frame 2 initializes a count variable:

```
var count=6;
```

Frame 5 contains conditional statements to duplicate the `mouth` movie clip. To ensure that the `mouth` movie clip stays on top of the depth stack, a `swapDepths` method is called every time a duplicate `mouth` is made:

```
if (i < count){
  _parent.mouth.duplicateMovieClip(["mouth"+i], i+50);
  _parent["mouth" + i]._xscale= Math.floor(((100-
➥(i*10))/100)*100);
  _parent["mouth" + i]._yscale= Math.floor(((100-
➥(i*10))/100)*100);
  _parent["mouth" + i]._y= _parent.mouth._y +(30*i);
  _parent["mouth" + i]._alpha= Math.floor(((80-
➥(i*10))/100)*100);
  i++;
  _parent.mouth.swapDepths(90);
//trace(i)
  }else{
    stop();
    }
```

Frame 8 of the `oracleCtrl` movie clip returns the play head to frame 5.

To create drama and spectacle, and a control for the `oracleCtrl` movie clip, I created a pulsing 'energy orb' (instance name `pulse`) at the apex of the painting. I wanted lines of force drawn across the screen if the orb was clicked: this next batch of code controls the pulsing action of the orb, plays the `oracleCtrl` movie clip, and inscribes energy lines across the oracle:

```
pulse._alpha = 0;
pulse.pulse = 3;
//
pulse.onEnterFrame = function() {
  this._alpha += this.pulse;
  if ((this._alpha>=100) || (this._alpha<=0)) {
    this.pulse = -this.pulse;
  }
};
pulse.onPress = function() {
woop.stop("wooop");
  woop.start(0, 3);
  oCtrl.play();
  this.lineStyle(1, 0xFF6600, 50);
  this.moveTo(100, 0);
  this.lineTo(100, 200);
  this.curveTo(200, 300, 200, 100);
  this.curveTo(200, 100, 200, 300);
  this.curveTo(300, 200, 200, 100);
  this.curveTo(300, 400, 200, 100);
};
```

Flash MX can import QuickTime movies, and I was determined to find some way to take advantage of this: the fact that the oracle needed a 'portal' into another dimension provided the perfect opportunity. First I built a 3D model of a bio-morphic form, animated it, and saved it as a QuickTime movie, before importing this into the library, selecting Embed Video in Macromedia Flash Movie from the options list. Then I opened up the `container` movie clip and placed the embedded QuickTime movie in frame 1, adjusting the span to fit the length of the imported movie by clicking the relevant option in the prompt. The opacity of the `container` movie clip is initialized to zero using the `onClipEvent(load)` event. The movie clip is masked with a shape that mirrored the blue celestial body to the left of the oracle, and the opacity of the container is triggered by clicking on the `mouth` or `mask1` movie clips. Both movie clips used this code syntax:

```
container._alpha= required value;
```

Lines of Force

To create the lines of force inscribed by the oracle I use the `lineStyle`, `moveTo`, and `lineTo` methods to draw lines across the oracle when the masks are clicked. The following code is attached to the center mask `mask1`:

```
mask1.onPress = function() {
    drums.stop("drummin");
    drums.start(0, 3);
    this.lineStyle(0, 0xFF3300, 30);
    this.moveTo(200, 0);
    this.lineTo(300, 200);
    this.lineTo(100, 200);
    this.lineTo(200, 0);
    this.moveTo(300, 150);
    this.lineTo(100, 150);
    word = "change your place, change your luck";
    container._alpha = 20;
    mouth._x = Math.random()*600;
    mouth1._x = Math.random()*600;
    mouth3._x = Math.random()*600;
};
```

Sound

The oracle needs sound to create the mood of mystery and awe around its presence. On a new layer, `thunder`, I initialize four sound objects for the sounds I've chosen:

```
woop= new Sound();
woop.attachSound ("wooop");

thunder= new Sound();
thunder.attachSound ("thunder");

drums= new Sound();
drums.attachSound ("drummin");
drums.start(0,6);
```

```
hum= new Sound();
hum.attachSound ("humm");
```

These sound objects can be activated from whatever movie clip I chose, provided that their activation conditions are met. For instance, the mouth movie clip activates the sound of thunder when you click on it. The drums sound object is initialized to play and loop six times once the oracle starts to play. To add a bit more drama, a sound file of shattering glass is attached to frame 5:

```
mouth.onPress = function() {
  if (this.hitTest(_xmouse, _ymouse, true)) {
    this.gotoAndPlay(5);
    container._alpha = 50;
    thunder.stop("thunder");
    thunder.start();
  }
};
```

Covering boards

I wanted covering boards to mask the presence of the oracle from sight until you knocked (or clicked!). The covering board was positioned on stage, converted to a movie (woodslat), and given the instance name cPlaque0:

From the main movie's code frame, the duplication is initialized when the movie starts. This code is attached to the movie clip, setting its visibility to zero when it's clicked:

```
cPlaque0.onPress = function() {
  this._visible = 0;
};
```

In frame 2 of the code layer, I've implemented a preload sequence using the getBytesLoaded and getBytesTotal methods to make sure the movie is loaded before playback:

```
if (getBytesLoaded() == getBytesTotal()) {
  play();
} else {
  gotoAndPlay(1);
}
```

Completion

The final piece shows how Macromedia Flash MX allows you to build up a presentation that uses a central script to control almost everything by using callbacks that are defined in a single place. Although the visuals are a scattergun stream-of-consciousness work in the vein of a painting, the scripting is centralized and self contained, allowing the artist to go wild on the visuals while keeping the code under control.

Rather than the Flash 5 model of coding, where you have events buried everywhere and have trouble finding them ('Was that `bug01` that I attached the `onLoad` event to, or was it `butterfly235`, and where the heck is it anyway?'), you have a single main listing that you can even print off in one go for debugging and development. A single script also makes for easier breakpoints and more advanced debugging, and you are less likely to miss that pesky bit of code embedded three movie clips deep that sets `_root.flag = true` when it should be setting `_parent.flag = true`!

Of course, the scripts in this example stop short of the full-on Flash MX OOP approach, but that would tend to slow down the artistic spontaneity of the piece anyway. Anyway, as we've seen in this book, give it a few months and someone else will have written all those little scripts to make the bugs crawl and the flies swarm as components, and the real artists won't even have to bother with the code if they don't want to; you'll be able to just drag and drop a component, forget about it, and start mixing some paint together for the next masterpiece!

For completeness, we now include the full code listing that you'll see on the main timeline of `Oracle.fla`:

```
// Create initial covering plaques...
cPlaque0.onPress = function() {
  this._visible = 0;
```

```
};
for (var b = 1; b<7; b++) {
  cPlaque0.duplicateMovieClip(["cPlaque"+b], b+90);
  this["cPlaque"+b]._y = cPlaque0._y+(cPlaque0._height*b);
  this["cPlaque"+b].onPress = function() {
    this._visible = 0;
  };
}
// Draw 'ray of energy'...
ray0.colors = [0x6BD812, 0xDE650C];
ray0.alphas = [30, 30];
ray0.ratios = [0, 0x00];
ray0.matrix = {a:300, b:0, c:0, d:0, e:200, f:0, g:100, h:100,
➥i:1};
ray0.beginGradientFill("linear", ray0.colors, ray0.alphas,
➥ray0.ratios, ray0.matrix);
ray0.moveto(-10, 200);
ray0.lineto(10, 200);
ray0.lineto(25, 550);
ray0.lineto(-25, 550);
ray0.lineto(-10, 200);
ray0.endFill();
// Draw background lines on the stage...
this.createEmptyMovieClip("line", 1);
line.lineStyle(0, 0x22B4C8, 70);
line.moveTo(400, 300);
line.lineTo(300, 100);
line.lineTo(200, 100);
line.lineTo(200, 400);
line.lineTo(600, 100);
line.lineTo(200, 100);
//
stop();
// ----------------------------------------------------
// INITIALIZE VARIABLES
// sVel = spin velocity of ray
// bugSpd = speed of bugs
// screen = screen size
sVel = 8;
bugSpd = 3;
screen = new Object();
screen = {top:0, left:0, bottom:500, right:900};
//
// ----------------------------------------------------
// INITIALIZE EVENTS FOR ANIMATIONS
//
//   Instance Description
//   blip    is the little animation that occurs at the
//           mouse position when you click anywhere.
```

```
//  mouth     the original oracle mouth.
//  ray0      is the rotating 'ray of energy'.
//  fly       is the original instance of the fly swarm
//            that flit around when you press the leftmost
//            mask.
//  mask0..3 are the three masked faces.
//  cPlaque0       is the top board.
//  bottomRung     is the bottom board.
//  pulse          The pulsating globe (top middle of stage).
//  bug            The Linkage ID of the bug movie clip
//
blip.onMouseDown = function() {
  this._x = _xmouse;
  this._y = _ymouse;
  this.play();
};
mouth.onPress = function() {
  if (this.hitTest(_xmouse, _ymouse, true)) {
    this.gotoAndPlay(5);
    container._alpha = 50;
    thunder.stop("thunder");
    thunder.start();
  }
};
//
ray0.onEnterFrame = function() {
  this._rotation += sVel;
};
//
fly.onEnterFrame = function() {
  this._rotation = Math.random()*360;
  this._x = Math.random()*400;
};
//
mask0.onMouseMove = function() {
  if (this.hitTest(_xmouse, _ymouse, true)) {
    fly.duplicateMovieClip(_root["fly"-i], i-40);
    --i;
  }
};
mask0.onPress = function() {
  hum.stop("humm");
  hum.start();
  mouth._x = Math.random()*600;
  mouth2._x = Math.random()*600;
  mouth5._x = Math.random()*600;
  word = "listen to your heart";
};
//
mask1.onPress = function() {
```

```
      drums.stop("drummin");
      drums.start(0, 3);
      this.lineStyle(0, 0xFF3300, 30);
      this.moveTo(200, 0);
      this.lineTo(300, 200);
      this.lineTo(100, 200);
      this.lineTo(200, 0);
      this.moveTo(300, 150);
      this.lineTo(100, 150);
      word = "change your place, change your luck";
      container._alpha = 20;
      mouth._x = Math.random()*600;
      mouth1._x = Math.random()*600;
      mouth3._x = Math.random()*600;
    };
    //
    mask2.onRelease = function() {
      if (this.hitTest(_xmouse, _ymouse, true)) {
        drums.stop("drummin");
        drums.start(0, 3);
        this.lineStyle(2, 0xFF9900, 20);
        this.moveTo(200, -5);
        this.lineTo(-600, 200);
        word = "life is a series of moment by moment experiences";
        mouth._x = Math.random()*600;
        mouth4._x = Math.random()*600;
        mouth6._x = Math.random()*600;
      }
    };
    //
    bottomRung.onPress = function() {
      mouth._x = 500;
      mouth0._x = 500;
      mouth1._x = 500;
      mouth2._x = 500;
      mouth3._x = 500;
      mouth4._x = 500;
    };
    // initialize pulse...
    pulse._alpha = 0;
    pulse.pulse = 3;
    //
    pulse.onEnterFrame = function() {
      this._alpha += this.pulse;
      if ((this._alpha>=100) || (this._alpha<=0)) {
        this.pulse = -this.pulse;
      }
    };
    pulse.onPress = function() {
      woop.stop("wooop");
```

```
    woop.start(0, 3);
    oCtrl.play();
    this.lineStyle(1, 0xFF6600, 50);
    this.moveTo(100, 0);
    this.lineTo(100, 200);
    this.curveTo(200, 300, 200, 100);
    this.curveTo(200, 100, 200, 300);
    this.curveTo(300, 200, 200, 100);
    this.curveTo(300, 400, 200, 100);
};
//
// duplicate bugs and add events to each copy...
for (b=0; b<30; b++) {
  // create bug clone...
  _root.attachMovie("bug", ["bug"+b], -b);
  _root["bug"+b]._x = 820+(Math.random()*20);
  _root["bug"+b]._y = 150+(Math.random()*150);
  // initialize bug clone...
  _root["bug"+b].localBugSpd =
Math.floor(Math.random()*5)+bugSpd;
  _root["bug"+b]._alpha = 60;
  // give bug clone an onEnterFrame call-back function...
  _root["bug"+b].onEnterFrame = function() {
    this._y += this.localbugSpd;
    if (this._y<(screen.top+100) || this._y>(screen.bottom)) {
      this.localbugSpd = -this.localbugSpd;
      this._rotation += 180;
    }
  };
}
```

I think this listing shows one of the practical benefits of having all your scripts in one place; you can get a feel for the overall movie's shape and functionality, especially if you comment your code liberally. So, that's my little example. I hope you have as much fun with MX as I've been having!

Spank, the Monkey, by Hoss Gifford

Anyone remember www.flamjam.com/spank/? Since Halloween 2001, more than a million people have *spanked my monkey*. This figure suggests that there's a fair chance that you are one of those people that have taken great pleasure at the site. But some people don't quite feel as satisfied as they would like to be after a good *spanking* session – they long for more!

I have lots of emails to prove this, most of them asking if I could make a version of Spank the Monkey with their boss's face, company logo, wife's backside, and so on, in place of the monkey. Well, here's your chance. With the magic of Flash MX you can spank whoever, or whatever, you want to spank!

Who needs Generator?

Macromedia Generator was a fantastic tool that allowed you to do many incredible things. The majority of its functionality was based around creating and serving dynamic Flash content. The thing is, most people want to use it for one simple task – embedding images dynamically into SWF files.

If, like me, you've been meaning to learn how to use Generator properly for years, but have never got around to it, you can now sit back with a smug look and watch the strain on the faces of all the Generator experts as they discover that it is not supported by Flash MX!

The functionality that people used most in Generator is now standard in Flash – so we can now build a *dynamic* version of Spank the Monkey.

Spank the Monkey MX

Three new features make it possible for us to make Spank the Monkey dynamic:

- The ability to dynamically load assets
- The drawing API
- The extra mask functionality

As with all projects, I like to start out by clearly defining my goals – this makes it easier to know when you have failed, and saves you from flogging a dead horse. It's sad when a horse dies, and I don't think flogging it helps *anyone*.

In Spank the Monkey, you drag one movie clip over another, and if the movement is fast enough it triggers an animation where the second movie clip exits stage left. That's it, nice and simple. This second movie clip contains a photo of my pet, Spank – a small, inflatable monkey. So with this new version of the game we are looking to allow the user to replace the photo of Spank with an image of their own.

Here's a summary of how it's done:

1. User inputs location of new image

2. User resizes image

3. User draws outline of person/object in image

4. Flash MX masks the image using this outline

It's quite a simple series of tasks that you'll pick up fast – but there are a few pitfalls that are easy to plunge into. Don't worry though, I've fallen in a few times already so I can tell you where not to tread!

The set up

To make it easier to see what is happening, here is a diagram of the structure of the movie clip `_root.spank_mc` at the start of our movie. As you will see in the sample file, the movie clip `imageMask_mc` is set to be the mask for the movie clip `imageHolder_mc`, which currently holds the picture of Spank. `imageMask_mc` contains another movie clip called `maskTemp_mc`, which is just a big rectangle that allows the entire Spank picture to show through:

Furthermore, with regard to the scripting in this example, `spank_dynamic.fla`, it's worth noting that:

- All the functions are defined in frame 1 of the functions layer.

- The scripts that control everything are on the keyframes of the actions, buttonInits, & labels layer. These scripts make use of the previously defined functions, thus keeping most of the code in frame 1 of the FLA.

Acquiring a new image

The first thing we need to do is get the new image into the movie. We do this by using our trusty old `loadMovie` command. We start by putting an input text box on stage containing the variable `imageUrl` at `_root` level (frame 1 of the interface layer). Next is a movie clip that acts like a button that the user hits once they've pasted or typed in the URL for the image.

The button scripts are located on frame 1 of the layer named actions, buttonInits, & labels, and they refer to functions that are defined in layer functions. As an aside, it's worth noting that the functions have to be defined before the button scripts are themselves defined, hence we make sure that the functions layer is above the actions... layer.

With Flash MX we finally have the ability to use keyboard shortcuts to copy, cut, and paste text in and out of text boxes in Flash movies. Previously, users would have had to use the right-click menu to paste a URL into our input text box.

The enclosed sample movie does a small amount of error checking in that it prefixes the URL with `http:/` if it isn't already there (this is, however, far from foolproof...). It then uses `loadMovie` to load the image into the movie clip `_root.spank_mc.imageHolder_mc` with the following line:

```
spank_mc.imageHolder_mc.loadMovie(imageUrl);
```

The field that the user typed their image location into supplies us with the variable, `imageURL` – simply a text string containing a URL to an image, such as the somewhat sinister image at www.h69.net/scary_hoss69.jpg.

We now move to a new frame labeled `loadImage` on `_root`, which has a loading bar for the new image. We use standard `imageHolder_mc.getBytesTotal` and `imageHolder_mc.getBytesLoaded` to calculate how much of the image has loaded. This doesn't differ from code you would have used in Flash 5 to load in a SWF.

It's important to ensure that the image has fully loaded before you try to manipulate it in any way. This is one of those pitfalls I was mentioning earlier.

Once the picture has loaded in we center it over where Spank was and move to another frame (labeled `resize` in the FLA) on `_root` that has buttons to scale the new image up and down. The chances are that your image isn't going to be just the right size, making this resize functionality quite useful. As with all the 'buttons' in the movie, I am using a movie clip with functions attached by the code on the actions, buttonInits, & labels layer.

The 'buttons' here are instances of a movie clip that sets its own `_alpha` to 0, hiding itself while remaining functional. Take note that this is not the same as setting `_visible = false`, which would hide the clip but also stop its code from working. Another potential hazard avoided!

Once happy with the resizing of their image, the user continues to the next labeled frame on `_root` (drawMask) where they are instructed to click points around the outline of their image to mask out the background.

Drawing an outline for the mask

It's time to whip out your drawing API. We now have a large movie clip button on stage over the loaded image. Clicking on it starts the drawing of our outline for the mask. What we have actually done is created a new, empty movie clip called `display_mc` just inside `spank_mc` to show the lines we are going to draw for the mask. If we were to draw the lines directly into the mask itself we would not be able to see the actual lines because they are part of the mask. So, instead we draw them in a display clip and store the x, y point data for each click in a couple of arrays so that we can redraw the lines into a movie clip in the mask once we're finished. Take note of this line of code:

```
display = _root.spank_mc.display_mc;
```

This stores the full path to `display_mc` in the variable display, so that we can keep our code nice and short in later functions. It also makes life easier if we have to change the path at a later date.

Function `drawLineToPoint` (defined in frame 1 of layer functions) does the actual line drawing and storing of point data. The first click of the mouse stores the x and y coordinates in the `maskArrayX` and `maskArrayY` arrays respectively, and we also place an instance of the movie clip `greenCircle_mc` on stage to mark this first point. Further clicks draw lines between the last click and the new click with `display_mc.lineTo (x,y)`.

The function `shapeComplete` is used to check if the user has clicked within a predefined distance from the first click, a kind of 'snap to' that you get in many drawing programs (including Flash). I've set my snap to distance to 5 pixels, which means if you click within 5 pixels of the first click, in both the x and y axis, it will close the shape ready to create the mask.

> I've used the drawing API in a very basic way here, using only straight lines between the points that the user clicks on around the object. Why don't you try adding the functionality of drawing curves (see Chapter 8) to create a smoother outline?

Creating the mask

Now that we have all the point coordinates stored in our arrays to draw the mask, it's time to tidy up and get masking. The function `displayMask` does all the work here. Let's take a look at what it does:

```
spank_mc.imageMask_mc.createEmptyMovieClip ("mask_mc", 69);
```

The first line creates an empty movie clip inside the mask `imageMask_mc` called `mask_mc` at a depth of 69.

To simplify my code I then assign the full path for this new clip to the variable `targ`, making my code shorter in the lines that follow. I then tell Flash that the shape I'm about to draw should be filled (the color isn't important because it's just defining the mask area):

```
targ = spank_mc.imageMask_mc.mask_mc;
targ.beginFill(0xFF0000, 100);
```

We now set up the drawing to start at the first points stored in the arrays:

```
targ.moveTo( maskArrayX [0], maskArrayY [0] );
for (i=1; i<pointCount; i++) {targ.lineTo( maskArrayX [i],
➥maskArrayY [i] );};
```

The next line loops through all the points in the arrays, drawing from point to point until it has a finished, filled shape.

Now for some tidying up:

```
display.removeMovieClip();
spank_mc.imageMask_mc.maskTemp_mc._x -= 1000;
spank_mc.point0.removeMovieClip();
```

The first line above removes the clip that displayed the lines as we drew them (`display_mc`). The next line hides our big dumb mask that we started with (`maskTemp_mc`) by placing it off stage. Then we remove the `greenCircle_mc` clip called `point0` that marked the position of our first click.

Finally we go to a new frame on `_root` (masked) with a button to redo the mask (perhaps if it looks a little messy and you want to try again), and another button to start spanking:

```
_root.gotoAndStop("masked");
```

For completeness, here's what the full `displayMask` function looks like:

```
function displayMask () {
  spank_mc.imageMask_mc.createEmptyMovieClip ("mask_mc", 69);
  targ = spank_mc.imageMask_mc.mask_mc;
  targ.beginFill(0xFF0000, 100);
  targ.moveTo( maskArrayX [0], maskArrayY [0] );
  for (i=1; i<pointCount; i++) {targ.lineTo( maskArrayX [i],
➥maskArrayY [i]);};
  display.removeMovieClip();
  spank_mc.imageMask_mc.maskTemp_mc._x -= 1000;
  spank_mc.point0.removeMovieClip();
  _root.gotoAndStop("masked");
};
```

Here's an illustration of the structure of `spank_mc` at the end:

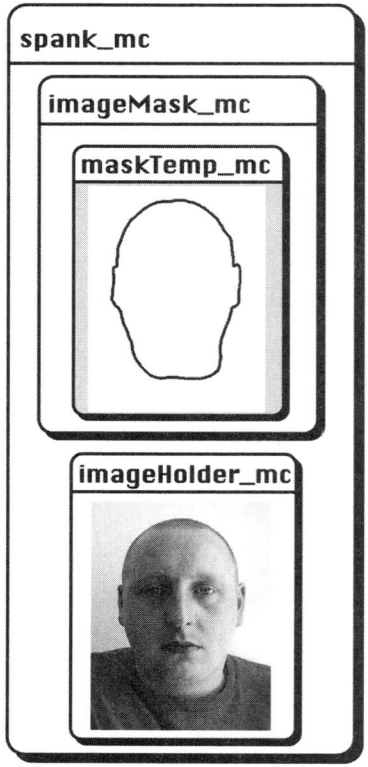

Ready to start spanking

In this example, we've created a mask for a bitmap dynamically, but there's nothing stopping the user extending this idea to create the mask via something like a data table, so that images could be loaded in, a mask created via a loaded set of numbers, and the final masked image used for all sorts of effects. The FLA could let the user use the masked bitmap effectively like a textured brush in a drawing program; in fact, numerous possibilities can be derived from this one slightly ludicrous game!

So, at the end of all of this scripting we have achieved our main objectives – the user has placed their own image into a movie clip, resized it, and then masked it off.

To turn this file into the finished 'Dynamic Spank the Monkey' game you just need to do some fairly standard Flash 5-compliant coding. Take a look at `spank_dynamic.swf` to see the finished product in action – as an exercise, why not see if you can add the scripting that will allow you to finish off our beta version `spank_dynamic_beta1.fla`?

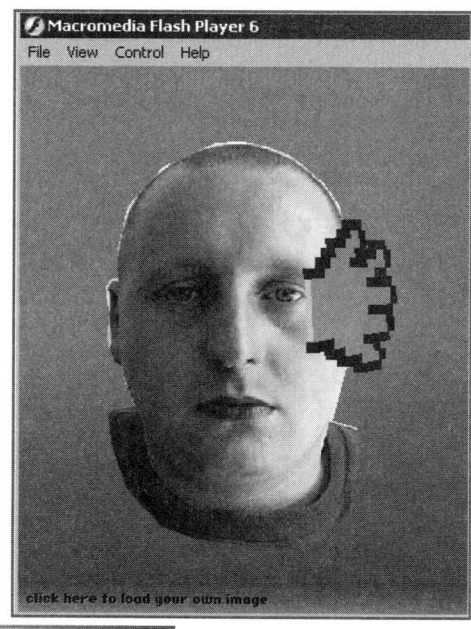

In the finished version we can see that the hand is a frame-by-frame animation inside a movie clip that you can drag around the screen. The speed and direction of your drag determines the frame of the animation – giving the impression of the hand experiencing wind resistance. Simple collision detection between Spank (or whoever you choose to put in his place) and the hand triggers an animation in which Spank flies off the screen, and leaves text congratulating the *spanker* on their actions. Just make sure that your spanked clip instance stays on the timeline at all times (even if it moves off the edge of the movie), otherwise it will default back to the original image of the monkey.

Reflections

These two examples should have given you some ideas of your own for utilizing the vast pool of new functionality that Macromedia Flash MX offers. Although your own journey into Flash MX is really just beginning, the introduction provided by this book will put you in a prime position to confront your future design challenges.

Appendix

Appendix: Common Errors

This appendix summarizes some of the commonest mistakes and pitfalls you are likely to encounter when converting from Macromedia Flash 5 coding to the new MX scripting techniques. It is based on my own experiences with Flash MX and discussions with other MX users, as well as common questions posed by the MX test team. This appendix is aimed at advanced Flash 5 scripters who are eager to get the most out of the new MX functionality.

We'll look at the following common problem areas:

- Errors caused by scope
- Errors caused by changes or additions to events' functionality
- Depth and the drawing API
- Issues with components and low level calls

Errors caused by scope

There are three major issues in Flash MX that may cause problems to the Flash 5 user:

- The new global level
- Using callback functions as event scripts
- The scope of code inserted between `#initclip` and `#endinitclip` in components

The global level

If you create a variable with a `_global.foo = "I am global"` statement, the variable can be accessed from any timeline by simply calling it `foo`. If you create another variable `_root.myClip.foo = "I am not global"`, you should consider the following points:

- If you refer to `foo` anywhere except from the timeline `_root.myClip`, you will be referring to `_global.foo`, and its value will be `"I am global"`.

- If you refer to `foo` from `_root.myClip`, you will be referring to the version of `foo` that's equal to `"I am not global"`. This will effectively hide the global version because you are calling from within the scope of the version of `foo` that is not defined as global.

- If you refer to `_root.myClip.foo` from anywhere, you will be referring to the version of `foo` that's equal to `"I am not global"`. This is because you are referring to the specific scope of this non-global version of `foo`.

This means that a global variable and a local variable of the same name can hide the value of the other if you are not careful.

Flash MX Upgrade Essentials

The only practical solution to avoiding conflicts between global and other variables is to make sure that they never happen! There are a couple of ways to do this:

- Always precede global variables with g. Thus foo becomes gFoo.

- Use a namespace. Create a global object in _global called myNameSpace, where myNameSpace is a name that is personal to you. Then create all global variables as properties of myNameSpace. For example:

```
_global.shamB = newObject()
shamB.foo = "my personal global"
```

The latter method is preferable for component creation, because if you and everyone else use the g prefix, there are bound to be conflicts between like-named globals created by different authors. Namespaces make this much less likely, and also allow you to debug your components in isolation, even if you are using them in a FLA that uses other components.

Callback events

Flash 5 allowed you to attach event scripts directly to an instance (such as myClip):

```
onClipEvent (enterFrame) {
  //code
}
```

The corresponding Flash MX style relies on callbacks:

```
myClip.onEnterFrame = function() {
  //code
};
```

An important thing to bear in mind is that if you refer to this.myVariable and myVariable in the Flash 5 coding style, the following are true:

- You are referring to the timeline that the code is defined on if you omit this
- You are referring to the timeline of myClip if you include this

For the Flash 5 event, it didn't matter whether you used this or not, because the two timelines were the same thing: the timeline of myClip.

Flash MX events, on the other hand, do not necessarily have to be defined on the myClip timeline. They can be defined on any timeline, but will usually be defined on _root. Whether or not you now use this becomes important – you will either be scoping _root.myClip (if you use this) or just _root (if you don't).

You always need to be aware of this when using callback functions, and it is a common cause of initial confusion for Flash 5 users adapting to MX. Using the callback style is a good idea because so much of Flash MX relies on it. Anyway, personal experience shows that it is actually an easier and less error-prone style of coding.

Scope of #initclip

The standard place that code in #initclip... #endinitclip sections will run is before frame 1 of a main timeline (assuming that you have exported the component for ActionScript). This means that it will run before anything other than _global and _root exist. The scope of #initclip... #endinitclip is therefore not the component that it is in, but _root. The best way of visualizing this is to assume that the code is run while the component is still in the library, and there is nothing on the timeline yet other than _root and _global.

You can also use #initclip... #endinitclip on frames other than frame 1 of _root, but this is not recommended. The #initclip... #endinitclip is really designed for defining prototypes and using registerClass() to create object structures that the component requires to be in place at _root and _global before the component comes into existence in the SWF timeline.

Errors caused by enhancements to events

In this section we'll examine typical mistakes that may occur because of the following changes and additions to the Flash events' functionality:

- Callbacks

- Object.watch

- Sound.OnSoundComplete

Callbacks

As well as the issues of scope, there are other things to be aware of with callback events:

- Defining onLoad events after the instance has been created will mean that the script never runs. This is a fiendishly easy error to make. For instance, you might define this event attached to an instance called myClip:

  ```
  myClip.onLoad = function(){
    //code
  };
  ```

  This will cause //code to run only if the script appears on the same frame as the one where myClip first appears. If it occurs before, there is nothing to attach the callback to, and if it occurs afterwards, the onLoad event has already occurred. For example, if //code was defined as...

  ```
  this.x = 10;
  y = 23;
  ```

  ...this means that myClip.x = 10, and y = 23.

- The effects of defining multiple identical events is different. Consider the script on the following page:

```
onClipEvent(enterFrame){
  // code 1
};
onClipEvent(enterFrame){
  // code 2
};
```

Will execute both // code 1 and // code 2, whereas

```
myClip.onEnterFrame = function() {
  // code 1;
};
myClip.onEnterFrame = function() {
  // code 2;
};
```

will only execute // code 2 because you can only have one callback per event, and this is the last one you define – earlier events will be overwritten.

Object.watch

An important thing to notice about watchers is that they do not get deleted if the thing that they are watching (the 'watch-point') gets deleted. The following points should clarify this:

- You can create a watch before you create the watch-point. The first time (and every subsequent time) you redefine the watch-point the watcher event will be invoked because watch-point definition is seen as a 'change'. Although this can cause problems if you don't expect it, it does give you a rather elegant way to define your watch-point as soon as you create it!

- The only way to kill a watch is via the Object.unwatch method.

sound.onSoundComplete

Issues with the accuracy of a sound.onSoundComplete event have been noted for sounds that begin on frame 1 of _root. If you are having trouble creating accurate sound synch with this, we recommend you look at leaving the first few frames of _root empty.

A second issue with onSoundComplete is that it is largely independent of the frame rate, but you may encounter problems at very low or very high frame rates. Flash actually looks for an onSoundComplete event at ten times the frame rate (which is fast enough to be instantaneous for most listeners). You may also see issues at very high frame rates, where there is too much going on and all event-based scripts may suffer because of this, particularly onSoundComplete because the human ear is very sensitive and can discern discontinuities in sound much better than the eye can detect discontinuities in motion. You may also see problems at very low frame rates, because even if you multiply a slow frame rate (below about 5fps) by ten, that's still slow enough to be discernable.

Depth and the drawing API

The use of the drawing API relies on a good understanding of depth. If you find that you are creating content that doesn't appear on the stage, the following information may help:

- Flash assigns a depth numbering per timeline. The numbering scheme goes from -16384 to 16384 (it actually goes further but these ranges may become unsupported in the future).

- Depths equating to negative numbers (and 0) are reserved for content placed on stage at authoring time. You can't use `removeMovieClip` on negative depths, which is why you can't remove content placed on the stage at run-time (although a sneaky way around this is to swap a negative depth with a positive one via `swapDepths` and then delete the content!)

- Positive numbers (1 to 16384) are usable by ActionScript when duplicating or attaching content to timelines during run-time.

- Numbers outside this range may work, but should be assumed to be unsupported.

Components and text fields

The default Macromedia Flash MX components only listen to changes in methods, and not the old Flash 5 way of changing properties explicitly.

For example, supposing you had a text field `myText` with a scrollbar component attached to it, and the text field had a variable `txt`. If you try to change the text the text field is displaying with the following...

```
txt = "Components only listen to changes in methods";
```

...you will find that the scrollbar will not respond to the change in displayed text if it makes the text fill the current text field. To do this, you have to apply the text change using `myText.text`, because the scrollbar is listening to that:

```
myText.text = "Components only listen to changes in methods";
```

Summary

In general, ActionScript is distancing itself from the low-level code that makes direct calls to properties and variables, evolving into a more structured and elegant language that relies on standard object interfaces via methods. ActionScript is also moving towards single, easy to read scripts, maintained on the first frame of the timeline (for example), rather than little bits of hard-to-find code spread throughout the FLA.

So with the release of Macromedia Flash MX, it seems that voodoo-scripting and hacking are things of the past – long live structured programming!

Index

Index

The index is arranged hierarchically, in alphabetical order, with symbols preceding the letter A. Many second-level entries also occur as first-level entries. This is to ensure that users will find the information they require however they choose to search for it.

#endinitclip 374, 382
#initclip 374, 382
  scope 419
3D graphics
  creating with Distort modifier 73

A

abstraction 374
accessibility 9, 253
  creating accessibility 254
  Microsoft Active Accessibility
  (MSAA) model, 254
  screen reader 254
Accessibility panel 6, 36, 254
  Global Accessibility Properties 256
Actions panel 30-32
  accessing panel 98
  advanced configuration 108
  altering basic appearance 101
  altering code formatting 102
  auto complete 104
  auto format 104
  check syntax function 103
  code hinting 105
  docking to Reference panel 31
  docking/floating 96
  Expert mode 95
  help features 103
  line numbering 99
  maximizing/minimizing 97
  naming conventions 107
  new functionality 32
  Normal mode 34, 95
  pinning Actions panel 99
  preferences 100
  toolbar 34
ActionScript 33, 141
  advanced scripting 20
Add Action button 34
Add Guide Layer icon 47
advanced components
(tutorial) **350-359**
  actions layer 354, 357
  adding description 351
  adding drag and drop 350
  bouncee parameter 352

changing component icon 351
component snapping to
  instance 352
creating icon 350
debugging 355
defining screen limits 354
initializing variables 354
linking SWF to component 358
live preview 355
onEnterFrame event 354, 357
parameters 351
path 353
setting speed of bounce 354
testing FLA 355
text 356
advanced components
 See also advanced components
 (tutorial)
  adding live preview 355
  adding drag and drop 349
  adding script 353
  targetInstanceName property 349
Americans with Disabilities
Act 254
anchor points 78
anchors 249-250
angle points 91
animask (tutorial) **121-122**
  keyframes 121
  mask layer 122
  masked layer 122
  overlapping gradient 122
  running movie 122
  shape tween 121
  viewing in Flash 5 122
animated buttons 131
animation
  setInterval event 320
  watchers 390
Answers Panel 6
Arrow Selection tool 70
Arrow tool 85
attached button script 143
attachMovie method 65
auto complete 104
auto format 104

B

basic checkbox (tutorial) **220-222**
  adding dynamic text field 222
  change handler 221
  component value 222
  creating layers 220
  getValue method 221
  initial value 221
  initializing checkbox 223
  label placement 221
  soundCheck change handler 224
Book icon 35
bookmarks 249
bow ties 77
  anchor points 78
  tangent handles 78
  tangent lines 78
Break Apart option 8, 69
breakpoints 17, 34, 267, 270
  adding breakpoints 273
  single stepping 275
Browser back button 249
Browser control 9, 20, 243
  anchors 249
  Back button 249
  shared objects 257
  Stage object 245
  viewing anchors 251
button and frame event
animation (tutorial) **150**
button event animation
(tutorial) **148-149**
button movie clip (tutorial) **126,**
182
  adding alpha to hit area 183
  adding instance of mc.hitArea 184
  adding keyframes 185
  adding new button graphic
    state 186
  adding new label 186
  adding stop action 130
  adding stop function 183
  button hit area 128
  button instances 188
  button Up, Over, and Down
    states 127
  code hints 129
  converting to movie clip 129

creating new movie clip 182,
creating text button 127
defining hit area 127
defining mc.button 126
defining rollOut state 187
editing button in library 126
graphics layer 184
graphics to match keyframes 185
labeling frames 127
movieClipButton.fla 188
onRollOut function 187, 188
placing hit area over text 184
resizing hit area 185
button movie clips 126
animated buttons 131
animated hit areas 131
button states 134
listeners 132
navigation elements 132
onLoad event 134
onRelease 135
reset function 134
states layer 134
timeline 132, 133
button object 142, 181
See also buttons in sequence
(tutorial)
See also button event animation
(tutorial)
See also button and frame
event animation (tutorial)
attached button script 143
attaching event scripts to buttons
142
creating customized buttons 333
disabling buttons 145
enable/disable hand cursor 146
enabled property 144
enterFrame event 150
errors 144
instance names 146
limitations 151, 182
onRelease event 142
reasons for using 181
reducing alpha setting 145
remote button script 143
visible property 147

buttons 333
See also custom buttons
(tutorial)
See also button object
buttons in sequence (tutorial)
147-148

C

callbacks 305, 418
See also listeners
center points 89, 91
change handlers 221-222
Character Options window 44
check syntax function 103
CheckBox component 209
check boxes 220
See also basic check box
(tutorial)
change handlers 224
classes 367
See also objects
code formatting 102
code hinting 105, 129
Color Mixer panel 6, 36
Color Swatches panel 30
combo box (tutorial) **234-235**
combo boxes 234
**Component Parameters panel
35, 212**
**Component Property inspector
45**
**component skinning 14, 208,
331, 335**
See also default skins (tutorial)
changing default skins 339
compatibility with
FStyleFormat 336
customizing skins 344
default skins 336
gel version of default skins 337
graphics 338
scrollbar skin 337
Component Skins folder 335
components 1, 14, 205, 207
See also scrollbar (tutorial)
adding functionality to clips 208

advanced components 331, 349
change handlers 221
checkboxes 220
combo box 234
converting smart clips 208
creating components with no
physical appearance 208
creating custom components
for Flash 5 users 236
customizing default
components 331
drag and drop components 213
errors 421
event handlers 219
linkage components 216
list box 230
live preview 208
new functionality 208
OOP 374
push buttons 224
radio button 226
sliders 215
using default components 212
Components panel 6, 35, 209
changing appearance of
component sets 211
changing component skins 211
Component Skins folder 210
Core Assets – Developer Only
folder 211
default components 209
drag components onto stage 210
FCheckBox Skins folder 211
workflow 209
compression 2
See also video object
Convert to Symbol window
default behavior 56
registration points 55
cookies
shared objects versus cookies 257
curves (tutorial) **194-196**
bow ties 196
clear method 195
control point 195
createEmptyMovieClip
method 194
curveTo method 194
mouse position 195

custom buttons (tutorial) **333–334**
custom components
  creating Flash 5 file 236
  Display in Components panel checkbox 237
  Export for ActionScript option 238
  installing components 237
  saving as installed components 238
  Tool Tip Text option 238
custom skins
  applying style format 348
  commenting out code 348
  creating elements 346
  custom elements 347
  elements 344
  guide layer 347
  registering instances 348
  registering FStyleFormat 345
custom styles 333

D

debug options 267
  trace action 267
  type action 268
  typeof action 268
debugger 171, 267, 268
  See also linear scripts
  See also script (tutorial)
  See also distributed timelines (tutorial)
  breakpoints 270
  Call Stack pane 270
  code optimization 278
  Locals tab 270
  multiple scripts 281
  pausing movies 270
  Remove All Breakpoints icon 270
  run-time debug data 268
  script pane 270
  scripts calling scripts 278
  Step In icon 271
  Step Out icon 271, 277
  Step Over icon 271
  stepping through code 268

Stop Debugging icon 270
SWD files 268
testing movies 269
Toggle Breakpoint icon 270
default skins (tutorial) **339–343**
  adding list box and combo 343
  adding new layer 340
  copying replacement skin 339
  dragging gel graphics 339
  opening gelSkin.fla as library 339
  replacing symbols 339
  rescaling skin 339
  rounding buttons 341
  testing movie 342
  testing scrollbar 342
Delete Selected Actions button 34
Diagnostics icon 34
Distort modifier 11, 69, 72
  creating faux 3D graphics 73
  isometric 3D graphics 76
Distribute to Layers function 51
  tweening text 54
distributed timelines (tutorial) **281**
  adding breakpoint 283
  creating layers 282
  depth order 284
  layer order 284
  order of execution 282
  starting debugger 283
docked panels 25, 28
  floating stacks 31
Document Property inspector 40–41
drag and drop components 213
Drawing API 18, 179, 412, 421
  See also lines (tutorial)
  See also curves (tutorial)
  See also elastic band (tutorial)
  See also filling shapes (tutorial)
  co-ordinates 191
  creating interactive drawing tool 196
  curves 189, 194
  depth 421
  drawing lines 189, 191
  errors 421
  fills 189, 201
  positioning paper 191

turtle graphics 189
dynamic text (tutorial) **118–120**
  changing text 120
  entering text 119
  Insert Target Path window 119
  rotating text 119
  setting dynamic text fields 119
  testing FLA 120
dynamic text fields 119

E

Edit Scene icon 47
Edit Symbol icon 47
elastic band (tutorial) **196**
  addListener method 199
  function scope 200
  keyboard 199
  listener 200
  mouse positions 199
  onKeyDown function 200
  paper movie clip 198
  pen movie clip 198
  penToggle method 199
  points 199
  splitting paper 198
elements 344
Envelope modifier 11, 69, 77
  anchor points 78
  bending body parts 82
  bow ties 77
  conforming text to defined path 84
  creating morphing animations 80
  curves 77
  distorting text 84
  tangent handles 78
  tangent lines 78
  vector graphic elements 79
errors 417
  callbacks 418, 419
  components 421
  events 419
  scope 417
  watchers 420
event handlers 305, 311, 419
  See also change handlers

event model 311
event sound 252
events 305, 419
  See also particle (tutorial)
  custom event handling 306
  errors 419
  listeners 311
  timer events 318
Expert mode 32, 95
Export options 63

F

faux 3D graphics 73
Fill Transform tool 69, 88
  angle points 91
  center points 91
  linear fill 88
  radial fill 90
  realistic light source highlights 92
  shape points 91
  size points 91
filling shapes (tutorial) 202-204
  assigning points to arrays 204
  beginFill method 203
  clear method 204
  corner points order 202
  createEmptyMovieClip
  method 202
  curveTo method 203
  drawing square path 202
  endFill method 203
  enterFrame method 204
  pen settings 202
fills 201
Find Text icon 34
Flash MX 1, 25, 305
  backward compatibility 3
  components 1
  enhancements 1
  event model 305, 311
  Expert mode 32
  features not supported 27
  Generator 28
  loading content directly 251
  OOP 365
  quick launch icons 27

speed 318
stage size 247
unsupported actions 3
user interface 3, 25
workflow 3
Flash player 288, 372
  clear method 289
  embedded video codec 2
  loading video 288
  Local Storage options 258
  OOP considerations 372
  slider 258
  SWF compression and system
  memory 289
floating panels 25, 28
floating stacks 31
font formatting
  kerning 115
font mapping 113
  substituting fonts 115
  warnings 114
Format Options window 44
  indent option 117
  kerning option 115
  line spacing 117
  text type option 116
  tracking option 116
Frame Property inspector
  Named Anchor checkbox 45
Free Transform tool 69
  creating faux 3D graphics 73
  Distort modifier 69, 72
  Envelope modifier 69, 77
  move 72
  Rotate modifier 69, 71
  Scale modifier 69, 71
  Skew modifier 69, 71
fscommand
  See shared objects
FStyleFormat object 331
  changing global style 332
  creating customized buttons 333
  customizing skins 344
  default style 332
  elements 344
function scope (tutorial) 200-201
functions 200
  See also function scope (tutorial)
  using without OOP 372

G

Generator 28
getters 387
global depth 177
  getDepth function 178
  setDepth function 178
  stacking order 178
global functions 176
  libraries 177
  modular code 177
global levels 20, 173, 417
  definition 178
  errors 417
  Math object 174
  movie clip object 174
  predefined Flash actions and
  methods 179
global variables 174
  creating 175
  local variables 175
  naming conventions 175
  when to use global variables 176
globalStyleFormat
  applyChanges method 332
  changing global style 332
Group Property inspector 39

H

help features 103
highlights 92
  creating realistic light source
  highlights 92

I

images
  loading content directly 251

Import Video Settings window
290
  audio 293

encoding video frames 292
Import audio check box 293
Keyframe interval slider 291
Quality slider 291
Scale slider 292
Synchronize video to
Macromedia Flash document
frame rate checkbox 292
indenting text 117
inheritance 367
Insert Layer Folder icon 47
Insert Layer icon 47
Insert Target Path icon 34
instance names 42
interface
 See user interface
internal script events 311
isometric 3D graphics 76

J

JPEGs 251

K

kerning 115
Key object 312
 See also keys (tutorial)
  onKeyDown listener 312
keyframe intervals 292
keys (tutorial) **312-314**
 adding inertia effect 314
 addListener method 313
 animating ship 313
 creating space ship 312
 initializing FLA 313
 keyDetect object 313
 multiple event handlers 314
 onKeyDown event 313
 registering keyDetect as
 listener 313

L

layer folders 8, 47-50
 closing all layers 50
 creating 49
 distributing to layers 51
 hiding 50
 locking 50
 nesting folders 49
 stacking order 50
layers 8
 break apart functionality 8
 folder structure 9
 shared libraries 9
leading text 117
Library 8, 47, 54
 accessing library 61
 automatic updating 61
 centralized library files 60
 controlled manual updating 62
 creating symbols 55
 default library folders 57
 docking/floating 55
 enhancements 54
 Export options 63
 multiple libraries 61
 sharing assets 57
 sharing at run-time 63
 sharing libraries during
 authoring 58
 symbol icons 55
line spacing 116, 117
Line tool 84
linear fill 88
 center point 89
 direction 89
 Envelope modifier 80
 width 89
linear scripts (tutorial) **271-277**
 adding breakpoints 273
 braces 273
 continuing to next breakpoint 274
 counter updating 277
 deleting breakpoints 275
 fruitEaten array 276
 fruitEaten list 272
 single stepping 275
 starting debugger 274
 Step Out icon 277

 viewing error 272, 275
 viewing global values 274
lines (tutorial) **191-193**
 cleaning up excess lines 193
 clear method 193
 createEmptyMovieClip
 function 191
 defining pen 192
 lineStyle property 192
 lineTo method 192
 moveTo method 192
linkage components 216
list box (tutorial) **231-233**
 adding colors 232
 adding label 232
 adding number values 233
 Data field 233
 getValue method 233
 Labels field 231
 listHandler change handler 232
 Select Multiple field 234
 Values window 232
list boxes 230
 See also list box (tutorial)
listeners 20, 132, 205, 246
 See also individual objects
 available events/methods 312
 definition 311
 multiple event handlers 314
 requirements for adding 312
live previews 208, 355, 359
load image functionality 251
 loaded sound 252
 loadSound action 252
 soundType 253
local shared object (tutorial)
259-263
 adding data 260
 creating local file 259
 data method 260
 debugging 263
 defining local data object 260
 flush method 261
 getSize method 262
 Local Storage settings 259
 pass property 261
 SharedObject object 260
 storing data 260
 testing 261
 username property 261

warning 261
local variables 175, 200
looping sound (tutorial) **325-326**

M

Macintosh users 26
Macromedia Flash MX
 See Flash MX
Macromedia Generator
 See Generator
margins 29
masking 113
 See also animask (tutorial)
 See also moiremask (tutorial)
animated masking 121
 dynamic masking 123
Media Property inspectors
 Edit button 41
 Swap button 41
methods 141
 using events as methods 305
Microsoft Active Accessibility
model (MSAA) 254
modifiers 69
modular programming 177
moiremask (tutorial) **123-125**
 circles as movie clip 125
 creating concentric circles 123
 dragging the mask 125
 filling rings 124
 layers 125
 onClipEvent handler 125
movie clip buttons
 See button movie clips
movie clip masks
 See masking
movie clip object 173, 289
 button events 181
 button object uses 181
 clear method 289
 createEmptyMovieClip
 method 180
 creating new movie clips 180
 Drawing API 179
 global level 173
 inherited button events and

properties 173
 movie clips as buttons 173
 movie clips as masks 173
 new events and properties 181
 smart clips replaced with
 components 173
movie clips 48, 113
 creating button movie clip 126
 scroll panes 216

N

naming conventions 106
navigation
 movie clip buttons 132
Normal mode 32, 95

O

Object model 205
Object object
 registerClass method 369
 watch method 388
object-oriented programming
 See OOP
objects 18, 113
 attaching events to objects 141
 extending via prototypes 367
 inheritance 367
 shared objects 257
 watchers 386
on sound complete (tutorial) **324**
onSoundComplete event 420
OOP (object-oriented
programming) 365
 See also skater component
(tutorial)
 #endinitclip 374
 #initclip 374
 abstraction 374
 components 374
 extending classes 367
 modular code 374
 order of execution 374

using functions without OOP 372
Oracle (case study) **395-404**
 adding sound 402
 adding speech and sight 400
 beginGradientFill method 397
 bugs 397
 code listing 404
 covering boards 403
 concept 396
 creating pulse 401
 creating stream of flying
 insects 399
 drums sound object 403
 flies 399
 getBytesLoaded method 403
 getBytesTotal method 403
 if conditional statement 400
 lines of force 402
 lineStyle method 402
 lineTo method 402
 localBugSpd variable 398
 looping animation 400
 Math.random functions 398
 mouth instance 400
 moveTo method 402
 onClipEvent handlers 398
 preload sequence 403
 ray of energy 397
 removeMovieClip method 399
 sVel variable 397
 swapDepths method 401
Oval tool 88

P

panels 25
 closing panels 30
 default layout 5
 default panel layout 28
 docking areas 28, 29
 docking panels 29
 docking/undocking 5
 drag areas 5
 floating stacks 31
 knurled drag bar 32
 maximize/minimize switch 30
 new functionality 32

Operating System bar 32
particle (tutorial) **306-310**
  apply method 307
  attachMovie action 307
  creating physical appearance
   of ball 309
  onEnterFrame event 307
  onPress event 307
  particle function 307
  remote script 307
Pin icon 35
pixel-snapping 13
preferences 100
preloading video (tutorial) **298-299**
Property inspector 5
  Actions panel quick-launch
   icon 7
  context sensitivity 27
  context sensitive Help icon 7
  docked panel 38
  documents 40
  group 39
  Help button 38
  media 41
  quick-launch buttons 38
  shape 38
  show/hide arrow 7, 38
  tools 40
  workflow organization 37
props 344
prototype object 367
  See also skater (tutorial)
  See also rotation component
   (tutorial)
  adding movie clip object 369
  advantages of using 385
  constructor 369
  creating custom classes 369
  independent motion
   simulation 370
  methods 369
  modifying default object
   prototypes 381
  properties 369
  registering object 369
Publish Settings window 41
Push buttons 224-225

Q

quick-launch buttons 38

R

radial fill 90-91
Radio button 226
  See also radio control (tutorial)
   Symbol Properties window 226
radio control (tutorial) **226-230**
  adding animation scripts 229
  assigning buttons 226
  colorGroup buttons 228
  colorHandler change handler 229
  component argument 230
  creating actions, controls and
   animation layers 226
  defining squareCol object 229
  initializing FLA 230
  onEnterFrame 229
  speedGroup buttons 228
  speedHandler change handler 229
Reference panel 6, 107
  docking to Actions panel 31
remote button scripts 143
remote scripting 307
resize (tutorial) **248**
  browser dimensions 249
  Flash stage dimensions 249
  FlashStageX 249
  FlashStageY 249
  onResize function 249
Rotate modifier 69, 71
rotation component (tutorial)
381-383
  #initclip/#endinitclip 382
  deleting callback function 382
  extending the clip 383
  fadeMe method 383
  rotateMe method 381
  starting/stopping rotation 381
  state argument 381
  step argument 381
  stop method 383
  timeline 382

S

Scale modifier 69, 71
Scene panel 251
scenes 250
  create new scenes 250
scope
  errors 417
  _root as default scope 307
screen readers 254
scripting 17
  See also Actions panel
  callback functions 305
  order 375
  scope 307
scripts (tutorial) **278-281**
  adding breakpoint 279
  debugging script 279
  defining functions 279
  local values 281
  stepping in 280
  tax function 278
  taxPercent and taxAmount
   variables 278
scroll pane
  See also scroll pane (tutorial)
  scrollbar versus scroll pane 216
scroll pane (tutorial) **217-219**
  altering parameters 218
  creating static text field 217
  dragging scroll pane instance
   onto stage 218
  floating panels 219
  identifying movie clip 217
  scaling text 217
scrollbar
  defining parameter values 214
  help text 214
  parameters 214
  sliders 215
  snaps to areas 213
  Target TextField 214
scrollbar (tutorial) **213**
selection (tutorial) **315-318**
  adding focusControl object as
   listener 317
  defining callback function 316
  dynamic text field 316
  focusControl object 316

for loops 317
newFocus 316
oldFocus 316
onSetFocus event 316
real-time error detection 318
setting colors 316
text fields 316
variables 316
Selection object 315
  See also selection (tutorial)
  onSetFocus selection listener 315
  text fields 315
  variable paths 315
set interval (tutorial) **319-320**
set interval animation
(tutorial) **320-322**
  adding setInterval script 321
  setInterval event 322
  speed of animation 322
setEvents method 306
setInterval event 318, 320
setters 387
shape points 91
Shape Property inspector 38
shape tweens 80
shared objects 20, 257
  See also local shared object
  (tutorial)
  cookies versus shared objects 257
  Flash Player 6 259
  uses 257
SharedObject object 259
sharing library assets 57
  attachMovie method 65
sight-impaired users 36, 254
single stepping 275
skater (tutorial) **370-372**
  adding constructor 370
  attaching prototype to movie
  clip object 371
  attachMovie method 372
  creating skater 370
  generating skaters 372
  linking 370
  makeTarget function 371
  onEnterFrame callback
  function 371
  onLoad callback function 371
  registerClass method 371
  registering prototype 371

skater object 371
  using functions without OOP 372
skater component (tutorial) **376**
  #initclip 376
  adding icon to timeline 378
  attachMovie method 379
  for loop 379
  library linkage ID 377
  makeSkater function 377
  making skaterDefinition a
  component 378
  registering skater object 377
  skater prototype 377
  skaterDefinition movie clip 376
Skew modifier 69, 71
skinning
  See component skinning
sliders 215
  See also sliders (tutorial)
sliders (tutorial) **215-216**
smart clips
  components versus smart
  clips 207
  converting to components
  208, 236
Sorenson Spark codec 287, 291
  loading video into Flash
  player 288
Sorenson Squeeze 287
sound 251
sound buffer 253
sound handling 311
sound object 323
  See also on sound complete
  (tutorial)
  See also looping sound (tutorial)
  See also sound sequence
  (tutorial)
    loadSound method 253
    looping sounds 324, 325
    onSoundComplete event 323
    sequencing sounds 305
    start method 253
    synchronizing sounds 323
sound sequence (tutorial) **327-328**
Spank, the monkey (case study)
408-413
  acquiring new image 410
  button scripts 411

  centering image 411
  concept 409
  creating mask 412
  displayMask function 412
  drawing outline for mask 412
  drawLineToPoint function 412
  Generator 409
  lineTo function 412
  loadMovie method 410
  maskArrayX/Y arrays 412
  resizing image 411
  set up 410
  shapeComplete function 412
spinner watcher (tutorial) **390-392**
  defining size object 391
  getScrollPosition method 391
  horizontal/vertical properties 391
  oldval/newval values 393
  onEnterFrame event 391
  setting up scrollbars 391
  smoothing spinner move-
  ments 392
  watcher callbacks 391
stage (tutorial) **245-247**
  adding dynamic text fields 245
  listeners 246
  onResize listener event 247
  setting scale and dimensions 246
  shifting between scale modes 247
  swfHeight variable 245
  swfWidth variable 245
Stage object 245
  See also stage (tutorial)
  See also resize (tutorial)
  dynamically resizing stage 248
  scaleMode property 247
streaming sound 252
streaming video (tutorial) **295-301**
  adding frames 295
  adding second instance 297
  adding tint effects 301
  bandwidth profiler 296
  creating streaming buffer 296
  dragging video instance onto
  stage 295
  preloading 297
  resizing new video object 297
  testing movie 298

video keyframe interval 296
Stroke Style window 39
style formats 332
Subselection tool 85
support 22
SWD (shockwave debug) files
scripts from FLA 269
Symbol Property inspector 42
changing behavior of symbols 42
Color dropdown menu 42
instance names 42
radio buttons 226
symbols
creating 55
dragging between libraries 56
System Capabilities object
hasAccessibility 255
properties 244

T

tangent handles 78
tangent lines 78
templates 15
text 54, 84, 113
accessibility 36
conforming to a path 84
distorting 84
enhancements 12
font formatting 115
font mapping 113
tweening 54
text field form (tutorial) **154-163**
adding functions and vari-
ables 158
adding help box 157
adding help text field 158
animating text field 158
backgroundColor property 155
color Hex values 155
converting variable to
number 156
creating input fields 154
creating invisible button 157
errors 156
full script 162
graphic authoring

environment 163
heightInput variable 154
hideHelp function 160
highlighting active text field 155
if/else statements 156
labeling text fields 155
mytext2 154
onKillFocus event 156
onSetFocus event 155
showHelp function 159
tab order 161
visible property 159
text field object 151
See also text field properties
(tutorial)
See also text field form (tutorial)
adding text events 154
backgroundColor property 153
onChanged event 153
onKillFocus event 153
onScroller event 153
onSetFocus event 153
password property 153
remote scripts 151
text field properties (tutorial)
151-152
text format object
See also text format options
(tutorial)
altering defaults at run-time 164
default formats 164
formatting options 165
text format options (tutorial)
165-170
alertText object 166
animating text fields 168
creating text and actions
layers 165
defining colors 166
disabling password text 169
help text 166
infoText object 166
initializing text fields 167
normalText object 166
onChanged event 168
onKillFocus event 168
onSetFocus event 168
passField 165, 168
passInput variable 165
password property 169

text formatting considerations 170
userField 165
userInput variable 165
text instances 119
text objects 113, 151
See also dynamic text (tutorial)
accessing text dynamically 118
Text Property inspector
Add Border Around Text icon 44
Line Type option 43
Make Text Selectable icon 44
Position dropdown menu 44
Render As HTML icon 44, 45
target field 44
Text Direction icon 44
Text Spacing value 44
Text Type dropdown menu 43
URL field 44
timeline 5, 8, 305
button movie clip 132, 133
default position 47
docking/floating 48
Insert Layer Folder icon 47
layer folders 48
scripting 305
visual changes 47
timer events 311
See also set interval (tutorial)
See also set interval animation
(tutorial)
setInterval event 318
tool modifier options 40
Tool Property inspector 40
toolbox 10, 69
**See also individual tool
names**
tracking 115, 116
Transform tool 11
turtle graphics 189
draw command 190
move command 190
tweening 80, 84
text 54

U

user interface 3
docked panels 25
extensibility 9
floating panels 25
Mac users 26
panel functionality 32
panels 4
Property inspector 27
users
accessibility 253
browser control 243
shared objects 257
System Capabilities object 243

V

variables
defining 175
naming conventions 175
video 15
video codecs 287
video object 287
See also preloading video
(tutorial)
adding video to Flash
timelines 295
compression 291
controlling via timeline 294, 300
embedded video 293
importing video 289
mixing vector graphics 300
property-based animation 300
Sorenson Spark codec 287
streaming video 300
video settings 291
workflow 287, 289
view options switch 34

W

watcher (tutorial) **388-390**
adding counter 388
adding watch definition 389
conversion 390
degC property 388
watchers 311
See also watcher (tutorial)
See also spinner watcher
(tutorial)
adding watchers 388
animation 390
callback functions 388
definition 386
errors 420
getters and setters 387
Window Eyes screen reader 254
workflow 3
www.ayobinitie.com 395
www.flamjam.com/spank 408

DESIGNER TO DESIGNER™

friends of ED writes books for you. Any suggestions, or ideas about how you want information given in your ideal book will be studied by our team.

Your comments are valued by friends of ED.

For technical support please contact support@friendsofed.com.

Freephone in USA	800.873.9769
Fax	312.893.8001
UK contact: Tel	0121.258.8858
Fax	0121.258.8868

Flash MX Upgrade Essentials - Registration Card

Name ....
Address ....
City ....State/Region ....
Country ....Postcode/Zip ....
E-mail ....
Profession: design student ☐ freelance designer ☐
part of an agency☐ inhouse designer ☐
other (please specify) ....
Age: Under 20 ☐ 20-25 ☐ 25-30 ☐ 30-40 ☐ over 40 ☐
Do you use: mac ☐ pc ☐ both ☐
How did you hear about this book?...
Book review (name)..
Advertisement (name) ....
Recommendation ....
Catalog ....
Other ....
Where did you buy this book? ....
Bookstore (name) ....City..............................
Computer Store (name)..
Mail Order..
Other...

How did you rate the overall content of this book?
Excellent ☐   Good ☐
Average ☐   Poor ☐
What applications/technologies do you intend to learn in the near future?..
....
What did you find most useful about this book? ....
....
What did you find the least useful about this book? ....
....
Please add any additional comments ....
....
What other subjects will you buy a computer book on soon?
....
....
What is the best computer book you have used this year?
....
....

Note: This information will only be used to keep you updated about new friends of ED titles and will not be used for any other purpose or passed to any other third party.

DESIGNER TO DESIGNER™

NB. If you post the bounce back card below in the UK, please send it to:

friends of ED Ltd.,
30 Lincoln Road,
Olton,
Birmingham.
B27 6PA

NO POSTAGE
NECESSARY
IF MAILED
IN THE
UNITED STATES

BUSINESS REPLY MAIL
FIRST CLASS   PERMIT #64   CHICAGO, IL

POSTAGE WILL BE PAID BY ADDRESSEE

**friends of ED,
29 S. La Salle St.
Suite 520
Chicago Il 60603-USA**